AF564507

Human Capital Into Financial Capital

Human Capital Into Financial Capital

Dr. S.K. PANNEER SELVAM
Assistant Professor, Department of Education
Bharathidasan University, Tiruchirappalli, Tamil Nadu

RANDOM PUBLICATIONS
NEW DELHI (INDIA)

Human Capital Into Financial Capital

ISBN 978-93-5111-532-8

Published in 2015 in India by

RANDOM PUBLICATIONS

4376-A/4B, Gali Murari Lal, Ansari Road
New Delhi-110 002
Phone : +9111-43580356, 011-43142548, 011-23289044
e-mail : sales@randompublications.com
info@randompublications.com
randomexports@gmail.com

Reprint 2021

Type Setting by : Shah Computer Graphics, Delhi-110094
Printed at : Replika Press Pvt. Ltd.

Contents

8

9

10

12

13

15

16

19

20

21

Topics and Contributors

1. Management of Micro-Enterprises in N.E. Region of Assam with special reference in Sonitpur District of Assam

   Balin Hazarika, Kaliabor College, Dist. Nawgaon (Assam)
   Dipanjan Chakraborty, Darrang College, Tezpur (Assam)

2. Emerging Ecosystem for Entrepreneurship in India with special reference to Finance

   Bindiya Soni
   NIRMA University, Ahmedabad

3. An Empirical Study on the Factors of Entrepreneurs Suggested to Bootstrapped Entrepreneurs

   B N Padmaja Priyadarshini, Vels University, Chennai
   N Panchanatham, Annamalai University, Chidambaram

4. SHG – A Significant Tool for Co-operative Entrepreneurship in Rural West Bengal

   Debasish Sarkar, Manish Ur Rahman, Biswajit Bhowmik
   Goenka College of Commerce and Business Administration, Kolkata

5. The Role of RRBS in Entrepreneurship Development

   Jitendra Kumar Sharma
   Seth Moti Lal Post Graduate College, Jhunjhunu (Rajasthan)

6. EGAON: Credit Facilitation to Rural Entrepreneurs with Mobile Services Intervention

   Kasina V Rao & R M Sonar
   Indian Institute of Technology, Mumbai

1

Management of Micro-Enterprises in N.E. Region of Assam with special reference in Sonitpur District of Assam

Abstract

The third world countries are still facing some socio-economic problems like unemployment, poverty, inflation; low productivity etc. in India, despite over sixty years of development, about 30 percent of the total population I.e., around 30 million is still leaving below poverty line. In order to improve their living standard, they are to be productive employed. Out of the three employment generating sectors, the agriculture sector is not a position to accommodate such huge unemployed youth. There is a growing worldwide appreciation of fact that micro- enterprises play a catalytic role in the development process of global economies by creating employment generation, self employment and entrepreneurship culture among the youth. In view of this, the government of India has stressed the development of micro-enterprise as a strategy for employment generation and promotion of income generating among the below poverty line people, and promotion of self-employment and entrepreneurship culture among the local youth. This has been recognized both by government and other development agency. With the evidence of fact, many banks and financial institutions have evolved micro finance schemes to address the financial needs of micro-enterprises.

Introduction

The third world countries are still facing some socio-economic problems like unemployment, poverty, inflation; low productivity etc. in India, despite over sixty years of development, about 30 percent of the total populations I.e., around 30 million are still leaving below poverty line. In order to improve their living standard, they are to be productive employed. Out of the three employment generating sectors, the agriculture sector is not a position to accommodate such huge unemployed youth. There is a growing worldwide appreciation of fact that micro- enterprises play a catalytic role in the development process of global economies by creating employment generation, self employment and entrepreneurship culture among the youth. In view of this, the government of India has stressed the development of micro-enterprise as a strategy for employment generation and promotion of income generating among the below poverty line people, and promotion of self-employment and entrepreneurship culture among the local youth. This has been recognized both by government and other development agency. With the evidence of fact, many banks and financial institutions have evolved micro finance schemes to address the financial needs of micro-enterprises.

Definition of SME

Since the word "micro" represents small, the MSMED act, 06(micro, small and medium enterprise development act.2006, ministry of small scale industries, notification, July 18, 2006) defines that the enterprise engage in the manufacturing or production of goods, investment in plant and machinery does not exceed twenty five lakh rupees and enterprise engage in providing or rendering of services, the investment in equipment does not exceed ten lakh rupees.

Significance of micro-enterprise

The SME sector is one of the fastest growing industrial sectors all over the world. It has been showing outstanding performance over five decades as a highly vibrant and dynamic sector of the Indian economy is well indicated by its 95 percent share in the total industrial units in the country, 40 percent of production in the manufacturing sector, 80 percent of industrial employment, about 45 percent of national export and an estimated employment to the order of 295 lakhs during 2005-06. The main significance of SME is:

1. The SME is capable of generating high degree of employment with low capital investment. During the period from 1991 to 1998, it has created almost 42 lakhs of new jobs whereas the entire organized industries and government was able to create 14.3 lakhs jobs only. i.e., a ratio of 3:1 in employment generation.
2. SMEs are labour intensive, it is evident of fact that average SMEs unit require about Rs. 25,000 per unit of per employment, whereas large scale unit needs Rs. 3 lakhs for providing employment to one person.
3. SMEs unit particularly agro-based units eco-friendly and hence, capacity of experiencing ecological and economic sustainability.
4. The SME sector has special significance in North Eastern region-which is one of the 'A' category backward regions in the country. The huge storage of natural resources i.e., locally available raw-materials can be utilized properly through the development of this sector.

Development of micro- enterprises in Northeastern Region and Assam: A profile

The North-Eastern Region (NER) of India comprise of Arunachal Pradesh, Mizuram, Manipur, Meghalaya, Nagaland, Tripura, Sikkim and Assam. Excluding Sikkim, the entire NER covers 2, 55,089 sq.kms area, which is 7.8 percent of the total geographical area of the country. As per the population census 2001, the total population of NER is 3, 65, 00,108 person which is 3.5 percent of the total population of India. As far as the growth of SSEs in North Eastern Region is concern it is seen that the region has 67,398 SSE units as on march 2001 which is only 2% of the total SSEs in the country as whole. Though the region's share in the all India total have been showing increased trend this growth do not satisfactory in terms of the available resources, huge labour force, demand base in the region, the scope of border trade etc.

While looking at the development of small enterprises in the region, the following external factors are needed to be considered.

1. The major tea production, plywood and oil industry are started since preindependence period but no ancillaries units are setting up based on semi-product of said industries.
2. The region is basically concentrated by outsider as a trading centre;

therefore no proper growth of entrepreneurship took place in the state.

3. The availability of capital is another big problem for entrepreneurship development by the evidence of credit deposit ratio. The total assistance by banks and financial institutions in NE till 2000 was Rs.1460.5 crores, which was only 0.58% of the total loan sectioned in the country.
4. The enterprises are starting their business operation without proper scanning of market and availability of raw-material.
5. The industrial estate, area and growth centre are located mostly in the area where communication is a big problem and those institution are far from commercial activities.
6. The traditional skill of the entrepreneurs has not been upgraded to meet the market demand in the state.

Table1.1

Growth of MEs in North Eastern Region

year	NER	India	% of NER to India
1971	991	239128	0.4
1981	9832	523180	1.88
1985	13816	854843	1.62
1986	16452	950334	1.73
1987	19770	1048253	1.89
1988	20337	1158765	1.76
1990	25525	1378485	1.86
1999	47654	3212000	1.48
2001	67398	3311000	2.03

Source: Smeindia

The state of Assam geographically from the core of North-Eastern states and is endowed with vast deposit of mineral resources like petroleum, natural gases, coal, limestone, forest and water resources but it has been considered as an industrially "A" category backward state of India. The existing industrial profile of Assam is very lopsided picture. There is less than 2% of countries large and medium scale industries and about 1% of the country small enterprises in the

Assam. As far as the small enterprise development concern in Assam, it is seen that the state has 49.691 registered units as on March, 2005, which is only about 1% of the total enterprises in the countries as a whole. Though the state share in the all India total have been increasing trend, this growth do not justify in terms of the available resources, manpower and market in local and Global trade.

Table-1.2

Year	No. of units	Nos. of Employment	Production in Lakhs	Fixed Investment (Rs. In Lakhs
1995-1996	29,617	120,568	60,020	57,968
	(10.14)	(19.92)	73,350	(9.23)
1996-1997	32,084	131,049	81,752	60,022
	(15.00)	(10.00)	(17.51)	(9.23)
1997-1998	34,241	141,636	89,265	75,045
	(11.65)	(13.35)	(7.16)	(83.39)
1998-1999	36,465	150,957	109,460	87,397
	(9.37)	(9.88)	(14.56)	(6.33)
1999-2000	38,286	158,064	147,021	91,335
	(10.14)	(9.29)	(10.40)	(4.43)
2000-01	40,402	168,324	163,034	96,627
	(8.20)	(8.08)	(14.57)	(3.34)
2001-02	42,930	179,863	179,411	101,693
	(6.50)	(8.08)	(11.45)	(25.02)
2002-03	45,270	190,977	198,375	106,561
	(6.90)	(6.58)	(9.19)	(16.46)
2003-04	47,624	202,746	218,072	113,753
	(5.00)	(4.71)	(22.62)	(4.51)
2004-05	49,691	212,142	1,47,021	120,873
	(4.99)	(6.49)	(34.31)	(5.80)

Note: Both SIDO and Non-SIDO units as on 31st March of the respective year and figure in brackets refer percentage over previous year

Sources: Directorate of Industries, Assam

Review of literature on small enterprise

So far, a number of studies in this area of research have been conducted by researchers, academician, and non- government agencies. Before going details of the study, some view of different authors has been quoted in the context on small enterprise

R.P. Sinha on "Some Problems of Small Scale industries" (1979) observed that the government purchase schemes in Bihar were not encouraging to development of small entrepreneurs in the region. He recommends the setting up of a "development consortia" and creation of a trade centre to boost the marketing of SSE's products.

T.Subbi Reddy, in his study (1981) observed that nearly eighty percent of the entrepreneurs not aware about government schemes. He emphasized the wide publicity of government schemes through advertisement media and suggested the subsidy must be simple.

Manohar U. Despande (1982) viewed involvement of development agency regarding management expertise so, that extended entrepreneurial environment among local youth.

Inderjeet Dagar (1993) revealed that management of human resource is important factor for the development of SSEs. He recommended systematic and scientific management of human resources development.

S.K.Bansal (1992) advocated few mechanisms i.e. net worth to fixed assets, net sales to turnover, net sales to gross working capital etc. with the help of the device, the financial institution should ensure before sanctioning of loan about the future prospects of the produce and service.

A.K. Sharma (1976) stated that sixty percent of surviving units were not managing their finance properly. According to him, availability of bank finance would solve the problems of small entrepreneurs in the region.

N.B.Dey (1980) mentioned that most of the entrepreneurs do not attend any regular courses on management. He recommends that the entire development agency involved for the development of small enterprise should rightly come forward to ensure speedy utilization of fund for true purpose.

P.Baishy (1986) revealed that cottage industries are gradually under developed due to lack of innovation in technology. He opined that cottage and small scale industries can provide more employment opportunities in the region.

P.C. Goswami (1985) advocates that development and expansion of secondary sector must be related to agricultural and allied activities.

B.K.Sharma (1987) suggested entrepreneurs should be encourage to come for resource based industries and North Eastern council should take initiative in developing appropriate model for industrialization in the Region.

P. Barthakur (1997) observed that finance was the most important problem faced by the most of the entrepreneurs. He viewed that capital investment subsidy could play a positive role in entrepreneurship development in the region and its re-introduction may help in accelerating in the process of industrialization in the region.

Atanu Baruah (1998) stated that educated youth in the region prefer white collared jobs rather entrepreneurship as a career. He has also mentioned that entrepreneurs in the region is still ignored the service sector, which is one of the employment contributory sector of other parts of the country. This study is design to focus on more areas of sustainable small enterprises development and adopted strategic management comprehensive policy framework.

Need for the study

The study will make the assessment of the management of the micro-enterprise in an industrially backward region, in Assam as general and Sonitpur district in particular. The purpose behind is that a study of this nature of the region would be useful to give an actual insight problems and prospects associated with the emergence of small enterprise. On the other hand, the study would be enable entrepreneurs to take the necessary measured for setting up small unit that would be healthy right from their inception by way of not allowing any scope for their sickness even to the great extent subsequently

Objective

The main objective of this paper is made to analysis the present managerial problems faced by small enterprises and to highlight the need for improvement management pattern of micro-enterprise in Assam, in general and Sonitpur district, in particular.

Methodology

Keeping the above objectives in mind, a sample 200 micro enterprises of the district were selected for the study. Design of the study was exploratory type and the data is collected from primary and secondary sources. Primary data were collected through questionnaire schedule and personal interview.

Secondary data is collected from directory of industries of Assam, DIC Sonitpur district, NABARD, Research paper, government bulletins etc.

Paper Design

For convenience, this paper is divided into four sections. The first section represents introduction, definition, significance of the study and give the conceptual framework of the paper. The second section deals with analysis of growth of SME in North- Eastern Region compared to India and Assam in terms of unit, investment, production and employment during 1971 to 2001 and 1995 to 2005. And third section analysed the problems associated with the micro Paper Presented at 9th Biennial Conference held at EDI, Ahmedabad during 16 18 February 2011 enterprise in Sonitpur district of Assam. The fourth section i.e., last section represents findings and recommendations.

District profile

Sonitpur district of Assam (India) **is** spread over an area of 5235.2 sq kms. In terms of area it is second largest district of Assam. It is situated in the middle of the state of Assam. The population of the district is 16.77 lakhs and density of population is 315 per sq km. as per the 2001 census. The total strength of the working population in the district is 4.64 lakhs which is 28 percent of the total population. Agriculture alone accounted 64 percent of the total workforce. This reveals the industrial backwardness of the district. Traditional dependence on agriculture is one of the reasons for lack of entrepreneurship among the educated youth. They are mostly concentrated white collared job. Absence of major industries in the district is also partly responsible for lack of entrepreneurial activities.

Major findings

The data collected through questionnaire/personal interview administrated with 200 small units in the state were analysed as per the objectives of the study. The salient findings of the study are as follows:

1. A majority 70.50% of the entrepreneurs belong to age group of 20-40 years remaining 29.50% were above 40 years. More than one third of them (37%) were matriculate or intermediate. 31.50% entrepreneurs were graduates of different disciplines. Only insignificant 4.00% was post graduate. A majority 62% of entrepreneurs were without any past occupation. It is because due to busy either studying or remained unemployed. 74.84 of them were belonging to Assames origin. A greater majority (87%) were proprietorship business. The study reveals that the total earning of 42% were less than Rs.25.000/, followed by 45% were found in between Rs.25000-35.000 p.a. and remaining percentage of them were above Rs.35000/-The reasons for low level of earning per year is that the majority of them were first generation entrepreneurs and they have less experience in business.(APP.table.1.3).
2. Internal Problems faced by the entrepreneurs in Assam: Socio-personal problems: - Most of the respondents stated that they have weak collateral Position due to weak family background. They are belief that business is not for Assamese people as like Marwaris,

Gujarati and Bengali. It was observed that due to less migratory nature, most of the entrepreneurs prefer to start their units near to their residence which is reduce risk taking capacity of them. (APP. Table-1.4)

3. Managerial problems: Majority of the entrepreneurs faced the problems of labour turnover and lack of skilled worker and remaining of them expressed labour absenteeism. Road are the only means of communication. Due to lack of board gauge railway communication, the price of the raw materials and finished products is always increasing high.(APP.Table-1.5)
4. Technical problems: The problems of poor record keeping was ranked highest in technical problems followed by lack of managerial experience, inadequate of land, poor equipment and lack of agency to guide. It was observed that due to lack of proper accounting and business planning of the entrepreneurs are keeps darkness regarding their financial requirement. Even, most of them are lavishly expenditure their business in family purposes such as celebration of festival, ceremony and rituals etc. As regards, training programme attended by entrepreneurs, it was surprising that 71.00% of them were not attended any course training programme which reflects unhealthy sign of importance and impact of modern management practices.(APP.Table-1.6 and 1.7)
5. Financial management problems: Most of the entrepreneurs faced the problems of price fluctuation, excessive documentations and security asked by financial institutions, long period of loan disbursement by bank, non availability of loan and subsidies. Majority of the units procured funds from financial institutions and indigenous bank. But it was observed that the share of loan latter is quite high. The reason being the latter involves relatively less formalities, though the rate of interest charged is much higher than the former.(APP.Table-1.8)
6. Marketing problems: Inadequate promotion, competition with big industries, low demand, less marketing expertise and limited marketing scope were the major marketing problems of small entrepreneurs in the district. Majority of the respondents were fixing their products price on cost plus and a few on skimming pricing. There were great differences between product price of SSEs and big industries. It was notice that the pricing change has been done mostly by the intermediaries.(APP.Table- 1.9).
7. Problems of Government Assistance: Majority of the small entrepreneurs in the state expressed that office bearer of development agency

become dishonest and exploitive in every step of starting units. Red-tapism is found at various levels. Technical help and assistance provide by them is found very poor.(APP.Table-1.10)

Recommendations

Small enterprise plays a significance role in the growth of our economy. In order to run industrial development in the region, following few recommendations are put forward for improvement of management of small enterprises in the state.

1. The goverment needs to focus more on setting up of Agro- based industries using the resources based on primary sector (agriculture) in the region and big industries to support ancillary SSE units which will, in turn, boost SSEs in this backward region under globalisation.
2. The government should simplify the official formalities through organising training programmes where the procedure of motivational training, selection and loan disbursement should be completed under a single roof.
3. The subsidising policy of the government needs to be rationalized on the basis of some criteria like project viability, entrpreneurs' experience and capacity instead of getting subsidy on receiving credit.
4. A trained psychologist in every motivational program can be used to increase the confidence of local entrepreneurs.
5. EDP need to be re-oriented based on successful entrepreneurs from inside and outside the region for development of self- confidence.
6. Entrepreneurs should use competition as a booster under globalisation for management improvement instead considering it as a threat for quality improvement.
7. To guide SSEs, a special cell should be made available in all the financial agencies which entrepreneurs can be approach at any time to discuss their financial problems.
8. Regarding securities, margin money, documentation, banks should be flexible in case of potential entrepreneurs and they should be educated about the concept of securities. In the same way, entrepreneurs should also be educated about the different financial schemes of the banks.
9. The micro enterprises are not sound to go for big promotional strategies. Joint venture promotional strategy is effective for local SSEs of similar product

10. Association of related SSEs for pricing of finished products will reduce competition. It will remove the middle men intervention and decrease the price of the product

Management opportunities for development of small enterprises in North Eastern region

1. North eastern Region is the gateway to East and South East Asia for India having more than 98% borders with Bhutan, Bangladesh, China and Myanmar and balance 2% area connected to mainland India. In the era of economic liberalization and growing cross border trade and at the wake of "LOOK EAST POLICY" of government of India, N.E region is a located wide marketing opportunity for small enterprises with the south East Asia.
2. N.E region is always been famous for bamboo, cane, brass, bell metal, wood, handloom weaving of Endi, Muga and Mulberry Silk industry. But these industries are starving for market. Now market is unlimited with Asia and world market. The arts and crafts industries in north eastern region is now to attract attention of the world market
3. North East is having great potential for small industries development related to oil and gas, limestone, coal based industries. Its location and rich forest are congenial to develop agro and forest based industry. The growing orchards and soil condition are ideal for development fruits processing industries. The region is endowed with huge water resources potential for power, fishery. Water sports and waterways etc. huge fresh water resources and favorable atmosphere and climatic condition set the tune for development of agriculture and allied sectors potential to develop agro based industry. North east has the potential of organic agricultural sector and organic food has a very huge demand in international market.
4. North east is a land of contrast and diverse resources. Its scenic beauty, climatic conditions, festivals, rich cultural heritage, wild lives and rich bio- diversities are unparallel in the world. North east can easily become a place of tourist interest from all over the world.
5. North east produce number of professional from it reputed universities and education institutions. These professional are now employed at various industries and institutions all over the country and in the world.

Now there is challenge to change the mind-set of these younger qualified and professional youth from service oriented to "entrepreneur". Acceptance of above challenge and taking location advantage north eastern states could produce centres for higher education for its neighboring countries like Bangladesh, Bhutan, Nepal, Myanmar and even Thailand etc.

Table-1.3

BACKGOUND OF ENTREPRENEURS

Profile	No. of Entrepreneurs	Percentage
Age		
20-30	48	24.00
31-40	93	46.50
41-50	36	18.00
50 & above	23	11.50
Educational Background		
Up to IX	54	27.00
Metric & Intermediate	75	37.50
Degree	63	31.50
Postgraduate	8	4.00
Past Occupation		
No occupation	124	62.00
Business	16	8.00
Agriculture	46	23.00
Services	14	7.00
Ownership		
Proprietorship	174	87.00
Partnership	24	12.00
Co-partner	2	1.00
Earning rate		
Below Rs. 20000	67	33.50
Rs. 20000 to 40000	69	34.50
Above Rs 40000	64	32.00

Source : Field Survey

Table-1.4

Socio-personal problems

Item	No.	%
Weak collateral position	78	52
Lack of confidence to business	77	51.33
Lack of migratory nature	27	18.00
Lack of family support	35	23.33

Note: Data indicate multiple responses

Table-1.5

Managerial Problem

Item	No.	%
Labour absenteeism	30	20.00
Transportation problem	41	27.33
Labour turnover	45	30.00
Lack of skilled labour	55	36.66
Outdated technologies	441	27.33

Note: Data indicate multiple responses

Table-1.6

Technical problems

Item	No.	%
Lack of proper accounting	110	73.34
Lack of managerial experience	88	58.67
Inadequate land plots and premises	44	29.34
Lack of development agency support	33	22.00
Inadequate equipments	32	21.34

Note: Data indicate multiple responses

Table No. 1.7

TRAING PROGRAMME ATTENDANT

Sl. No.	Items	No. of Entrepreneurs	Percentage
1.	Self Development	142	71.00
2.	Managerial	17	8.50
3.	Technical Training	41	20.50

Source: Field Survey

Table- 1.8

Financial Problems

Items	No.	%
Lack of working capital	57	29.68
Price fluctuation of product	68	35.41
Lack of Bank finance	51	26.56
High credit sales	50	26.05

Note: Data indicate multiple response

Table- 1.9

Marketing problems

Item	No.	%
Lack of knowledge	46	30.67
Inadequate promotion	44	29.34
Low demand	24	16.00
Competition	38	25.34

Note: Data indicate multiple responses

Table-1.10

Problem of Govt. Assistance

Items	No.	%
Red Tapism at various level	65	43.34
Development agency become dishonest	50	33.34
Poor Govt. assistance	20	13.34
No response	15	10.00

Note: Data indicate multiple responses

References

1. Prasad.C.S, Laghu Udyog Samachar, Development Commissioner (SSI) ministry of SSI, govt. of India, New Delhi,2001,p-23.
2. Bhandari.P, Problems and Prospects of SSI in North-East, The Assam Tribune Nov-9,2006.
3. Rajendra Prasad.T, and Suthamma, Perspectives of SSI & Employment Generation in Karnataka. Southern Economist, Jan-15, 2003, vol-41.
4. Sing.M.P, Growth and Development of SSI, Laghu Udyog Samachar, vol.xxii & xxiii, Ja-Sept.1998.
5. Saikia. Sunil, Small Scale Development in North Eastern Region. (edit. Book).2005.
6. M.K. Prasanna, Strategy for Attracting young people to become Entrepreneurs Gauhati commerce college, 2008.(seminar)
7. S.G. Purohit and H.G. Jambagi. Planning for Agri-Business under WTO, Southern Economist, August, 2003.

2

Emerging Ecosystem for Entrepreneurship in India with special reference to Finance

Abstract

Today world is experiencing the entrepreneurial revolution. Economic and technological advancements opened up a new horizon for entrepreneurship development. The growing economy and right eco-system provide more supportive environment for practicing entrepreneurship than before. However, there are plenty of challenges that an entrepreneur has to face. Raising startup capital for a business venture has always been a bigger challenge, particularly for knowledge based and innovative ventures. Beginning with resource constraints for such ventures, this paper attempts to present a comprehensive scenario of available funding options such as bootstrapping techniques, incubation centres, angel investors, venture capital and private equity; for aspiring entrepreneurs in knowledge based sectors. There are many scattered empirical studies on such funding options that describe the traits of these institutions individually but only few studies analyze such institutions and mechanisms comprehensively. The study also relates the stages of venture development such as seed, startup, expansion and early expansion with the funding options as mentioned above. Further, the availability of incubation centres, angel capital, venture capital and private equity in India, has also been discussed. The paper concludes with various programmes and events initiated to encourage the emerging entrepreneurs in the country such as business plan competitions; events of National Entrepreneurship Network (NEN) The Indus Entrepreneur (TiE) and Headstart.

Introduction

Setting up a business is a formidable task. There are plenty of challenges that an entrepreneur has to face. Raising startup capital for a business venture has always been a bigger challenge for aspiring entrepreneur. This is espccially true for firms in knowledge based industries. Various observers describe today's global economy as one in transition to a 'knowledge economy', or an 'information society' where resources such as know-how are more critical than other economic resources like labour and capital as recognized by neo-classic economics (Skyrme, 1997; Houghton and Sheehan, 2000). In India, also new economy is driven by technology development, wherein major investments are being made in the knowledge based industries with substantially low investments in land, building, plant and machinery. These knowledge based industries often start with just an idea hence, the asset/collateral-based instruments adopted for the hard core manufacturing industries, are proving to be inadequate for the knowledge based industries.

From the entrepreneur's perspective, the available financing sources could be considered as debt versus equity (Zimmere and Scarborough, 2005), however, debt financing is not an option for such firms as these enterprises are characterized by significant intangible but limited tangible assets, a period of negative returns and uncertain prospects. These characteristics make a debt financing difficult (Povaly, 2007). Similarly, high quality and useful information on their activities and prospects may be difficult or very costly to obtain externally resulting into lower level of capitalization. All these factors lead to serious moral hazard problems that must be controlled by an outside investor, and that cannot adequately be dealt with pure debt-type contracts (Sagari, 1992). Thus, alternative source of finance is required to enable these ventures to pass from the startup to expansion phase. Within this context, probably the equity capital such as angel capital, venture capital and private equity are the financing mechanism that will fit with the financial and managerial needs of such innovation based entrepreneurship. Besides the equity gap of these firms with high growth potential, these funding options may also fill the competence gap as the involvement of these fund providers, in the companies that they invest in goes beyond the provision of financial resources (Isaksson, 2006).

In addition to these equity options, the entrepreneurs can also employ innovative techniques such as bootstrapping that reduces the need for external funding to a greater extent at the initial stage of venture development. Further, the facilities of incubation centres may also meet the financial and non financial needs of the ventures at seed stage of venture development. All these funding options and mechanisms for fostering the innovation based entrepreneurship have been reviewed in detail in the following sections of the study.

Purpose of the Study

Through this conceptual study, a systematic attempt has been made to add to the scientific understanding of the options available to the start-ups from the grassroots level i.e. bootstrapping, to the most advanced late stage financing i.e. venture capital/private equity. The paper makes a detailed foray into the role played by equity investors such as angel investors and venture capitalists (VCs). In the process of understanding their contribution to the development of the start-up firm, the study also differentiates among these two types of investors. Further, the current scenario in the country with respect to venture capital/private equity has been highlighted based upon the secondary information available from the study conducted by various research outfits like Venture Intelligence etc. Recent developments for practicing entrepreneurship as discussed in the later part of the paper will help the emerging entrepreneurs to explore various options for financial and non-financial assistance.

Literature Review

Reflecting the overall importance of equity capital to entrepreneurship, it has received considerable academic attention. Various scholars from different disciplines have conducted studies from different perspectives in the area of bootstrapping techniques, incubation centres, angel capital and venture capital.

In this section, an attempt has been made to trace the development of literature related to these options, from the detailed descriptive studies that dominate early work to the theory driven analysis.

Bootstrapping Technique

In the early 1990s, scholars began to name bootstrap finance explicitly. Over the last few years several definitions have been published, but the first pointed reference appeared in the *Harvard Business Review where in*

Bhide (1992) focused on bootstrapping in the earlier stages and defined it as "launching ventures with modest personal funds." Freear, Sohl, and Wetzel (1995) extended the use of bootstrap financing to firms' rapid growth stage rather than exclusively in the earliest stages of an enterprise's life. Van Auken and Neeley (1996) found that sole proprietorships and firms requiring high capital investment relied on bootstrap financing to a greater extent than other firms.

Freear *et al.* (1995) found that 95% of the firms they studied had used bootstrap financial methods to varying degrees. More recently, Winborg and Landstrom (2001) studied the bootstrapping methods used by Swedish firms. They derived six classifications of bootstrapping methods namely owner provided financing and resources, accounts receivable management methods, sharing or borrowing of resources from other firms, delaying payments, minimization of resources invested in stock through formal routines and use of government subsidies.

Business Incubation

Many researchers have defined incubators in many ways. As described by Albert and Gaynor (2001) Albert *et al.*, defined an enterprise incubator as a "collective and temporary place for accommodating companies which offers space, assistance and services suited to the needs of companies being launched or recently founded". They classified the research on incubators into descriptive, prescriptive, and evaluative research. The *descriptive works* define incubation, classify different types of incubators, identify key features of specific types of incubators and set out the lifecycle of an incubator. *Prescriptive works* are aimed at informing key stakeholders, primarily sponsors and incubator management. These studies illustrate the role of incubators in economic development, identify features of successful incubation programmes, examine other issues facing incubator management, and set out best practice guidelines and methodologies aimed at informing incubator managers on effective ways of running incubators. *Evaluative works* establish the metrics by which incubation programmes can be evaluated. They try to quantify the impact of incubators on firms they work with.

Angel Capital

In contrast to the large volume of academic research on the role of venture capitalists, comparatively little work has been done on angel investors. In 1999, Mason and Harrison identified three different generations research on business angels: *First generation studies* were focused upon studying attitudes, behaviour and characteristics of angels. These studies were replicated in other countries in the world though initiated in the United States in the 1980 (Brettel, 2003; Hindle and Lee 2002; Hindle and Wenban, 1999; Landstorm, 1993; Reitan and Sorheim, 2000). In the *second generation studies*, researchers started to make a systematic inquiry into investment decision making process of angels with application of various theoretical concepts like agency theory, social capital, signaling etc (Feit, 1995; Prasad *et al*, 2000; Saetre, 2003; Sorheim, 2003; Van Osnabrugge, 2000). Finally, *third generation studies* present those areas, where further research is needed in terms of certain methodological and theoretical issues with new research designs, such as case studies and longitudinal research.

Venture Capital/Private Equity (VC/PE)

The terms venture capital and private equity are used interchangbly in the literature. In fact, venture capital is a subset of a larger private equity asset class which includes venture capital, leveraged buy-outs, management buy-ins and buy-outs, bridge and mezzanine investments. In this study, the discussion is restricted to the concept of venture capital only. The institutional venture capital market was established by the end of 1940s in US; however, scholarly interest in the venture capital began only in 1970s and expanded substantially since the late 1980s (Mason and Harrison, 1999). Since 1970s most of the academic researchers tried to describe and understand venture capitalists‘ decision making process (Silva, 2004). In western countries, the venture capital process has been described in numerous academic studies (Sweeting, 1991; Bygrave and Timmons, 1992; Tyebjee and Bruno, 1984; Fried and Hisrich, 1994).

Tyebjee and Bruno (1984) proposed simplistic and descriptive five-stage model of venture capital investing (i.e. deal origination, screening, evaluation, deal structuring, post investment activities). Fried and Hisrich (1994) extended the previous research by Tyebjee and Bruno by investigating venture capitalists' decision making in more detail. However, there are very few studies in the context of Asian countries. Notable among them, are by researchers like, Rah *et al.* (1994), Pandey (1996), Pandey and Jang (1996), Mishra (2005), in the context of countries like Korea, India and Taiwan.

Sapienza and Villanueva (2007) have identified certain dimensions that have been studied extensively and the ones that have been relatively neglected. The dimensions basically include the stages in the venture capital cycle, the perspective of the entrepreneur/venture capitalist and the type of the venture capital. These dimensions have been represented in the following diagram.

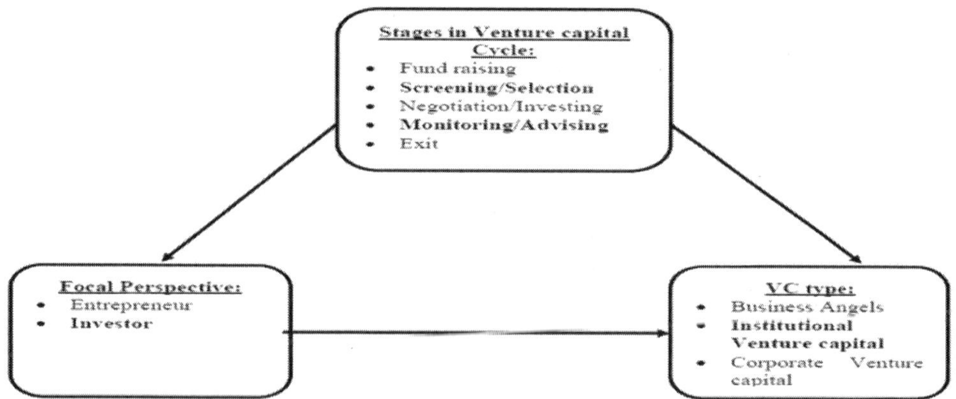

Figure 1 Areas Investigated/Neglected in Venture Capital Research Focal Perspective:

(Source: Adapted from Sapienza, Harry and Jaume Villanueva (2007), "Conceptual and theoretical reflections on Venture Capital research", in edt. Vol. by Landstorm, Hans, Handbook of Research on Venture Capital, Edward Elgar, USA.)

The figure above indicates that the available literature on venture capital focuses upon institutional venture capital, from the investor's perspective and in the selection as well as monitoring stage in venture capital cycle. (These areas are marked in Bold). Studies by Tyebjee and Bruno, 1984; MacMillan *et al.*, 1985; MacMillan *et al.*, 1987; Sandberg and Hofer, 1987; Timmons and Bygrave, 1986; Gorman and Sahlman 1989; MacMillan *et al* 1989; Maula *et al* 2005; Dolvin 2005; Ehrlich *et al* 1994; Busenitz 2004; Gabrielsson and Huse 2002; Sweeting and Wong 1997; Gomez-Mejia 1990; focused on these areas.

Stages of Venture Development and the Funding Options

Start-ups need different forms of financing at different stages of the development of their ventures. These stages include seed stage, start up stage, early expansion, expansion and late stage.

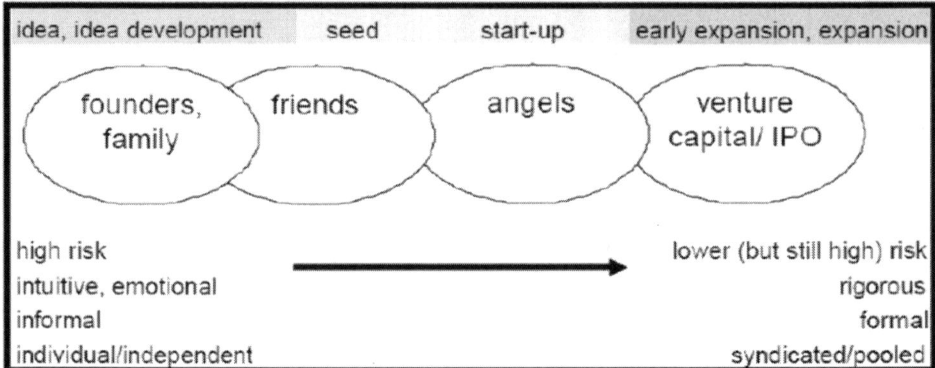

Figure 2 Development Phases and Sources of Financing

(Source: "New Zeland's Angel Capital Market- Supply side" (2004): A Report prepared by Infometrics for the Ministry of Economic Development)

It can be seen from the above figure that when the investment risk is high during the development stage and seed stage; the founder's family and friends are typically financing the deal but the resources made available by them are often limited. So as the deal move close to the startup stage, business angels begin to enter into the picture (Benjamin and Margulis, 2001). Venture capital funds typically invest in companies that have the seed and early stage developments and are looking for expansion capital. This is because by investing at later stages, there is less risk in the company and potentially less time to harvest. Also the size of today's venture funds does not allow them to make smaller investments (Bradley *et al*, 2002). Fixed costs of project screening and monitoring make it uneconomical for venture capitalists to make small investments. In order to deal with the uncertainties in the startup investments (characterized in the form of asymmetric information, moral hazard problems, higher intangible assets etc.), venture capital firms tend to focus on a few industries that they get to understand very well (Gupta and Sapienza, 1992).

Besides, self funding, angel capital and venture capital, the start-ups can resort to bootstrapping techniques and the facilities of incubation centres at the seed and start-up stage. The characteristics of all these options are discussed in the following section.

Bootstrap Financing

For a long time researchers and policy-makers have argued that small businesses face severe problems in attracting external capital. Hence, entrepreneurs have exploited variety of funding sources and used different techniques including "*Bootstrap Financing*" (Neeley, 2003). Bootstrap financing is particularly important at the start up and in the early years of venture when capital from debt financing (i.e. in terms of higher interest rate) or from equity financing (i.e. in terms of loss of ownership) is more expensive or unattractive or even inaccessible (Hisrich and Peter, 2002). It works on the same principle of 'A penny saved is penny earned.' It is a collection of methods to minimize the need to seek outside financing by a start up (Donde, 2007). A wide variety of bootstrap financing techniques are available to business owners, including the use of credit cards, delaying payments, sharing of equipments and employees with other businesses, working from home, partnering rather employing and leasing (Auken, 2005). These techniques reduce overall capital requirements and improve cash flow.

Incubation Centers

Entrepreneurs in all societies need support on the way from the translation of an idea to a business entity creation, particularly for small and medium size firms (SMEs). The support is critical if individuals or firms contemplate entering into untested product, process and market. These start ups should be provided with some type of nursery at the inception stage, otherwise violent competition with large business firms will not allow them to survive and grow. Incubation is widely considered to be one such dynamic mechanism that accelerates the growth and development of these SMEs and also encourages people with ideas for new products or services to start their own businesses.

In the medical field, an incubator (in·cu·ba·tor/ in´ku-bat-er) is an apparatus for maintaining optimal conditions (temperature, humidity, etc.) for growth and development, as one used in the early care of premature infants, or one used for cultures. The infant is kept in a special incubator till it can withstand the normal environment. The incubation stage, thus, refers to a limited period association. In the context of business development/new enterprise creation, the concept of the incubator is applied more for the ultimate fruition of project ideas which have a high degree of uncertainty. The aim of the incubator is to facilitate the survival of such firms, and also to nurture them for the growth and success, by providing the inputs needed by the firms at different stages. In some cases, an innovator or a scientist may not be inclined to become an entrepreneur for developing a business enterprise. He rather prefers to concentrate more on innovations. Hence, the role of business application or commercialisation has to be played by yet another person who is interested in a business venture. Here the incubators learn the mission of the innovator, and attempts to find out an entrepreneur who can convert the innovation into a business proposition (Nagayya, 2005).

Incubators, also named as Technology Centres or Innovation Centres, are one of the most successful approaches being used in the past 25 years all over the world to promote and support entrepreneurs and SMEs. The formal concept of business incubation began in the USA in the 1960s. It later developed in Europe through various related forms (e.g. innovation centres, pépinières d'entreprises, and techno poles/ science parks) during the 1980s. Incubation programmes have boomed since the early 1980s. Today, several thousand incubators are in operation worldwide (Sun *et al*, 2007).

The spectrum of services offered in an incubator is extremely varied, ranging from strategic business planning, to administrative services, to guidance on issues of intellectual property rights particularly in the case of technology incubators. Regardless of their type, however, most incubators provide the following kinds of services;

1. Below market rental space on flexible terms
2. Sharing of equipment and services that would otherwise be unavailable or unaffordable. Such services are typically divided into three major categories. (i) Offices and communication services such as typing, photocopying and phone answering. (ii) Business services such as business planning and financial planning and (iii) Facilities and equipment services, including a reception area, conference rooms and computers. Not only do these services save young entrepreneurs money, but also save them time. Entrepreneurs can focus on getting their products and services to market faster than competitors rather than searching for the resources they need to build their companies.
3. Additional information on and access to various types of financial and technical assistance
4. Provision of an environment where small businesses are not alone, thereby reducing the anxiety of starting a new venture.
5. Increased business tenants' visibility to community.

6. Elimination of building maintenance responsibilities. This allows new entrepreneurs freedom from maintenance of furniture and equipment and of such areas as loading docks, lunch areas, conference room and reception areas (Kuratko& Hodgetts, 2005).

India has made commendable progress in terms of the growth of scientific and technology culture. As a response to the perceived potential, some encouraging steps have been adopted by policy makers. In the recent past the Department of Science and Technology, Government of India, has initiated a number of institutional based programmes. These include the mechanisms of Science & Technology Entrepreneurs Park (STEP) and the recently launched Technology Business Incubator (TBI). The National Science and Technology Entrepreneurship Development Board (NSTEDB) of the Department of Science and Technology has played significant role in the Indian Business Incubation arena. The NSTEDB has already catalyzed and supported several Science and Technology Entrepreneurs Parks (STEPs), Technology Business Incubators (TBIs), in addition to many Entrepreneurship Development Cells (EDCs) in different parts of the country. So far 15 Technology Business Incubators have been set up at various institutions.

In addition, there are 17 Science and Technology Entrepreneurs' Park and 50 other such mechanisms promoted by various agencies including the State Governments.

The Ministry of Communication and Information Technology is establishing Software Technology Parks (STPs) through the Software Technology Parks of India (STPI) all over the country. The main objective of the Software Technology Parks scheme is to boost the software exports from the country using high-speed data communication links. So far, 35 STPs including 19 international gateways have been set up.

The Department of Biotechnology (DBT) is promoting Micro-propagation Technology Parks (MTPs) for providing an interface between the research institutions and industry and biotechnology parks to provide opportunities for women entrepreneurs through the application of environment friendly biotechnologies. DBT has set up two MTPs, one at Tata Energy Research Institute (TERI), New Delhi and another at National Chemical Laboratory, Pune. A biotechnology park for women has been set up by DBT at Chennai in collaboration with the state government.

The Indian STEP and Business Incubator Association (ISBA) were set up in 2004 as a registered professional body to promote business incubation in India. ISBA aims to promote business incubation activities in the country through exchange of information, sharing of experience, and other networking assistance among Indian Business Incubators, Science and Technology Entrepreneurs Parks (STEPs) and other related organisations engaged in the promotion of start-up enterprises.

Business Incubation in the county is poised for a strong growth with both government and private sectors seeing good prospects in promoting the ideas that have robust commercial potential. As reported by the bureau of *The Economic times Ahmedabad* (4th Feb, 2008 pp18), earlier it was only the ministry of science and technology that was funding business incubation, but now other ministries too have begun the practice and with the private players also supporting the commercially viable ideas, the incubation business is set for significant growth. ISBA, which is the apex professional body, supporting business incubators across the country, has about 100 incubation centres, and the numbers are expected to double within the next two years, while the private business incubation centres are about a dozen at present. However, these numbers do not match upto global levels, considering the figure that US has about 1500 incubation centres, China has about 800 and even South Korea has about 400 such centes.

Business Angels

In contrast to the large volume of academic research on the role of venture capitalists, comparatively little work has been done on angel investors. Angel investors are high net- worth individuals who invest their personal capital in a small set of companies. They typically invest “seed capital” (Denis, 2004).

Business angels tend to be private individuals, who often have started their own successful firms in the past and are now looking to invest some of their money and experience gained into a small entrepreneurial firm. Angel investors are first driven by the beauty of the business idea and then return on investment.

Hence, they can put in as little as few lakhs of rupees to as much as several crores (Cherian, 2007). Many invest for the love of innovation and creativity; others invest to ‘give back’ to the community that may have nurtured their success; and still others see it as an opportunity to mentor younger entrepreneurs who may be facing similar issues that the angel has tackled previously (Jensen, 2002).

In the 1920s and 30s, the term 'angel investor' was the nomenclature used to describe individuals or wealthy families, who because of their belief in the importance of culture and entertainment in the time of economic turmoil, helped finance Broadway shows. But although the terminology may not have existed prior to 1920s or 30s, angels were active up to thousands of years before their broad way followers. The gross number of transactions, the concealed nature of angels, and the relatively small investment size, all contribute to the difficulty behind building a formal picture of the marketplace, historical or otherwise (Bradley *et al*, 2002).

However, the funding importance of BAs has become even greater in recent years as VCs, professional investors of institutional money, in the US and the UK started to shift their investment focus away from start-ups and early-stage firms, in favour of safer and more mature ventures (Sapienza *et al.*, 1996).

Angel investors perform the key role of plugging the gap between what the entrepreneur can raise to get the firm off the ground and the level at which institutional investors and creditors will invest (Benjamin and Margulis, 2001).

Business angels are hard to study as there are many one-shot and intermittent investors (Baty and Sommer, 2002). The Center for Venture Research at the University of New Hampshire has created a profile of the 'typical' angel investor. Here are some predominant characteristics:

1. Angels tend to invest close to their home base, usually no further afield than a half-day's drive;
2. Individual angels rarely invest more than a few hundred thousand dollars in total;
3. Angel investors tend to be older, wealthier and better educated than the average citizen, yet a large number are not millionaires;
4. Angels anticipate an average annual return of 26% on their investments;
5. Angels expect that up to one-third of their investments will fail, resulting in significant capital losses;
6. Angel investors reject 7 out of every 10 deals that cross their desks; deals are rejected for a variety of reasons, including poor growth potential, overpriced equity and inexperienced management team (Jensen, 2002).

Angel investing is a global activity. That is, angel investors exist in every emerging market across the globe. Angel investors, however, are not commonly cross border investors. Angels tend to be 'touchy-feely' with their investments. They like to be able to reach out and touch their holdings. As such, most angel investments occur within a couple of hundred miles of the angel. The angel's close proximity to his or her private investment portfolio eases monitoring responsibility and promotes the value added aspect of angel-entrepreneur relationship. The market is too localized today to cross international borders (Bradley *et al.*, 2002).

Angel investments are private transactions that are not subject to any public disclosure. In addition, unlike the venture capital market, there is little institutional infrastructure supporting the angel market. For all of these reasons, data on angel investments are difficult to obtain (Denis, 2004). In India, Indian Angel Network, found in 2006 and based at Delhi, is providing a common platform for the emerging entrepreneurs to interact with the successful and established entrepreneurs (popularly known as angel investors) so that they can receive funding and their guidance towards building a quality and scalable organization. Other such networks include Mumbai Angels and Chennai Fund.

Though it is very hard (but not impossible) to measure the economic impact of angel investors' actions, it is equally true that the impact is huge. The angel market is being forced to evolve as high net-worth individuals participate. The structure of the market is changing adapt to both the new passive nature of inexperienced angels as well as to the increased demands of the traditional investor. Nonetheless, the angel investor remains a staple in the emergence of start-up companies (Bradley *et al.*, 2002).

Venture Capital

Venture capital investing is popularly referred to as the 'business of building businesses' (Benjamin and Margulis, 2001).Venture capital means many things to many people. It is in fact nearly impossible to come across one single definition of the concept. *Jane Koloski Morris*, editor of the well known industry publication, Venture Economics, defines venture capital as 'providing seed, start-up and first stage financing' and also 'funding the expansion of companies that have already demonstrated their business potential but do not yet have access to the public securities market or to credit oriented institutional funding sources (Chary, 2005). *The European Venture Capital Association* describes it as risk finance for entrepreneurial growth oriented companies. It is investment for the medium or long term to maximize returns. It is a partnership with the entrepreneur in which the investor can add value to the company because of his knowledge, experience and contact base (Kumar, 2005). According to a definition of *National Venture Capital Association (NVCA)* "Venture capital (VC) is money provided by professionals who invest alongside management in young, rapidly growing companies that have the potential to develop into significant economic contributors. Venture capital is an important source of equity for start-up companies. Professionally managed venture capital firms are generally private partnerships or closely-held corporations funded by private and public pension funds, endowment funds, foundations, corporations, wealthy individuals, foreign investors, and the venture capitalists themselves (Retrieved from http://www.nvca.org/def.html).

In reality, there is a difference between the US definition of VC and the European definition. This difference stems from the field of specialization of the VC firm and its preferences regarding the development stage of firm that invested in. The definition of venture capital as it is used in the US comprises three types of investing- seed, startup, and expansion investment and excludes buyouts. In the United States, private equity firms supplying buyout and restructuring funds to the large established funds are not accepted as being "proper" venture capitalists and as such are subsequently not accepted as members of North America Venture Capital associations (NVCA) In Europe, on the other hand, these types of VC firms are accepted as "proper" venture capitalists and thus are accepted as members of the corresponding association (Centindamar, 2008).

Professor I M Pandey has given a comprehensive definition in the Indian context. According to him, Venture capital is an investment, in the form of equity, quasiequity and sometimes debt-straight or conditional (i.e. interest and principal payable when the venture starts generating sales), made in new or untried technology, or high risk ventures, promoted by a technically or professionally qualified entrepreneur where the venture capitalist, expects the enterprise to have a very high growth rate, provides management and business skills to enterprise, expects medium to long term gains and does not expect any collateral to cover the capital provided (Pandey, 1996).

From the above mentioned definitions, it can be said that venture capital is a non-conventional, risky finance to new ventures based on innovative entrepreneurship. It is basically capital investment that includes both equity and debt and carries substantial risk and uncertainties. This investment is made in novel or untried concepts, promoted by technically or professionally qualified entrepreneurs. Here, the risk taken by the investor (Venture capitalist) is offset by participation in the future success of the firm as part owner. And the Venture capital firms are firms that are specialized in co-investing equity with the entrepreneur to fund an early stage (seed and start-up) or expansion venture.

These firms not only provides with capital, but also with the necessary competence to help the entrepreneurial firms to grow.

VC firms devote significant management resources to understanding new technologies and markets, finding promising startups in those spaces, providing them with financial resources, and coaching them through the early part of their lives (Davila Antonio *et al.*, 2001). In order to deal with the uncertainties in the startup investments (characterized in the form of asymmetric information, moral hazard problems, higher intangible assets etc.), venture capital firms tend to focus on a few industries that they get to understand very well (Gupta and Sapienza, 1992).

As noted in the definition by Prof. I M Pandey, venture capitalists take an equity position in the company and play an active role in the governance of the firm (Sapienza and Gupta, 1994). They generally sit in the board of directors and periodically monitor performance (Sahlman, 1990). This monitoring goes beyond what a traditional financing institution would do and includes spending time at the companies, frequent meetings with managers, and being involved in the definition of the companies' strategies, hiring decisions and top management compensation. In addition, venture capitalists bring their experience in evaluating the prospects of startups through their screening of potential investments (Hall and Hofer, 1993).

While VC investment involves high risk, they likewise involve high potential for return (Benjamin and Margulis, 2001). Venture capital fills the void between sources of funds for innovation and traditional, lower-cost sources of capital available to ongoing concerns. Filling that void successfully requires the venture capital industry to provide a sufficient return on capital to attract private equity funds, attractive returns to its own participants, and sufficient upside potential to entrepreneurs to attract high quality ideas that will generate high returns. Put simply, the challenge is to earn consistently superior returns on investment in inherently risky business ventures (Zider, 1998).

Usually, private equity investors do not primarily invest their own capital, but rather raise the majority of their funds from institutions and high net worth individuals. Particularly large institutional investors such as pension funds are likely to want long run, relatively illiquid private equity investments in their portfolio, given high return expectations. These institutions often do not have the professional staff or the expertise to make such investments themselves and hence channel capital to private equity funds, which have developed the necessary expertise and resources (Povaly, 2007). Typically, institutional investors, such as pension funds are limited partners. While the general partners work for the venture capital firms and run such firms. They are called venture capitalists. VC firms offer limited partners number of advantages over investing directly in startups themselves. Because these firms invest in many start ups, limited partners are more diversified. They also benefit from the expertise of the general partners. For this, General partners normally charge fees, taken normally as a percentage of the positive returns they generate. They also generally charge an annual management fee of about 2% of the fun's committed capital (Berk *et al*, 2008).

As such there is no difference between venture capital and private equity as far as their functioning is concerned. However, private equity is usually associated with the later stage, buyout and acquisition financing while venture capital is associated with early expansion financing.

To sum up the discussion, the accumulated evidence on venture capital investment highlights the basic features like an equity participation of the "outside" investors, a long-term investment horizon and an active, on-going involvement (hands-on approach) in the business of the investee company.

Difference between Angel Investors and Venture Capitalists

Both, angel investors and the VCs, invest in early stage companies and take equity stake in the ventures. Both these investors take active investment approach. However, people who do angel investing are different from the mainstream VCs. From the aforesaid discussion on venture capital and angel investors, it is now possible to differentiate between these two sources of equity on the following points.

Source of capital

Angel investors are high net-worth individuals and therefore invest their own capital in the ventures. While the venture capitalists are general partners. They raise funds from limited partners who are institutional investors such as pension funds. Thus, they invest others' money.

Stage of investment

Angel investors invest at the seed stage (concept development) while the VCs prefer to invest in the growth companies at the early and later stage of the venture development as there is less risk in such companies and potentially less time to harvest.

Amount of investment

Angels invest small amounts of approximately the size entrepreneurs require to achieve their intermediate milestone as their capacity to invest as an individual is limited. On the other hand, VCs only invest larger amounts, given that they manage larger funds and thus seek to invest in larger projects.

Motive of Investment

The investment decisions of both the investors are driven by the financial returns. However, angel investors do not solely invest for return on investment. They are more driven by emotional returns than monetary returns. These include, helping the other entrepreneurs, giving back to the society and joy of building businesses.

Approachability

The angel investor market is fragmented, lacks the structured efficiency and sophistication of the institutional market place. Therefore they are difficult to approach. However, venture capital marketplace is a highly institutionalized process, designed to bring together those with massive amounts of money to invest and those whose ideas are promising enough to warrant its receipt. So, compared to angel investors, VCs are easier to approach.

Due Diligence

Angel investors are not professional investors. They are not very rigorous in indentifying, screening and evaluating the proposals. While the VCs are professional investors and they spend lot of time and give more importance to due diligence of the potential investment proposals.

Scenario of Venture Capital Industry in India

Prior to 1997, the private equity (PE) market was very small and mostly based on official funding from the government and multilateral agencies such as World Bank. The actual growth was observed during early days of dotcom boom with entry of Foreign Institutional Investors (FIIs) (Adilakshmi and Jampala, 2007).

The flow of risk capital in India has increased substantially since year 2000. Subsequent to IT bubble, the seed stage funding declined substantially. However, the market started recovering during 2004. Table 1 provides the picture of venture capital/private equity operations in the country.

Table 1 Phases of Growth of Indian Risk Capital

	Phase I	Phase II	Phase III	Phase IV
Particulars	Pre-1995	1995-1997	1998-2001	2002-2005
Total funds (US$ mn)	30	125	2847	5239
Number of funds	8	20	50	75
Primary stages and sectors	Seed, Early Stage and Development Diversified	Development-Diversified	Early Stage and Development Telecom and IT	Growth/Maturity Diversified
Primary sources of funds	World Bank, Government	Government	Overseas Institutional	Overseas Institutional
Seed/early-stage (US$ mn)	5	15	657	250
Number of transactions	10	20	273	58
Development (US$ mn)	25	110	2186.1	3107
Number of transactions	20	45	273	288
Growth/Maturity (US$ mn)			21.9	1882
Number of transactions			2	100
Total number of transactions	20	65	548	446
Average investment (US$ mn)	1	2	5.2	11.75

(Source: *Report of the committee on Technology Innovation and Venture Capital (2006), based on TSJ Media, IVCA Publications, Retrieved from www.planningcommission.gov.in/reports/genrep/rep_vcr.pdf, accessed as on January, 2009)*

Table 1 shows that the supply of finance took off after year 1997. But there is a sharp drop in early stage financing after the end of the internet boom (1998- 2001) (Dossani and Desai, 2006) and the bulk of the money was invested into late stage development (Report of the committee on Technology Innovation and Venture Capital, 2006). In the year 2000, at the height of the internet boom, fund raising activity in the US touched its peak. When the dotcom bust happened in 2001, and was followed by events such as 9/11 and the US economic slowdown, fund raising activity declined dramatically. India felt the ripple effects of the Internet bust harder, since more than 90 per cent of the country's private equity money came from the US (Sengupta, 2006).

Consequently, during year 2001-2003, these investors started investing in more mature companies in an effort to minimize the risks. The average deal size more than doubled from $4.14 million in year 2000 to $8.52 million in year 2001, while number of early-stage deals fell sharply from 142 in year 2000 to 36 in year 2001. Late-stage deals and Private Investments in Public Equity (PIPEs) declined from 138 in year 2000 to 74 in year 2001, and investments in internet related companies fell from $576 million in year 2000 to $49 million in year 2001. This decline broadly continued until year 2003 (Aggarwal, 2006). By early year 2004, fundraising in the US, which accounts for more than 60 per cent of the world's private equity market, had begun to stabilize. The ripple effects were soon felt in other parts of the world, including emerging markets like China and India (Sengupta, 2006).

As shown in figure 3, the number of deals and the total dollars invested in India has been increasing substantially. The VC investment continuously increased till the year 2001 and then drastically reduced upto year 2003. Due to high growth prospects of Indian economy and largely soaring stock markets, investors renewed their interest and started investing again in year 2004. It is evident from the figure 5.0 that US $1650 million in investments were made in year 2004 surpassing the $1160 million in 2000 by almost 42%. These investments reached US $2200 million in year 2005. Venture capital finally made a comeback in India after 2005. During the year 2006 and 2007, there was a substantial growth of almost 241% and 89% respectively in value of investment. In absolute terms, the number of deals and the value of the investments were just 280 and $1160 million in

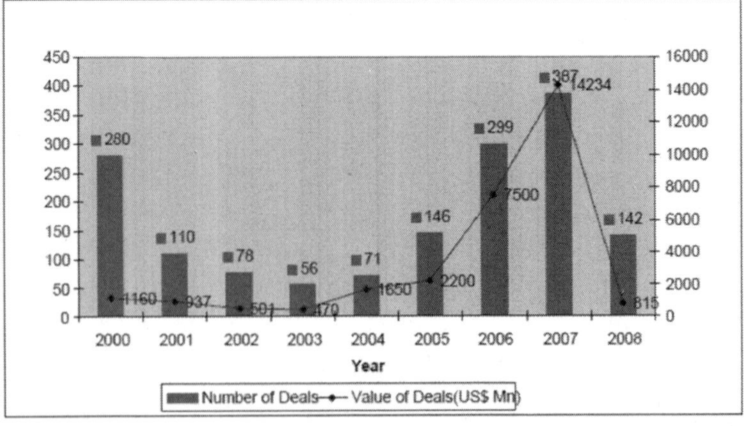

Figure 3 Total Number and Value of VC and PE Investments

year 2000, which increased to 387 and $14234 million in year 2007, respectively.

(Source: Selvakumar and Kethraj (2009), Venture Capital for Startups", *Facts for you*, 29(5), 29-32)

In the year 2008, the development of the VC market was adversely affected due to American sub-prime mortgage crisis. As per Venture Intelligence's estimates, investments during 2008 were at $815 million in 142 deals. American venture capital investments globally halved in the March quarter of 2009, dripping to a five year low of $1.87bn, while in India it was down by 29% (*The Economic Times, Ahmedabad*, 8th May, 2009, pp 5). It was a challenging time for VCs as liquidity markets were virtually shut down in the face of economic crises and cash strapped limited partners were reluctant to back new venture funds without substantial returns (Retrieved from *http://fis.dowjones.com/VS/1Q09GlobalVC.html*, accessed as on January, 2010).

The markdown in valuations and slow growth of equity market throughout year 2008 as well as in the beginning of year 2009 has raised serious consideration for Indian VC/PE industry. With companies scaling back their expansion plans and the earnings outlook for quite a few companies turning uncertain; VC/PE players have raised their share-holdings in the listed companies where they already hold a stake-through open market purchases, rather than pumping money directly into new companies (Vasudevan and Zachariah, 2009).

Of course, the future is difficult to predict because private equity investments are based on a complex combination of macroeconomic, microeconomic, and financial policy-related factors, which affect the rational and emotional sentiments of the investor community. Yet, the overall outlook for VC/PE investments in India seems to be quite promising. Despite the interim ups and downs, the VC/PE industry has made a significant progress over time. PE flows have been driven by the continuous allocation of risk capital from developed to developing economies such as India (Mukhrerjee, 2007).

Ecosystem for Entrepreneurship - Recent developments

Today, youngsters in India are mainly knowledge entrepreneurs unlike the first generation entrepreneurs who were mere traders. But such individuals lack conducive environment for successfully converting their ideas into innovations. However, this ecosystem is developing gradually with creation of many programmes, events and forums. One such organisation is *The Indus Entrepreneur* (TiE) with a global network of entrepreneurs and professionals. TiE was formed in 1992 in Silicon Valley by a group of successful entrepreneurs, corporate executives, and senior professionals. There are currently over 11,000 members and more than 2,500 charter members in 53 chapters across 12 countries. TiE provides top notch programs, marquee events, forums, special interests groups, networking with the industry and mentoring programs for members to benefit from (Retrieved from *www.tie.org › Home › About TiE,* accessed on December, 2009*)*.

Today aspiring entrepreneurs have many opportunities to interact with other entrepreneurs and investors through events like *Startup Saturday* and *Bar- Camps.* Startup Saturday is a monthly community driven forum and an initiative by the HeadStart group. It is held in Ahmedabad, Mumbai. Kolkata and Hyderabad; on every second Saturday of the month. A Startup Saturday provides a forum for entrepreneurs to discuss, present, network and learn from peers, prospective customers, adopters, partners and investors. Bar-Camp is an ad-hoc gathering born from the desire for people to share and learn in an open environment. These camps are organized and evangelized largely through the web; anyone can initiate a Bar-Camp using the BarCamp wiki. It is a new kind of technology 'unconference'- organized by attendees, for attendees. Attendees are strongly encouraged to give a demo, a session, or help with one. In India many such camps are being organized from time to time in cities such as Delhi, Mumbai, Hyderabad and Ahmedabad. *National Entrepreneurship Network* (NEN) is one more community driven initiative for the emerging entrepreneurs. Established in 2003, NEN represents India's largest and most dynamic community of new and future high-growth entrepreneurs, with over 70,000 members in 30 cities. It provides critical support to start-ups and early-stage entrepreneurs through high-impact entrepreneurship education; access to mentors and experts; fast-track access to incubation and funding; and learning tools and materials. It partners with over 470 top-tier academic institutes in India to help them develop vibrant entrepreneurship ecosystems on campus, which develop and support new and future entrepreneurs. In addition, it runs Entrepreneurship Week India, the country's largest entrepreneurship-awareness campaign. In 2009, E Week India featured over 3500 events with more than 350,000 participants. NEN was cofounded by IIT Bombay; IIM Ahmedabad; BITS, Pilani; SP Jain Institute of Management & Research, Mumbai; Institute of Bioinformatics and Applied Biotechnology, Bangalore. The programs can range from entrepreneur talks, to games and exercises, to full and short courses, mentoring, incubation, and networking events.

Today the new age entrepreneurs have access to web platforms such as *Plugged- In.* Plugged-In provides a networking to the entrepreneurs with the investors such as angel investors and VCs. Besides, many premier management and technology institutes in the country such as IITs and IIMs organized business plan competitions every year. Here, entrepreneurs get an expert advice from the investors, academicians and successful entrepreneurs on their proposed and actual venture ideas. Besides, serving as a crucial networking links, these competitions might also help the entrepreneurs in connecting with the investors and raising funding from them later.

To sum up, it may be said that on one hand, the quality of the enterprise is on ascending curve with growing number of young technically qualified entrepreneur's added while on the other hand, scope for young entrepreneurs has increased along-with various opportunities as discussed above.

Conclusion

Entrepreneurship in India has become revolutionary over a period of time. Once upon a time, starting up a business in India was a difficult task but the situation has changed for better. During the earlier times, economic growth was also slow, job and business opportunities were mainly overseas, there were infrastructure bottlenecks and government was relatively unsympathetic to business needs in general. Similarly, funds for early stage and growth companies were very limited as banks and financial institutions were not keen on providing loans and credit facilities to knowledge based enterprises. However, the situation has been a lot more favourable now for the new age entrepreneurs.

The paper provides a conceptual idea about various funding options available to these entrepreneurs for starting and growing their ventures in future. In addition to the funding sources, the study also discussed the recent developments in the field of entrepreneurship. This information sometime is loosely available in newspaper articles, research papers and magazines. This paper provides a ready compilation of the information which may benefit emerging entrepreneurs who may lack knowledge and skills regarding the financing of their ventures.

References:

1. Adilakshmi, Polavarapu and Rajesh Jampala (2007), "Private Equity

the growing Importance in Indian Capital Market", *ICFAI Reader*, 10(8), August, 18-24.

2. Aggarwal, Alok, (2006), "Is the venture capital market in India getting overheated?" August, Retrieved from *http://www.venturewoods.org/wpcontent/ uploads/2007/10/evs-article-indian-pe-market-sept-21-2007- version-5.doc,* accessed as on May, 2009.
3. Albert, Philippe and Lynda Gaynor (2001), "Incubators-growing up, moving out- A Review of the literature", Chair of high tech entrepreneurship, *CERAM Sophia Antipolis*, Retrieved from *www.ceram.fr/v3/R7_modules/R7- 5.../R7.../ACF8E09.pdf,* accessed as on December, 2008.
4. Auken Howard Van (2005), "The use of bootstrap financing among small technology based firms", *The ICFAI Journal of Entrepreneurship Development*, 2(2), June, 22-32.
5. Baty, Gordon and Sommer Bruce (2002),"True then, true now: a 40-year perspective on the early stage investment market", *Venture Capital*, 4(4), 289- 293
6. Benjamin, Gerald and Joel Margulis (2001), *The Angel Investor's Handbook*, Vision Books Private limited, New Delhi.
7. Berk, Jonathan and DeMarzo Peter (2008), *Financial Management*, Dorling Kindersley (India) Pvt. Ltd, Delhi.
8. Bhide, A. (1992), "Bootstrap Finance: The Art of Start-Ups", *Harvard Business Review,* November-December, 109-117.
9. Bradley, William, Gerald Benjamin and Joel Margulis (2002), *Angel Capital*, Capstone Publishing, United Kingdom.
10. Brettel, M (2003), "Business Angels in Germany: A research note", *Venture Capital*, 5(3), 251-268.
11. Busenitz, Lowell W, James O Fiet and Douglas D Moesel (2004), "Reconsidering the venture capitalists' "value added" proposition: An interPaper Presented at 9th Biennial Conference held at EDI, Ahmedabad during 16 18 February 2011 organizational learning perspective", *Journal of Business Venturing, 19, 787- 807.*
12. Bygrave, William and Jeffery Timmons (1992), *Venture Capital at the Crossroads*, Harvard Business School Press, USA.
13. Centindamar, Dilek (2008), "*Introduction*", in Centindamar, Dilek (eds.), *The growth of Venture Capital- A cross cultural Comparison,* Jaico Publishing House, Mumbai.
14. Chary, T Satyanarayana (2005), *Venture Capital Concepts and Applications,* Macmillan India Ltd, New Delhi.
15. Cherian, Jacob (2007), Starting Up, *The Economic Times*, 30th November, 9.

16. Davila, Antonio, George Foster and Mahendra Gupta (2001), "The Impact of Rounds of Venture Capital Funding on the Growth Strategy of Startups", November, Retrieved from *http:/gsbapps.stanford.edu/researchpapers/library/RP1727.pdf,* accessed as on December 2008.
17. Denis, David (2004), "Entrepreneurial finance: an overview of the issues and evidence", *Journal of Corporate Finance,* 10(2), 301-326.
18. Donde, Ritwik (2007),Starting Up, *The Economic Times,* 6th April, pp 9
19. Dossani, Rafiq and Asawari Desai (2006),"Accessing Early Stage Risk Capital in India", South Asia Initiative, Retrieved from *http://www.indiavca.org/upload/library/7 Dossani Stanford India VCTrends 2006.pdf* accessed as on April, 2009.
20. Ehrlich, S. B., A. F. De Noble, T. Moore, and R. R. Weaver (1994)," After the cash arrives: a comparative study of venture capital and private investor involvement in entrepreneurial firms", *Journal of Business Venturing,* 9(1), January, 67-82.
21. Fiet, J. O. (1995), "Risk avoidance strategies in venture capital markets", *Journal of Management Studies,* 32(4), July, 551-574.
22. Freear, J., J.E. Sohl, and W.E.Wetzel Jr (1995), "Who Bankrolls Software Entrepreneurs?" Retrieved from *Frontiers of Entrepreneurship Research 1995 Edition, http://www.babson.edu/entrep/fer/papers95/freear.htm,* accessed as on February, 2009.
23. Fried, V. and R. Hisrich (1994), "Towards a model of venture capital investment decision-making", *Financial Management,* 23(3), Fall, 28-37.
24. Gabrielsson, Jonas and Morten Huse (2002), "The venture capitalist and the board of directors in SMEs: roles and processes", *Venture Capital,* 4(2), 125- 146.
25. Gomez-Mejia, L. R., D. B Balkin, and T. M. Welbourne (1990)," Influence of venture capitalists on high tech management', *Journal of High Technology Management Research,* 1(1), 103-121.
26. Gorman, M and W. Sahlman (1989), "What do venture capitalists do?", *Journal of Business Venturing,* 4(4), 231-248.
27. Gupta, A and H. Sapienza (1992), "Determinants of Venture Capital firms; Preferences regarding the industry diversity and geographic scope of their investments", *Journal of Business Venturing,* 7 (5), September, 347-362.
28. Hindle, K. and R. Wenban (1999), "Australia's informal venture capitalists: an exploratory profile', *Venture Capital,* 1(2), 169-186.
29. Hindle, K and L. Lee (2002), "An exploratory investigation of Informal venture capitalists of Singapore", *Venture Capital,* 4(2), 169-181.

30. Hisrich Robert D and Michael P Peters (2002), *Entrepreneurship*, Tata McGraw-Hill Publishing Company Limited, Delhi, 380-31
31. Isaksson, Anders (2006), "Studies on Venture Capital Process" Umeå School of Business UMEÅ UNIVERSITY, *Studies in Business administration*, Serie B No.59, Retrieved from *http://urn.kb.se/resolve?urn=urn:nbn:se:umu:diva-851,* accessed as on February 2009.
32. Jensen, Mark (2002), "Angel Investors: Opportunity amidst Chaos", *Venture Capital*, 4(4), 295 -304.
33. Kumar, Aruna (2005), "Venture capital funds in India", Retrieved from *http://www.indianmba.com/Faculty_Column/FC159/fc159.html,* accessed as on April 2009.
34. Kuratko, Donald and Richard Hodgetts (2005), *Entrepreneurship-Theory, Process, Practice,* Thomsan South Western.
35. Landstorm, Hans (1993), "Informal Risk Capital in Sweden and some institutional comparisons", *Journal of Business Venturing*, 8(6), November, 525-540.
36. MacMillan, I.C., R. Siegel, P. N.Subba, Narasimha (1985), "Criteria Used by Venture Capitalists to Evaluate New Venture Proposals", *Journal of Business Venturing,* 1(1), 119-128.
37. MacMillan, I.C., L, Zemann.and SubbaNarasimha, P.N. (1987), "Criteria distinguishing successful from unsuccessful ventures in the venture screening process", *Journal of Business Venturing,* 2(2), 123-137.
38. Macmillan, I. C., D. M. Kulow, and R. Khoylian (1989), "Venture capitalists involvement in their investments—extent and performance", *Journal of Business Venturing*, 4(1), 27 – 47.
39. Mason, C. M. and R.T. Harrison (1999),"An overview of informal venture capital research", *Venture Capital*, 1(2), 95-100.
40. Mason, C. M and R.T. Harrison (1999), "Editorial Venture capital rational, aim and Scope", *Venture capital*, 1(1), 1-46.
41. Mishra, A.K. (2005), "Indian Venture Capitalists (VCs) Investment Evaluation Criteria", Retrieved from *http://129.3.20.41/eps/fin/papers/0507/0507002.pdf,* accessed as on April, 2009.
42. Mukhrerjee, Rupali, (2007), "Times Business", *The Times of India Ahmedabad*, July 18, 13.
43. Nagayya, D (2005), "Venture Capital- Recent trends in the Liberalization Context", The ICFAI journal of Entrepreneurship Development, 2(4), December, 27-40.
44. Neeley, Lynn (2003), "Entrepreneurs and Small Business Finance", Retrieved from *www.aoef.org/papers/2003/neeley.pdf,* accessed as on January, 2009.

45. Pandey, I M (1996), *Venture Capital: The Indian Experience*, Prentice Hall of India Private Limited, New Delhi.
46. Pandey, I.M. and A. Jang (1996), "Venture Capital for financing technology financing in Taiwan", *Technovation*, 16(9), September, 499-514.
47. Povaly, Stefan (2007), *Private Equity Exits*, Springer-Verlag Berlin Heidelberg, New York.
48. Prasad, D., G. Bruton and G. Vozikis (2000), "Signaling value to business angels: the proportion of entrepreneur's networth invested in a new venture as a decision signal", *Venture Capital*, 2(3), 167-82.
49. Rah, J., K. Jung, and J. Lee (1994), "Validation of the venture evaluation model in Korea", *Journal of Business Venturing*, 9(6), November, 509–524.
50. Reitan, B and R. Sorheim (2000), "The informal venture capital market in Norway: investor's characteristics, behaviour and investment preferences", *Venture Capital*, 2(2), 129-141.
51. Sagari, Silvia (1992), "Venture Capital Lessons from the developed world for developing markets", *International Finance Corporation Discussion paper* 13.
52. Sahlman, W., (1990), "The structure and governance of venture capital organizations", *Journal of Financial Economics*, 27(2), October, 473– 521.
53. Sandberg, W.R. and C.W. Hofer (1987), "Improving new venture performance: The role of strategy, industry structure and the entrepreneur", *Journal of Business Venturing*, 2(1), 5-28.
54. Sapienza, Harry and Jaume Villanueva (2007), "Conceptual and theoretical reflections on Venture Capital research", in Landstorm, Hans (eds.), *Handbook of Research on Venture Capital*, Edward Elgar, USA, 66-85.
55. Sapienza, H. J., S. Manigart, and W. Vermeir (1996), "Venture capitalist governance and value added in four countries", *Journal of Business Venturing*, 11(6), November, 439- 469.
56. Sapienza, H.J. and A. K. Gupta (1994), "Impact of agency risks and task uncertainty on venture capitalist-CEO interaction", *Academy of Management Journal*, 37(6), December, 1618- 1633.
57. Selvakumar. M. and M. Ketharaj, (2009), "Venture capital for start-ups", *Facts for You*, February, 29(5), 29-32
58. Sengupta, Snigdha, (2006), "Cover Story Private Equity Survey", *Business World*, August, 36-46.

59. Silva, Jorge (2004), "Venture capitalists' decision-making in small equity markets: a case study using participant observation", *Venture Capital*, 6(2/3), April–September, 125-145.
60. Skyrme, David (1997), "The Global Knowledge Economy and its implication for markets", Retrieved from *http://www.skyrme.com/insight/21gke.htm*, accessed as on May 2008.
61. Sorheim, R. (2003), "The pre-investment behaviour of business angles: a social capital approach", *Venture Capital*, 5(4), 337-64.
62. Sun, Hongyi, Ni Wenbin, Joseph Leung (2007), "Critical Success Factors for Technological Incubation: Case Study of Hong Kong Science and Technology Parks", *International Journal of Management* 24(2), June, 346-363.
63. Sweeting, R. C. (1991), "UK venture capital funds and the funding of new technology-based businesses: process and relationships", *Journal of Management Studies*, 28(6), November, 601-622.
64. Sweeting R. C. and C. F. Wong (1997), "A UK `hands-off' venture capital firm and the handling of post-investment investor-investee relationships", *Journal of Management Studies*, 34(1), January, 125-152.
65. Timmons, Jeffry A. and William D. Bygrave (1986), "Venture capital's role in financing innovation for economic growth", *Journal of Business Venturing,* 1(2), 161-176.
66. Tyebjee, tyzoon and Albert v. Bruno (1984), "A model of venture capitalist investment activity", *Management Science*, 30(9), 1051-1066.
67. Van Osnabrugge, M. (2000), "A comparison of business angels and venture capital investment procedures: an agency theory based analysis", *Venture Capital*, 2(2), 91-109.
68. Vasudevan, Naresh and Reena Zachariah (2009), *The Economic Times, Ahmedabad*, 5th March, 6.
69. Van Auken, Howard E and L. Neeley (1996), "Evidence of Bootstrap Financing Among Small Start-up Firms", *Journal of Entrepreneurial and Small Business Finance* 5(3), 235-249.
70. Winborg, Joakim and Hans Landstorm (2001), "Financial Bootstrapping In Small Businesses A Resource-Based View On Small Business Finance", *Journal of Business Venturing*, 16(3), 235-254.
71. Zider, Bob, (1998), "How Venture Capital works", *Harvard Business Review*, Nov-Dec, 131-139.

3

An Empirical Study on the Factors of Entrepreneurs Suggested to Bootstrapped Entrepreneurs

Abstract

Entrepreneurship refers to an individual's ability to turn ideas into action. It includes creativity, innovation and risk taking, as well as the ability to plan and manage projects in order to achieve objectives. Bootstrapping is entrepreneurship in its purest form. It is the transformation of human capital into financial capital. It typically involves the use of personal savings, credit card debt, loans from friends and family and other nontraditional forms of capital. The success of an enterprise hinges on the ability of its owner(s) to create and leverage financial resources. Bootstrapping generally involves the acquisition and control of resources (both tangible and intangible) through creative means. Emerging bootstrapped entrepreneurs encounter some pitfalls along the way. Hence, the main objectives of this descriptive type of research paper are given below:

1. To identify the factors that influence entrepreneurship.
2. To analyze bootstrapping in entrepreneurship.
3. To analyze the sustainability of bootstrapped entrepreneurs.

The study includes survey and fact finding enquiries of different kinds. Since this research focuses on the sustainability of bootstrapped entrepreneurs, it is designed as an empirical study. The important outcome of this study is to find out the factors which affect the sustainability of bootstrapped entrepreneurs and obtain a solution for the problem.

Introduction

Entrepreneurship is the process of creating something new with value by devoting the necessary time and effort, assuming financial, psychic, and social risks, and receiving the resulting rewards of monetary and personal satisfaction and independence.

This definition stresses four basic aspects of being an entrepreneur regardless of the field.

First, entrepreneurship involves the creation process – creating something new of value.

Second, entrepreneurship requires the devotion of the necessary time and effort.

Assuming the necessary risk (generally center around financial, psychological and social areas) is the third aspect of entrepreneurship.

The final part of the definition involves the rewards of being an entrepreneur. Coming to bootstrapped entrepreneurship, the definition taken from Wikipedia is:

Financial bootstrapping is a term used to cover different methods for avoiding using the financial resources of external investors. Bootstrapping can be defined as "a collection of methods used to minimize the amount of outside debt and equity financing needed from banks and investors"[11]. The use of private credit card debt is the most known form of bootstrapping, but a wide variety of methods are available for entrepreneurs. While bootstrapping involves a risk for the founders, the absence of any other stakeholders gives the founders more freedom to develop the company. Many successful companies including Dell Computers were founded this way. There are different types of bootstrapping:

1. Owner financing
2. Sweat equity
3. Minimization of the accounts receivable
4. Joint utilization
5. Delaying payment

6. Minimizing inventory
7. Subsidy finance
8. Personal Debt

Problem of Study

For the person who actually starts his or her own business, the experience is filled with enthusiasm, frustration, anxiety, and hard work. There is high failure rate due to such things as poor sales, intense competition, lack of capital, lack of family support or lack of managerial ability. Inspite of such a high failure rate due to n number of factors a handsome number of entrepreneurs sustain in the market. These inevitable factors can be adopted by bootstrapped entrepreneurs for their growth and sustainability in the environment for a period of long run.

Objectives of the Study

1. To identify the factors that influences the sustainability of entrepreneurship.

2. To analyze bootstrapping in entrepreneurship.

3. To help the bootstrapped entrepreneurs to understand the factors for sustainability.

Scope of the Study

The present research aims to help the bootstrapped entrepreneurs to get stable in the market by understanding the factors which are necessary for their sustainability which is a very essential quality for an entrepreneur.

Review of Literature

Mill (1984) suggested that risk taking is a key factor in distinguishing entrepreneurs from managers. It is believed that entrepreneurs take greater degree of risk especially in areas where they have control or competencies in realizing the profit. Many studies have included risk taking as a major entrepreneurial characteristic. Mitton (1989) confirmed that entrepreneurs eagerly undertake the unknown and uncertain circumstances, thus the entrepreneurial inclined individuals are expected to display more tolerance of ambiguity than others. As far as innovativeness is concerned, Mitton suggested that it is the focal point of entrepreneurship and an essential entrepreneur characteristic. Indeed entrepreneurial literatures show that entrepreneurs are significantly more innovative than non-entrepreneurs (Ho & Koh, 1992; Robinson & Sexton, 1994).

Entrepreneurs' personality traits have also been identified to have impact on organizational performance (Robinson & Sexton, 1994). Studies also found that personality traits such as locus of control and ambiguity tolerance influenced the business success directly and the business process indirectly (Entrialgo, Fernandez, & Vazquez, 2000). Kiggundu (2002) later added demographic variables to his study and found that personality traits have direct influence on the success of African entrepreneurs. Although studies on personality traits have played an important role in contributing to the success of entrepreneurs worldwide, nevertheless, personality traits have been criticized both on theoretical and empirical ground in the studies of entrepreneurship. Gartner (1988) in his research article entitled "Who is the entrepreneur?" mentioned that asking "Who" is the wrong question, but rather the personality of entrepreneur is only related to the success of business start-up through more specific mediating processes. This is due to the fact that these factors are not relevant if there is no action and initiative taken by the entrepreneurs.

Data Source

The target population for this study is the members of TIE Chennai (who are entrepreneurs in various areas). A letter was sent to nearly 400 members of TIE requesting for their participation in this survey and share their details. However, only 53 of them managed to participate in this study. Self completion questionnaire was utilized to collect data for this study. Secondary data was collected from various sources like books, magazines, journals and websites.

Limitations of the Study

1. The study is limited to 53 respondents only due to shortage of time.
2. As the sample is small the result cannot be generalized
3. There is hesitation on the part of the respondents towards full disclosure.

Data Analysis and Intrepretation

The major factors for sustainability in entrepreneurship are explained in one sample t-test. The result of one sample t-test is described as follows:

Inference

From the above table it is found that the mean value range from 2.20 to 4.92 with consistency. Standard Deviation less that 1 except the three variables with standard deviation greater than 1. The values of the standard error are also found to be consistent.

Table 1
One-Sample Statistics

	N	Mean	Std. Deviation	Std. Error Mean
EducationLevel	53	4.3019	.84546	.11613
InterPersonalSkills	53	4.4906	.57588	.07910
PriorWorkExp	53	3.8868	.64032	.08796
ParentsOwnBusiness	53	2.2075	1.00687	.13830
FeasibleBusinessPlan	53	3.2264	1.17082	.16082
StrategicPlanning	53	4.1132	.89142	.12245
RaiseCapital	53	3.4340	1.10086	.15122
FinancialPlanning	53	4.3962	.68891	.09463
SalesPromotion	53	4.7358	.48639	.06681
MarketUnderstanding	53	4.9245	.26668	.03663
MarketAnalysis	53	4.9057	.29510	.04053
EmployeeRecruitment	53	4.0755	.75572	.10381
HRPolicies	53	4.2453	.70454	.09678
PerformanceAppraisal	53	4.4906	.60836	.08356
EmployeeMotivation	53	4.7170	.49526	.06803
PersonalInitiative	53	4.8868	.37521	.05154

Table 2
One-Sample Test

	Test Value = 3					
	t	df	Sig. (2-tailed)	Mean Difference	95% Confidence Interval of the Difference	
					Lower	Upper
EducationLevel	11.210	52	.000	1.30189	1.0688	1.5349
InterPersonalSkills	18.843	52	.000	1.49057	1.3318	1.6493
PriorWorkExp	10.082	52	.000	.88679	.7103	1.0633
ParentsOwnBusiness	-5.730	52	.000	-.79245	-1.0700	-.5149
FeasibleBusinessPlan	1.408	52	.165	.22642	-.0963	.5491
StrategicPlanning	9.091	52	.000	1.11321	.8675	1.3589
RaiseCapital	2.870	52	.006	.43396	.1305	.7374
FinancialPlanning	14.755	52	.000	1.39623	1.2063	1.5861
SalesPromotion	25.982	52	.000	1.73585	1.6018	1.8699
MarketUnderstanding	52.538	52	.000	1.92453	1.8510	1.9980
MarketAnalysis	47.013	52	.000	1.90566	1.8243	1.9870
EmployeeRecruitment	10.360	52	.000	1.07547	.8672	1.2838
HRPolicies	12.868	52	.000	1.24528	1.0511	1.4395
PerformanceAppraisal	17.837	52	.000	1.49057	1.3229	1.6583
EmployeeMotivation	25.239	52	.000	1.71698	1.5805	1.8535
PersonalInitiative	36.609	52	.000	1.88679	1.7834	1.9902

The following t-test clearly mentions the significance of the factors of the sustainability in entrepreneurship.

Inference

All the test values are statistically significant.

ONE Way ANOVA is carried out to analyze microscopically to compare mean classification of the categorical analysis.

Influence of age of the Entrepreneurs on the Factors Of Sustainability In Entrepreneurship

The study encounters with four different classification of age of the entrepreneurs from 20 - 34, 35 – 49, 50 – 64 and above 65. Results of one way ANOVA is clearly presented below:

Table 3

ANOVA

		Sum of Squares	df	Mean Square	F	Sig.
HumanCapital	Between Groups	16.848	3	5.616	2.046	.120
	Within Groups	134.473	49	2.744		
	Total	151.321	52			
Planning	Between Groups	5.231	3	1.744	.816	.491
	Within Groups	104.655	49	2.136		
	Total	109.887	52			
FinancialAspect	Between Groups	2.853	3	.951	.503	.682
	Within Groups	92.618	49	1.890		
	Total	95.472	52			
MarketingAspects	Between Groups	68.018	3	22.673	.493	.689
	Within Groups	2253.227	49	45.984		
	Total	2321.245	52			
HRAspects	Between Groups	4.466	3	1.489	.852	.472
	Within Groups	85.647	49	1.748		
	Total	90.113	52			
PersonalInitiative	Between Groups	.141	3	.047	.320	.811
	Within Groups	7.180	49	.147		
	Total	7.321	52			

Inference

The above ANOVA table explains that all the factors are statistically significant with respect to the age of the entrepreneurs.

Influence of Educational Qualification of the Entrepreneurs on the Factors of Sustainability In Entrepreneurship

The study encounters with four different classification of educational qualification of the entrepreneurs from School Level, College Level, Professional Level and Others. Results of one way ANOVA is clearly presented below:

Table 4

ANOVA

		Sum of Squares	df	Mean Square	F	Sig.
HumanCapital	Between Groups	41.662	3	13.887	6.205	.001
	Within Groups	109.659	49	2.238		
	Total	151.321	52			
Planning	Between Groups	18.750	3	6.250	3.360	.026
	Within Groups	91.136	49	1.860		
	Total	109.887	52			
FinancialAspect	Between Groups	18.010	3	6.003	3.797	.016
	Within Groups	77.462	49	1.581		
	Total	95.472	52			
MarketingAspects	Between Groups	12.086	3	4.029	.085	.968
	Within Groups	2309.159	49	47.126		
	Total	2321.245	52			
HRAspects	Between Groups	.454	3	.151	.083	.969
	Within Groups	89.659	49	1.830		
	Total	90.113	52			
PersonalInitiative	Between Groups	.222	3	.074	.511	.676
	Within Groups	7.098	49	.145		
	Total	7.321	52			

Inference

The above ANOVA table explains that all the factors except Personal Initiative are statistically significant with respect to the educational qualifications of the entrepreneurs.

Influence Of Mode Of Mobilization Of Funds By The Entrepreneurs On The Factors Of Sustainability In Entrepreneurship

The study encounters with three different classification of the mode of mobilization of funds by the entrepreneurs viz., Own funds, Venture Capitalist, Angel Funding. Results of one way ANOVA is clearly presented below:

Table 5
ANOVA

		Sum of Squares	df	Mean Square	F	Sig.
HumanCapital	Between Groups	41.662	3	13.887	6.205	.001
	Within Groups	109.659	49	2.238		
	Total	151.321	52			
Planning	Between Groups	18.750	3	6.250	3.360	.026
	Within Groups	91.136	49	1.860		
	Total	109.887	52			
FinancialAspect	Between Groups	18.010	3	6.003	3.797	.016
	Within Groups	77.462	49	1.581		
	Total	95.472	52			
MarketingAspects	Between Groups	12.086	3	4.029	.085	.968
	Within Groups	2309.159	49	47.126		
	Total	2321.245	52			
HRAspects	Between Groups	.454	3	.151	.083	.969
	Within Groups	89.659	49	1.830		
	Total	90.113	52			
PersonalInitiative	Between Groups	.222	3	.074	.511	.676
	Within Groups	7.098	49	.145		
	Total	7.321	52			

Inference

The above ANOVA table explains that all the factors except Human Capital are statistically significant with respect to the mode of mobilization of funds by the entrepreneurs.

Study on the Reltionship Between Bootstrapped Entrepreneurship and Years of Sustainability in the Business

Table 7

Correlations

		NO OF YEARS IN BUSINESS	BUSINESS BY OWN MONEY
NO OF YEARS IN BUSINESS	Pearson Correlation	1	.251
	Sig. (2-tailed)		.070
	N	53	53
BUSINESS BY OWN MONEY	Pearson Correlation	.251	1
	Sig. (2-tailed)	.070	
	N	53	53

Inference

The relationship between entrepreneurs starting their business by their own money and sustaining in the market is positively correlated to an extent of 0.251.

Study on the Relationship Between Amount Invested By Bootstrapped Entrepreneurs And Years Of Sustainability In The Business

Table 8
Correlations

		Years in Business	Initial Investment
Years in Business	Pearson Correlation	1	.048
	Sig. (2-tailed)		.731
	N	53	53
Initial Investment	Pearson Correlation	.048	1
	Sig. (2-tailed)	.731	
	N	53	53

The relationship between the amount invested initially by bootstrapped entrepreneurs and sustaining in the market is positively correlated to an extent of 0.048.

Major Pitfalls in Entrepreneurship Journey

The problems faced by the entrepreneurs and their mean ranks are categorized according to Friedman's test as follows:

Inference

The above test explains clearly that the major pitfalls for sustainability in entrepreneurship are :

1. Rejection of Business Plan
2. Lack of Government Support
3. Lack of Mentorship

4. Lack of Technological Updation
5. Lack of Experience
6. Cash Flow Problems
7. Lack of Family Support

Table 9

Ranks

	Mean Rank
FamilyDistraction	5.18
CashflowProblem	5.39
Competitions	5.38
LackofExperience	5.47
LackofMentorship	5.58
HeavyCollateralReq	5.14
RejectionOfBusinessPlan	5.87
HighEmployeeAttrition	5.55
LackofGovtSupport	5.78
LackofTechnologyUpdate	5.67

Summary & Findings

1. The age of the entrepreneurs are influenced on the factors of sustainability in entrepreneurship
2. Educational qualification of the entrepreneur has an influence on all the factors except Personal Initiative qualifications of the entrepreneurs.
3. Human Capital is the only factor which is influenced by the mode of mobilization of funds by the entrepreneurs.
4. The relationship between entrepreneurs starting their business by their own money and sustaining in the market is positively correlated to an extent of 0.251.
5. The relationship between the amount invested by bootstrapped entrepreneurs and sustaining in the market is positively correlated to an extent of 0.048.
6. The major problems faced by an entrepreneur for his sustainability are listed as :

i) Rejection of Business Plan

ii) Lack of Government Support
iii) Lack of Mentorship
iv) Lack of Technological Updation
v) Lack of Experience
vi) Cash Flow Problems
vii) Lack of Family Support

Suggestions

According to the study, Bootstrapped entrepreneurs are unable to sustain in the market due to various reasons. in order to get stabilized in their current entrepreneurship environment, they need to take necessary steps in formulating their business plan, identifying mentors, technological updating, manage their cash flows & fund flows. On top of everything family support is also an essential attribute for bootstrapped entrepreneurs.

Conclusion

Many start-up entrepreneurs do have the necessary skills and opportunity to create a giant "in the making" company, nevertheless, concerns such as the lack of education, experience, moral and financial support have always been the few major stumbling blocks or rather mental blocks holding them back from their journey to success. It is very clear that a large number of entrepreneurs affirmed personal initiative as one of the major key to success. It has also illustrated that entrepreneurs with high personal initiative will further enhance their management, improve business operation skills, and embark in a continuous learning and development attitude. Some of the entrepreneurs have given their view about their sustainability that it is a great task as it consists of risk, it expects a lot of family support, it is an understanding maker, it makes a paradigm shift, it needs financial support and infrastructure. The more and more entrepreneurs grow and sustain so is the national economy.

Bibiliography

1. Entrialgo, M. Fernandez, E., & Vazquez, C. J. (2000). Psychological characteristics and process: the role of entrepreneurship in Spanish SMEs. European Journal of Innovation Management, 3(3), 137-151.
2. Ho, T. S., & Koh, H. C. (1992). Differences in psychological characteristics between entrepreneurially inclined and non-entrepreneurially inclined accounting graduates in Singapore. Entrepreneurship, Innovation and Change: An International Journal,1,243-254.

3. Kiggundu, M. N. (2002). Entrepreneurs and entrepreneurship in Africa: What is known and what needs to be done. Journal of Developmental Entrepreneurship, 7 (3), 239-258.
4. Mill, J. S. (1984). Principles of political economy with some application to social philosophy. London: John W. Parker.
5. Mitton, D. G. (1989). The complete entrepreneur. Entrepreneurship: Theory and Practice, 13, 9-19.
6. Madhurima Lall, & Shikh Sahai (2006) Entrepreneurship, Excel Books, Chapter 5, 137 – 138.
7. Robert D Hisrich, Michael P Peters Dean A Sheperd (2007) Entrepreneurship Tata McGraw Hill Education Pvt Limited, Chapter 11, 326 – 329.
8. Vasant Desai (2006) Dynamics of Entrepreneurial Development & Management, Himalaya Publishing House, Chapter 3, 24 – 27.

4

SHG – A Significant Tool for Co-operative Entrepreneurship in Rural West Bengal

Abstract

The current concept of Global Village seems very apt even in this 21st century marked by modernization and hi-tech revolution as the world is predominantly rural till date, especially the developing world. About 69% of the people of low income countries live in rural areas and in South Asia the figure stands at 72%. Thus, more than three quarters of the world's population lives in rural areas and more than a half of the world's poor are expected to do so in 2025. As is well known, that rural population is a major population segment in India. According to the 2001 Census of India, 72.2% of the total population is rural. The rural economy still accounts nearly 40% of India's GDP. Share of exports coming from rural economy in GDP is also on the increase. Major contribution to exports comes from the agricultural and allied sectors such as handloom, power loom, gem & jewellery, handicrafts, carpets, leather and mineral products, all of which have at least one primary rural production base. However, despite the strong base of our rural economy, there is consensus that more than 250 million people remain poor in India, even after 63 years of Independence, irrespective of the debate on the methodology and indicators used for poverty estimates. A humble attempt has been made in this paper to review the status of cooperative entrepreneurship in rural West Bengal.

Keywords: SHG, Cooperative entrepreneurship, rural population, rural economy.

Introduction

The current concept of Global Village seems very apt even in this 21st century marked by modernization and hi-tech revolution as the world is predominantly rural till date, especially the developing world. About 69% of the people of low income countries live in rural area and in South Asia the figure stands at 72%. Thus, more than three quarters of the world's population lives in rural areas and more than a half of the world's poor are expected to do so in 2025. As is well known, that rural population is a major population segment in India. According to the 2001 Census of India, 72.2% of the total population is rural. The rural economy still accounts nearly 40% of India's GDP. Share of exports coming from rural economy in GDP is also on the increase. Major contribution to exports comes from the agricultural and allied sectors such as handloom, power loom, gem & jewellery, handicrafts, carpets, leather and mineral products, all of which have at least one primary rural production base. However, despite the strong base of our rural economy, there is consensus that more than 250 million people remain poor in India, even after 63 years of Independence, irrespective of the debate on the methodology and indicators used for poverty estimates.

Objective of the Study and Data Source

The objective of the study is to review in general the overall progress of SHGs movement in West Bengal over the last decade. Data have been collected mainly from secondary sources. They include Ministry of Self Help and Self Employment, Govt. of West Bengal, NABARD, SIDC, SIDBI, SUDA etc.

The Malice of Rural Indebtedness

The rural scene in India has several other special features. Agriculture is the mainstay of the rural population and its seasonal nature reflects itself in lack of work for many during the lean agricultural season. Also much of the economic activities are carried on in household enterprises and self-employment. The distinguishing feature of the household enterprises is that economic activities take place in a wider complex of family activities with intermittent participation by members of the household, particularly women and children. Therefore, the employment scene in rural India is marked by the prevalence of both chronic and short term employment in the sense of involuntary unemployment as well as visible and invisible underemployment. This growth in this rural unemployed force further complicates the poverty estimates (Table 1) and hinders the development efforts.

Table 1: Incidence of rural poverty (major states) (2004-05)

State	Percent of rural population below poverty line
Andhra Pradesh	7.5
Assam	17.0
Bihar	32.9
Chhattisgarh	31.2
Gujarat	13.9
Haryana	9.2
Himachal Pradesh	7.2
Jharkhand	40.2
Karnataka	12.0
Kerala	9.6
Madhya Pradesh	29.8
Maharashtra	22.2
Orissa	39.8
Rajasthan	14.3
Tamilnadu	16.9
Tripura	17.0
Uttar Pradesh	25.3
West Bengal	24.2
All India	21.8

Source: NSSO 2004-05 survey

Poverty is the main cause of the indebtedness of the Indian farmers. The farmer needs huge amount of financial support for adopting new technologies, use of High Yield Varieties Seed, fertilization of fields etc. However increase indebtedness, idiosyncrasies of monsoons or natural calamities will create an insurmountable debt trap for these all poverty-stricken small and marginal farmers of rural India. They lose both ways- Get a low price while selling their produce but have to pay high prices while buying inputs. Socially this indebtedness creates a class of landless labourers and tenants in the place of independent farmers.

To overcome this problem measures should be adopted for (a) Settlement of old debt; (b) Reduction on dependence on money lenders and (c) Control of new loan. In some of our States Legislations have been passed to prevent farmers from selling their lands to professional money lenders who are not farmers. At the same time measures have been taken to control the activity of the farmer.

In 1975 the Government of India had declared a moratorium on the recovery of debt by money lenders from farmers, landless labourers and rural artisans. *Liquidation of rural indebtedness* and *abolition of bonded* labour were two dynamic aspects of the 20-point economic program declared in the year 1975.

Recent Development in Rural Finance: Micro Finance

Micro credit or micro finance is a novel approach to "banking with the poor". In this approach, very successfully tried in Bangla Desh (thanks to the initiatives of Dr. Mohammed Younis, the founder of Grameen Bank and also awarded with Nobel Prize for his unique effort to eradicate rural poverty) ,bank credit is extended to the poor through Self Help Groups (SHGs), Non-Government Organisations (NGOs), credit unions, etc. Micro credit attempts to combine lower transaction costs and high degree of repayments. This is essentially because of the involvement of potential beneficiaries of rural credit in the credit delivery system. The SHG-bank linkage programme, introduced and encouraged by NABARD is now implemented vigorously by more than 30,000 branches of commercial banks, RRBs, and cooperative banks in over 500 districts in 30 states and Union Territories of India.

At the end of March 2007, as many as 2.9 million SHGs are now linked with banks and 7,000 NGOs are associated with the scheme. It is estimated that, at the end of March 2007, 20 million very poor families were brought within the fold of formal banking services. The notable feature was the active women participation - 90 per cent of the groups linked with the banks were exclusively women groups. Also there was strong repayment performance – at more than 95 per cent of the loans disbursed. The disbursement of bank loans to SHGs was ' 18,040 crores in 2006-07 ('11,400 crores in the previous year). The average loan per SHG came to nearly '30,000 and the average loan per family came to '1,770.

Micro-finance initiatives have shown that banking with the poor is a viable proposition. Micro-credit has been hailed as the best method of creating additional employment and removing poverty. NABARD has been playing a catalytic role in terms of promotional support to NGOs and also in nurturing quality SHGs. It has launched a pilot project (2005-06) for promotion of micro enterprises among the members of matured SHGs.

Self-help Groups (SHGs): A Major Catalyst for Rural Economic Development

Alternative development thinkers emphasize participation, self-reliance and self-help as basic human rights (Friedman 1992, Rahman 1993). Development involves changes in the awareness, motivation and behaviour of individuals, in the relations between individuals as well as between groups within a society (Burkey, 1993). These changes can come from within individuals and groups through self-help, and not necessarily from outside. The experiences of self-reliance have led to attempts to build local level organizations like, cooperatives, credit societies, neighborhood or community development associations, water sharing associations or women's groups. The Neo-liberal paradigm has also incorporated self-reliance as a strategy for building people's entrepreneurial spirits and absorption into the capital market (Fernando 2006).

In other words, self help approach is the opposite of waiting for government to deliver services and has a collective connotation (Krause, 2004). Against this backdrop, the group-based model of self-help is widely practiced for rural development, poverty alleviation, entrepreneurship development and empowerment of women. Self-help Groups (SHGs) are playing a major role in rural India today. Self-help, as a strategy for social development, places emphasis on self-reliance, human agency and action. It aims to mobilize people, to give them voice and build people's organizations that will overcome barriers to participation and empowerment. Central to the idea of self-help is the formation of groups, concept of a 'community' and the development of egalitarian relationships that will promote people's well-being. The self-help model in India facilitates institution-building in the form of people's organizations in the form of groups, clusters and federations. The poor, however, seldom organize themselves. It is an assisted self-help (Uphoff and Esman, 1984) process where the State, the financial institutions and the nongovernmental organizations (NGOs) play an important role in mobilizing and assisting the poor and the needy. While the policies of the external agents of development places emphasis on building institutions to assist the poor and women, the practice-oriented reality has to deal with the structural barriers that people, women and the organizations face. At the level of practice, the outcomes of self-help depend on building mutually beneficial relationships, negotiating power and gaining control.

The spread of SHGs in India has been phenomenal. It has made dramatic progress from 500 groups in 1992 (Titus, 2002) to some 1,618,456 groups that have taken loans from banks. About 24.25 million poor households have gained access to formal banking system through SHG-bank linkage programme and 90% of these groups are women only groups

(NABARD, 2005). The NABARD (2006) homepage declares that more than 400 women join the SHG movement every hour and an NGO joins the micro-finance programme every day.

It is clear from Table 2 that the trend of SHG promotion under SGSY between 1999-2000 and 2007-08 in the country indicates that the number of SHGs formed in 2007-08 (306688) was about 104% of the number of SHGs formed during 1999- 2000 (292426).

The annual growth rate of formation of SHGs has not shown any definite increasing or decreasing trend over the years. During the year 2000-01, i.e. the second year of formation of SHGs in India, witnessed a negative growth of – 23.6% as compared to the previous year.

Table 2: Physical progress under SGSY since its inception on 1.4.1999

Particulars	1999-00	2000-01	2001-02	2002-03	2003-04
SHGs formed (Nos.)	242426	223265 (-23.6)	434387 (94.5)	398873 (-8.2)	392136 (-1.7)
Percent of women SHGs	NA	NA	NA	55.4	59.5
SHGs involved in economic activities	29017	26317 (-9.3)	30576 (16.2)	35525 (16.2)	50717 (42.8)

Particulars	2004-05	2005-06	2006-07	2007-08	Total

SHGs formed (Nos.)	266230 (-32.1)	276414 (3.83)	246309 (-10.9)	306688 (24.5)	2786728
Percent of women SHGs	72.0	77.1	71.7	75.5	-----
SHGs involved in economic activities	68102 (34.3)	80130 (17.7)	137931 (72.1)	181386 (31.5)	639701

Particulars	1999-00	2000-01	2001-02	2002-03	2003-04
Total funds available	1962.0	1608.2	1299.5	1178.2	1214.9
Total funds utilized	959.9	1117.9	970.3	921.1	1043.4
Total Credit Mobilized	1056.5	1459.4	1329.7	1184.3	1302.1
Total subsidy disbursed	541.7	701.9	665.6	605.9	713.4
Credit subsidy ratio	2.0	2.1	2.0	2.0	1.8
Total investment	1598.2	2161.3	1995.3	1790.2	2015.5
Per capita investment	17113	21480	21283	21665	22471

Note: (a) NA Not available; (b) Figures in the parentheses are annual growth rates

Source: Monitoring Division of Ministry of Rural Development, GoI.

During 2001-02, there was a high positive growth rate of SHG formation (94.5%) whereas the next three years experienced negative growth at -8.2, -1.7 and - 32.1 % respectively. During 2007-08, the SHG formation marked an increment of 24.5%. On the other hand, the number of SHGs assisted increased more than sixfold from 29,017 in 1999-00 to 181386 during 2007-08. In case of SHGs, which have taken up economic activities, there has been a positive increment in the linkage of SHGs to self-employment activities except in the year 2000-01.

As on October 1, 2008, 7.06 lakhs SHGs have been linked with credit and taken up economic activities. Table 3 indicates that on an average an amount of ‘ 1601.1 crore is available under the SGSY programme. The matching credit mobilized so far is 1563.1 crore. The cumulative subsidy disbursed is ‘7630.4 crore during the last ten years under the programme. This implies that the credit subsidy ratio is only 2:1 which is well below the government norm of at least 3:1. While the total investment has been estimated to be ‘ 23,040, it is however, below the desired level of the government's indicative and targeted per capita investment of ‘ 25,000 per beneficiary (MoRD, 2007).

There are also agencies, which provide bulk funds to the system through NGOs. Thus organizations engaged in micro finance activities in India may be categorized as wholesalers, NGOs supporting SHG Federations and NGOs directly retailing credit borrowers or groups of borrowers. The spread of the SHGs again show that it is highly concentrated in the southern part of the country with very few in the north and the east. Over half a million SHGs have been linked to banks over the years but a handful of States, mostly in South India, account for almost 60% of this figure (Harper, 2002; NABARD, 2005). Andhra Pradesh has over 42%, Tamil Nadu and Uttar Pradesh have 12% and 11% respectively, and Karnataka has about 9% of the total SHGs (Chakrabarti, 2004). Thus, the rise of the movement has been very high in the Southern States, and very minor in Haryana and in the North-East.

Table 4 shows the percent of credit disbursed to all the states under SGSY and the credit availability in the regions of high poverty and backwardness like Jharkhand, Bihar, Orissa, Madhya Pradesh, and West Bengal (as shown in Table 1 from NSSO data on poverty) happens to below.

Per capita credit for rural poor available under SGSY suggests that the poorer states received lower level of per capita credit, while the states with lower incidence of rural poverty received relatively higher levels of institutional credit in 1999-2000. The per capita credit levels have, however sown impressive gains in 2007-08. Andhra Pradesh registered a remarkable rise in this area since per.

SHG member credit rose from ‘3,635 to ‘22,406 during this period and with only a 2.9 % share in the national rural poverty, its share in the national SGSY credit disbursement increased from 8.9% in 1999-00 to 10.1 % in 2007-08.

The rise in the share of credit disbursement in case of Uttar Pradesh can also be accorded to its high percent of rural poor along with its reasonable performance in the area of per capita credit. However, states like Bihar have registered an alarming fall in the share of credit disbursement in 2007-08 to 5.5% from 10.3% in 1999-00 despite a high percent of rural poor (15.2%) and a reasonably good performance in per capita credit during the period. A similar treatment with West Bengal is unjustifiable.

Table 3: Financial progress under SGSY since its inception on 1.4.99 (Crore)

Particulars	2004-05	2005-06	2006-07	2007-08	Total
Total funds available	1511.2	1558.5	1724.6	2394.2	14451.3
Total funds utilized	1290.8	1338.8	1424.2	1966.0	11032.4
Total Credit Mobilized	1658.2	1823.2	2291.2	2760.3	14864.9
Total subsidy disbursed	858.8	904.8	971.1	1289.1	7252.3
Credit subsidy ratio	1.9	2.0	2.4	2.1	2.04
Total investment	2517.0	2728.0	3262.3	4049.4	22117.2
Per capita investment	22555	23698	19281	28764	198310

Source: monitoring division of ministry of rural development, GoI.

Table 4: State-wise share of credit disbursed and per capita credit under SGSY (major states)

States	bank credit per assisted swarozgaris		credit disbursed		rural poor 2004-05 percent
	1999-2000	2007-2008	1999-2000 percent	2007-2008 percent	
Andhra Pradesh	3,635	22,406	8.9	10.1	2.9
Assam	7,176	13,396	0.8	4.8	2.5
Bihar	2,347	14,856	10.3	5.5	15.2
Chhattisgarh	6,153	21,721	3.5	3.6	3.2
Gujarat	13,844	16,168	2.1	2.3	2.9
Haryana	4,446	27,724	2.8	2.0	1.0
Himachal Pradesh	13,150	25,350	2.1	0.8	0.3
Jharkhand	1,432	9,242	5.3	3.2	4.7
Karnataka	16,986	18,462	3.2	5.6	3.4
Kerala	12,069	20,620	4.7	2.4	1.5
Madhya Pradesh	2,312	27,382	10.3	9.6	8.0
Maharashtra	18,331	17,171	14.6	7.8	7.7
Orissa	8,686	20,068	8.9	6.4	6.9
Rajasthan	12,567	30,498	5.8	4.9	4.0
Tamil Nadu	10,917	16,623	7.0	5.3	3.5
Tripura	NA	11,314	0.9	0.5	0.3
Uttar Pradesh	13,705	18,735	9.7	20.1	21.4
West Bengal	6,203	12,845	6.8	1.6	7.8
All India	5,383	18,113	100	100	100

Source: Department of rural development, MoRD, GoI.

Characteristics of SHGs

Self-help group (SHG) is generally an economically homogeneous group formed through a process of self-selection with membership ranging between 10 and 20. SHGs have well defined rules and by-laws, hold regular meetings and maintain records, savings and credit discipline. These are self-managed institutions characterized by participatory and collective decision-making. They usually start by making voluntary thrift on a regular basis, which are a form of contractual savings. They use this pooled resource (as quasi-equity) together with the external bank loan to provide interest-bearing loans to their members.

Such loans provide additional liquidity or purchasing power for use in any of the borrower's production, investment, or consumption activities. SHGs broadly have three stages to evolution viz., (a) Group formation to evolve into a self managed peoples' organization at grassroots level; (b) Linkage with banks and capital formation through the revolving fund, skill development for management and activity; and (c) Taking an economic activity for income generation. Under SGSY, SHG has following characteristics:

1. A SHG may consist of 10-20 members. In the case of minor irrigation and in the case of disabled persons, the number may be a minimum of five.
2. All members of the group should belong to families below poverty line.
3. The group shall not consist of more than one member from the same family.
4. A person shall not be a member of more than one group.
5. Group members usually create a common fund by contributing their small savings on a regular basis.
6. Groups evolve flexible systems of working (sometimes with the help of the (SHPI)) and manage pooled resources in a democratic manner.
7. Groups consider the loan requests in periodic meeting and competing claims on limited resources are settled by consensus.
8. Loans are mainly given on trust with minimum documentation and without any security.
9. The loan amounts small, frequent, issued for short duration and are mainly for unconventional purposes.
10. The rates of interest vary from group to group and the purpose of loan. It is higher than that of banks but lower than that of money-lenders.

11. At periodic meetings, besides collecting money, social and economic issues are also discussed.
12. The group should maintain on its own or with the help of the facilitator the basic records such as minute's book, cash-book, loan ledger, attendance register, general ledger, bank-pass-book and individual pass-book.
13. Defaults are rare due to the 'collateral' of peer pressure and intimate knowledge of the use of credit.
14. By and large, the SHG will be an informal group. However, the groups can also register themselves under the Societies Registration Act, the State Co-operative Act or a Partnership Firm Act. The SHGs can be further stabilized and strengthened by forming federation of groups.

Thus, self-help group is a voluntary group valuing personal interaction and mutual aid as means of altering or ameliorating problems. The SHGs offer a unique opportunity for dispensing cheap credit (complementing the existing banking system) at the doorstep of the poor with almost assured repayment at the terms and requirements of the poor. The SHGs follow collective decision-making on issues like meetings, thrift and credit decisions. The participative nature of the group makes it a responsible borrower.

Self-help Groups and Income Generation

The steady deterioration in the employment situation, particularly in rural areas, had become a matter of national concern and figured high in the economic agenda by the late eighties. "The past experience", it was argued, "had demonstrated that the approaches of treating employment as a by-product of growth or seeking solutions of the unemployment problem in special employment programmes as such are inadequate" (Planning Commission, 1990).

Moreover, the desired outcome of development is aggregate and sustainable positive change in productivity and income that leads either directly or indirectly to economic possibility for growing numbers of poor and low-income people. Enterprise development or income generation is not only about credit delivery to the poor, but also about generating additionality, long-term possibility and eventually mobility out of poverty.

It is only by such integrated approach can the threats of globalization faced by the rural sector be turned into opportunities. Lending a few rupees for consumption or other purpose does not fit into this bill, even though it may be helpful to the poor client or his household. Against this background, the Micro Finance Institutions (MFIs) are supposed to provide Enterprise Development Services. The current emphasis on Micro Finance Institutions is not just for credit delivery alone. In fact, the minimalist approach of Micro Finance states that by its very definition, MFIs are mandated to provide one missing piece in rural development i.e. credit. Whereas, the integrated approach argues that simple financial intermediation in the rural areas is not expected to be sufficient to make them participate in and contribute to the process of development.

Thus, for micro finance to succeed and produce sustainable results, financial intermediation should be accompanied by social intermediation, micro enterprise development services and social services. Social intermediation includes group formation, leadership training and cooperative learning.

Enterprise development services include marketing, business training, production training and sub-sector analysis. While, social services involve health, education and literacy.

In the present context, all the services are to be facilitated by the SHPI. It may utilize the services of MFIs for financial intermediation and provide other intermediation through its own efforts or through convergence of services etc. Under *Swarnjayanti Gram Swarozgar Yojana*, for SHGs Group Social Intermediation is followed whereby, most of the services are facilitated by the SHPI for building the institutional capacity of groups and investing in human resources of their members so that groups can being to function on their own, with less help from outside. Individual *swarozgaris* are provided financial intermediation and if they wish to, they can have access the enterprise development services through its group for their income-generating activities.

SHGs in West Bengal: A Review

Even though the SHG movement has had a late start in the state of West Bengal, off late it has gained tremendous momentum. It is estimated that there are more than three and a half lakh SHGs in the State, out of which little more than 1.5 lakh SHGs have been formed under the Swarnajayanti Gram Swarojgar Yojana (SGSY) alone. The two major programmes which had been supporting the movement are 1) the SGSY and 2) the NABARD supported SHG-Bank Linkage programme. Apart from these two programmes, the Forest department has facilitated large number of SHGs in areas where their programmes are under implementation and more and more women are now being able to actively participate in FPC and EDC for their own economic development as well as giving a new vigour in forest protection and preservation. Other attempts like Swayamsiddha (IWEP - upgraded IMY) by government through West Bengal Women Development Undertaking is a woman focused SHG initiative to enhance economic, health, nutrition, education status for women using access to microcredit and convergence for services. As of now, the scheme targets 3900 women SHGs in 39 block level federation - though target surpassed long ago, and uses both government and non government facilitation in the scheme. The Backward classes Welfare Department is also assisting the scheduled castes and scheduled tribes, and other backward classes to form self-help Groups for economic development by providing training, infrastructure, and institutional finance.

There are similar programmes for Minorities implemented through the Minorities Development and Finance Corporation. The Cottage and Small Scale Industries Department has a scheme named Deen Dayal Hathkharga Protsahan Yojana to provide support to Handloom Weavers through self-help Groups recognised by state handloom cooperation and Apex Handloom Weavers' Co-operative Society in the form of capacity building, infrastructure and financial assistance. Similar support is provided to self-help groups of artisans through another scheme known as Baba Sahib Ambedkar Hasta Shilpa Vikash Yojana. Under the watershed projects being implemented by the Panchayat and Rural Development Department, formation of self-help groups and user groups has been conceived as grass root level organisations. Director of sericulture has been implementing a scheme (Sen, 2000) under which support is provided to self help groups in the form of capacity building and institutional finance. The department of Food Processing & Horticulture is also encouraging groups of small and marginal farmers. Animal Resource Development Department uses SHG concept to organise and strengthen poor and marginal section of the society into women's dairy cooperatives, which are ultimately linked up with marketing co-operatives and processing industries. Under the non-government category, organisations like CARE promoted informal SHG banking. The process is based on identifying and empowering selected Self Help Promotion Institutions (SHPI) in promotion and nurturing SHGs and initiate SHG-banking.

Presently, about 7,000 groups have been promoted by partnering SHPIs under CASHE project of the CARE and the institutionalisation of federations with a focus on community owned sustainable micro-finance model, is providing a lot of learning experience for the sector. Alternative microfinance institutions are also being developed by MF promoters such as STDBI. The three categories listed above have different channels for obtaining finance and pay different rates of interest.

An at-a-glance profile of how the SHGs have been doing in the state is given below.

1. Savings of the SHGs under SGSY: ‘ 107 crore (approximately)
2. Savings of the SHGs under NABARD: ‘ 97 crore (approximately)
3. No of SHGs under SGSY to have passed Grade I: 1,42,490
4. No. of SHGS under SGSY to have passed Grade II: 36,595
5. No. of SHGs under SGSY to have got cash credit loan: 1,15,000
6. Amount of such cash credit: ‘ 250 crore (approximately)
7. No. of SHGs under NABARD to have got first input of loan: 1,93,086
8. Amount of cash credit for NABARD SHGs: ‘ 395 crore (approximately)
9. Refinance amount for NABARD SHGs repaying first input of loan: ‘ 127·43 crore (approximately)
10. No. of SHGs under the State Cooperation Department getting loan: 70,000 (approximately)
11. Amount of such loan: ‘ 115 crore (approximately) Paper Presented at 9th Biennial Conference held at EDI, Ahmedabad during 16 18 February 2011

Recovery Status of selected Employment generation schemes as on March 2010 in comparison to March 2009 are as under

Table 6: Recovery Status of Employment Generation Schemes in West Bengal:

Sector	-			Amt. ` in crore		
	March 2009			March 2010		
	Demand	Recovery	%	Demand	Recovery	%
PMRY	125	30	24	146	36	24
SJSRY	17	6	35	24	9	38
BSKP	119	60	50	125	59	47
REGP	101	60	59	96	49	51
SCP/TSP	64	32	50	120	56	47
SGSY(Individual)	37	18	49	36	19	52
SGSY (Gr)	139	99	71	197	136	69
SHG	228	205	90	353	287	81

Source:SLBC

Bangla Swanirbhar Karmasansthan Prakalpa

Under a separate programme called Bangla Swanirbhar Karmasansthan Prakalpa (BSKP), in the year 2006-07, out of 9,058 cases sponsored to the West Bengal State Cooperative Bank, disbursement was made to 6,354 cases involving a sum of ' 91·90 crore, out of which an amount of ' 17·26 crore was spent towards payment of subsidy, and the rest amount of ' 64·64 crore was bank loan. Since the inception of the BSKP, approximately 32,000 beneficiaries have so far been provided with loan. In the current financial year, certain amendments have been made in the guidelines of BSKP, of which the major aspects have been :

a) The upper age limit has been enhanced from 40 years to 45 years.
b) The ceiling of subsidy in respect of individual entrepreneurs and groups have been increased from ' 50,000 and ' 1·25 lac respectively to '1 lac and '2·5 lac respectively. For the number of savings-linked SHGs under the two major programmes,

Table-7: District-wise Groups formed under SGSY and NABARD

Districts	No. of groups formed under SGSY	No. of groups formed under NABARD
Murshidabad	7900	16568
Darjeeling	2561	2232
Malda	9173	9546
Uttar Dinajpur	4422	8816
Dakshin Dinajpur	8224	10451
Birbhum	3312	21701
Hooghly	12572	17606
Purba Medinipur	18695	9853
Paschim Medinipur	3038	3757
Jalpaiguri	14044	10786
Howrah	3243	6380
Coochbehar	9130	12181
Nadia	6356	24836
Bankura	6940	12881
Purulia	10046	3938
Burdwan	10514	15672
North 24-Parganas	11270	23066
South 24-Parganas	8944	20402

Source: Ministry of Self Help and Self Employment, Govt. of West Bengal

Self-Help Groups and Economic Development

Contrary to popular belief, the poor households are engaged in myriad types of micro enterprises which are linked to their livelihood. As a source of employment, the micro enterprise has a lot of potential because of its ease of entry and low startup capital. It also plays a significant role in self-employment when employment in organized sector or even wage employment is scarce. The micro-credit support extended to the self help groups together with other extension support such as skill up gradation, enhancing entrepreneurial abilities along with providing necessary infrastructures and marketing support helps the SHGs to cross the barriers that keep them below the poverty line. The table below is an illustrative list of the various types of activities taken up by the SHGs, who have passed Grade I level formed Under SGSY in the State. Support of professional bodies are being taken for upgrading skills of the SHGs for improving quality of the products as well as to meet the tastes of the people. A tie-up has been made with the National Institute of Fashion technology (NIFT) for training selected SHGs engaged in manufacturing of certain products like Kantha Steech Sarees, handicrafts, leather goods etc. The Comprehensive Area Development Corporation (CADC) is also extending training support to all those engaged in primary sector activities like agriculture, horticulture, animal husbandry etc for augmenting their income. Many groups have been found to take up agricultural activities by taking land on lease for raising suitable crops during the period when the owners normally keep it fallow. To supplement both income and nutritional support to the people, particularly the women and the children a very large number of groups, irrespective of their prime economic activities, have been given training on vegetable cultivation for developing good kitchen garden and even to use the roofs of their huts for growing vegetables.

They have been also given seeds of common vegetables, which have been very popular and an annual feature in the training exercise. Many SHGs have been given training on nursery-raising for supplying planting materials to the Panchayats for social forestry, which has become a good source of income for those group members. The Panchayats have excavated large number of tanks out of National Food for Work programme and other employment generation programme. Order has been passed by the L&LR department allowing the SHGs to be given lease of those tanks, owned by the government for growing fish.

Many groups have taken up composite culture of taking up pisciculture, duckery and horticulture on such leased in tank including its embankments. Other inputs like Chicks, piglets and kids have also been distributed in large numbers by the Animal Resources Development department and the DRDCs of the Zilla Parishads. In districts covered under RSVY such inputs have been distributed in large numbers out of RSVY fund in most of such districts. Small infrastructures like working sheds, machines for making Saal leaf plates, go down for storing Sabai grass etc in areas of Bankura, Purulia etc where such grass is grown as well as larger infrastructure like food processing centre, paddy processing facilities etc have also been constructed in large numbers for helping the groups in pursuing their economic activities. In quite a few districts the SHG groups have started selling rice processed by group members to the agents of the Food Corporation in fulfilling their procurement target. Providing marketing support to the SHGs for selling their products is another important support that is being provided by the State government and the local bodies. Fairs are organized in the districts and the State head quarter for promotion of sale of products of the SHO groups. Some of them also participate in fairs outside the State. However, much more is required to be done in this regard and the business enterprises of the State have been approached through their organizations like then Confederation of Indian Industries for developing linkages between the SHGs and those enterprises for helping the SHGs in improving and selling their products as well as to augmenting their marketing skills. Very recently a few organizations have shown their interests, which is yet to take concrete shape. A quick glimpse of such activities conducted by SHGs in different districts of rural Bengal as a measure towards eradicating poverty is depicted here-

Table-8: Activity-wise number of SHGs

Serial no.	Name of activities	No. of SHG
1	Agriculture	2,607
2	Animal Husbandry	17,336
3	Paddy Processing	4,632
4	Vegetable & Mushroom cultivation	571
5	Horticulture	42
6	Nursery	895
7	Floriculture	284
8	Fishery	2,708
9	Food Processing	597
10	Milch Cow	316

11	Zari embroidery	2,980
12	Kantha stitch & Embroidery	455
13	Silk, Tasar & Handloom	1,590
14	Jute Products	307
15	Readymade Garments/Tailoring	578
16	Imitation Jewellery	148
17	Leather Products	109
18	Sericulture	74
19	Betel vine	1,590
20	Minor Irrigation	96
21	Boutique	145
22	Mat Making	167
23	Dhoop Making	90
24	Cane & Bamboo Products	248
25	Marine Jewellery	53
26	Detergent & Phenyl Making	44
27	Wig Manufacturing	3
28	Bee Keeping	95
29	Wood Products Manufacturing	36
30	Carpentry	20
31	Bell metal utensils manufacturing	19
32	Shola works	8
33	Bel Mala	25
34	Pottery	44
35	Spice Making	30
36	Plate making (shal leaf)	160
37	Babui rope	70

Source: Govt. of West Bengal, West Bengal, July 2008.

Self-Help Groups as extended arms of the Primary Agricultural Co-operative Credit Societies (PACS)

In West Bengal, Self-Help Groups are reckoned as Co-operatives within a Cooperative. They are informal groups of 5-20 persons of the same low level of economic condition, belonging to the same locality or hamlet. Open and voluntary membership, democratic control of members, participation of members in economic activities of the Group, autonomy and independence, education, training and information, cooperation amongst different groups and concern for the community — all the seven Co-operative Principles do exist in these Groups. Since these are un-registered informal groups, and the PACS' cannot finance non-member units, the State Government, in exercise of the power conferred upon it u/S. 69(1)(d) of the West Bengal Co-operative Societies Act, 1983, permitted the PACS' to enrol Self-Help Groups as members of the PACS. This was done as a part of the programme for implementation of Business Development Plan, introduced pursuant to the recommendations of the Agricultural Credit Review Committee (Khusro Committee), which envisaged that the plan for every deposit, credit and trading activity of the PACS should have two prongs—individual members and Self-Help Groups. Later on NABARD sponsored SHG programme acted as a booster and the Self-Help Groups in the Co-operative Sector in West Bengal assumed the shape of a movement in the State. Through periodical meetings, equal doses of savings at the end of every week, fortnight or month, rotation of leadership, united fight against the evils in the family and the community, group dynamism develops amongst the SHG members over months of existence and they become eligible for credit-linkage through the PACS' which organize and nurture them. The central Co-operative Banks act as the facilitators and the State Co-operative Bank as the coordinator.

The special case of West Bengal

West Bengal is known for mobilising the highest number of small savings accounts. Living up to the reputation, the state has maintained its lead too in terms of micro savings of self help groups (SHGs). Even states like Andhra Pradesh, Tamil Nadu and Karnataka — where the SHG movement flourished the most — are behind West Bengal in this regard. This is according to the latest micro-finance report published by the National Bank for Agriculture & Rural Development (NABARD).

The primary reason behind this trend is a practice followed by nearly one-third of the over 6 lakh SHGs in the state which are developed and nurtured by the cooperative sector. Unlike in other states, SHGs under the cooperative ambit do not recycle their thrift as loans to the members. And so, their savings kitty keeps growing.

The cooperative sector accounts for around one-third of the SHGs operative in West Bengal. And the cooperative sector typically does not allow recycling of the savings of SHGs for on lending to their own members. This is one of the reasons why average loans to SHGs are one of the poorest among all other states. According to the latest statistics, the average savings per group is the highest in West Bengal. As on March 31, 2009, the 6,09,439 groups in the states have collectively deposited ' 1233.28 crore in banks, showing an average savings of ' 20,235 per group.

By contrast, Andhra Pradesh has 12.81 lakh groups with a total '1191.93 crore of savings. Tamil Nadu and Pondicherry collectively have

7.30 lakh groups with '577.31 crore worth of deposits, while Karnataka has over 4.57 lakh SHGs with ' 566.87 crore of deposits in banks.

Normally according to NABARD norms, SHG members can use their savings for lending to their own members. And so their collective savings kitty keeps shrinking periodically in most states unlike in West Bengal.

Conclusion

In order to promote entrepreneurship as a means to eradicate rural poverty, the SHGs play the vital role of catalyst in this form of endeavor. However, there were numbers of traditional and informal ways of forwarding credit before the emergence of the SHGs. All of them provided very little attention to the question of both empowerment and sustainability. Along with this there was a casual approach towards the accountability of the credits leading to adverse impact on both repayment as well as further outreach.

The conclusion that emerges from this study is that SHGs are playing a vital role in the rural empowerment, though most of the SHGs are formed as female groups (86%). However, the most highlighting feature of this mode as compared to other sponsored credit system is that it imparts the knowledge of managing money to its subscribers before they go for availing any loan from the banks. Moreover the SHG approach does not involve any subsidy, hence it can sustain with its own strength. Besides, in financing SHGs, the requirement of collateral by banks has been replaced by peer group pressure and hence this approach has enabled social and economic inclusion of women by waiving the requirement of collateral. The study also shows that whole scenario of SHGs flourishing in West Bengal is not at all satisfactory in comparison to southern and western part of the country. But though it took off very slowly the Self-help group movement in West Bengal has acquired considerable quantitative momentum over the years.

Another significant outcome of the study is that people are not interested in subsidy while forming SHGs as the NABARD scheme does not provide any subsidy while SGSY provides the same. Therefore, it is observed that for development of entrepreneurship in rural economy, the financing through SHGs acts as an important impetus.

Policy Implications:

Some of the important recommendations for development of SHGs as a primary tool for financing rural entrepreneurship may as follows-

1. Necessary trainings are to be imparted to the budding rural entrepreneur as well as SHGs for up gradation on the basis of the assessment, adoption of new technology etc.
2. The bankers should assess the technical skill and managerial skill of these SHGs in general and budding rural entrepreneur in particular.
3. Orientation programs may be organized regarding the group objectives, their responsibility, elements of book keeping, knowledge of market, identification and appraisal, familiarity with product costing and product pricing, acquaintance with project financing by banks as well as some basic skills in the key activity identified.
4. Other significant factors to be addressed are gender equality and propoor development.

References

1. Datt R. and Sundharam K.P.M. (2009), Indian Economy, S. Chand, New Delhi
2. Maheshwari S R (1995), Rural Development in India, sage Publications India Private Ltd., New Delhi
3. Ahlin, C and Robert Townsend (2003), 'Selection Into Across Credit Contracts: Theory and Field Research,
4. Anand, Jaya S. (2002), "Self-Help Groups in Empowering Women: Case Study of Selected SHGs and NHGs",
5. Bali S., Ranjula and Fan Yang Wallentin (2007), " Does Micro Finance Empower Women ? Evidence from Self-Help Groups in India", *Working Paper* 2007:24, Department of Economics, Uppsala University, August 2007.
6. Besley, T and S. Coate (1995), 'Group Lending Repayment Incentives and Social Collateral', *Journal of Development Economics*, 46, pp.1-18.
7. Coleman B.E (1999), 'The Impact of Group Lending in Northeast Thailand', *Journal of Development Economics*, 60, pp.105-141.
8. Dasgupta, R (2001), 'Working and Impact of Rural Self-Help Groups and other Forms of Micro Financing: An Informal Journey Through Self-Help Groups', *Indian Journal of Agricultural Economics*, 56, no. 3.pp. 370-386.
9. Deshmukh- Ranadive, J. (2004), Women's Self-help Groups in Andhra Pradesh: Participatory Poverty Alleviation in Action, Washington, DC: World Bank.
10. Discussion Paper No. 38, Kerala Research Programme on Local Level Development, Centre for Development Studies, Thiruvananthapuram.

11. Ghatak M and T.W Guinnane (1999), 'Economics of Lending with Joint Liability: Theory and Practice', *Journal of Development Economics,* 60, pp.195-228.
12. NABARD (2002), 'Ten Years of SHG-Bank Linkage: 1992-2002', NABARD and Micro Finance.
13. Lahiri-Dutt and Samanta (2006), 'Constructing Social Capital: Self-Help Groups and Rural Women's Development in India', Geographical Research, 44 pp. 285- 295.
14. Namboodiri. N.V and R.L Shiyani (2001), 'Potential Role of Self-Help Groups in Rural Financial Deepening',*Indian Journal of Agricultural Economics,* 56, pp.401-409.
15. Pitt. M.M and S.R Khandekar (1998), 'The Impact Of Group Based Credit Programmes On Poor Households In Bangladesh: Does The Gender Participants Matter? *Journal of Political Economy,* 106, 958-996.
16. Satish P (2005), 'Mainstreaming of Indian Micro Finance', *Economic and Political Weekly,* Vol XL pp. 1731-1739.
17. Sen A (1973), On Economic Inequality, Oxford University Press, Delhi.
18. Smith, D. H and K Pillheimer (1983), 'Self-Help Groups as Social Movement Organisations: Social Structure and Social Change', Research in Social Movements, Conflicts and Change, Vol 5 No 2
19. Verman P, Mahendra (2005) ' Impact of Self-Help Groups on Formal Banking Habits', *Economic and Political Weekly,* Vol XL No 17 pp.1705-1713.
20. Working Paper No. 03-23, Department of Economics, Vaderbilt University, www.vanderbilt.edu/econ, LAT ACCESSED ON 12.07. 2010
21. Yunus M (2004), Grameen Bank, Micro Credit and Millennium Development Goals, EPW, Vol. 39, 4077-4092.

5

The Role of Rrbs In Entrepreneurship Development

Abstract

The Rural Development in India is one of the most important factors for the growth of the Indian economy. India is primarily an agriculture-based country. Agriculture contributes nearly one-fifth of the gross domestic product in India. In order to increase the growth of agriculture, the Government has planned several programs pertaining to Rural Development in India. Rural Development in India-Organizations:

Department of Rural Development in India
Haryana State Cooperative Apex Bank Limited
National Bank for Agriculture and Rural Development
Sindhanur Urban Souharda Co-operative Bank:
Rural Business Hubs (RBH)
Council for Advancement of People's Action and Rural Technology (CAPART)
National Bank for Agriculture and Rural Development

The Role of Regional Rural Banks in Rural Entrepreneurship

In order to meet the global demand and the new challenges thrown to the Indian industry and also to generate employment at village level, entrepreneurship development has to be given a priority. In order to accelerate the growth of industries generate employment and utilities the national human potential there is a need to channelize the youth and women of the country for useful and productive purpose. There is also a need to motivate the guide the youth to enable them to take a step forward and take up a carrier of self employment and setup a small or micro enterprise as an entrepreneur.

The RRBs have, further, to play a crucial role in our rural economy, as they have to act as alternative agencies to develop entrepreneurship ability and provide institutional credit in rural areas. In course of time, they are intended to eliminate money-lenders altogether. The sponsor banks also need to closely monitor the performance of their sponsored RRBs and provide timely guidance to them for entrepreneurship development wherever necessary.

The Rural Development in India is one of the most important factors for the growth of the Indian economy. India is primarily an agriculture-based country. Agriculture contributes nearly one-fifth of the gross domestic product in India. In order to increase the growth of agriculture, the Government has planned several programs pertaining to Rural Development in India.

The Ministry of Rural Development in India is the apex body for formulating policies, regulations and acts pertaining to the development of the rural sector. Agriculture, handicrafts, fisheries, poultry, and dairy are the primary contributors to the rural business and economy.

The introduction of Bharat Nirman, a project set about by the Government of India in collaboration with the State Governments and the Panchayat Raj Institutions is a major step towards the improvement of the rural sector. The National Rural Employment Guarantee Act 2005 was introduced by the Ministry of Rural Development, for improving the living conditions and its sustenance in the rural sector of India.

Rural Development in India-Organizations

1. Department of Rural Development in India: This department provides services such as training and research facilities, human resource development, functional assistance to the DRDA, oversees the execution of projects and schemes.
2. Haryana State Cooperative Apex Bank Limited: The main purpose

of the Haryana State Cooperative Apex Bank Limited is to financially assist the artisans in the rural areas, farmers and agrarian unskilled labor, small and big rural entrepreneurs of Haryana.

3. National Bank for Agriculture and Rural Development: The main purpose of the National Bank for Agriculture and Rural Development is to provide credit for the development of handicrafts, agriculture, small scaled industries, village industries, rural crafts, cottage industries, and other related economic operations in the rural sector.
4. Sindhanur Urban Souharda Co-operative Bank: The main purpose of the Sindhanur Urban Souharda Co-operative Bank is to provide financial support to the rural sector.
5. Rural Business Hubs (RBH): RBH was set up with the purpose of developing agriculture. The Rural Business Hubs Core Groups helps in the smooth functioning of the Rural Business Hubs.
6. Council for Advancement of People's Action and Rural Technology (CAPART): The main purpose of this organization is to promote and organize the joint venture, which is emerging between the Government of India and the voluntary organizations pertaining to the development of the rural sector.

National Bank for Agriculture and Rural Development

The main purpose of the National Bank for Agriculture and Rural Development is to provide credit for the development and publicity of small scaled industries, handicrafts, rural crafts, village industries, cottage industries, agriculture, etc. The NABARD also supports all other related economic operations in the rural sector, promotion of sustainable growth in the rural sector. The NABARD also plays the role of a contributor to the rural development by the means of promoting institutional development, facilitating refinance to loan providers in the rural sector, inspection, monitoring, and evaluation of client financial corporations. National Bank for Agriculture and Rural Development (NABARD) was established as the premiere rural development bank.

The Regional Rural Banks in India has actively contributed to the growth of the rural sector. The growth of the rural industries in India and the development of the rural business and economy have been dependent largely on the investment and financial aids provided by the Regional Rural Banks in India.

However, IT is now widely recognised that access to credit is critical for cultivators operating in a market setting. Nevertheless, before the nationalisation of banks, key sectors of the economy including agriculture remained thoroughly neglected in terms of availability of institutional credit.

Whereas the industrial sector at that time accounted for about 15 per cent of national output, it appropriated two-thirds of commercial bank credit, whereas the agricultural sector contributing about half of national output was almost completely neglected by the commercial banks.

One of the most important objectives of government policy since the nationalisation of 14 commercial banks in 1969, was to extend and expand credit not only to those sectors which were of crucial importance in terms of their contribution to national income and employment, but also to those sectors which had been severely neglected in terms of access to institutional credit.

The sectors that were initially identified for this purpose were agriculture, small industry and self-employment. These sectors were to be accorded priority status in credit allocation by the banks.

As a consequence, policies such as interest rate controls and pre-emption of resources through directed credit programmes aimed at agriculture and the small scale sector increased in magnitude during this period. There was also a concerted effort at substantially expanding the reach of the banking system, especially to the rural areas. The success of policy in terms of branch expansion, mobilisation of household savings, diversification of lending targets and direction of credit to the priority sector was substantial.

Table 1: Expansion of Regional Banking: 1975-2010

Year:-	Dec.1975	Dec.1980	Dec.1985	March2006	March2010
No.of Banks (RRBs)	6	85	188	196	82
Branches of RRBs	17	3279	12606	14,443	15,475

Source: NABARD Reports

The following one-and-a-half decades saw large-scale efforts to increase the number of banks, bank branches, and disbursements nationwide. (See Table 1) By 2006, there were 196 RRBs with over 14,443 predominantly rural branches in 476 districts with an average coverage of three villages per branch. These banks had disbursed over Rs. 3,500 crore in credit and mobilized over Rs. 4,100 crore in deposits. Perhaps the most significant achievement of the RRBs during this period was in enabling the weaker sections of the rural community access to institutional credit. The bulk of the loans from RRBs were to the priority sectors, which accounted for over 70 per cent of the total. Agriculture and allied activities took up more than 50 percent of the total advances. In addition, the RRBs were instrumental in extending credit for poverty alleviation schemes.

1. For further improving the financial health of RRBs, the Government of India started the process of structural consolidation of RRBs by amalgamating RRBs sponsored by the same Sponsor Banks within the State. The process of amalgamation is almost complete. As on date, there are 82 RRBs (46 amalgamated and 36 stand alone) with a branch network of 15,475 branches covering 619 districts, 26 States and 01 Union Territory (Pondicherry).

The RRBs have shown improved performance in many areas. The total loan outstanding of RRBs as on 31 March 2010 was Rs.83,562 crore whereas the deposits amounted to Rs.1,42,814 crore. The ground level credit flow of RRBs has improved from Rs.43,367 crore to Rs.56,268 crore thereby recording an appreciable growth rate of about 30%. A significant part of their performance is substantial lending to the priority sector. RRBs are mandated to lend 60% of their loans to the priority sector. During the last three years, RRBs have not only achieved the target fixed for the purpose but have maintained priority sector loans above 80%.

The Role of Regional Rural Banks in Rural Entrepreneurship

Entrepreneurship is regarded as one of the important determinants of the industrial growth of the country. The dearth of the entrepreneurial and managerial skill is one of the most common problems being faced by all under developed economies. Entrepreneurship is to promoted to help alleviate the unemployment problem, to overcome the problem of stagnation and to increase the competitiveness and growth of business and industries. Various attempts have been made to promote and develop entrepreneurship. By giving specific assistance to improve the competence of the entrepreneur, so as to make him an entrepreneur, so that more people become entrepreneurs.

In order to meet the global demand and the new challenges thrown to the Indian industry and also to generate employment at village level, entrepreneurship development has to be given a priority. The entrepreneurs should possess required skills, ability to grasp opportunities which offer economic advantages, orientation towards applying knowledge to maximize gains, business skills, and leadership qualities and above all confidence that one can make things happen. In this context a trained entrepreneur has a number of advantages. In order to accelerate the growth of industries generate employment and utilities the national human potential there is a need to channelize the youth and women of the country for useful and productive purpose. There is also a need to motivate the guide the youth to enable them to take a step forward and take up a carrier of self employment and setup a small or micro enterprise as an entrepreneur.

The Regional Rural Banks in India is the major investors in different types of operations in the rural areas. The concept of rural banking in India dates back to the time when the banking sector was set up in India. Regional Rural Banks in India was set up with the purpose of facilitating the promotion of rural business in India. The Regional Rural Banks in India are spread all across the country and have been playing an important part in the development and growth of the rural business and economy. The development of the rural sector is important for the economic growth of India. As India is an agrarian economy, the growth of the rural sector and the promotion of agricultural sector would give the economy a boost.

The State Bank of India is one of the major commercial banks having regional rural banks. There are 30 Regional Rural Banks in India, under the State Bank of India and it is spread in 13 states across India. The number of branches the SBI Regional Rural Banks is more than 2000.

The main purposes of the Regional Rural Banks are to financially assist the artisans in the rural areas, farmers and agrarian unskilled labor, and the small rural entrepreneurs.

Apart from above as we know that Rural India continues to suffer from lack of employment and self-employment opportunities owing to its narrow economic base. For addressing unemployment problem, considerable success can be achieved in developing rural poor through entrepreneurship development approach which focuses on selectively utilising local talent, appropriately developing them through training intervention and linking them with relevant business opportunities. Regional Rural Banks can play an important in this regard to implement Rural Entrepreneurship Development (RED) Approach, in collaboration with NGOs by imparting training to rural people . One of the major hurdles is faced in this process is non-availability of required and timely financial support to trained entrepreneurs, which can be solved by RRBs. It is , therefore, concluded that the desired success can be achieved by imparting best possible training inputs, and availability of funds from banks to trainees.

Keeping this in view, RRBs can conduct workshops for rural people to make them aware of the Entrepreneurship approach and the role which is to be played by the RRBs.

Objectives of workshop can be followed:

2. To share rural entrepreneurship development experience and approach
3. To provide orientation to the participants regarding rural entrepreneurship development strategy as a viable alternative, role of NGOs and the support systems
4. To expose the participants to various phases of RED training intervention
5. To provide a common platform to NGOs and support system officials, to discuss various issues pertaining to success of RED activity
6. To evolve a future course of action for rural entrepreneurship development and involvement of NGOs and the support system for maximum impact.
7. These programmes should be attended by officers of Regional Rural Banks/ SFC branches operating in areas where REDPs have been or are to be implemented in collaboration with NGOs, would generate positive response from the support system officials for trained potential entrepreneur.

There is a growing concern for economic development and this strengthens interest in entrepreneurship with primary focus on exploring practical measures to augment the supply of entrepreneurs, i.e. persons with competence and aptitude to initiate, nurture and expand industrial enterprises. This will result in the belief in education and training to inculcate and develop entrepreneurial capabilities in people so that they could set up their own enterprises.

Conclusion

The following concluding remarks may be made based on the overall analysis carried out in the paper. The RRB though meant basically for the poorer sections was found to be serving not only all the segments of the rural society but also the major portion of its loans had gone to the households in the better-off categories. Moreover, the regular accessibility to the RRB was found to be restricted mainly to better-off households. This is attributable mainly to the emphasis put by the RRB on the security based lending. The system or practice of considering the individual and not the household as the borrowing unit had not only enabled the richer sections to borrow from the RRB in the name of rural poor but also had helped them to garner a major share of its loans. Though the bank had brought in a considerable number of poorer households into its ambit, their coverage is attributable more to the selection of such households by the government agencies under various poverty alleviation schemes rather than to bank's own initiative. Incidentally, most of them have also not been able to sustain their access to the bank. As a result, the RRB was found to be serving mainly the better-off sections who could sustain their dealings with it unlike the poorer households.

Given the common lending policies pursued by the RRBs, the following conclusions may be drawn. The RRBs which were created as institutional innovation for the rural poor, however, did not come out with any radically different policy or strategy to reach out to their clientele. Unlike the Grameen Bank of Bangladesh, the RRBs in India have followed mainly the established security based lending and hence, their success as an institutional innovation/reform appears to be of a limited nature only. Since their basic policy remained the same, the outcome was in no way significantly different from that of other institutions like the co-operatives and the commercial banks.

This suggests that what becomes important for serving the rural poor by the institutional credit agencies is not their form but their policies and this has to be reckoned with in any future institutional policy reform for the rural poor. The RRBs have, further, to play a crucial role in our rural economy, as they have to act as alternative agencies to develop entre-preneurship ability and provide institutional credit in rural areas. In course of time, they are intended to eliminate money-lenders altogether. However, they were not set up to replace cooperative credit societies but to supplement them. In the last 32 years, RRBs have been active participants in programmes designed to provide credit assistance to identified beneficiaries. Under the new 20 –point programme, IRDP and other special programmes for scheduled castes and tribes have been launched. They are also implementing differential rate of interest scheme for the weaker sections; physically handicapped persons who are gainfully employed can secure the finance from the RRBs for the purchase of artificial limbs, hearing aids, wheeled chairs etc.

The sponsor banks also need to closely monitor the performance of their sponsored RRBs and provide timely guidance to them for entrepreneurship development wherever necessary. Keeping in view the expectations from the RRBs, the training and capacity building of rural people need to be given utmost priority. A Committee should be set up by NABARD for the identification of areas, in which training is to be given by RRBs to rural people. All the RRBs should prepare a comprehensive plan for meeting the training needs of rural people. A mechanism should be created for providing funding support to RRBs for conducting this training programme duly involving NABARD, sponsor banks and the RRB itself.

References

1. Velayudham, T.K., and Sankaranarayanan, V. (1990)"Regional Rural Banks and Rural Credit: Some issues", Economic and Political weekly, Sep.22Thingalaya N.
2. K. (2000):"The Other Side of Rural Banking" BIRD Lucknow.
3. Report on Trends and Progress of Banking in India (Various Issues) Reserve Bank of India, Mumbai, URL (www.rbi.org.in)
4. Reddy, Y. V. (2000): "Rural Credit: Status and Agenda", Reserve Bank of India. Bulletin, Nov.
5. Nitin Bhatt and Thorat Y.S.P. (2004): India's Regional Rural Banks: The Institutional dimension of Reforms
6. National Bank News Review, NABARD April Sep.
7. Mohan Jagan (2004): "Regional Rural Banks Need a shot in the Arm", Financial Daily from The Hindu group of publications March 19th edition.
8. Bose, Sukanya (2005): "Regional Rural Banks: The Past and Present Debate", Macro Scan,
9. Jain, Khanna, Tiwari, Banking and Finance, 2007-08, V.K. Enterprises, New Delhi.
10. Gupta, Vashishtha, Swami, Banking and Finance, 2007-08 Ramesh Book Depot, Jaipur, Delhi
11. A.Vinayak Reddy, G. Bhaskar, 2005, Rural Transformation in India, The Impact of Globalisation, New Century Publications, New Delhi, India.
12. People's Democracy Weekly Organ of the Communist Party of India (Marxist) Vol. XXVIII No. 02, January 11, 2004
13. Biswa Swarup Misra, The Performance of Regional Rural Banks (RRBs) in India: Has Past Anything to Suggest for Future? Reserve Bank of India Occasional Papers, Vol. 27, No. 1 and 2, summer and Monsoon 2006.

6

Ekgaon: Credit Facilitation to Rural Entrepreneurs With Mobile Services Intervention

Abstract

The potential to develop new markets in financial, agriculture, health, education and social networking services is enormous in rural India, where about 60 percent of people live-in. Information and credit play a major role in rural areas productivity and its economic and social upliftment in general. Even the credit access to the most disadvantaged sections of the society is the direction from Reserve Bank of India. Inadequate credit in time brings down the productivity and leads to development divide. The solution is a technology based intervention business model can invent new ways to achieve minimum credit services reach to rural citizens. This paper discusses a case Ekgaon, is one such initiative whose major objective is to facilitate credit to rural entrepreneurs by its mobile based tools. The mobile services intervention providing a chance for credit in-time facilitation to improve rural citizens living conditions with adopted innovative business plans. Finally observed benefits of socio-economic in nature are looked into so such services assist to bridge the development divide.

Introduction

The potential to develop new markets in financial, agriculture, health, education and social networking services is enormous in rural India, where about 60 percent of people live-in. They are not just consumers, but are also producers even at bottom of the pyramid. They have real service necessities and this has a bunch of market potential. Till date innovation in markets such as supply chain management, marketing and customer interactions are studied. But innovation of process in different services or a part of the service is helpful to deliver towards development of the needy, is the researchable point. Credit to small vendors at rural areas with innovative microfinance process, brings productivity and its economic and social change. Reserve Bank of India's (RBI) policy too directs towards it. Inadequate credit in time brings down the productivity and leads to development divide. The solution is a technology based intervention business model can invent new ways to attain minimum credit services reach to rural citizens.

Development strategies do not give desired results as user needs based like the Grameen microfinance. Armed with intellectual property rights global trade policies of developed countries are pushing ill-prepared markets of developing countries towards liberalisation for widening their markets (CFU, 2010). Knowledge revolution brings a new beginning towards information driven business models. This in-turn created a virtual global market without boundaries in providing e-commerce and IT enabled services bringing telecommunications and information gateways together. In-turn created newer and mainly cost effective service delivery platform through mobiles, to provide new personalized information and services. But the costs at connectivity, software, ownership and services reach shortened the excitement in pilots towards their sustainability. The spread of mobile signal across country with growing adoption rate by people have opened up an opportunity. There is something driving the people to adopt mobiles into their personal life.

Social and market driven are providing a chance to invent new ways through creative business models to achieve minimum services reach to rural citizens. The path breaking development initiatives are become essential on both side of the divide. Most of the initiatives in this path started to target rural areas failed within pilot stage as they could not understand the user needs and services. Every initiative does not able to provide all the services, but it has strength on a particular service. These aspects include:

1. Providing know how and content (advisory services) for the day to day activities such as agriculture, rural artifacts etc.
2. Providing localized market prices of the produce to farmers and others.
3. Providing social info-communication networking channel among villages nearby.
4. Providing the financial advisory services to badly needed rural people.

The above four major services together form the basic development needs of any rural citizen in India. These services are formed on user needs which are affordable, understandable, acceptable and usable to them. By providing all four components, we can expect to see the changes in socio-economic development.

Such positive changes are to be enhanced, negative changes are to be contained and finally, the untouched issues are to be looked into. One of such initiative named Ekgaon technologies seen closely here, to learn the innovation aspect in terms of its philosophy, goals, business model, and services in work which are bringing benefits to the rural people with mobile based interventions. It work towards increasing efficiency of value chain process, enabling access to financial services, technology and strategy consulting for primary producer communities in south Asia (I4d, 2010). It has been into mobile rural accounting and mobile tracking of transactions for small rural financial organisations. When 60 percent of the Indian population has no access to financial services (or no bank account), that presents both a challenge and an opportunity (Brian, 2010). The main problem in rural financial services is the non-availability of accurate, timely and needed information for decision making at higher levels (i4d, 2010).

Ekgoan is an excellent initiative in IT innovation for social impact, which is making a difference in rural lives using IT tools, to stop leakages of funds in social financial systems. Using mobile based applications providing villagers an opportunity to perform banking transactions in their native language and have an access to much needed information from the government. Working through this process, wherein simple technology has made noteworthy experience in proactive transparency in the delivery of social security services through a right based community driven approach. Regular audits and studies by government have identified that there is a need for greater transparency at all levels of service delivery to ensure entitlements reach the intended recipients. The big challenge before it is to provide financial services to almost 600 million people, at the lowest possible cost. This requires a competent technology platform with innovative business model should offer low operational cost and allow scale for wider distribution of services.

Background

An enterprise has a mission to use ICT to empower lives in rural areas taken birth in twenties by two entrepreneurs, who first opted for financial services, but also plans to offer other information related services. The name ekgaon reflects, one village is the origin of human civilization, the smallest unit of socio-cultural and administrative structure in the world, and is often synonymous with the idea of an interdependent community of individuals, like a family (ekgaon, 2010). It believes that what is best for a village is indeed best for the sustainable development of the whole world. Ekgaon functions as an IT services provider for rural India, designing and developing technology and information systems to address the varying needs of developing communities.

Its applications have been into mobile rural accounting and mobile tracking of transactions for small rural financial organisations. And also created innovative interface designs for semi-literate population through image capture, numeric and audio output allows customers to capture more information accurately, without having to rely on banking correspondents. One of its founding members VPS Aditya state about ekgaon, is creating the atmosphere to co-develop solutions with local participation is its end goal and its greatest operational strength. It partners with microfinance institutions, NGOs, NBFCs (non-banking financial companies), banks and insurers. The company works closely with selfhelp groups (SHGs). By April, 2010 it has 50000 customers in India (Brain Pereira, 2010) is an example for the smart IT investment not only pay off for the business itself, but for their customers as well. It has potential to further scale and act as a direct link between citizens and their government by using mobile phones as a portal for all kinds of government services. RBI encourages 'Banking Corresponding Mechanism (BCM)' is the aim of ekgaon to allow financial inclusion. SHG model has its inherent strength as a micro-banking institution at village level before BCM (i4d, 2010).

The acceptance of new technology has been reluctant and half-hearted by microfinance institutions (MFIs) as they are unwilling to modify operational models with it. The real intention of using technology is not for increasing efficiency of the system or improving profitability. But for doing something exciting and getting new funds for the projects they initiate, as per ekgaon experience (Asma Azmi, 2010) on them. The vision of ekgaon is to transform the way rural producers compete in increasingly globalised markets by increasing their incomes and provide results for their families. Despite these challenges, ekgaon gone for new improvements in technologies such as biometrics, confirmation sms, a visual screen on mobile phones that confirms transactions, and for can't read, audio messages that communicate financial information.

Reach to all the customers and all the places by a small company are quite difficult. Technology provided a solution to solve the reach problem and partnerships work for across the regions. The solution is supposed to be enterprise version or cloud based MIS solution where small microfinance organisations can work within the network without much investment. It is a winwin solution for ekgaon and its partners at local level using services organisations.

The final beneficiary is the end user who is going to get benefited from microfinance products. To make it happen, a ground observation at each individual's problem identification letting them drive development. The case evidently look into the scale for financial inclusion in India, technological and regulatory aspects, security aspects for leveraging mobile and ICT technologies for financial inclusion. It also discuss about the mobile environment – that include not only the bankers, service providers and customers but also the community at large, involving governments, regulatory authorities and other stakeholders.

Literature Review

Microfinance will continue as a practical tool for development, but also that it will become a considerable choice for financing innovation in developing economies. It has been long proposed as an instrument (or set of instruments) relevant to stimulating entrepreneurship in developing countries and deprived regions (Yanuar and Ian, 2009). For effective microfinance services – both in product and process respects – requires technological (and organisational) linkage and market possibilities. The link has to align the product and its delivery with the user's location, situation, and requirements (Yanuar and Ian, 2009). Mobile technology is a unique channel helps in this service delivery where it not only serves the youth and also the poor in rural areas. Technology in itself does not lead to social change; people decide how a particular technology will be used and, depending on the political and socio-economic environment in which they live, adapt it accordingly (Kling, 1999). But implementation of technology by organisations has three areas, even half-heartedly (Asma Azmi, 2010):

1. The quality of technology that is going to be implemented
2. The chosen technology should work efficiently with the MFI model
3. The organisation intent of using such technological solutions

But to utilize technology efficiently well by the organisations, sometimes the operational models are to be modified to get better results. But in practice, it won't happen, leading to half-baked solution which doesn't provide required results as expected. The conscious lack of technological coordination among service providers leads them to use proprietary technology platforms even at higher overhead costs, aiming to monopolize geographical sections of the rural market. This expensive counterproductive make customer is forced to pay higher prices at the end. Slowly expectation of users rise and they start demanding cutdown prices, but it happens in negative leads to customer to start weaning away (Marco Iannone, 2008).

If a cooperative model is adopted by telecom operators with banks, non-banked 600,000 villages can able to get into branchless banking with mobile services, which becomes the new personalised information and services gateway. Mobile based payments based on mobile transaction benefits (see Table-1) include cost reductions, improved efficiency and, in longer term (i.e. from the 2 year onward), higher revenues (Marco Iannone, 2008).

Table 1 Mobile transaction benefits

Appropriate technologies that seek to make the development process consumer and producer driven are best equipped to design rural and community owned platform for finance, health, marketing, social networking and agricultural services. However such technologies are scare and lacking. Inclusive growth is accorded high importance in recent years in order to extend offering of affordable financial services to people at the grass root level. Microfinance institutions should direct asset transfers to women residing in poor households, to enable them to establish a reliable income source and 'graduate' them into regular microfinance groups. When executed effectively, it can-relieve suffering, bring dignity, become sustainable, and inspire supporters (Sam Daley and Harris, 2006).

Products and Services

Ekgaon undertake multiple products (see Table-2) based on various technological platforms to cater the specific objective of the implementing

	Quantifiable	Qualitative
Short-term	Credit officer to save time, to be spent on customer acquisition Administrative staff to save time on registration and reconciliation Reduced opportunities for fraud for treasurers and credit officers Fewer customers late on payments or defaulting Reduced cost of stationery	More accurate data More timely and reliable error detection Increased security as credit officers no longer handle cash More timely reporting More accurate auditing
Long-term	Opportunity to reduce meetings Lower cost of acquisition, and more effective word-of mouth Customers to open more products with MFI Customers to be more loyal Lower turnover of staff, especially field staff Opportunity to expand individual lending Opportunity to develop new products	Opportunity to expand the agenda of a meeting to other topics Opportunity to disassociate payments from meetings Leaner business processes Customers to be more engaged Staff to be more engaged Reputational value with partners and investors
Benefits are shown: Lower costs, Greater efficiency and Higher revenues.		

organisation. These applications are real time driving force of the initiating objectives and play critical role of reach anytime, anywhere, and anyone in their own language where ever the end user wants to utilise it. Ekgaon's work includes delivery on mobile phone enabled financial, agriculture, weather services and technology solutions for storing indigenous knowledge and strategic consulting for a range of private, public and citizen sector organisations.

In the words of ekgaon CEO, "the challenge is not about the cost of technology, it is about the intent" (Asma Azmi, 2010). This vision has clearly made them to go for open source based software because their market survey found the purchase price should be around five thousand range. Organizations need simple software, which their human resource can download and install it easily to make it work for them. Most of them need technology and solutions but they don't have the capacity to run them on their own. Hence, ekgaon came up with a platform like enterprise or cloud computing where no need to invest money in servers and computers, but can perform transactions like an email account using applications hosted by it at usage charges. Pay-as-you use model benefit most small microfinance firms and brings all to one platform hosted by ekgaon irrespective of any boundary. It is most cost effective model to the benefit of all partners.

The software produced is of IDRBT standard so it doesn't allow microfinance organizations to make changes in their accounts. The software works very transparently as is also seen by the user when the agent or a BC performs the transaction before them. The tools in software provide such as:

- Biometrics, mobile pins and confirmation sms – going back and forth to the customer
- Confirmation screen on the mobile phone – customer can read transactions
- A voice over–which reads out the content for those who cannot read

Ekgaon has created interface designs for semi-literate people through image capture, numeric and audio output. The innovative use of interface design allows customers to capture more information precisely, without having to rely on banking representatives. All these make a point of sense, safe in using the device for their transactions. It is providing critical, safe, local, timely and customized information to users via mobile phones and other technologies also.

A. Solution steps

Step-1: An NGO or MFI field officer visit rural areas, to help villagers with microfinance (microcredit, savings, etc) transactions.

Step-2: The required transaction is performed with their mobile phone based software (one mobile). Total operation happens in a span of 2 to 3 seconds.

- Once the transaction is complete the information is stored on the mobile as an encrypted sms
- The encrypted sms is now transmitted across the mobile network to the centralized servers
- The sms is decrypted on the server in real time and stored as information

Step-4: The field officer then issues a receipt to the client using a portable thermal printer.

Step-5: The partner finance organisation (known as the federation) does the settlement with bank.

Step-6: The bank access the information on the server to analyse their portfolio and settlements.

Table 2 Information types of mServices

Information provided		
Know-how	Financial inclusion Financial efficiency	Options for enterprise microfinance solutions. MIS solutions for accounting, client and portfolio management. Mobile application platform for financial service delivery at doorsteps.
Context	Financial services Citizen services Agro-advisory services	Enterprise MIS solution for accounting, client and portfolio management - One MIS Mobile application platform for (retail & group) financial service delivery at doorsteps - One Mobile Monitoring citizen services Old age pension Widow pension Differentially aided pension Public grievances Rural health services Rural education - Teachers and students attendance Scholarship for rural students Mid day meal programme Offering crop value chain advisory and information services to enhance productivity of the farms Crop weather alerts E-commerce mandi Crop disease alerts Agri-finance & credit information Agri-input suppliers information Soil nutrient management advisory services Crop markets prices, commodities futures and spot prices
One Network	B2B services B2C services	B2B and B2C e-network connecting franchisee, partners and service providers to clients.
Pipeline	Remittance services Microfinance product scoring Health insurance	Mobile/Epos technology solution for remittance delivery Scoring product for retail and corporate microfinance clients Enterprise MIS solution for cashless health insurance

B. **One MIS**: It is also known as Self help MIS or Mahalaxmi MIS, as it allows managing the accounts of SHGs in an easy manner. It is freeware software which enables greater community ownership of SHG members on their financial services and is particularly useful for those who are not literate enough. The best part of it is, keeping account of seven books in one book made it quite simple and easy to utilise (Matthew Fox, 2010). Rural users transfer paper-based information to roaming smart-phone middleware, which uploads the data to remote storage for distribution in various ways (Tapan Parikh, 2007).

C. **One Mobile**: Mobile application platform for financial service delivery at low cost and the value associated with its voice services. The interface can be addressed with most Indian languages apart from its usage durability and technical support for maintenance in rural areas. One MIS application on the server which handles portfolio management and microfinance transactions at back end with wireless connectivity to mobile networks. The front-end technology solution (on the mobile phones) is used by banks and financial institutions to connect to their customers. This front end tool is known as 'one mobile'.

Business Model

The key of any business model is to keep registered users intact and increase the user number based on service performance. The implementers are going to get benefitted with large volume of users within same umbrella for such services. The ripple effect of this is socio-economic development of rural communities on one side and providing better governance from urban to rural areas on other side.

These benefits are going to be seen only when the services are well reached as per user's needs and requirements. Services are seen as affordable, understandable, reach to users, and satisfy localized needs on day-to-day basis by solving their concerns. If any business model fits better between these two points, it is a success venture like ekgaon to use mobile technology intervention bringing socio-economic upliftment to users.

a. Business partners

In any value chain customers and partners form a lifeline to make the initiative perform and achieve its objectives. Ekgaon is building a platform to sell information that would help the rural community take better decision on financial, citizen and agricultural activities as per day to day needs. The partners' contribution leads to the info-services delivery to the needy rural user at affordable cost and his door step through mobile (see Table-3).

b. Financial contribution

The mobile and other technological based services reach to users at a cost in their selected regional languages. The choice of the services is given to the customer at the time of registration time. Depending on the type of the card purchased, services are accordingly provided for a specified duration. These services shows how a mobile phone can be utilised as a development tool for the world's poor who are unreachable till date. The services provide a chance for the rural users to take decisions better in the area chosen. The share of amount among partners is based on their contribution to the service. But the franchise (or agents) will get Rs.5.00 more from the price mentioned on the cards to do their market (see Table-4).

Table 3 Customers and Partners in business chain

Customers and Partners in business chain		
Financial services	Banks Microfinance institutions (MFIs) Non Banking companies (NBFCs) Financial institutions & investors	Providing services that include credit, savings, remittance, insurance, investment and mortgage. Mobile based enterprise solution for information management system
Citizen services	Government departments NGOs Resident welfare associations	Monitor delivery of government programs and services entitled to the citizens through web & mobile applications
Agro-advisory services	Agri-departments & Universities Farmer's organisations Cooperatives Federations Agri-input suppliers Insurance companies Banks Credit organisations Multi-commodity firms - MCX	Agriculture crop knowledge for advisory services Commodity market price information Prices of input and produce Distribute weather information Soil nutrient management Customised crop management advise for farmers
Main Partners	Postal circle Multi-commodity exchange of India (MCX)	Providing local access, training and support Building confidence on services Encouraging customers to adopt and use it

c. Working model

The rural market is a virgin terrain and has unrestricted potential with diverse challenges. The biggest against them is price position (Shukla, 2009). India is a price-conscious market and offering costly services could be hard. The reach of mobile diffusion can create a market base within two years such that every player in this segment can get the required customer base. The working model (see Figure-1) made up of three segments which are undertaken towards the services providing to end users. The activities are independent of each other and provide critical input to the services. As per Vijay Pratap Singh, CEO Ekgaon wants to grow from present 11,000 customers to 5 million in 3-year time.

Table 4 Financial Model

Category	Example	Typical information needs
Nature of delivery	sms-text / voice recognition / interactive voice response system (IVRS) / web-technologies	Choice of delivery method for literate/non-literate user
	Crop, Financial and other service selection	Customer has to choose a major service with add-on services from 8-9 services
Payment options (Colour card)	ce of the card is FIXED: For entire crop period Irrespective of land size For any seasonality	Blue card: Retail card priced at Rs.100.00 Green card: Single crop card priced at Rs.120.00 Gold card: Three crop card priced at Rs.240.00

Observed benefits from ekgaon

Ekgaon undertakes projects with microfinance institutions, NGOs, NBFCs (nonbanking financial companies), banks and insurers as its partners. The observed benefits have been recognized through various awards to the project initiatives. They clearly show its operational value to the end user benefit. The technological applications offer low operational cost and allow scale for wider distribution of services. Bringing ICT to the benefit of the masses by enabling financial inclusion and increasing efficiency of self help groups' microcredit federations is one major achievement. A multi-stakeholder partnership in ICT for development has a huge potential for bringing in change and efficiency; but most of the development organisations fail to exploit the full potential since their interest lay in putting money in technology but not to invest in operational efficiency. Hence it is finding difficult to see the real impact of technology intervention in microfinance sector either on organisations utilizing technology or the end users are served with services through them get benefited much. Ekgaon platform and software allows banks, insurance companies and other service organisations, to access information about customers which helps them redesign their products and services, while keeping customer data highly protected. It is allowing rural service providers, rural customers and producers to access each other either in a transparent, efficient and competitive way. The mobile based software brought compatibility with banks and MF institutions effectively to get better results.

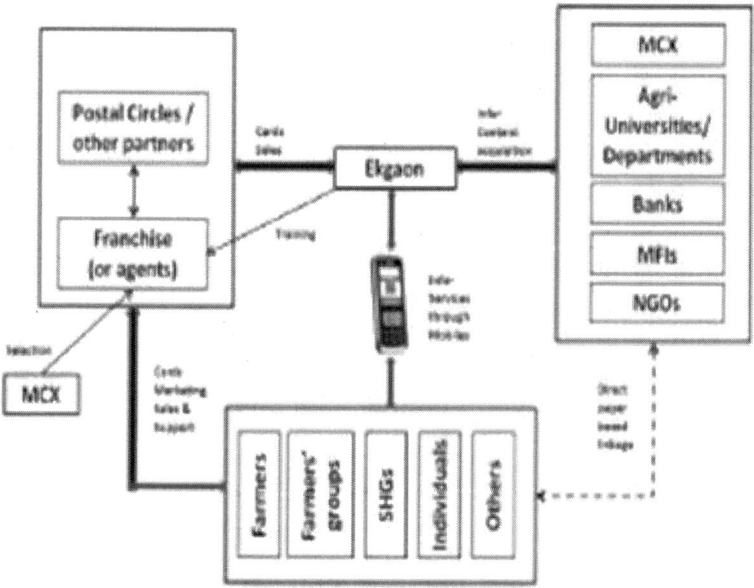

Figure 1 Working Model

Conclusion

By using technology for feeling the pulse of people and putting the last first is ekgaon's achievement. Such recognition reaffirms the larger role of such innovations making development reach to the poor. The motivation of ekgaon team is to create an impact which brings large change for the people for whom it was planned. Ekgaon is a testimony to the idea that smart IT investment can not only pay off for the business itself, but for their customers as well. Its initiatives pertaining to microfinance, rural credit and mobile service framework is enabling financial inclusion at different levels of community engagement and resource coordination. The technology has created not only transparency in tracking social entitlements but also proved that effective mechanism for delivery of services through mobile phones as a portal. This shows, ekgaon providing a competent technology platform offering low operational cost and allowing scale for wider distribution of services. More of such innovative solutions with mobile platform can make ekgaon a leading mobile phone service provider. The impact of such services on rural people is future scope of the work.

References

1. Azmi, Asma. (2010). Cloud computing is way forward for smaller microfinance organisation-Ekgaon. Available at: http://www.microfinancefocus.com/news/2010/08/09/cloud-computingis- way-forward-for-smaller-microfinance-organization-ekgaon/, accessed on 20 October 2010.
2. CFU. (2010). ICT for communities. Available at: http://www.microfinance.in/en/ict, accessed on 3 November 2010.
3. Daley, Sam & Harris. (2006). State of the microcredit summit campaign report 2006. Microcredit summit 2006.
4. Ekgaon. (2010). Ekgaon – One village one world. Available at: http://www.ekgaon.com/about_us, 12 October 2010.
5. I4d. (2010). Ekgaon technologies India. I4d Magazine: January – March Edition, available at: http://www.i4donline.net/articles/currentarticle. asp?articleid=1862&typ=Features, accessed on 12 October 2010.
6. Iannone, Marco. 2008. Mobile transactions: as guide for MFIs: Mobile Transactions Publications.
7. Kling. (1999). What is social informatics and why does it matter? D-Lib Magazine, January, Vol.5, No.1.
8. Nugroho, Yanuar & Miles, Ian. (2009). Mini study 06 – Microfinance & Innovation. Intelligence and Policy studies: Global review of Innovation, INNO-GRIPS.
9. Parikh, Tapan S. (2007). Designing an architecture for delivering mobile information services to the rural developing world. Doctoral dissertation, University of Washington.
10. Pereira, Brain. (2010). Ekgaon chooses mobile platform to empower villagers. Available at:http://www.informationweek.in/Mobile/10-04 06 ekgaon_chooses_mobile_platform_to_empower_villagers.aspx, accessed on 11 October 2010.
11. Shukla, Akhilesh. (2009). Rural changes: Voicendata publication. Available at: http://voicendata.ciol.com/content/service_provider/109120204.asp, accessed on 23rd February 2010.

7

Inclusive Growth Through Insupreneurship: A Study With Reference to Life Insurance in India

Abstract

India boasts of 16% of the world population, but has only 1.68% of the world insurance market as at 2006 (Source: World Insurance Report by Capgemeni). Around 21% of insurable population of India is covered by the all twenty and odd life insurance companies and there is a mine of opportunity untapped in the rural areas. Lack of entrepreneurial skills on the part of insurance distributors, particularly agents, is one of the causes resulting in deprivation of life insurance to the rural people and thus they are not part of inclusive growth. The needs of the customers are not analyzed before canvassing life insurance and hence insurance is almost always sold and never bought. In order to analyze the insurance needs and the canvassing pattern, a survey is conducted and responses are gathered from 500 customers and 200 agents of Bangalore and Kolar rural districts. The data is tabulated and by applying SPSS package, necessary statistical tests are conducted to analyze the trends.

The results indicate that all the rural credit is not insured even though the borrowers have inclination to cover the loans. The retirement needs of the rural people are seldom addressed by the insurance agents and the canvassing of policies was more determined by high commission yielding policies. The occupational niceties of the daily agricultural laborers have peculiar problems and paying capacities and they are never recognized. Above all the knowledge levels of agents are not perceived in good esteem by the customers resulting in lack of interest in life insurance policies. This also has lead to high attrition rate of agency force (47.67% in 2007-08) in the insurance sector.

As the insurers and the agents are using "yesterday's techniques for today's problems", it is highly imperative to take a second look and equip agents with entrepreneurial skills. Innovation and application of new methods is the key for spreading the message of life insurance to the nook and corner of India. An attempt is made in this article as to how entrepreneurial skills can help develop viable alternatives in mass rural coverage and help in inclusive growth of the rural people.

Introduction

Apraaptasya praapanam yoga; Praaptsya rakhanam kshema"- thus says Shankara in his commentary on Bhagavadgita (Geetha Bhashyam). Yoga means getting the things one has not got and Kshema means protection of things one has got. The sum and substance of the two are the essence of insurance. Life insurance is a social security tool. This is more pronounced in rural areas that promote and sustain the life links of the economy. The various programs of the government promoting agriculture and tiny industries, the scientific agricultural practices, the agrarian reforms, the empowerment of village panchayats and such other activities have created reasonable disposable incomes in the hands of the rural folk.

For sustaining the growth of rural sector it is imperative to design insurance protection to each and every earning member of the household. "70% of India live in rural areas but have no access; or have negligible access to insurance.

Due to wide geographical disparity and high distribution costs, insurers have been chary of venturing into this territory. Coupled with a tariff regime which assured them of good profits, they have been concentrating only on urban market. With increasing rural incomes and improving infrastructure, rural and micro insurance offers immense possibilities. But with opportunities, this sector throws various operational challenges as well, for the insurers — rural and social sector insurance should not be approached as a legal or statutory requirement, but as a business opportunity.

With proper safe guards, this sector can contribute immensely to the top line as well as bottom line.

Doing well while doing good is very much possible" (Gopinath,K). Insupreneurship on a large scale is the key for inclusive growth and stability of rural economic life. An attempt is made in this article to focus on the potential insurance market, the gap between the available potential and potential tapped the present marketing techniques of the insurance companies, the hindrances for rural insurance protection and finally the need for innovative practices to overcome the hindrances.

The great hiatus

World Insurance Report, 2008, while dealing with Indian life insurance, observes that 'despite recent growth, there is still tremendous untapped potential in the Indian insurance sector. India accounts for 16% of the world population, but accounted for only 1.68% of the world life insurance market in 2006. India is also far behind world averages in terms of insurance penetration, and insurance density. A mere 20% of the insurable population aged 20 to 60 years is currently covered by life insurance'. 'Only 14% of the population is covered by any type of health insurance, of which only 15 to 20% are covered by insurance players.

As a result only about 1.5% to 2% of total health care expenditure in India is covered by insurance players' (Boston Consulting Group Report,

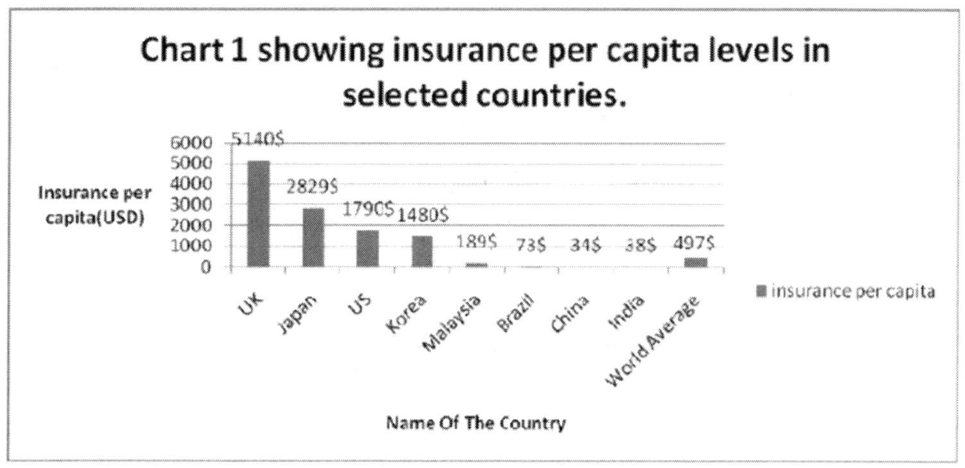

2007). 'Approximately 10 to 11% of the working population in India is covered by formal old age security mechanisms' (Oasis Report, 1999). All

these reports suggest under utilization of the insurance market by the players. The low per capita levels of life insurance in India when compared to some of the advanced countries can be seen from the following chart.

Source: Chart prepared on the basis of the data of the "The World Insurance Report, 2008by Capgemini".

The reports further indicate that it is the low income groups who really need insurance are deprived of insurance. The following chart 2 clearly illustrates the point.

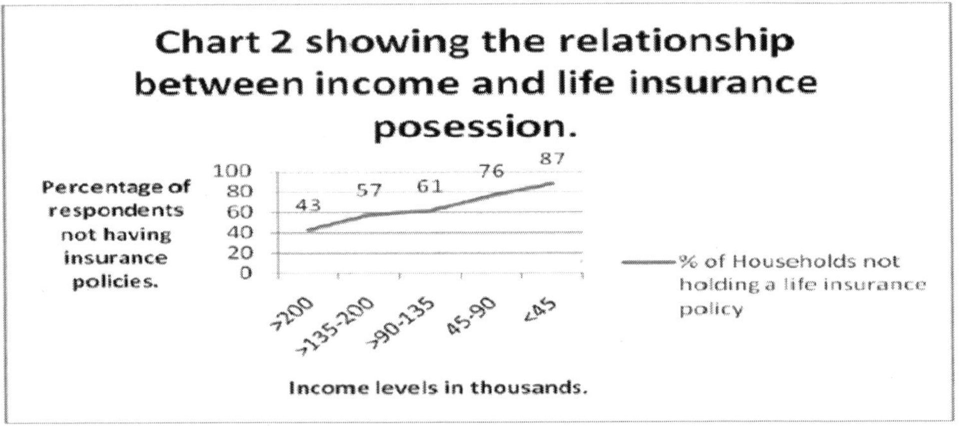

Source: Survey of 4125 individuals in BCG's next billion consumer research,2007, BCG analysis. The Boston Consulting Group Report, 2007, page no 16.

Current growth of life insurance sector- An urban phenomenon

Life insurance continues to remain a 'Push Product' in India (Vijayan). The Maslow's need analysis does not fit life insurance as one of the needs of the populace. Insurance is a subject matter of solicitation and it is still sold and not bought by the people. The distributive mechanism of the life insurance companies has of course undergone tremendous change in the last one decade, particularly after the opening of the industry to the private players. Apart from the traditional Agency Channel, new channels are opened up by the insurance companies. The Bank Assurance, Micro Insurance, Group Insurance, Multi Level Marketing, Mobile Insurance and E Insurance have paved for the tremendous growth of the sector. But it is not wrong if we can say that the focus is on urban market and the message of insurance has not trickled down to rural areas. There is exponential growth in life insurance industry after it is thrown open to private players in 2000.

During 2001 to 2007, the life insurance industry registered a growth of 41% in new business sum assured with premium registering 28% growth. If we analyze the growth carefully, it is evident that the growth is fueled largely by Unit Linked Policies (ULIP) and single premium policies. While the ULIP business grew from 41.77% to 70.30% from 2005-06 to 2007-08, the traditional business declined from 58.23% to 29.70% in the same period.

The implication is that the growth emanated from semi urban and urban centers and also from the affluent segments of the rural areas as the minimum ticket size of a ULIP policy is generally Rs 10000 per year. The rural poor who are at the bottom of the pyramid with lesser disposable incomes may not find it convenient to take up these types of policies. The growth story of life insurance industry has not seriously attempted for inclusive growth which is the paramount need today. The table1 clearly illustrates the trends of life insurance business.

Table1 showing trends of life insurance business.

	ULIP Business %			Non-linked business%		
	2005-06	2006-07	2007-08	2005-06	2006-07	2007-08
Private companies	82.30	88.75	90.33	17.70	11.25	9.67
LIC of India	29.76	46.31	62.31	70.24	53.69	37.69
Industry total	41.77	56.91	70.30	58.23	43.09	29.70

Source: IRDA Annual Report as at 31st March, 2007.Page no 16&17.

If we see the pattern of growth in terms of expansion of offices, again the trend is urban biased. The table 2 illustrates this aspect.

Current marketing techniques for inclusive growth

Insurers who begin to transact insurance business in the year 2000 or later are required to underwrite 7%, 9%, 12%, 14% and 16% respectively in the first five years of operations in the rural sector. With regard to social sector, they are required to issue 5000, 7500, 10,000, 15000 20,000 policies on different lives in the first five years respectively.

In order to meet the IRDA obligations, the life insurance players have evolved certain marketing techniques. The marketing techniques currently practiced are broadly similar with all the private players which can be analyzed under the following Heads.

Table 2 showing distribution of offices of life insurance as on 31/03/08					
Insurer	Metro	Urban	Semi-urban	Others	Total
Private	628	1169	2692	1902	6391
LIC	311	468	848	895	2522
Total	939	1637	3540	2797	8913

1. Insurance awareness programs.
2. Development of brand image.
3. Striving to build the trust by developing customer relationship.
4. Introducing innovative products.
5. Leveraging the synergies of other financial and social institutions.
6. Societal marketing with a view to gain the attention of customers, particularly of rural areas.
7. Sales promotion campaigns through suitable incentive/reward systems to intermediaries.
8. Innovative advertisement mechanisms.
9. Training of resources to meet the challenges of insurance marketing.
10. Deploying IT solutions aiming to meet the ever rising customer expectations.
11. Relaxations of procedures in claims settlement.

As the object of this paper is more towards finding insupreneurial ideas for more rural coverage than to discuss each marketing technique, it is enough to state that these techniques have not yielded desired results and total insurance coverage for all insurable population has remained a dream. It is rightly commented by Philip Kotler that "Marketing entered into the consciousness of different industries at different times — Marketing spread most rapidly in consumer packaged goods companies, consumer durable companies, and industrial equipment companies in that order – Bankers initially showed great resistance to marketing but in the end embraced it enthusiastically. *Marketing has begun to attract interest in the insurance industry and the stock brokerage industry although marketing is still poorly understood in these industries"* (Shirodkar). "Marketing conveys many things to many people. The problem is, very often the marketer uses yesterday's techniques for today's market. In LIC major marketing activity is conducting agents meetings, mainly the ongoing sales competitions. These meetings do not attract new faces. Another activity is the follow up of agents on phone. Whether these activities are wholesome remedies for bringing optimal results in competitive era? Activities like putting up canopy stalls at busy locations, mass canvassing in one residential complex, adopting survey techniques in marketing, conducting insurance awareness camps with the help of insurance beneficiary, event marketing connected to birth of child, marriage etc, conducting lapsed service camp in big apartment complexes, encouraging the agents to do tele-marketing from their residences, doing the mail marketing to addresses in various directories, conducting five to ten cold canvassing in a week as a planned activity, strategic move for cross selling, up selling and so on, are not thought of. The need of the hour is innovativeness and the present day marketers are not prepared to have a different kind of approach to marketing" (Swaminathan). "Insurance will have to overcome its sluggishness, if there is to be a culture of innovation within the industry. Understanding how population change is central to the life insurance industry, and global changes currently underway are providing a once in a century opportunity for life insurers" (Saroj Dikhale).

Hindrances for inclusive growth

Lack of insurance awareness in the rural areas, lackadaisical interest shown by insurance companies and low knowledge levels are the main reasons apart from many other reasons for the large size untapped life insurance market that we see today. In order to assess these factors, a survey has been conducted over 500 policy holders of Bangalore rural and Kolar rural districts of Karnataka during 2009. A Chron Back Alpha test is also conducted to check the reliability of the instrument and as the Alpha value is 0.70, the responses have been taken as reliable representing the whole population. The findings are as follows:

In order to analyze the responses of beneficiaries (62 questions constituting 11 major areas of life insurance market viz, insurance awareness, product expectations, Agents' knowledge levels, effectiveness of advertising, rural interest of the companies, customer satisfaction etc) from the beneficiary questionnaire, a factor analysis is undertaken. Since these 62 questions constitute 11 major areas of life insurance market, eleven variables are taken in to consideration for undertaking the factor analysis. This is also in view of the fact that these 62 questions are not asked randomly but were grouped in to eleven separate headings and responses are obtained as eleven variables represent eleven areas of life insurance market.

Insurance Awareness in Rural Areas

For the 500 beneficiaries the minimum score is 16 and the maximum score is 21. Seven variables are analyzed to establish the awareness levels of the rural customers. The results indicate that the responses range between 2.28 (16/7) to 3 (21/7).It means the responses are lying in between 'somewhat disagree' to 'neither agree nor disagree' category. It can be concluded that the awareness of life insurance in rural areas is very low and average percent of preferences on all variables is 54.09% only and is shown in table 3. It indicates that they are not aware of the structure of ULIPs, claim procedures, methods of surrender and they could not differentiate micro insurance and rural insurance.

Table 3 showing variables in respect of the awareness level factor

N	Minimum	Maximum	Mean	Std. Deviation	Variance
500	16	21	18.93	1.55	2.41

Here the minimum and maximum shows variability in terms of range of scores where the least score obtained in the group for 7 questions is 16 and the highest score in the group is 21.

Knowledge Levels of Agents

For the 500 beneficiaries the minimum score is 4 and the maximum score is 7.Four variables are analyzed to establish the knowledge levels of the agents. The results indicate that the responses range between 1(4/4) to 1.75(7/4).It means the responses are lying in between 'strongly disagree' to 'somewhat disagree' category. It can be concluded that the knowledge levels of agents in rural areas are perceived by the beneficiaries in low esteem and average percent of preferences on all variables is 30.18% only and is shown in table 4. It indicates that the agents have not explained all products before selling a particular product and also they are not quite knowledgeable.

Here the minimum and maximum shows variability in terms of range of scores where the least score obtained in the group for 4 questions is 4 and the highest score in the group is 7.

Table 4 showing variables in respect of agents' knowledge levels.

N	Minimum	Maximum	Mean	Std. Deviation	Variance
500	4	7	6.04	1.12	1.25

Rural Interest of the Companies

For the 500 beneficiaries the minimum score is 17 and the maximum score is 23. Seven variables are analyzed to establish whether all companies are really interested in rural business. The results indicate that the responses range between 2.42 (17/7) to 3.28 (23/7).It means the responses are lying in between 'somewhat disagree' to 'neither agree nor disagree' category. It can be concluded that the companies are not really showing any interest in spreading insurance message in rural areas and average percent of preferences on all variables is 57.39% only and is shown in table 5. It indicates that all companies have no rural centric policies and all companies have no agents in rural places.

Table 5 showing variables in respect of rural interest of the companies.

N	Minimum	Maximum	Mean	Std. Deviation	Variance
500	17	23	20.09	1.62	2.64

Here the minimum and maximum shows variability in terms of range of scores where the least score obtained in the group for 7 questions is 17 and the highest score in the group is 23.

The results clearly indicate that insurance companies prefer urban areas with the result the insurance awareness levels in rural areas are far from satisfactory. The low knowledge levels also contribute to inadequate insurance coverage in rural areas.

Search for entrepreneurial solutions for inclusive growth

"Entrepreneurship is the most powerful economic force known to human kind. The 'entrepreneurial revolution' that captured our imagination during the late 1990s has now permeated every aspect of business thinking and planning. The applications of creativity, risk taking, innovation, and passion lead the way to economic development far greater than anyone could imagine. The twenty-first century presents newer and sometimes more complex challenges than ever before conceived; however the entrepreneurial drive and determination of our yet to be discovered 'dynasty builders' will be our greatest solution"(Kuratko & Hodgetts). An Insupreneurial pitch of the highest scale is the need of the hour.

In order to maximize insurance coverage in rural areas, the companies need to aim at inclusive growth strategy so as ensure maximum life insurance coverage without losing the profit motive. For inclusive growth old and tried marketing techniques such as routine Agents' Meetings, 'One size fits all' products, media advertisements etc may not work as the life insurance coverage sought to be covered is to financially excluded ,non bankable and sometimes media dark population of the rural hinterlands. Out of box solutions and short and long term techniques are to be forged in order to spread the message of life insurance and value creation in cash poor low income society. Some of the suggestions are:

1. The low levels of life insurance awareness are evident from the analysis of the primary. With a view to educate the customers and raising the awareness levels, apart from the existing techniques such as mobile publicity vans and publicity in print and electronic media, *the industry can create a consortium of life insurance companies with the involvement of IRDA for educating the rural people on a mass scale. Social marketing technique is to be used to market the idea of insurance* before the individual life insurance company steps in to the business. This consortium has to organize exhibitions, slide shows, short films and such other activities in the village markets frequently.
2. Rural India is a mixture of opposites. We witness raising affluence of some and at the same time financially excluded lot of people on the other side. We need insurance advisors who are ambidextrous enough to cater to the rural rich and also rural poor. The rural agent has to equip himself with the subject of wealth creation as well as social insurance coverage. *It is therefore suggested for all the insurance companies to form a consortium and establish an Insurance Academy for training the agents of rural areas for initiating an exclusive training activity and devise curriculum to rural agents across India.*
3. The IT initiatives presently practiced by the life insurance companies are inadequate to rural life insurance coverage and it is discussed in chapter 4 and 5. In order to generate insurance awareness and spread the coverage of life insurance, *Insurance companies need to establish ITC model e- choupal webs in rural areas and start*

disseminating life insurance awareness in local languages. Electronic reminders for payment premiums can be issued and the premium calculator for different products can be installed. Video conferences can be arranged in this model where the company representative chat with the villagers and personally explain the features of the new products. Companies can issue credit cards to rural policyholders and provision can be made for paying premiums through credit cards. Life Insurance companies are recommended to develop data ware housing for each village of all districts comprising the income, caste, religion and occupation details and make use of the data for recruitment of agents from stratified data, designing need based products , positioning of the products and such other marketing initiatives. The Bank Assurance profile of Indian Life Insurance Companies is far from satisfactory. In India only 2% of the captive customers of the banks are given insurance through bank assurance against the global bench mark of 50 to 60%. *It is suggested for the life insurance companies to have tied up with all regional and cooperative banks and tries to cover all the liabilities of the indebted people. Most of the village households have loans for one reason or other and it is a profitable venture if each loanee is covered by insurance in order not to bequeath the debt in case of any untoward eventuality. The life insurance companies should educate the cooperative societies for getting formal approval by cooperative members for the mandatory insurance scheme for all loans sanctioned by them. The commission can be paid to co operative societies. Insurance companies should also launch easy to understand bank assurance specific exclusive products for facilitating the bank managers to push the sales in an easy fashion.*

4. The alternate premium collection mechanisms, viz, ECS, Internet payment, Salary Saving Schemes may not work with unbankable and financially exclusive population. *Insurance companies through consortium of all insurers collect premiums through mobile vans at the village markets and through 'Collecting Banks'.*
5. *Insurance companies should start giving reward points for each repeat purchase and for each recycling of maturity claim which can be redeemed when the last policy results in to claim by way of maturity or death. This model may be christened 'Generations Relationship Rewards Scheme (GRRS)'.* This ensures loyalty on the part of the customer towards the company at no extra expense. 'The prototype available in Coffee Day (Coffee card), IOC (Petro card) and Bharath Petroleum (Petro card) can be made use of by the insurance

companies also. For this the companies should start looking at the customer in totality and not as a Policy number. *Preparing and perfecting a unique customer ID for a policy holder with various policies is a pre requisite for the success of this model.*

6. For the low income agricultural labor group it is necessary to devise collection mechanism on daily base since their incomes are labor driven. Daily wage earners can spare a few rupees daily but find it difficult to pay a bulk premium at a time. *Insurance companies need to design policies with daily pigmy collection mechanism and position the products to agricultural labors.*
7. With a view to spread the message of life insurance on a wider scale in each and every village, *the life insurance companies need to prepare branch socio economic profile of each branch office with all details of caste / religion/ income/ occupation composition of all villagers and try to appoint agents from each stratum to tap the business from each group. Since caste / religious loyalties play vital role in the rural social spectrum, it is necessary to make use of this strategy for better advantage. The Black Spot villages (where there is no agent of any company) need to be identified and agents are to be appointed in such villages. Since opinion leaders play an important role in purchase decisions, companies need to enlist the opinion leaders as their Sales Force.*
8. There is dearth of products suiting to rural psyche. Except a few products of a few companies, the general product design of all companies has no exclusive rural orientation with a unique selling proposition. The lack of need based products is also one of the reasons for low levels of rural coverage. In order to design need based products, insurance companies are advised to survey the rural market thoroughly to assess the needs. *A family policy covering all members of the family can be launched in order to cover maximum people at a stroke. We have prototypes of such policies in foreign countries .Insurance companies have to design hybrid products with the convergence mechanism of micro credit, micro insurance and micro savings. Since the people at the bottom of the pyramid are exposed to risks relating to vagaries of nature with unpredictable timings in income generations, the insurance companies should design premium holiday products, deferred premium payment products , seasonal premium payment products and 'any time any amount' premium payment products specially designed to suit the needs of the rural people Comprehensive insurance policies covering the life of the individual and his other needs viz, crop, scooter, house, travel etc as riders can*

be thought of by the life insurance companies by ceding the risk of general insurance subject matters to general insurance companies. In this model the insurance company acts as a single window mechanism for all insurance needs. Life insurance companies have to design region specific innovative products taking the emotional needs of the rural people, viz, son's education, daughter's marriage, pilgrimage, funeral expense needs and position the products to different segments.

9. In order to become more customer friendly, *the life insurance companies need to introduce employee appraisal linked branch service index meters in all branches where each and every service activity is measured according to scale by the robust IT department monitoring from the head office.* The Service areas relate to issue of flawless policy bond, change of address, sending premium notice, mode correction, registering nominations & assignments, settling survival benefits before date, loan sanctioning, fund switching , claim settlement, free look cancellation, courteous response to queries, disciplinary actions against mis-selling and a host of service related things. *Printing policy bond in regional language and communicating in regional language avoiding insurance jargons create right chord to relate the company to the rural customer.*
10. Jeb Brugman and C.K.Prahlad, while emphasizing the role of NGOs in spreading insurance, argue that 'while companies have discovered the importance of NGOs as paths to markets, social groups have realized that carefully calibrated business models can unleash powerful forces for good. Their interactions have created new links between business innovation and social development. Companies and NGOs are increasingly going into business together, pursuing scale and profits, social equity, and empowerment as part of an integrated value chain Some NGOs are positively thriving where state-owned or multinational companies have failed. Two years ago, when the Indian insurance giant, Life Insurance Corporation, found it difficult to collect premiums and pay claims in rural areas in the state of Andhra Pradesh, micro credit federations took over the business.

    Their extensive knowledge of customers and their superior reach allowed the NGOs to grow the market rapidly. They operate quite profitably, earning an average gross margin of 27%'. This observation is an eye opener for the life insurance players and *they can have tie ups with the gross root NGOs on a large scale, perhaps with all NGOs working at the rural areas for the distribution of the insurance products.*

Conclusion

Insurance penetration in rural India is far from satisfactory is an undisputed fact. The lack of insurance awareness, the low levels of Corporate interest, the low knowledge levels of agents, lack of market research, 'one size fits all product' range and above all the following yesterday's techniques to today's problem by the companies have resulted in depriving insurance to the needy poor. It is high time for the insurance companies to shed the sluggishness and embrace entrepreneurial ideas for spreading the gospel of life insurance in the rural areas. "The need of the hour is the thinking of 'Suraksha' in place of 'insurance', 'promise' in place of 'Policy', 'peace of mind' in place of 'risk cover', 'care and concern' in place of 'contractual obligations' and 'well wisher & friend' in place of 'agent and broker'(Venkata Ramana Rao)". Only Insupreneurship on large scale is a key for heralding the protective coverage that is insurance.

Bibliography

1. Brugman, Jeb & Prahlad, C.K, 2007, "Cocreating Businesses' New Social Compact", Harvard Business Review, February, 2007, Page no 4 to 14.
2. Dikhale, Saroj, 2009,"Future Creates the Present – Insurance 2020", Yogakhsema, May, 2009, Page no 12.
3. Gopinath, K, 2009, "Rural and Social Sector Insurance", IRDA Journal, April, 2009- Page no 17.
4. Kuratko, Donald F and Hodgetts, Richard M, 2007, "Entrepreneurship in the new millennium", Cengage Learning India Private Limited", page no 11.
5. Maslov, Abraham, 1970, Analysis of Hierarchy of Needs, "Toward a Psychology of Being' edited by Richard Lowery.
6. Ramana Rao, Venkata, 2008, "Life Insurance Awareness in Rural India- Micro Insurance Lessons to Learn and Teach"- Bima Quest, Volume 8, January, 08, Page 57.
7. Sankaracharya,Adi , Geetha Bashyam, Ramakrishna Mutt Publication, 1999 translated by Krishna, A.G.
8. Shirodkar, S.M, 1992, - "Marketing and Public Relations", IC-88, published by Insurance Institute of India, Page no 44.
9. Swaminathan,K,2010- "Marketing- Think Beyond the Routines", Yogakshema, Jan, 2009.
10. Vijayan, 2010, "Insurance remains a Push Product"- an interview appeared in Financial Express dated 4th November, 2010.

8

Rural Women Entrepreneurship through Self-Help Groups and Micro-Finance Institutions: Do they really lead to Economic Development of Poor Women?

Introduction

Economic independence is one of the pre-conditions for the women to gain equal status in day-to-day life along with their male counterparts. Identifying the importance of economic empowerment and eradication of financial exclusion of the rural women, several governments in India have been implementing various developmental programmes and schemes. Recently, Self- Help Groups (SHGs) have become one of the vehicles of development to empower rural poor women economically by lending credit facilities through rural banks and providing a space to create various entrepreneurial activities in the rural areas. These groups are positively altering the lifestyles of the rural women in terms of their occupations, earnings, involvement and participation in the society. The SHG movement has been so highlighted particularly in Andhra Pradesh which brought a radical change in the position of rural women from that of daily-wage laborer to an entrepreneur. Simultaneously, Micro-Finance Institutions (MFIs) have also been playing an active role in the rural regions where the rural banks do not exist; and lending credits to the poorest sections without any delay with simple procedures. But recently, some of the SHG women in Rural Andhra Pradesh are committing suicides and some of them are migrating to the nearby towns due to their inability to repay the borrowed money from the MFIs who are charging high rate of interest unlike rural banks has led to several critics. In these circumstances the paper explores the possibilities and potentialities of SHGs to emerge as an institution of rural entrepreneurship and promoting women as a rural entrepreneur through SHGBank Linkage Programme. Parallel to this, it also examines does MFIs really making rural women as a self-employed entrepreneur in the rural areas or is it pushing women in more vulnerable conditions due to the pressure on repayments with high interest rates?

Economic development is one of the prerequisites for the people who are in the clutches of poverty, especially poor women, to ameliorate their status and live a dignified life in the society[1].

Though, since independence various central and state governments have being given policy attention to rural development and economic upliftment of the rural poor, it has not been fulfilled due to poor public service delivery system, delay in the proper implementation of government programmes, unaccountable and corrupt government officials. In addition, most of the rural poor in general and women in particular are illiterate, unemployed and unaware of development policies and welfare programmes etc. because of which they have been excluded to access basic minimum needs. Due to these difficulties, a major proportion of the rural women have been working as daily-wage laborers in the agricultural and various other fields. In the absence of work (agricultural related work exists only in particular sessions) they would remain without any earnings. The unpredictability and inconsistency of earnings, therefore, compelled them to remain bound in the shackles of poverty and dependent on their male counterparts. The problem is further compounded by rapid feminization of poverty[2] which renders the rural women into a more vulnerable group vis-à-vis others.

In these circumstances, women entrepreneurship has been recognized as one of the alternative source to address the rural women unemployment and further to contribute for their economic growth. In fact, development and empowerment of rural women depends on their level of participation in various developmental activities at the grassroots. Faraha Nawaz (2009) says, involvement of rural women in various entrepreneurial activities bestows them to empower themselves in different fields. Particularly, in rural areas establishment of various entrepreneurial activities enables women to earn sustained incomes that have the potential to release them from the clutches of poverty. In this regard, it is imperative to recognize that the provision of extending loans to the poorer sections in the rural areas through the formal banking system i.e. by the SHGBank linkage or Micro-Finance Institutions (MFIs) enable the rural poor in development of entrepreneurship qualities, increase the employment opportunities that further not only lead to their socio-economic enrichment but also include them in the mainstream.

Entrepreneur and Entrepreneurship

An entrepreneur can be defined as one who initiates and establishes an income generating activity that makes him as a self-employer. Entrepreneur never constrains himself just with that, he would not rest unless he revolutianalize the whole system where they involve.

Entrepreneurship therefore denotes the establishment of new income-generating activity in a society (Begum, 1993 & Nawaz, 1999). These lines denote that entrepreneurship is a set of business activities being performed by the entrepreneur. In the globalization era, the rapid expansion of Information and Communication Technology (ICT) has marginalized the unskilled laborers and made them as unemployers. Particularly in the rural periphery, the malady of unemployment both for men and women become one of the major impediments for their socio-economic development. In these circumstances, entrepreneurship becomes one of the solutions to address the problem of unemployment among the rural youth that certainly brings positive changes among in their economic status.

Thus access to the financial services to the rural poor, particularly to the rural women through SHGs brought forefront the importance of rural women entrepreneurship. SHG-Bank Linkage or Micro-Finance Institutions (MFIs) are the major funding sources (micro-finance) for the SHGs and these groups are the basic platforms to the rural women to start various entrepreneurial activities.

SHG-Bank Linkage and MFIs: Major Sources of Micro-Financing for Rural Entrepreneurship

There are three major sources of financing for the rural entrepreneurs in India i.e. Informal lenders (money lenders, friends, relatives, etc.); semi-formal finance (NGOs and MFIs); and Rural banks (SHG-Bank linkage)

Nawaz (2009). In that, SHG-Bank linkage through rural banks and MFIs through private agents are the major financing source. However, the channel for lending micro-finance is mostly through SHGs. Since the mid-1980s, micro-finance has become a favored intervention for poverty-alleviation in developing and underdeveloped countries (Leach & Sitaram, 2002:575). It has also become a novel way of extending credit to the rural poor and improving their income levels (Vatta, 2003:432). It is a credit facility that provides (through SHG-Bank linkage, NGOs, MFIs) to the rural poor women and encourages them to start small scale entrepreneurial activities to reduce their acute poverty vis-à-vis expanding their income levels.

SHGs become one of the important players in development of entrepreneurial activities in the rural areas and due to its pro-active role it gained the attention of policy makers and governments in various states. The basic purpose of the SHGs is to improve the conditions of the poor and marginalized sections, particularly those who are unable to obtain credit from money-lenders. It is above preparing them to employ themselves as well providing employment for those in need. It allows them to transcend themselves from job seeker to job giver. As a whole it elevates their livelihoods. It encourages the rural women to establish various entrepreneurial activities through micro-credits so as to pull them out of poverty trap.

Suguna views SHG as

A small economically homogeneous group of rural poor which is voluntarily ready to contribute to a common fund to be lent to its members as per group decision; and it works for group solidarity, self-help, awareness, social and economic empowerment in the way of democratic functioning. (2006:15) Simultaneously, MFIs emerged as a result of civil society initiatives that have also played a major role in bringing micro-finance to the forefront (Shylendra, 2006: 1960). These institutions aim at lending micro-credits to a large number of rural poor to establish various entrepreneurial activities with simple procedure and without any delay. The repayment to these Institutions is based on weekly installment (in rural banks the repayment is monthly-wise) and duration of repayment is 50 weeks. These institutions have become popular in the rural areas where there is no accessibility of rural banks and reduced the rural poor need to approach money lenders and indebtedness to them for years. These institutions have also the credibility that they become second-best option for the rural poor both in terms of interest rates and financial services after the rural banks (Shylendra, 2006:1962); and providing micro-credits to the rural poor women (as a group) at lower interest rates as compare with moneylenders[3].

Self-Help Groups and Micro Finance Institutions in Andhra Pradesh: An Overview

The Government of Andhra Pradesh has introduced the concept of SHGs in 1980s as a strategy to address poverty, and in particular a reduction in feminization of poverty and empowerment of women in rural areas [Bapuji et al., (2008), Das (2005), Ramalakshmi, (2003), Reddy, C.S. et al., (2005)]. As of now, there are 9, 33, 585 SHGs in Andhra Pradesh covering the total participation of 1,06,60,968 rural poor women and 22 districts in the process of micro-financing the poor women[4]. During the 2008-2009 financial years Rs.11037 crores has been targeted as loan mobilization under SHG-Bank Linkage Programme and an amount of Rs.7203. 53 crores have been managed[5]. Andhra Pradesh government through the formation of SHGs and its SHG-Bank linkage model has been targeted rural poor women as a special group and providing micro-finance facilities with a subsidized rate of interest and encouraging women to create various entrepreneurial activities.

Andhra Pradesh is also one of the states which has the highest penetration of MFIs in India and started operating since 1996. It is home to some of India's biggest MFIs such as SKS, Spandhana, Basix and Share etc are began operations (Johnson & Sushmita, 2010: 11). Since 2000, the MFIs in AP have started their expansion rapidly with total numbers of borrowers more than doubling each year, and by the year 2005, AP become one of the focal points for MFIs in India[6].

According to Sa-Dhan, a network body of India's MFIs, the total MFIs in India are 264 having total loan outstanding Rs. 18,343.9 crores from 2.67 Crore active borrowers. Up to 31st March, 2010, AP has the maximum outreach of borrowers with 62.5 lakh the borrowed amount is Rs. 16, 466 Crores.

Rural Women Entrepreneurship through SHGs and MFIs

In recent times, SHGs and MFIs are seen as instrumental in both women's empowerment and poverty eradication by creating various entrepreneurial opportunities with the help of micro-finance. In the field study[7] it is observed that most of the rural women on an average were borrowed Rs. 50,000-60,000 from SHGs. It is observed that, before joining SHGs, most of these women were coolies and daily labors or housewives. They did not have access to capital to start their own small business ventures. If they get money from money-lenders, the interest rate used to be very high and they were unable to repay the money within the time-frame. That is the reason most of the women from poorer households worked as coolies and daily wage labours rather using their entrepreneurial knowledge. In such a way a lot of human capital which has the gist to undertake entrepreneurial activities has been wasted. But the instigation of SHGs and with the financial assistance from the SHG-Bank linkage the scenario has changed, as it led to for a significant improvement in the economic conditions of the rural poor.

After joining SHGs, the rural women have started various entrepreneurial activities such as daily farming, sari painting, tailoring, bangle stores, tea shops and interestingly meat shops too, they have also spent their money in agricultural activities and livestock raring. Some of them are holding semi initiations where they are employing 5-10 people from underprivileged sections. They are now in a position to earn money on a regular monthly basis according to the business they have chosen. Most of the women entrepreneurs are earning on an average Rs. 1000-2000 per month. However, the amount which they are earning now is a positive sign for the economic upliftment of the poor who are in the clutches of poverty. Given the above, the impact of SHGs on economic aspect is very clear, as observed by author during the field visit; there is an incredible change which can be seen through their material well being.

Most of the SHG members claimed that they joined the SHG because microcredit facilities not only for establishment of entrepreneurial activities but also are useful when urgently needed or in emergencies.

In addition to the entrepreneurial development, SHG women in the rural areas are concentrating on community development and addressing village level issues. It was observed that the SHGs are making an impact in the village by trying to address the problems of basic amenities such as water, public service delivery of ration goods, proper maintenance of primary and Anganvadi schools, roads and health facilities. This does not always mean that the SHGs are taking care of all the tasks mentioned above, but out of their elevated awareness levels, they are demanding that the local institutions of the panchayat and their grassroots leaders should do it so. If the SHG members feel any problem or shortage of any of the above services, along with other villagers, they are opting for dharnas as a way of protest to claim their basic amenities. It is observed that women who are active in the SHGs are also participating in social issues such as purified water facilities, health services, nutritious food in Mid-day meals, infrastructure facilities in the villages, activities taking up for Clean & Green in the villages etc. They are organizing group meetings in order to solve the problem in the villages.

The Government of Andhra Pradesh has identified the increased level of awareness among the women and started channelizing them to utilize in order to ensure the developmental activities that are aimed at eradication of extreme poverty in the rural areas are through. Having such objective the Govt. of Andhra Pradesh started implementation of several programmes with the help of SHGs. These programmes include Pavala Vaddi Scheme, Indira Kranthi Patham, Abhaya Hastham, Janashree Bima Yojana (JBY), Pesticide Management programme (NPM), Scholarship Facilities for the children of SHG women and Deepam Scheme.

Role of MFIs and its impact on Rural Poor

MFIs are also providing financial assistance to the rural women to start any new entrepreneurial activity. Unfortunately, apart from the huge success part there are women who have taken loans from these institutions been using for their consumption needs and agricultural activities instead of using for small business ventures. Sometimes the women are used to handover their loan to their husbands for the improvement of his business activity. In addition, most of the rural women were taken a number of loans for their children's education. Ahmad (2008:261) rightly said that if the micro-credit is used directly for entrepreneurship development and for future savings of a woman entrepreneur, certainly it will lead to their socio-economic development and financial inclusion. However if the resources are used up for other activities other than entrepreneurial opportunities, the actual purpose of the micro-credit cannot be fulfilled.

There are several allegations charged that at the beginning MFIs in India have started as non-profitable organizations, which aimed at lending credits to the rural poor to establish various entrepreneurial activities, but in recent times, the MFIs have converted as a profit based organizations and doing as well as expanding their business at the cost of rural people's money. Besides they are also charging high interest rates by adding service and other charges, and following unethical ways to recover the loans by using intimidation and abusive language (Shylendra, H.S., 2006). They are also encouraging the poor people by providing multiple lending, where the rural banks are strictly not. This is also one of the reasons the rural poor are attracting towards MFIs rather than rural banks. Kumar (2006) argued that because of such practices, MFIs are causing a huge burden on the rural poor and certainly that pushing them to a vicious cycle of debt, poverty and even deaths. Recently, Andhra Pradesh has witness 30 suicides by the rural poor borrowers during September, 2010 to November, 2010, due to their inability to repay the exorbitant interest rates charged by the MFIs (Lalita Iyer, 2010).

Although the micro financing scheme started in an efficient manner by the professionalized NGOs and MFIs; there are innumerable NGOs which are totally new to the micro financing sector, leading to duplication of programmes which ultimately causes the beneficiaries to be indebted (Loganath, 2006). It is observed that there are about 40 very small lending institutions in Andhra Pradesh, which merely give and take money. These Institutions are not familiar with the concept of MFIs that made the rural poor to take credits from multiple sources. As it mentioned, the MFIs follow the weekly repayment schedule to recover the debts from the borrowers put a lot of pressure on them to continue with regular repayments. Sometimes the borrowers are depending upon other lending sources (other MFIs or money-lenders) to repay the MFI loans to retain their access (Sinha and Matin 1998). Whereas in the SHG-Bank linkage models the SHG members take the responsibility to recover the debts from the borrowers (usually SHG members). Therefore, there is less scope to use coercive methods unlike the MFI agents.

Some critical observations and suggestions on Micro-Finance and SHGs

Andhra Pradesh is considered to be one of the states which have been operating SHG-Bank Linkage and MFIs network successfully. Even here many short comings are noticed in the functioning of SHG in fulfilling its stated objective i.e. economic upliftment through entrepreneurial activities. Though many of the short comings that we will now discuss may not be applicable to Andhra Pradesh in particular, there are commonalities in the Andhra Pradesh and other state experience. Many are of the view that micro-credits do not reach the poorest sections that are in an urgent need of financial assistance. The reason for the exclusion of the poorest sections is held to be the discrimination by the loan officers (Simanowitz & Walter, 2003:36). Even if they get the loan amount it is hardly sufficient to create income-generating activities for all the entrepreneurs. It is observed in the field study by the author that some of the women from SC and ST groups are lagging behind the women from OBC or other castes which are observed to be more enterprising and active. There is a need to promote better interaction among all the rural women to take better advantage of the facilities extended and to promote social harmony.

Most of the poorest women are facing difficulties in joining and continuing in a SHG. Due to their extreme poverty, they often come under stress in meeting the repayment schedules and thus feel compelled to withdraw as their non-payment adversely affects the whole group. Galab & Rao (2003: 1282) points out that some of the poor are not obtaining loan from the SHG-Bank linkages because their credit worthiness is under question. This ultimately results in lower utilization of loans and in turn may threaten the very sustainability of SHGs. It was rightly affirmed that [Madheswaran and Dharmadikary (2001:442)] too much of financial discipline or strict repayments and penalties for delays, prevent the poor from joining a micro-credit scheme or could limit the duration of their participation in it. Manimekalai (2004:173) in one of his field study on microfinance and women empowerment in the state of Tamil Nadu noticed that the stipulation of strict repayments made some of the members to borrow from informal sources (MFIs) with higher interest rates in order to re-pay the SHG credit.

According to Chowdhury (2009: 3) few factors are crucial for making credit more productive, in which the most important is, recipient's entrepreneurial skills. Mahajan (2005) added some other inputs such as identification of livelihood opportunities, selection and motivation of the rural women, business and technical training and establishing of market linkages all are crucial in making credit much more worthy. Both the authors hold that without a basic training in marketing skills, these women cannot properly utilize the credit. Consequently, they do not acquire maximum profits from the small business enterprises set up with credit from SHG or MFIs. Madheswaran and Dharmadhikary (2001:442) also draw our attention to the viability of non-farm economic activities or goods[8] in the long term. They claim that these non-farm goods made by the rural women and brought to the urban areas hardly meet the standards of the urban market thus affecting their incomes and in turn their capacities to repay the loans.

Hence there is a need for training to enhance the skills among rural women entrepreneurs and to ensure that goods produced meet the needs of the market. Das (2005:21) argued that, the southern region of India accounts for 64 percent of the functioning SHGs. The other regions like north-eastern, northern, eastern, western and central regions accounts for only 1%, 5%, 13%, 6% and 11% of functioning SHGs respectively. In view of these vast differences, there is a need to enlarge the scope of SHG-Bank Linkage programme in "13 priority states[9], which accounts for 70% of rural poor in the country" (Rao, 2010:24).

Therefore, the governments and various development agencies are called upon to promote SHGs for the rural poor in a vibrant manner and fill the imbalance between the SHGs across India.

Need of the hour

In order to improve the rural women entrepreneurship and to develop the rural women socially or economically there is urgent needs of some of the measures that can be address the problems of rural poor in lending credits form MFIs. It is significant to point out that the government of Andhra Pradesh has passed an ordinance called as "The Andhra Pradesh Micro Finance Institutions (Regulation of money lending) Ordinance, 2010[10] to regulate the excess interest charges and to stop the coercive tactics taken up the MFI agents to recover the repayments which led to more than 30 suicides by the SHG women and other borrowers. As it mentioned, lack of training is one of the obstacles to the rural women on how to use the micro-finance in a most profitable way. Most of the rural women are establishing petty shops and buying their livestock with the borrowed amount but they don't have proper training facilities. This setback seriously affects the efficiency of the rural women entrepreneurs. Therefore, special training programs need to be taken at the grassroots level to train and educated the rural entrepreneurs to make better worth from the entrepreneurial activities.

Lack of proper banking facilities is also one of the problems where most of the rural poor are compelled to depend upon the private MFIs though they are charging high interest rates. Therefore, it is foremost important for various state governments to intervene and take initiatives to establish more rural banks in the rural areas. The delay in disbursement of loan made the rural women to depend upon the private MFIs, hence, government should also take necessary steps to provide micro-finance that too without any delay in disbursing the loan amount.

Nowadays, MFI agents are using unethical methods to recover the debt amount from the borrowers; there is also need to follow a flexible recovery methods and monthly repayments instead of weekly. So that the rural entrepreneurs get sufficient time to earn the money through their various entrepreneurial activities including dairies and repay the debt amount, otherwise again they have to depend upon other lending source to repay the credit. Another important aspect that requires attention is the need to modify the procedures for applying, seeking credit and release of the credit from the banks. The existing procedures for obtaining bank loans for rural illiterate women (for instance, most of the Scheduled Tribe and Scheduled Caste women in the field area are unable to acquire bank loans) are still a major problem resulting in denial of the financial benefits they are entitled to thus diminishing their interest in lending money from the banks.

Conclusion

Faleye (1999) rightly pointed out that women entrepreneurship opportunities and their entrepreneurship qualities not only reducing poverty by increasing productivity, but also about women's emancipation and empowerment. In this regard, SHG as an institution of entrepreneurship, which not only develops women's entrepreneurial capacity but also as a form of collective action (team work & collective decision-making), strives for each and every individual's empowerment. Certainly, the private MFIs support them financially to establish various entrepreneurial activities. In fact, MFIs are one of the credit lending institutions in the rural areas where the rural banks are do not exist; and lending credits to the poorest sections without any delay with simple procedure.

But the high interest rates of the MFIs is one of the serious concerns that leading the women to commit suicides.

Through the entrepreneurial activities rural mass have an opportunity to transform from daily wage earner to self-employed entrepreneur, if the SHGs and MFIs lend money to them with subsidized interest rates and simple procedures. Andhra Pradesh government's initiative of Pavala Vaddi is made half-way succeeded in the establishment of income-generating activities by the rural poor; but at the same unless there is an urgent concern to disburse the loans without long interventions. It is the time to look at the concept of SHGs and MFIs in a long term perspective because these intermediaries have the potentiality to create various entrepreneurial activities to the rural unemployed poor women that not only paved for their all-round empowerment but also reduction of feminization of poverty as well restrictions on recovery practices being used by the MFI agents. For more details see "The Andhra Pradesh Micro Finance Institutions

(Regulation of money lending) Ordinance, 2010, Government of Andhra Pradesh.

References

1. Ahmad, Rais. (2008): "*Role of Micro-Finance in Empowering Women*" in Ajit Kumar Sinha (ed) (2008), "*New Dimensions of Women Empowerment*". Deep & Deep Publications, New Delhi.
2. Begum, R. (1993): "Entrepreneurship in Small-scale Industry: A Case Study of Engineering Units", *Dhaka University Journal of Business Studies*, Vol. 25. pp. 89-126.
3. Chowdhury, Prabal Roy & Ray, Jaideep (2009): "Public-private partnership in micro-finance: Should NGO involvement is restricted?". *Journal of Development Economics*, Vol. 90 (2). pp. 200-208.
4. CGAP Annual Report (2009): "*Advancing Financial Access for the World's Poor*", World Bank, pp. 1-64.
5. Das, Rimjhim Mousumi (2005): *"Micro-Finance through Self-Help Groups: A Boon for the Rural Poor"* in Verma, S.B; Pawar, Y.T (ed), "*Rural Empowerment through SHGs, NGOs and PRIs"*, Deep & Deep Publications, Pvt, Ltd, New Delhi.
6. Das, Sabyasachi (2005): "*Self-Help Groups and Micro-Credit Synergic Integration*", in Verma, S.B; Pawar, Y.T (ed), "*Rural Empowerment through SHGs, NGOs and PRIs"*, Deep & Deep Publications, Pvt, Ltd, New Delhi. pp 27-37.
7. Faleye, G.O. (1999): "*Women and Accountability*", A case study of the Family support programme in Osun-State, MPA project.
8. Galab, S & Chandrasekhara Rao, N (2003): "Women's Self-Help Groups, Poverty Alleviation and Empowerment", *Economic and Political Weekly*, Vol.38, No.12, pp.1274-1283
9. Johnson, Doug & Sushmita Meka (2010): *"Access to Finance in Andhra Pradesh"*, CMR Report Series No.3, Centre for Microfinance Research Banker's Institute of Rural Development. Pp.1-53.
10. Kumar, S. Nagesh (2006): 'The Making of Debt Trap in Andhra Pradesh', *The Hindu*, April 20.
11. Sinha, Saurabh and Imran Matin (1998): 'Informal Credit Transactions of Microcredit Borrowers in Bangaldesh', *IDS Bulletin*, 29 (4), pp 66-80. 2011
12. Madheswaran, S; Dharmadhikary (2001): "Empowering rural women through self-help groups: Lessons from Maharashtra rural credit project ", *Indian Journal of Agricultural Economics*, Vol.56 (3). pp. 427-43.

13. Manimekalai, K. (2004): *"Impact of Various Forms of Micro-Financing on Women"*, Submitted to Department of Women and Child Development, Ministry of Human Resource Development, Government of India. pp. 1- 232.
14. Nawaz, Faraha (2009): *"Critical Factors of Women Entrepreneurship Development in Rural Bangladesh"*, Bangladesh Development Research Working Paper Series, Bangladesh Development Research Centre, pp. 1- 16.
15. Premchander, Smita (2005): Competing Perspectives of Women and Micro-Finance Institutions: Rethinking Organizational Forms and capacity Building", April 8-14, *Mainstream*. pp. 11-17.
16. *Qazi Moin, (2005): "Self-Help Groups: Poised for a New Role in Rural Development", in* Verma, S.B; Pawar, Y.T (ed), "*Rural Empowerment through SHGs, NGOs and PRIs"*. Deep & Deep Publications, Pvt, Ltd, New Delhi. pp 38-48.
17. Ramalakshmi, C. S. (2003): "Women Empowerment through Self-Help Groups". *Economic and political Weekly*. Vol. 36(12). March - April.
18. Reddy, C.S. and Sandeep Manak (2005): "*Self-Help Groups: A Keystone of Microfinance in India-women empowerment & social security*". Mahila Abhivruddhi Society, Andhra Pradesh (APMAS), Hyderabad. pp. 1-19.
19. Available at: www.empowerpoor.org/downloads/SHGs-keystone-paper. pdf
20. Reghuvanshi, K. (1982): "Appropriate technology to help rural women". *Kurukshetra*, July, 36 (2): 18-21
21. Suguna, B. (2006): *"Empowerment of Rural Women through Self-Help Groups"*, Discovery Publishing House, New Delhi.
22. Shylendra, H.S., (2006), "Micro Finance Institutions in Andhra Pradesh: Crisis and Diagnosis", *Economic and Political Weekly*, May. Pp. 1959-63.
23. Sylendra, H.S. (2008): "Role of Self-Help Groups", *Yojana*, January 2008, pp. 25-31. 2011
24. Thorat, Y.S.P (2005): *"Micro-Finance in India: Sectoral Issues and Challenges", NABARD, Mumbai. pp. 1-10.*
25. Vatta, Kamal (2003): "Microfinance and Poverty Alleviation". Economic and Political Weekly. Vol. 38(5). pp. 432-433.

9

Focus Markets, New Generation Entrepreneurship: India's Options in Lac

Abstract

This paper proposes India to diversify and expand her international trade beyond the conventional markets and include LAC (Latin America and Caribbean) region as focus market for India's potential trade and investment growth. The LAC region emerging trends seem favorable with more and more creative EXIM policy schemes like Focus Market are set to boost India's prospect in the region. This paper focuses on "Focus Market" approach and dynamics of government of India's current EXIM policy, our international trade and business opportunity analysis for Indian prospective entrepreneurs in LAC region and LAC economic and market growth trajectory. Arguments in this paper is based on case study method, LAC market analysis, examination of India's international trade policy, India's current engagement profile and comparable international experiences like Sino –LAC engagement paradigm.

Introduction

Amritsar to Argentina the distance is only peanuts. Thanks to Simmer Pal Singh, the young Amritsar agriculture graduate who came to Argentina in 2005 to buy peanuts and settled down to cultivate nuts instead. Singh is now General Manager, Argentina with Singapore based Olam International - the $5 billion global supply chain of agricultural products and food ingredients. Singh now cultivates over 12,000 hectares of peanut farms and 5,000 hectares of soya and corn in Cordoba province, Argentina and with his Argentine success, Olam International has become the sixth largest agro player in the world from its twenty-sixth ranking. Nick named as peanut king, the handsome Sikh youth with his elegant turban is presumed to be a real king and not surprisingly, many Argentineans inquire where they can buy turbans to mimic Pal and his privileged profile in the community.

Singh's success in Argentina is not an isolated event. Indian MNCs in the last five years are active in whole of Latin America. India's Belgaum based Shree Renuka Sugars recently negotiated a 51% share purchase in a Brazilian sugar plant Equipav SA Acucar e Alcool at a cost of $250million (Rs.1150 Cr). Along with the Brazilian sugar major's debt, the transaction makes it to a deal of over $1.2billion-largest deal by any Indian sugar group. While India is the world's largest consumer of sugar, Equipav SA Acucar e Alcool has been the 7th largest sugar manufacturer of the world. Very interestingly, Renuka clinched the deal in a field of five bidders which included Noble Group from China and Bungee from USA. This is the second acquire for Renuka in Brazil and with this, Renuka became the third biggest sugar company in the world, number one sugar firm in India and among the top five in Brazil. Along with Renuka, there are now three other Indian sugar MNCs - Bajaj Hindustan; Rajshree Sugar and Godavari Sugar Mills with investments of over $700 million in Brazil alone.

These deals however, in the context of globalization of Indian industries opens up a far larger trade corridor in faraway Latin America and Caribbean region (LAC) which hitherto had remained outside Indian MNCs expansion agenda.

Neither the government of India nor Indian Inc. had meaningfully enlisted LAC into India's international trade map. Interestingly now, more than 35 Indian MNCs, in the last five years, have shown newer direction to India's international trade prospect away from India's traditional focus markets of USA, Western Europe and Middle East.

While these are larger Indian success stories in Latin America, the region still remains a virgin land for serious Indian trade and business engagement. This paper focuses on "Focus Market" approach and dynamics of government of India's current EXIM policy, our international trade and business opportunity analysis for Indian prospective entrepreneurs in LAC region and LAC economic and market growth trajectory. Arguments in this paper is based on case study method, LAC market analysis, examination of India's international trade policy, India's current engagement profile and comparable international experiences like Sino –LAC engagement paradigm.

Why Go Lac

Indian household is now too familiar with basket of forcign goods including Chinese garlic, New Zealand apples and Russian grapes etc. Automobile to nuclear energy and vegetables to foreign degrees, India is a large consumer market for global vendors. Globalization has brought in a range of international products and investments to India. On the other hand, one wonders how much of Indian investments and products are making it to global markets. India's international trade though is not doing poorly in international markets, we have to go a long distance to match with countries like China or even some of the South East Asian countries who are venturing into newer markets anywhere in the world. India's global export currently is around \$168billion and we import over \$250billion worth of goods and services - a trade deficit of over \$80billion (GOI, 2009). Though our trade deficit is more due to import of oil and petroleum products, it makes a case to bridge the trade deficit as early as possible.

We have always felt that LAC is hemisphere away from India and lost time and corresponding opportunity. While the American economic meltdown precipitated India's trade diversion need, Chinese trade and investment success in LAC demonstrated the regional trade prospect in LAC. Spreading from Mexico in the north, Caribbean Islands in the east and down to Chile in south, forty three countries and 560million people in the Western Hemisphere constitute the geographic and market profile of LAC.

Additionally, while India, Brazil and South Africa (IBSA), Brazil, Russia, India and China (BRIC) and Brazil, South Africa, India and China (BASIC) countries do appear as emerging paradigms of new international power alignment in the years ahead and set to redefine global engagement dynamics based on seer strength of knowledge driven economic development where India remains as a common thread, it is imperative that India and Indian MNCs factor LAC towards a growth model both economic as well as political.

Additionally, in a comparative case analysis China's growth model becomes a lesson for emerging economies around the world. China entered into LAC as late as 1997 more to nullify growing Taiwanese influence in the region and in the lookout of market. Today China is the second largest exporter of LAC and shares around 14% of LAC export market (Alberto, 2010). As per Inter-American Development Bank, Sino-LAC trade is growing by 31% from 2000 onwards through the economic meltdown (Alberto, 2010). It may be noted that China's exports to LAC is over $120billion compared to India's export of little over $ 6.5billion only. It makes a strong case therefore that India open up more seriously to LAC prospcct.

Finally, it is perhaps very important to note the new found economic strength of LAC. China now is the fourth largest destination for cumulative LAC exports. LAC exports to China have grown from 3.8% to over 370% thanks to China's burgeoning consumption appetite and income growth and commodity boom in LAC. It indicates LACs economic growth to reciprocate in trade terms and set sustainable two way trade – a healthier economic model.

Exim Policy Orientation Shift

Government of India's EXIM policy has gradually come out of conservatism and now links export and import of India's products in international market as a tool to achieve mainly three objectives- economic development, doubling India's percentage share of global merchandize trade and finally international trade driven employment generation. Successive EXIM policies have gradually been promoting and facilitating instruments than prohibiting and regulating documents. The result has been very satisfying. In the last five years our exports witnessed robust growth to reach a level of US$ 168 billion in 2008-09 from US$ 63 billion in 2003-04. Our share of global merchandise trade was 0.83% in 2003; it rose to 1.45% in 2008 as per WTO estimates. Our share of global commercial services export was 1.4% in 2003; it rose to 2.8% in 2008. India's total share in goods and services trade was 0.92% in 2003; it increased to 1.64% in 2008. On the employment front, studies have suggested that nearly 14 million jobs were created directly or indirectly as a result of augmented exports in the last five years. Now government of India sets a bench mark of 15%annual export growth and export target of US$ 200 billion by March 2011. By 2014, India targets to double exports of goods and services. The long term policy objective for the government of India is to double India's share in global trade by 2020(GOI, 2009). To achieve the bench mark targets, new and creative initiatives and schemes have been floated to facilitate Indian foreign trade entrepreneurs and Focus Market is one such theme.

India's Focus Market- Approach and Dynamics

It is evident that government of India sets two major targets i.e. to achieve $200billion export target by 2011 and over $330billion export in the next 3-4 years by 2014; and double India's international trade share by 2020. A range of new initiatives have been initiated towards this ambitious objective. This paper takes Focus Market and allied instruments to expand entrepreneurial prospect in international trade. New EXIM policy focuses on trade diversification to mitigate fall outs of economic recession to Indian exports in the developed economies.

Towards this end, New EXIM policy identifies 26 new markets around the world under Focus Market Scheme. These include 16 new markets in Latin America and 10 in Asia-Oceania. Focus Market Scheme is added with Focus Sectors, Focus Products, Towns of Export Excellence, Export of Green Products and Market Linked Focus Product Scheme (MLFPS). The schemes have been incentivized to motivate exporters along with Market Development Assistance (MDA) and Market Access Initiative (MAI).

The incentive available under *Focus Market Scheme* (FMS) has been raised from 2.5% to 3%. The incentive available under Focus Product Scheme (FPS) has been raised from 1.25% to 2%. A large number of products from various sectors have been included for benefits under FPS. These include, Engineering products (agricultural machinery, parts of trailers, sewing machines, hand tools, garden tools, musical instruments, clocks and watches, railway locomotives etc.), Plastic (value added products), Jute and Sisal products, Technical Textiles, Green Technology products (wind mills, wind turbines, electric operated vehicles etc.), Project goods, vegetable textiles and certain Electronic items(GOI, 2009).

Market Linked Focus Product Scheme (MLFPS) has been greatly expanded by inclusion of products classified under as many as 153 ITC (HS) Codes at 4 digit level. Some major products include; Pharmaceuticals, Synthetic textile fabrics, value added rubber products, value added plastic goods, textile made ups, knitted and crocheted fabrics, glass products, certain iron and steel products and certain articles of aluminum among others. Benefits to these products will be provided, if exports are made to 13 identified markets (Algeria, Egypt, Kenya, Nigeria, South Africa, Tanzania, Brazil, Mexico, Ukraine, Vietnam, Cambodia, Australia and New Zealand). It may be noted that two major countries of LAC are covered in this scheme. More importantly, trading with Brazil provides scope to trade with South American MERCOSUR member countries like Brazil, Argentina,

Paraguay, and Uruguay which are otherwise covered under Indo – MERCOSUR Preferential Trade Agreement (PTA) and corresponding duty discount ranging from 10% to 100% in over 450 products (GOI, 2009).

MLFPS benefits also extended for export to additional new markets for certain products. These products include auto components, motor cars, bicycle and its parts, and apparels among others. A common simplified application form has been introduced for taking benefits under FPS, FMS, MLFPS and VKGUY (Vishesh Krishi and Gramodyog) products. Higher allocation for *Market Development Assistance* (MDA) and *Market Access Initiative* (MAI) schemes is also being provided to make the package more export oriented.

India's Focus Lac Programme

India's LAC engagement is less than a decade old. Indian private sector has driven the momentum followed with government of India's Focus Latin America policy initiated in 1997. Focus LAC is a special trade promotion initiative of the Ministry of Commerce, government of India and implemented in collaboration with trade and industry institutions in India. Under this vision, there are a number of proactive measures, including financial support for Indian companies to explore the LAC market for participation in trade fairs, market studies, BSMs etc. Financial support is also given for LAC region importers to visit India. The support is provided through Export Promotion Councils and trade and industry bodies only and not directly to individual companies.

As an extension of India's Focus LAC initiative, India's Preferential Trade Agreement (PTA) with MERCOSUR partners and a separate PTA with Chili is an encouraging development towards Indo-South American trade. Being effective from June 2009, Indo- MERCOSUER PTA provides for progressive duty reduction in over 450 export-import products in the following manner - Duty discount for 452 Indian exports to MERCOSUR countries: (10 % -394products) (20% - 45 products) and (100% - 13 products). Duty discount on 450 MERCOSUR exports to India - (10 % - 93products), (20%-336products) and (100 % - 21 products) (GOI, 2009).

India and Chile signed a PTA in 2006. Under the PTA, India has offered to provide fixed tariff preferences ranging from 10% to 50% on 178 tariff lines at the 8 digit level to Chile; the latter have offered India a similar range of tariff preferences on 296 tariff lines at the 8 digit level. The products covered in the mutual offers account for more than 90% of the value of total bilateral trade amounting to $0.447 billion, which took place between the two countries during 2004-05(GOI, 2009).

The products on which India has offered tariff concessions relate to meat and fish products (84 tariff lines), rock salt (1 tariff line), iodine (1 tariff line), copper ore and concentrates (1 tariff line), chemicals (13 tariff lines), leather products (7 tariff lines), newsprint and paper (6 tariff lines), wood and plywood articles (42 tariff lines), some industrial products (12 tariff lines), shorn wool (3 tariff lines) and some others (7 tariff lines).

In return, Chile's offer covers some agriculture products (7 tariff lines), chemicals and pharmaceuticals (53 tariff lines), dyes and resins (7 tariff lines), plastic, rubber and miscellaneous chemicals (14 tariff lines) leather products (12 tariff lines), textiles and clothing (106 tariff lines), footwear (10 tariff lines), some industrial products (82 tariff lines) and some other products (5 tariff lines).

Additionally, a trilateral trade corridor prospect via Indo-MERCOSUR-South Africa (IBSA-India, Brazil, South Africa) and SACU (South Africa Customs Union) are very promising steps to boost Indian trade prospect in the region. The following institutional arrangements already exist with countries of the Latin American region to further enhance our trade prospect i.e. Indo-Argentine Joint Commission; Indo-Argentine Joint Trade Committee; Indo-Mexican Joint Commission; Indo-Brazilian Commercial Council; Indo-Cuban Joint Commission; Indo-Cuban Trade Revival Committee; Indo-Suriname Joint Commission and Indo-Guyana Joint Commission. What emerges out of the combined initiative is over $16billion worth of trade in the region where it was nearly negligible a decade ego. Brazil is our biggest trade partner in the region with an export of around $2.5billion in 2007-08.

Brazil, Colombia, Mexico, Chile, Argentina and Panama have emerged as the top five trading posts for India. However, Indian presence is now beginning to be visible in most countries of the region today. Very interestingly, while Indian exports are around $6.535 billion to LAC market, LAC cumulatively exports back around $7.135 billion to India-an indication of trade reciprocity and sustainability.

Indian Mncs in Lac

Indian MNCs FDI in LAC is approximately around $11billion. More than thirty-five Indian majors have already set up their posts in the form of factories, subsidiaries, joint ventures or BPO's in over ten countries in the region. Steel, energy, IT, pharmaceuticals, chemicals, sugar and infrastructure sectors are some of the front line sectors of Indian investment in the region. While India has sold seven helicopters to Ecuador recently, Indian battery driven Reva car is driving the streets of Colombia and Costa Rica today. Steel majors like Mittal Group, ESSAR, Jindal Group, IT majors like Infosys, HCL, Patni Computer Systems and TCS, have not only established their ventures but seem to have expansion plans too. In the energy and oil sector, IOC, Reliance, ONGC Videsh, Bharat Petro Resources, Suzlon, Havells and Vijaya Electrical have already invested close to $ 4billion in the region. In the pharmaceutical sector, Ranbaxy, Dr. Reddy's Labs, Glenmark, Cellofarm, Zydus, Cadila, Manish Pharma, Torrent and Bilcare have invested in series of LAC countries like Peru, Venezuela, Ecuador, Colombia, Guatemala, El Salvador, Trinidad &Tobago, Jamaica Dominican Republic as well as big countries like Brazil, Argentina and Mexico. Series of other Indian industries see the region as an opportunity location (Viswanath, 2000).

Lac Trade Profile

LAC export and import profile is dynamic. LAC 2009-10 imports profile is in the following order – USA- 43%, EU-18%, Inter American-11%, China – 14%, Japan- 5% and others 9%. What is more revealing is that there have been visible losers and gainers in the last two years. LAC import from Inter American countries has reduced from 19% in 2007-08 to current 11% and other countries has increased from 2.6% to 9% in favour of a spectacular gain for China from 5.8% two years ago to 14% now. India in the whole process is a beginner with only around $6.535 billion of exports to LAC. While China has extended a full vision of global trade in general a strategic focus has been placed towards LAC which has resulted in the spectacular chine miracle in LAC.

Latin America and Caribbean is no more a zone of failed nations or banana republics. While ABC countries have gone past their troubled times, Brazil is the new emerging economy and perceived as one of the drivers of new international economic order. Mexico as a result of free trade association with USA and Canada (NAFTA) has been doing far better. The smaller countries of LAC are integrated into Common Markets - Andean Pact covering Bolivia, Peru, Colombia and Ecuador. MERCOSUR members are associated members of Andean Common Market. Central American countries are part of Central Amcrican common Market (CACM). The benefit of engagement therefore is the availability of market clusters.

The Wall Street Journal and Heritage Foundation economic survey 2009 tracks 183 countries in terms of their level of economic freedom. Ten specific freedom parameters covering economic and allied areas necessary in delivering economic freedom is profiled to arrive at economic freedom index of the countries. While economic freedom in Hong Kong is indexed as highest in the world with 90 score out of 100, followed by Singapore with 87.1 score, as many as 119 countries score is between 50 -70. Very interestingly, Chile is the 11th most economically free country next to the most industrialized countries of Western Europe and USA. While India and China figure as mostly un-free economies with a score of 54.4 and 53.2, along with Chile, 13 LAC countries figure in 60-70 score bracket indicating moderate economic freedom- a condition more suitable for growing trade and investment in those countries. While Mexico scores 65.8, larger countries like Argentina and Brazil, are in the order of India and China with 53.2 and 56.7 score (Economic Freedom Index, 2009).

Entrepreneurship Prospect – Lac

While the Indian trade prospect in LAC seems encouraging, the profile at this juncture can be said as at 'take off stage' only. What limits our trade diversion and growth prospect in LAC is our large scale unfamiliarity with the region coupled with misgivings about Latin American political and economic stability.

Together they have contributed towards lack of real time contact and market intelligence. The recent time success of Indian investments and industries in LAC indicates opportunity in those sectors. In addition to FDIs in range of industrial sectors, few other areas are also emerging as possible sectors for Indian investment.

Produce Market

Produce market has already emerged. Interestingly, an impressive produce market both in terms of consumption ability and export potentials is already building up outside the so called global developed markets in Asia, Central and Eastern Europe and Latin America with over 4.5 billion consumer bases. This phenomenon is no less than a significant paradigm shift in the global exportimport directions. These emerging markets are profiled with 3-5 times faster per capita income growth than the developed markets like United States, Western Europe and Japan. As exporters and importers, such markets have already registered 50-100% higher growth rate than the traditional developed markets. In this context while countries like India, China and Brazil are set to play larger roles, much of the integrated markets in Asia and Latin America would be global produce markets. The emerging trends seem to grow further in the next two decades accounting for more than 60% growth in Asia and Latin America's produce markets along with growth of their export potentials (Reardon, March, 2008). Super Market Syndrome The emerging produce market is a consumer hub and an economic model of super market dynamics. Beginning in late 1980s, the supermarkets are now redefining the scope of market behavior. The Super market development can be mapped into three waves. Globally regions that experienced the first such wave are South America, East Asia (outside Japan and China), Northern-Central Europe, Baltic region and South Africa. The second wave countries include, Mexico, Central America, much of Southeast Asia and Southern-Central Europe.

The third wave which is still unfolding include some countries in Central and South America, parts of Eastern and Southern Africa, "transition East Asia" (China and Vietnam), Russia, and India (Reardon).

As mentioned above, Latin American markets in all the three waves have shifted their market experience from conventional markets to super market dynamics giving rise to the scope of Super Market model consolidating its hold in the region. In total retailing and in food retailing, supermarkets are dominant. By 2001 they had a population-weighted average of 60% of food retailing, ranging from 45-75% in the largest and/ or highest-income countries in the region. Argentina, Brazil, Chile, Colombia, Costa Rica and Mexico- which may be referred as the 'leading-6', profiled as 86% of the income and 74% of the population of Latin America experienced this major paradigm shift (Reardon).

While Chinese import and export interests seem to have some distorting effect on emerging LAC trade specialization patterns and negatively correlate to their economies, India's trade specialization positively correlates with these markets (Lederman, 2006). Evidently therefore, India and Indian entrepreneurs must participate in this economy with industrial zeal.

Conclusion

In spite of the positive trends, we have to go a long distance to generate a China like prospect for India in the region. Striking as it may appear, India's exports to Hong Kong, Singapore and Belgium in 2007-08 stood at \$6.3billion, \$7.3 billion and \$4.2 billion as compared to \$ 6.5 billion of India's exports to whole of LAC in 2009. India needs a road map of entrepreneurial engagement with LAC region. As the second largest developing economy of the world, India must diversify her international trade in favor of emerging opportunity markets. Additionally India must invest in understanding of LAC, its institutions, its people, its resources, its socio-cultural dynamics and the contemporary developments that have changed the region from being failed nations in 1980s to growth models of today. It is therefore necessary that we engage the region in broader cooperation terms and set India favorably into a comprehensive collaboration mode with LAC to benefit from the ongoing economic globalization.

References

1. Govt. of India, (2009). Dept. of Commerce, Export-Import Data Bank country report, New Delhi.
2. Moreno, Luis Alberto, President, Inter-American Development Bank, 4th China-LAC Business Summit, April 2010, China Council for the Promotion of International Trade, Beijing.
3. Govt. of India, (2009). Dept. of Commerce, Export-Import Data Bank country report, New Delhi
4. Viswanathan, R (2000). Business with Latin America. www. business withlatinamerica.blogspot.com
5. Index of Economic Freedom 2009, Executive Summary, http://www.heritage.org/Index/pdf/Index09_ExecSum.pdf
6. Reardon Tom,(2008). Super Market revolution in Emerging Markets: Implications for Produce Industry, USAID News Letter, 57th Issue, 4 -8. www.usaid.gov/.../trade/trade_matters/LAC Trade Matters 57. pdf
7. Lederman Daniel, Marcelo Olarreaga & Eliana Rubiano,(2006).Latin America's trade specialization and China and India's growth. Development Research Group, The World Bank project repot from Chief Economist Office for Latin America and Caribbean, Banco Mundial, Carrera 7, 71-21, Bogotá, 3-4.
8. Also see, Kearney, A. T, (2009).Windows of Hope for Global Retailers. The 2009 A.T Kearney Global Retail Development Index, Chicago.

10

Economic Empowerment of the Poor: A Study on the Self Help Groups (Shgs) in West Bengal

Abstract

A major cause of poverty among rural people is lack of access for both individuals and communities to productive assets and financial resources. This is caused by the fact that the formal credit institutions that function smoothly in developed urban areas cannot cater to the credit need of rural poor due to lack of information about the borrowers, lack of proper collateral among the poor people, which are acceptable to the formal financial institutions, and there are enforcement problems in case of default. The failure of formal lending institutions and the apparent success of Bangladesh's Grameen Bank in reaching the rural poor have recently inspired numerous non-governmental organizations (NGOs) and governments of less developed countries to establish group-lending schemes to deliver credit at low cost and reasonable interest rates to small-scale rural entrepreneurs. India is no exception in this case. From 1 April, 1999 Government of India initiated a programme called Swarnjayanti Gram Swarojgar Yojana (SGSY) which is a self-employment programme of Ministry of Rural Development that aims at providing assistance to the BPL (Below the Poverty Line) rural poor for establishing micro-enterprises through bank credit and government subsidy to acquire an income-generating asset. Towards this end, SGSY has been designed to cover all aspects of self-employment such as organisation of the poor into self-help groups, training, credit, technology, infrastructure, marketing, and enabling the rural poor to take decisions on all issues concerning poverty eradication. This SGSY programme actually tried to link the rural poor to the formal micro finance institutions via self-help groups where groups will receive joint liability loans from formal credit institutions. A study by NABARD (National Bank for Agriculture and Rural Development) across 11 states showed many positive results on the impact of participation of rural poor in the SHGs. It shows that there have been perceptible and wholesome changes in the living standards of SHG members in terms of ownership of assets, borrowing capacities, income generating activities, income levels and increase in savings. It indicates that the average annual saving per household registered an increase over three-fold. At this backdrop, a study on the impact of SHGs in the state of West Bengal was conducted. Though the study is a desk study, it also shows satisfactory performance of SHGs in West Bengal.

Introduction

A major cause of poverty among rural people is lack of access for both individuals and communities to productive assets and financial resources. This is caused by the fact that the formal credit institutions that function smoothly in developed urban areas cannot cater to the credit need of rural poor due to lack of information about the borrowers, lack of proper collateral among the poor people, which are acceptable to the formal financial institutions and there are enforcement problems in case of default. The failure of formal lending institutions and the apparent success of Bangladesh's Grameen Bank in reaching the rural poor have recently inspired numerous non-governmental organizations (NGOs) and governments of less developed countries to establish group-lending schemes to deliver credit at low cost and reasonable interest rates to small-scale rural entrepreneurs (Coleman ,1999). India is no exception in this case.

From 1 April, 1999 Government of India initiated a programme called Swarnjayanti Gram Swarojgar Yojana (SGSY) which is a self-employment programme of Ministry of Rural Development that aims at providing assistance to the BPL (Below the Poverty Line) rural poor for establishing micro-enterprises through bank credit and government subsidy to acquire an income-generating asset. Towards this end, SGSY has been designed to cover all aspects of self-employment such as organisation of the poor into self-help groups, training, credit, technology, infrastructure and marketing and enabling the rural poor to take decisions on all issues concerning poverty eradication. This SGSY programme actually tried to link the rural poor to the formal micro finance institutions via self-help groups where groups will receive joint liability loans from formal credit institutions. Different theoretical results by Ghatak and Guinnane (1999) had shown that in closed communities where group members are known to each other, group lending promotes screening, monitoring, state verification and enforcement of repayment. Ghatak (1999) had shown that in closed village communities in-group formation stage, the members could choose safer partners that reduce their effective cost of borrowing and improve rate of repayments of loans to avoid the social sanction of his peer group (Basely and Coate, 1995)). Experiences of Grameen bank in Bangladesh have shown that availability of collateral free tiny loans for income generating activities for poor have a significant impact on the lives of poor families (Yunus 2004). A study by Pitt and Khandekar (1998) considered the impact of Grameen Bank and two other group-based micro credit programmes in Bangladesh on labour supply, schooling, household expenditure and assets. They found that the programme credit has larger positive impact on the behaviour of poor if the borrowers are women rather than men. Coleman (1999) in a study considered the impact of group lending programmes in North East Thailand. This survey had shown that the impact of village banks that provide group-loans in villages is insignificant on physical assets, savings, productions, productive expenditures, and on other variables. However, it has positive impact on women's high interest debt because a number of members had fallen into vicious circle of debt from moneylenders in order to repay their loans on village banks. It has positive significant impact on women's lending out with interest because some members engaged in arbitrage, borrowing from village bank at low interest and then lending out money at mark up. A study by Ahlin and Townsend (2003) considered the presence of joint liability loans versus individual loans on the basis of data gathered from Thailand. Their study showed that the wealth level; showed a 'U' shaped relationship with group loans, and it was also found that the lower the probability of success of the project, higher is the likelihood of taking a group loan. There have been many studies on the working of SHGs in different parts of India. These studies mostly covered the SHGs working in the States of Orissa, Andhra Pradesh, Maharashtra, Tamil Nadu, and Uttar Pradesh. A study by NABARD (National Bank for Agriculture and Rural Development) covering 560 SHG member households from 223 SHGs across 11 states, showed many positive results on the impact of participation of rural poor in the SHGs. It shows that there have been perceptible and wholesome changes in the living standards of SHG members in terms of ownership of assets, borrowing capacities, income generating activities, income levels and increase in savings. It indicates that the average annual saving per household registered an increase over three-fold (NABARD, 2002).

Objectives of the Study

The present study humbly attempts to assess:

i) the progress of SHGs in West Bengal,
ii) the social and economic impact of SHGs in West Bengal.

Methodology

The study is a desk study based on secondary sources of data. The scope of study is the state of West Bengal. The study covers all the districts in the state of West Bengal. Period of study is 2000 – 2010. Available up-to-date data have been used. They include books, journals, and reports. The sources include the Ministry of Self Help and Self Employment, Govt. of West Bengal, NABARD, SIDC, SIDBI, SUDA etc.

Nationalist Movement and Rural Development

Rural development received popular mass support, for the first time, with the entry of Mahatma Gandhi into Indian public life. Gandhi returned to India from South Africa in 1915, but it was in 1919 that he plunged into national politics. The Non–Cooperation movement, started by Mahatma Gandhi in 1920, was the first political attempt in India to mobilize the villagers and realize politics. Besides, Mahatma designed a comprehensive programme of rural development which included use of khadi, promotion of village industries, eradication of unsociability, provision of basic and adult education, prohibition of liquor, women's uplift, and propagation of the national language. The Congress Party symbolized its newly acquired rural orientation by holding its annual sessions in villages.

The new wave of the 'back to the villages 'movement quickly spread far and wide and a spurt in the voluntary activities in the field of rural development occurred. Rabindranath Tagore set up the Sriniketan Institute of Rural Reconstruction in 1921 with the aim of making the rural population 'self-reliant and self-respectful'. In the same year the Mantardam experiment was started in Madras under the leadership of 'Young men's Christian Association' to bring about the complete upward development towards a more abundant life for rural people, spiritually, mentally, physically, socially and economically. These were entirely voluntary efforts, but in the process, even the government attention began to turn to the villages. A most notable name, in this respect , is F.L. Brayne, the district collector of Gurgaon (then in Punjab, now in Haryana) , who started in 1927 a programme of rural reconstruction based on the ancient virtues of hard work, thrift, self-respect, self-control, self-help, mutual help and mutual respect. Similarly, in 1932, the princely state of Baroda launched a broad-based programme of rural amelioration to promote the will to live better and a capacity for self-help and self-reliance.

Rural Indebtedness

Poverty is the main cause of the indebtedness of the Indian farmers. The farmer has to borrow for various purposes because he has no past savings. Moreover the crops fail because of the failure of monsoons or natural calamities. He is forced to borrow when he needs to improve his farm related matters. Poverty forces him to borrow. Again it is poverty which forces him to pay little off his debt.

Increasing rural indebted as resulted in growing pauperization of the small and marginal Indian farmers. They lose both ways – Get a low price while selling their produce but have to pay high prices while buying inputs. Socially this indebtedness creates a class of landless labourers and tenants in the place of independent farmers.

To overcome this problem measures should be adopted for (a) Settlement of old debt; (b) Reduction on dependence on money lenders and (c) Control of new loan. In some of our States Legislations have been passed to prevent farmers from selling their lands to professional money lenders who are not farmers. At the same time measures have been taken to control the activity of the farmer.

In 1975 the Government of India had declared a moratorium on the recovery of debt by money lenders from farmers, landless labourers and rural artisans. *Liquidation of rural indebtedness* and *abolition of bonded* labour were two dynamic aspects of the 20- point economic program declared in the year 1975.

Recent Development in Rural Finance: Micro Finance

Micro credit or micro finance is a novel approach to "banking with the poor". In this approach, very successfully tried in Bangla Desh, bank credit is extended to the poor through Self Help Groups (SHGs), Non-Government Organisations (NGOs), credit unions, etc. Micro credit attempts to combine lower transaction costs and high degree of repayments. This is essentially because of the involvement of potential beneficiaries of rural credit in the credit delivery system. The SHG-bank linkage programme, introduced and encouraged by NABARD is now implemented vigorously by more than 30,000 branches of commercial banks, RRBs, and cooperative banks in over 500 districts in 30 states and Union Territories.

At the end of March 2007, as many as 2.9 million SHGs are now linked with banks and 7,000 NGOs are associated with the scheme. It is estimated that, at the end of March 2007, 20 million very poor families were brought within the fold of formal banking services. The notable feature was the active women participation-90 per cent of the groups linked with the banks were exclusively women groups. Also there was strong repayment performance–at more than 95 per cent of the loans disbursed. The disbursement of bank loans to SHGs was Rs. 18,040 crores in 2006-07 (Rs. 11,400 crores in the previous year). The average loan per SHG came to nearly Rs. 30,000 and the average loan per family came to Rs. 1,770 Micro-finance initiatives have shown that banking with the poor is a viable proposition. Micro-credit has been hailed as the best method of creating additional employment and removing poverty. NABARD has been playing a catalytic role in terms of promotional support to NGOs and also in nurturing quality SHGs. It has launched a pilot project (2005-06) for promotion of micro enterprises among the members of matured SHGs.

Shg Approach and Financial Inclusion

As an innovative credit channel, the Self Help Group (SHG) approach was introduced in 1992, to link poor people with bank credit. Under this programme, about 40 million families have been linked with banks up to March 2007 (NABARD). The distinguishing feature of this approach as compared to other sponsored credit schemes is the learning management of own money by the poor before availing bank loan. Moreover, the approach (not SGSY) does not involve any subsidy; hence, it is sustainable with its strength. A number of studies have found that SHG approach reduces the transaction cost banks and loan availing cost of borrowers. In financing SHGs, the requirement of collateral by banks has been replaced by peer group pressure and hence this approach has enabled social and economic inclusion of women by waiving the requirement of collateral. Some important highlights of SHG- achievements in India are as under.

I. Upto March 2007, 2.925 millions SHGs & about 40.95 million families have been linked with bank credit.
II. Of the total SHGs, women groups are 86 per cent.
III. During 2006-07, 0.686 million SHG linked with banks.
IV. During 2006-07 loan amount of Rs 664.3 million disbursed to SHGs.
V. Average Bank Loan per SHG is Rs 61000.
VI. Upto March 2007, Bank loan of Rs 180000 million provided to SHGs.

The state-wise outreach of the SHG programme in India is given in Table-1.

Table-1: State-wise cumulative credit linked SHGs as on 31 March

Sr No	States	2005	2006	2007	% to total in 2007	% of adults covered under SHGs
1	Andhra Pradesh	49,2927	587,238	683,619	23	21.64
2	Tamil Nadu	2,20,698	312,778	400,477	14	14.19
3	Karnataka	163,198	224,928	317,636	11	14.52
4	Orissa	123,256	180,896	234,451	8	15.58
5	Maharashtra	71,146	131,470	225,856	8	5.63
6	Uttar Pradesh	119,648	161,911	198,587	7	3.38
7	West Bengal	92,698	136,251	181,563	6	5.54
8	Rajasthan	60,006	98,171	137,837	5	6.78
9	Kerala	60,809	86,988	117,913	4	8.03
10	Assam	31,234	56,449	81,454	3	8.10
11	Bihar	28,015	46,221	72,339	2	2.47
12	Madhya Pradesh	45,105	57,125	70,912	2	3.16
13	Gujarat	24,712	34,160	43,572	1	2.11
14	Chhattisgarh	18,569	31,291	41,703	1	5.21
15	Jharkhand	21,531	30,819	37,317	1	3.80
16	Himachal Pradesh	17,798	22,920	27,799	1	10.91
17	Uttarakhand	14,043	17,588	21,527	1	6.74
18	Sub-total	1,591,350	2,199,616	2,873,035	98	7.78
19	All India	1,591,350	2,238,786	29,24,786	100	7.57

Source: Government of West Bengal, West Bengal, July 2008.

Note: The table shows that outreach of the programme is the maximum in southern states, which account for 52 per cent of the total SHGs in India and it may be one of the reasons for higher financial inclusion in terms of saving as well as credit accounts in this region. To test this relationship, at the first stage correlation was computed between the percentage of adults covered under SHGs, savings, and credit accounts per 100 adults respectively. In this exercise, the states with less than one per cent of adults covered by SHGs and the regional level data were excluded. The correlation coefficients were 0.417 and 0.596 in case of savings and credit accounts respectively.

Figure - 1: Percentage of Total SHG Credit Share in 2007

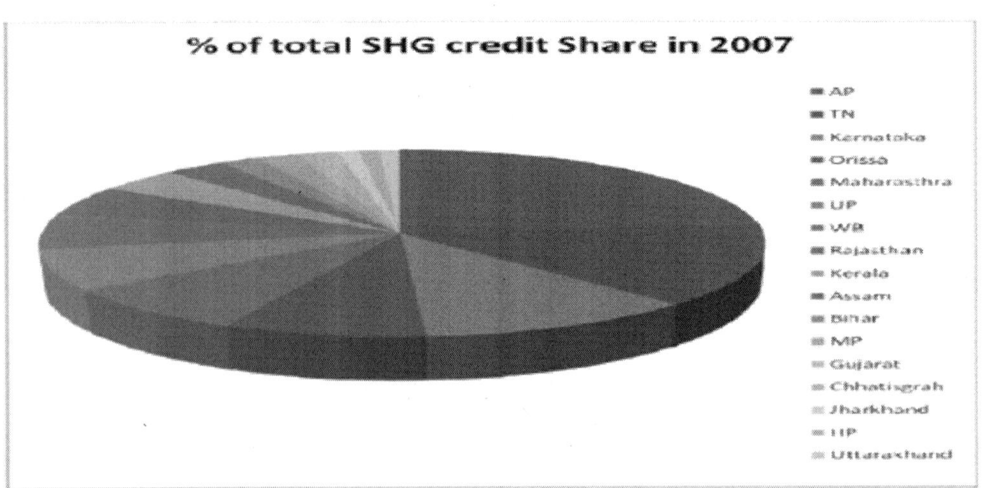

Source: Compiled from the data contained in Table - 1

Shgs in West Bengal

Even though the SHG movement has had a late start in the state of West Bengal, off late it has gained tremendous momentum. It is estimated that there are more than three and a half lakh SHGs in the State, out of which little more than 1.5 lakh SHGs have been formed under the Swarnajayanti Gram Swarojgar Yojana (SGSY) alone. The two major programmes which had been supporting the movement are 1) the SGSY and 2) the NABARD supported SHG-Bank Linkage programme. Apart from these two programmes, the Forest department has facilitated large number of SHGs in areas where their programmes are under implementation and more and more women are now being able to actively participate in FPC and EDC for their own economic development as well as giving a new vigour in forest protection and preservation. Other attempts like Swayamsiddha (IWEP - upgraded IMY) by government through West Bengal Women Development Undertaking is a woman focused SHG initiative to enhance economic, health, nutrition, education status for women using access to microcredit and convergence for services. As of now, the scheme targets 3900 women

SHGs in 39 block level federation - though target surpassed long ago, and uses both government and non government facilitation in the scheme. The Backward classes Welfare Department is also assisting the scheduled castes and scheduled tribes, and other backward classes to form self-help Groups for economic development by providing training, infrastructure, and institutional finance.

There are similar programmes for Minorities implemented through the Minorities Development and Finance Corporation. The Cottage and Small Scale Industries Department has a scheme named Deen Dayal Hathkharga Protsahan Yojana to provide support to Handloom Weavers through self-help Groups recognised by state handloom cooperation and Apex Handloom Weavers' Co-operative Society in the form of capacity building, infrastructure and financial assistance. Similar support is provided to self-help groups of artisans through another scheme known as Baba Sahib Ambedkar Hasta Shilpa Vikash Yojana. Under the watershed projects being implemented by the Panchayat and Rural Development Department, formation of self-help groups and user groups has been conceived as grass root level organisations. Director of sericulture has been implementing a scheme (Sen, 2000) under which support is provided to self help groups in the form of capacity building and institutional finance. The department of Food Processing & Horticulture is also encouraging groups of small and marginal farmers. Animal Resource Development Department uses SHG concept to organise and strengthen poor and marginal section of the society into women's dairy cooperatives, which are ultimately linked up with marketing co-operatives and processing industries. Under the non-government category, organisations like CARE promoted informal SHG banking. The process is based on identifying and empowering selected Self Help Promotion Institutions (SHPI) in promotion and nurturing SHGs and initiate SHG-banking.

Presently, about 7,000 groups have been promoted by partnering SHPIs under CASHE project of the CARE and the institutionalisation of federations with a focus on community owned sustainable micro-finance model, is providing a lot of learning experience for the sector. Alternative microfinance institutions are also being developed by MF promoters such as STDBI. The three categories listed above have different channels for obtaining finance and pay different rates of interest.

For the number of savings-linked SHGs under the two major programmes,

Table-2: District-wise Number of SHGs formed under SGSY and NABARD

Districts	No. of groups formed under SGSY	No. of groups formed Under NABARD
Murshidabad	7900	16568
Darjeeling	2561	2232
Malda	9173	9546
Uttar Dinajpur	4422	8816
Dakshin Dinajpur	8224	10451
Birbhum	3312	21701
Hooghly	12572	17606
Purba Medinipur	18695	9853
Paschim Medinipur	3038	3757
Jalpaiguri	14044	10786
Howrah	3243	6380
Coochbehar	9130	12181
Nadia	6356	24836
Bankura	6940	12881
Purulia	10046	3938
Burdwan	10514	15672
North 24-Parganas	11270	23066
South 24-Parganas	8944	20402

Source: Ministry of Self Help and Self Employment, Govt. of West Bengal; NABARD

Source: Compiled from the data contained in Table - 2

Figure - 2: Bar Diagram showing SHGs formed under SGSY and NABARD

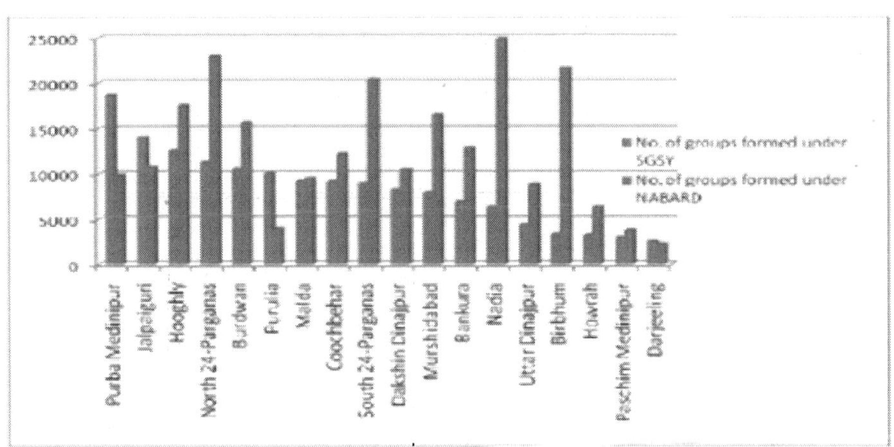

Shgs - Capacity Building Strategies

There are quite a few SHG based projects and programmes. Efforts are afoot to converge these initiatives. There are a number of service providers in the form of Extension agencies of different line departments, NGOs, who are functionally broad spectrum but have a limited scope for developing into a fully fledged, specialized institution for rendering capacity building services. The Panchayat and Rural Development Department have initiated steps for capacity building of all categories of SHGs. The department has a partnership with Non government organisations like CARE West Bengal in building up capacities of the SHGs. On an average, an amount of Rs. 12 crore is spent under the SGSY programme alone annually for training of the SHGs. This is exclusive of the investments being made by NABARD, the different line departments associated with SHG linked programme for capacity building of the SHGs. SHGs are also associated with programmes like Community Health Care Management Initiative, Mid-day meal, National Rural Employment Guarantee Act, ICDS etc. and undergo training and orientation on various issues focused on social sector and livelihood related developments.

Infrastructure for Shgs

Self Help Groups need infrastructural support to carry on their income generating activities. On an average a sum of Rs. 17 crore is spent annually under the SGSY programme alone for providing infrastructure support for enhancing livelihood opportunities of the SHGs. The Panchayat bodies also utilise resources available with them for constructing required infrastructures for the SHG groups.

A convergence model of SHGs in West Bengal is placed below.

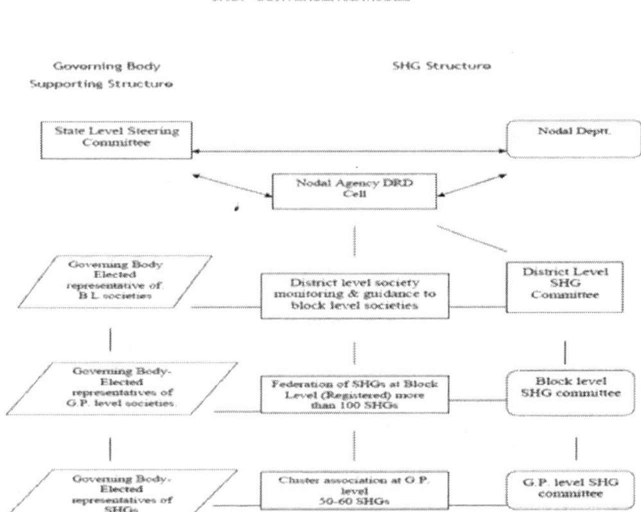

Source: Ministry of Self Help and Self Employment, Govt. of West Bengal

Self-Help Groups and Economic Development

Contrary to popular belief, the poor households are engaged in myriad types of micro enterprises which are linked to their livelihood. As a source of employment, the micro enterprise has a lot of potential because of its ease of entry and low startup capital. It also plays a significant role in self-employment when employment in organized sector or even wage employment is scarce. The micro-credit support extended to the self help groups together with other extension support such as skill upgradation, enhancing entrepreneurial abilities along with providing necessary infrastructures and marketing support helps the SHGs to cross the barriers that keep them below the poverty line. The table below is an illustrative list of the various types of activities taken up by the SHGs, who have passed Grade I level formed Under SGSY in the State. Support of professional bodies are being taken for upgrading skills of the SHGs for improving quality of the products as well as to meet the tastes of the people. A tie-up has been made with the National Institute of Fashion technology (NIFT) for training selected SHGs engaged in manufacturing of certain products like Kantha Steech Sarees, handicrafts, leather goods etc. The Comprehensive Area Development Corporation (CADC) is also extending training support to all those engaged in primary sector activities like agriculture, horticulture, animal husbandry etc for augmenting their income. Many groups have been found to take up agricultural activities by taking land on lease for raising suitable crops during the period when the owners normally keep it fallow. To supplement both SHG income and nutritional support to the people, particularly the women and the children a very large number of groups, irrespective of their prime economic activities, have been given training on vegetable cultivation for developing good kitchen garden and even to use the roofs of their huts for growing vegetables.

Table-3: Activity-wise number of SHGs in West Bengal

S.No	Name of activities	No. of SHGs
1	Agriculture	2,607
2	Animal Husbandry	17,336
3	Paddy Processing	4,632
4	Vegetable & Mushroom cultivation	571
5	Horticulture	42
6	Nursery	895
7	Floriculture	284
8	Fishery	2,708
9	Food Processing	597
10	Milch Cow	316
11	Zari embroidery	2,980
12	Kantha stitch & Embroidery	455
13	Silk, Tasar & Handloom	1,590
14	Jute Products	307
15	Readymade Garments/Tailoring	578
16	Imitation Jewellery	148
17	Leather Products	109
18	Sericulture	74
19	Betel vine	1,590
20	Minor Irrigation	96
21	Boutique	145
22	Mat Making	167
23	Dhoop Making	90
24	Cane & Bamboo Products	248
25	Marine Jewellery	53
26	Detergent & Phenyl Making	44
27	Wig Manufacturing	3
28	Bee Keeping	95
29	Wood Products Manufacturing	36
30	Carpentry	20
31	Bell metal utensils manufacturing	19
32	Shola works	8
33	Bel Mala	25
34	Pottery	44
35	Spice Making	30
36	Plate making (shal leaf)	160
37	Babui rope	70

Source: Government of West Bengal, West Bengal, July 2008.

They have been also given seeds of common vegetables, which have been very popular and an annual feature in the training exercise. Many SHGs have been given training on nursery-raising for supplying planting materials to the Panchayats for social forestry, which has become a good source of income for those group members. The Panchayats have excavated large number of tanks out of National Food for Work programme and other employment generation programme. Order has been passed by the L&LR department allowing the SHGs to be given lease of those tanks, owned by the government for growing fish.

Many groups have taken up composite culture of taking up pisciculture, duckery and horticulture on such leased in tank including its embankments. Other inputs like Chicks, piglets and kids have also been distributed in large numbers by the Animal Resources Development department and the DRDCs of the Zilla Parishads. In districts covered under RSVY such inputs have been distributed in large numbers out of RSVY fund in most of such districts. Small infrastructures like working sheds, machines for making Saal leaf plates, go down for storing Sabai grass etc in areas of Banker, Purulia etc where such grass is grown as well as larger infrastructure like food processing centre, paddy processing facilities etc have also been constructed in large numbers for helping the groups in pursuing their economic activities. In quite a few districts the SHG groups have started selling rice processed by group members to the agents of the Food Corporation in fulfilling their procurement target. Providing marketing support to the SHGs for selling their products is another important support that is being provided by the State government and the local bodies. Fairs, are organized in the districts and the State head quarter for promotion of sale of products of the SHO groups. Some of them also participate in fairs outside the State. However, much more is required to be done in this regard and the business enterprises of the State have been approached through their organizations like then Confederation of Indian Industries for developing linkages between the SHGs and those enterprises for helping the SHGs in improving and selling their products as well as to augmenting their marketing skills. Very recently a few organizations have shown their interests, which is yet to take concrete shape.

Shgs and the Primary Agricultural Co-operative Credit Societies (PACS)

In West Bengal, Self-Help Groups are reckoned as Co-operatives within a Cooperative. They are informal groups of 5-20 persons of the same low level of economic condition, belonging to the same locality or hamlet. Open and voluntary membership, democratic control of members, participation of members in economic activities of the Group, autonomy and independence, education, training and information, cooperation amongst different groups and concern for the community—all the seven Co-operative Principles do exist in these Groups. Since these are un-registered informal groups, and the PACS cannot finance non-member units, the State Government, in exercise of the power conferred upon it u/s 69(1)(d) of the West Bengal Co-operative Societies Act, 1983, permitted the PACS to enrol Self-Help Groups as members of the PACS. This was done as a part of the programme for implementation of Business Development Plan, introduced pursuant to the recommendations of the Agricultural Credit Review Committee (Khusro Committee), which envisaged that the plan for every deposit, credit and trading activity of the PACS should have two prongs — individual members and Self-Help Groups. Later on NABARDsponsored SHG programme acted as a booster and the Self-Help Groups in the Co-operative Sector in West Bengal assumed the shape of a movement in the State. Through periodical meetings, equal amount of savings at the end of every week, fortnight or month, rotation of leadership, united fight against the evils in the family and the community, group dynamism develop amongst the SHG members over months of existence and they become eligible for credit-linkage through the PACS which organize and nurture them. The central Co-operative Bank acts as the facilitators and the State Co-operative Bank as the coordinator.

An at-a-glance the profile of how the SHGs have been doing in the state is given below.

1. Savings of the SHGs under SGSY: Rs. 107 crore (approximately)
2. Savings of the SHGs under NABARD: Rs. 97 crore (approximately)
3. No of SHGs under SGSY to have passed Grade I: 1,42,49
4. No. of SHGS under SGSY to have passed Grade II: 36,595
5. No. of SHGs under SGSY to have got cash credit loan: 1,15,000
6. Amount of such cash credit: Rs. 250 crore (approximately)
7. No. of SHGs under NABARD to have got first input of loan: 1,93,086
8. Amount of cash credit for NABARD SHGs: Rs. 395 crore (approximately)
9. Refinance amount for NABARD SHGs repaying first input of loan: Rs. 127·43 crore (approximately)
10. No. of SHGs under the State Cooperation Department getting loan: 70,000 (approximately)

11. Amount of such loan: Rs. 115 crore (approximately)

Table - 4: SHGs and PACS in West Bengal

PARTCULARS OF SELF-HELP GROUPS FORMED BY THE PACS AS ON 31.03.2009 (RS IN LAKH)

SL. NO.	NAME OF THE RANGE	TOTAL NO OF SHG FORMED	NO OF MEMBER OF SHG	OF WHICH FEMALE MEMBER	TOTAL DEPOSIT RAISED	TOTAL LOAN DISBURSED	NO OF SHG OBTAINED CREDIT FACILITY	% OF RECOVERY	NO OF SHG STARTED ECONOMIC ACTIVITIES
1	BANKURA	12665	113459	109848	959.38	3379.18	9484	91	9484
2	BIRBHUM	1836	16150	13259	252.46	352	1101	96	
3	BURDWAN-I	7770	56708	43168	398.86	186.35	4023	89	4651
4	BURD-II	7068	56110	43020	442.36	867.1	3958	92	3405
5	BURDWAN-III	364	2646	1830	24.4	26.71	284	86	NR
6	COOCHBEHAR	6992	62509	57000	357.08	489.81	6434	97	NR
7	DK DINAJPUR	2584	23502	22542	242.36	671.55	1669	74	NR
8	DARJEELING	618	5605	5006	56.97	45.08	328	78	NR
9	HOOGHLY	29865	196262	196012	1875.74	7760.45	27215	99	NR
10	HOWRAH	5364	29145	26321	437.34	861.52	2409	98.28	NR
11	JALPAIGURI	2378	23374	22719	219.54	353.79	2124	33.69	NR
12	MALDA	12341	115487	101883	916.49	2130.17	9775	98.13	NR
13	MURSHIDABAD	12095	100301	90887	1529.93	4540.22	9388	92	NR
14	NORTH 24-PGS	2302	22540	8702	185.97	97.04	852	40	NR
15	NADIA	14156	127943	115384	1057.53	767.29	7703	97.28	NR
16	PASHIM MEDINIPUR	4825	43644	33798	392.48	363.62	2982	83.16	NR
17	PURBA MEDINIPUR-I	5670	44540	38621	420.65	864.92	3396	95.55	3396
18	PURBA MEDINIPUR-II	12549	98846	91724	954.03	582.78	6767	91	6767
19	PURULIA	2945	30768	29232	142.09	179.79	693	87	NR
20	SOUTH 24-PGS	5123	40849	38558	278.99	723.66	4618	97.72	NR
21	UTTAR DINAJPUR	8846	70126	63654	509.86	1354.18	6851	63	NR
	TOTAL	158336	1280514	1152168	11664.51	26597.21	112054		27703

Source: SLBC (State Level Bankers Committee, West Bengal)

The position of Savings and Credit Linked SHGs (both NABARD and SGSY) for the State of West Bengal for last 4 years is given below:

Table–5: Position of Savings and Credit Linked Shgs (both Nabard and Sgsy) for West Bengal

(Amt. Rs in crore)

Year	Target No.		Achievement-Deposit Linked No.	Achievement-Credit Linked	
	Deposit Link	Credit Link		No.	Amt.
2006-2007	150000	150000	101556	78730	373.03
2007-2008	150000	150000	134106	128148	388.50
2008-2009	150000	150000	109617	105450	450.88
2009 - 2010	150000	150000	117372	152067	615.13

Source: SLBC (State Level Bankers Committee, West Bengal)

Recovery Status of selected Employment generation schemes as on March 2010 in comparison to March 2009 is as under:

Table – 6: Recovery Status of selected Employment generation schemes as on March 2010

Amt. Rs in crore

Sector	March 2009			March 2010		
	Demand	Recovery	%	Demand	Recovery	%
PMRY	125	30	24	146	36	24
SJSRY	17	6	35	24	9	38
BSKP	119	60	50	125	59	47
REGP	101	60	59	96	49	51
SCP/TSP	64	32	50	120	56	47
SGSY (Individual)	37	18	49	36	19	52
SGSY (Gr)	139	99	71	197	136	69
SHG	228	205	90	353	287	81

Source: SLBC (State Level Bankers Committee, West Bengal)

Concluding Observation

There were numbers of traditional and informal ways of forwarding credit before the emergence of the SHGs. All of them provided very little attention to the question of both empowerment and sustainability. Along with this there was a casual approach towards the accountability of the credits leading to adverse impact on both repayment as well as further outreach. The conclusion that emerges from this study is that SHGs are playing a vital role in the rural empowerment, although most of the SHGs are formed as female groups.

1. The distinguishing feature of this approach as compared to other sponsored credit system is that it imparts the knowledge of managing money to its subscribers before they go for availing any loan from the banks.
2. Moreover the SHG approach does not involve any subsidy, hence it can sustain with its own strength.
3. In financing SHGs, the requirement of collateral by banks has been replaced by peer group pressure and hence this approach has enabled social and economic inclusion of women by waiving the requirement of collateral.
4. Of the total SHGs, women groups are 86 per cent.
5. It can be commented that the whole scenario of SHGs flourishing in West Bengal is not at all satisfactory in comparison to southern and western states. Though it took off very slowly the Self-help group movement in West Bengal has acquired considerable quantitative momentum. Room for improvement:
6. Assessment of technical skill and managerial skill by bankers.
7. Upgradation on the basis of the assessment, adoption of new technology may be patronized here. Necessary training are to be imparted.
8. Organizing some orientation programs regarding the group objectives, their responsibility, elements of book keeping, knowledge of market, identification and appraisal, familiarity with product costing and product pricing, acquaintance with project financing by banks as well as some basic skills in the key activity identified.
9. Gender equality and pro-poor development.

References

1. Besley, T and S. Coate (1995), 'Group Lending Repayment Incentives and Social Collateral', *Journal of Development Economics,* 46, pp.1-18.

2. Coleman B.E (1999), 'The Impact of Group Lending in Northeast Thailand', *Journal of Development Economics*, 60, pp.105-141.
3. Dasgupta, R (2001), 'Working and Impact of Rural Self-Help Groups and other Forms of Micro Financing: An Informal Journey Through Self-Help Groups', *Indian Journal of Agricultural Economics*, 56, no. 3.pp. 370-386.
4. Deshmukh- Ranadive, J. (2004), Women's Self-help Groups in Andhra Pradesh: Participatory Poverty Alleviation in Action, Washington, DC: World Bank. EDA and APMAS(2006), "Self-Help Groups in India A Study of the Lights and Shades" http://www. edarural. com/ documents/SHGStudy/ Executive-Summary.pdf
5. Ghatak M (1999), 'Group Lending Local Information and Peer Selection', *Journal of Development Economics,* 60, pp .27-45.
6. Ghatak M and T.W Guinnane (1999), 'Economics of Lending with Joint Liability: Theory and Practice', *Journal of Development Economics,* 60, pp.195-228.
7. NABARD (2002), 'Ten Years of SHG-Bank Linkage: 1992-2002', NABARD and Micro Finance.
8. Lahiri-Dutt and Samanta (2006), 'Constructing Social Capital: Self-Help Groups and Rural Women's Development in India', Geographical Research, 44 pp. 285-295.
9. Namboodiri. N.V and R.L Shiyani (2001), 'Potential Role of Self-Help Groups in Rural Financial Deepening', *Indian Journal of Agricultural Economics,* 56, pp.401-409.
10. Pitt. M.M and S.R Khandekar (1998), 'The Impact Of Group Based Credit Programmes On Poor Households In Bangladesh: Does The Gender Participants Matter? *Journal of Political Economy*, 106, 958-996.
11. Satish P (2005), 'Mainstreaming of Indian Micro Finance', *Economic and Political Weekly*, Vol XL pp. 1731-1739.
12. Sen A (1973), On Economic Inequality, Oxford University Press, Delhi.
13. Smith, D. H and K Pillheimer (1983), 'Self-Help Groups as Social Movement Organisations: Social Structure and Social Change', Research in Social Movements, Conflicts and Change, Vol 5 No 2.
14. Verman P, Mahendra (2005) ' Impact of Self-Help Groups on Formal Banking Habits', *Economic and Political Weekly,* Vol XL No 17 pp.1705- 1713.
15. Yunus M (2004), Grameen Bank, Micro Credit and Millennium Development Goals, *EPW*, Vol. 39, 4077-4092.
16. Government of West Bengal, West Bengal, (different issues)

11

Role of Banking Institutions in Promotion and Development of Microenterprises of Shgs

Abstract

Institutions are mechanism to perform certain functions of society. Individuals, groups and communities interact and experience various institutions in their day to day life. As life develops and society transforms, old institutions may wear out and new institutions may come up with new functions and role or they may need to be modified. Institutions have specific roles, functions and expectations to perform. They influence human life as well as impact on quality of life. For this reason their performance matters. Here the researcher through the data collection work for doctoral research has made efforts to know the various roles and functions performed by the institutions of stakeholders in respect of SHGs' microenterprises development. The research inquiries are about challenges faced and to know the necessary changes for efficient and proactive performances. The performance has been analyzed on the basis of functional performance indicators like policies and programmes, governance, professionalism, timely follow-ups, infrastructural facilities, networking, sustainability in providing support etc. The study was conducted in two blocks of Sindhudurg district of Maharashtra state in India. The methodology includes mixed methods with research design of the case studies- of SHGs and of their microenterprises by using Focused Group Discussions (FGDs), Focused Group Interviews (FGIs), interviews and observation tools. For this paper the researcher is focusing on the role of banks in microenterprises development of SHGs. Banks include Nationalized, District Cooperative and Regional Rural banks.

Introduction

Poverty and unemployment are twin problems faced by many nations in the world. Among the accepted Millennium Development Goals, poverty and hunger alleviation is that of prime concern for world's development task. To alleviate poverty of any kind, needs long term sustainable means for poor to earn and improve standard of life. Hence providing opportunities, resources, supportive strategies, means etc. becomes an important aspect of proactive response towards the above mentioned challenge. Short-term measures like food supply, monetary support, services have limited strength. So, we need to look for sustainable means to alleviate dual problem of poverty and unemployment.

Since 1960s much importance was given on enterprises development and self employment. In India big, small or medium enterprises and presently microenterprises are seen as a source or means to explore opportunities for employment and production. Various studies during in the 1980s mention that less availability of finance has been a major constraint for development of enterprise in general. Hence, 1990s onwards microfinance has been started as a provision to support or to act on the research findings. But many of the policy makers or programme planners might have forgotten that access to 'finance' was a limited aspect. Only making finance available and policies regarding it may not be improving the quality of the requirements of enterprises or it may not bring the change; but it needs more.

The capacity building of delivery agents, staff, supportive inputs to creditor/entrepreneurs, sustainability in providing finance, safety and security measures etc. need to be taken care of simultaneously. This paper attempts to explore the performance and experiences of banking institutions while delivering microfinance with special reference to microenterprises of SHGs in two major programmes of the country. The SGSY and NABARD's SHGs-Bank credit linkage programme. The researcher had extended interactions with various stakeholders like NGOs and the DRDA of the Sindhudurg district.

Banks' experience of Shgs promotion and development

Since 1999-2000, SHGs have been adopted as a strategy for financial inclusion in the country. Banks are one of the important stakeholders in the promotion and development of the SHG movement in India. Banks are providing saving and credit linkage and some of the facilities of banking to SHGs. This helps in getting financial literacy of poor, who are first time getting linked with banks through SHG. When SHGs open their saving bank account in any of the formal banks i.e. Regional Rural Banks (RRBs), District Credit Cooperatives (DCCs) or commercial nationalized bank, then only the SHG's formation gets a formal recognition. Until an SHG does not open the bank account in any of these mentioned financial institutions, SHG's formal existence is not accepted for providing any kinds of benefits of schemes or programmes. SHG's passbook is a kind of formal registration proof, which tells that a particular SHG is valid or not.

It is the 'Grameen Bank of Bangladesh' that has made 'group financing' a profitable transaction, for those who were hardly covered by the formal financial institutions. It was due to the belief that the *poor are non-credit worthy*. World's microfinance movement has used 'group financing' as a most efficient strategy, which mostly assures the good repayment and collective support for the poor and needy members of the group e.g. Bancosol, Bank Rakyat Indonesia (BIR) etc.

The groups formed by the poor and marginalized people for self help purpose are called SHGs in the India and now this fact is accepted by many countries too. SHG is an accepted form for the delivery of microfinance to poor by the government and non-governmental financial institutions in India. The 'group' works as collateral and peer pressure mechanism works effectively for its members. The group helps and motivates members for timely repayment of loan borrowed from the banks. This assures banks to get better recovery of the loan disbursed to the SHGs. In the study district RRBs, DCC and nationalized commercial banks are helping SHGs with microfinance. Ten years back banks were not ready even to open a bank account of SHGs. There was lot of confusion, ignorance as well as lack of motivation at bank level to support SHGs. But situation changed due to continuous push by the NGOs, members of SHGs and NABARD's trainings for bank officers. Training to bankers and simultaneously a good publicity and awareness of SHG's success became the factors responsible for the change. The RBI's policies and guidelines for banks have made clear that finance to SHGs has become a priority sector lending. Group financing is a new experience for banks.

And it has been found safe and profitable. Banks will be provided with the support of revolving funds by NABARD as it finances SHGs under the priority sector lending.

Micro saving and banks

Saving linkage of SHGs with bank provides members an access for safe savings of their thrift as well as credit from the formal banking system. This is a safe mechanism for poor to save as well as to take less costly loans than that of traditional money lenders without losing their petty assets and securities in emergencies. DCC and RRB are playing a role beyond by just providing savings and credit linkages to SHGs in the study areas. These banks are involved in formation of SHGs in their service area villages and work as Self Help Promotion Institutions (SHPIs) under the NABARD's SHG- Bank Credit Linkage Programme.

The DCCs and RRBs in the district have accepted this programme of NABARD and are getting the financial support as well as refinances against the lending done to the SHGs from NABARD. It helps these banks to spread their commercial customer network for their future business opportunities as well as to get access to funds from NABARD to increase their business. It helps to increase their financial capacity, especially when bank deposits are lesser due to the rural area locations and even to increase their regular lending business with the regular customers. When banks themselves are forming SHGs there is an ownership and psychological attachment, hence better support is provided to these SHGs. There is also a confidence among the banks when SHGs are formed by them and a bond develops. When these banks are making SHGs then those SHGs are generally of above poverty line (APL) people and generally people who do not have saving accounts in bank or not having any financial relations with banks in past. This serves the purpose of financial inclusion.

NABARD's objective behind the programme is for spreading the financial services of banks to the un-reached population of the country. And through the SHPIs, the banks are provided some incentives for doing this work, which was not the earlier function of banks. Nationalized commercial banks hardly become SHPIs as these banks hardly lack deposits with them for lending purposes. Some commercial banks like State Bank of India, Bank of Maharashtra form SHGs on their own, with involvement of their staff. For SBI, SHG formation and providing finance to SHGs has become a Social Corporate Responsibility. SBI, sometimes form SHGs with help of volunteers from the villages, own staff or by having collaboration with

NGOs. Due to the emerging challenges with SHGs, SBI has started appointing a field based staff with professional degree in rural development or agriculture disciplines to support people in service villages.

The professional interventions from the banking sector needs to be sustainable and should provide qualitative improvements in life of SHG members that they can wisely use available resources to transform their life.

NGOs under the NABARD's SHGs Bank credit Linkage programme perform the role with SHGs. If there are no NGOs in the service areas that role is played by SHPIs. But in addition to that they provide credit to SHGs which NGOs hardly provide unless a NGO having the status of SHPIs.

Gradation of Shgs

Gradation of SHGs is one of the supervision and monitoring techniques for evaluating SHG's performance and functioning before financing them. NABARD has prepared and given gradation forms to banks and to NGOs for rating the SHGs. As per the rating of the SHGs, the better graded SHGs are eligible to get credit support from the banks. The gradation indicates that they require inputs for further improvements. This helps SHGs to know their status. In the case of BPL- SHGs the DRDA, NGOs and bank staff jointly visit the SHG and do gradation at the SHG's place or at village panchayat office where village development officer and sometimes elected representatives of village panchayat are present. For APL-SHG, the bank or the concerned NGO does gradation and as per the grades it collectively decides to finance or not to finance. This brings seriousness among the SHG members; they become more responsible and better disciplined for the credit given to them. For APL –SHG often NGO's gradation and recommendation are accepted by banks for providing credit to SHGs as partners in formations and promotions of SHGs because of having less staff with banks to spare for this work.

Credit Linkage

Credit to SHGs, comes under the priority sector lending for banks. Before the SHGs, poor and marginalized or even little above the poverty line population, hardly used to have any transaction with bank. SHG has opened this platform for the excluded group of people by providing an opportunity to know and understand the banking system. Bank's primary function is to provide saving and credit linkage facility to SHG members. SHGs being strong and a more assured strategy for financing to the poor and marginalized they induce various changes to take place with present institutions; banks are not exceptions. They have also felt the need to bring the changes in their present practice and working.

Under the SGSY and NABARD's SHGs-Bank credit linkage programmes, banks are asked to provide finance to the SHGs if the rating of SHGs is good and satisfactory. If banks are not cooperative for credit linkage then NABARD's district development manager intervenes and pursues banks to finance SHGs. NABARD's district officer is supposed to maintain a record of credit linked SHGs in districts. However, at present such records are not available with the district officers of NABARD.

Microfinance support depends upon the SHG's BPL (Below Poverty Line) status or APL status (Above Poverty Line). For BPL-SHGs government's subsidy has been considered as a very important motivation. If the subsidy gets deposited in bank on SHG's name then banks provide the credit to BPL-SHGs in the district. Initial loans are given to BPL and APL- SHGs for basic domestic purposes. Using credit and its successful return with timely repayments is an indicator for knowing SHG's functioning and seriousness. This helps SHGs to build confidence for utilizing bank loan in group. It is a pre-testing of SHG's capacity of using a credit given by banks and its effective repayment. It is usually a small amount of loan up to Rs 20,000/ to Rs 25,000/- for BPL-SHGs and is called revolving fund. If this proved to be satisfactory then the SHG's demand for second loan for starting an income generation activity is considered. This has been given as a onetime sanction of loan for BPL-SHGs as per the government norms; the amount comes up to the Rs 2.5 lakhs where the half amount of the loan is a subsidy, which is given by the DRDA on behalf of Government of India and deposited in SHG's bank account. This amount is given to SHGs after the successful completion of their loan repayment from their economic activities.

For the APL SHGs there is no subsidy component. APL-SHG receives the bank loan against their saving amount for suitable purpose. For the APL-SHGs, the banks provide credit limit up to four times on SHGs' collative savings. It is usually twice, thrice or even four times to SHG's saving amount. If the repayment has been found successful, then banks are more liberal in sanctioning more amounts of loan to the SHG or even to individual members.

Banks are supposed to be responsible while providing the education and training inputs on keeping the books of accounts and books of business, which need to maintained by SHG members. But this has been hardly done by the banks in the study area. For BPL-SHGs, when the DRDA organizes training in general. Bankers are also called to provide training. But after the trainings stakeholders do not bother about its application and practice. During the gradation, it has been checked by the team of DRDA and bank staff. As transactions increase and the SHG starts using bigger amounts they find it difficult to maintain the books of accounts. Especially, if they lack habit of keeping proper records and accounts regularly in past. And many times, most of the stakeholders hardly take care of this factor. If any improper utilization happens it is difficult to trace. Banks say that there is shortage of staff to handle SHG's needs. Banks do not have any experience to work with groups especially that of poor and less educated and to guide them on development of microenterprises.

Grameen bank's situations and Grameen bank model's adoption as it is may need more moldings to the present approach, attitude, practice and convictions for the banking system in India. Commercial nationalized banks are hardly taking much interest in the promotion of SHGs and even financing them liberally. Banks see it as an additional work with insufficient staff. And past experience of government's anti-poverty programmes (IRDP) has made banks to be dormant on SHGs.

For SHG related work the bank staff need to move out from their offices, experience the struggles for setting up SHGs, visit locations and guide and supervise the members and help them to progress. Bank personnel have hardly done these types of work in their previous service. So accepting this as a job profile is difficult for most of the present staff.

In the district, many banks are unable to visit SHGs, even once a year where as it is mandatory for them to visit SHGs which they have financed. It definitely motivates SHG members and helps to build the healthy customer relationship with banks. But at present, it has been hardly practiced because many of the staff members are hardly aware and prepared for it. Usually for SHG's work bank managers are held responsible, who do not get time to do justice to his job. Regular administrative work assigned to him/her makes it difficult to visit SHGs in the service areas. Other staff in the bank do not take initiatives to support SHGs.

However, SHG's general performance really has moved bankers in these years, especially when women members of SHGs confidently interact with bank personnel. This change has been accepted very positively by many staff at banks in the district and also this has shared by many district coordinators of various banks with the researcher. Ten years back, banks were hesitant even to open their saving bank account with banks. But now, hardly any SHG faces any problem while opening of a bank account. Timely repayment by the SHGs has motivated banks to be positive with the poor. Finance to SHGs' women members helps banks to fulfill the target to finance the women section of the society.

Following tables are providing some factual information about the banks and related information in Sindhudurga district studied by the researcher to support this paper and discussions.

a-Table showing types of banks and No. of branches they have to work with SHGs

Sr.No	Banks	No of Branches
1	Nationalized	71
2	DDC-SDDC	70
3	RRBs- WKGB	15

Source: Lead banks' (BOI) district annual report of - March 2010

b-Bank wise distribution of the studied SHGs in the study area :

Banks	WOMEN		MEN	MIXED		Total
	BPL	APL	APL	BPL	APL	
Nationalized	7	3	4	2	1	17
Co-operative (SDCC)	-	2	1	1	-	4
Rural banks (RRBs)	1	-	-	-	-	1

c-Functional performance by the banking institutions for SHGs in the district

Banks	Nationalized	RRBs	DCCs
SHGs formation	Very rarely	Yes	Yes
Saving Linkage	Yes	Yes	Yes
Gradation	Only BPL-SHG	Yes	Yes
Credit Linkage	Yes	Yes	Yes
Business Guidance Cell	No	No	Very poor
Training	No	No	Few trainings*
Marketing support	No	No	Some times
Networking/ Federation of SHGs at bank level	No	No	Started but stopped
Infrastructural support	No	No	Sometimes

RRB- Wianganga Krishna Rural bank

DCC- Sindhudurga District Credit Cooperative Bank

* As bank works as SHPI and gets grants for it.

Methodology

For present study, various levels bank officers- the LDM, banks' district coordinators and concern banking personals have been interviewed. Bank managers and staff were requested for sharing their experiences, problems and challenges, while performing their role with the SHGs' microenterprises development task. The researcher had attended District Level Bankers Committee's (DLBC) meeting, to know bankers collective views and experiences while developing SHG's microenterprises through microfinance and understanding their roles and functions towards it. The Lead District Manager (LDM) had a good experience of the district's banking system as he takes quarterly review of them in DLBCs. The LDM has been found very cooperative, transparent and experienced one. The further issues and concerns related to the institution of bank are discussed here. Those helped to understand the field reality and banking practices clearly.

Data base of Shgs

The data of SHGs has not been maintained by most of the banks in the district.

Only Sindhudurga District Credit Cooperative bank (SDCC) was able to provide the data of SHGs with the bank. The bank does not keep separate records of BPL and APL SHGs, it has maintained together. Even NABARD and LDM's offices at the district could not able to provide any base line data regarding number of SHGs in the district to the researcher. A very poor record management and missing of records details of SHGs with banks was a surprise for the researcher.

Even though, SHGs come under the priority sector lending of banks in the country (RBI/NABARD's guidelines for banks). SHGs' long term relation takes place with banks than any other stakeholders, as SHGs are in need of getting regular financial support. Hence banks role and functions matters a lot for regular and sustainable progress of SHGs.

Discussions with Lead District Manager (BOI) and banks district coordinators

Each district has appointed a Lead Bank, which is a host commercial bank to do the monitoring and regulatory work of banking institutions; preparing yearly banking plan for the district and assigning targets to various banks those have branches in the district and achieve the goals collectively. Lead District Bank (LDB) conducts collective reviews of banks, working in the district as well as makes RBIs guidelines known to all branches. SHG is one of the components to be reviewed by LDM, especially for BPL-SHG and APL-SHGs in general. So it was important to get the district's picture more clearly from him, his sharing contributed lot. His seniority and very close involvement has helped the researcher to understand banks and their work with SHGs, in much better way.

His general sharing about the SHGs i.e. SHGs are helping for financial inclusion processes to take place in the district and now banks are moving towards opening of each individual SHG members' saving bank account in thc banks. Due to the SHGs formation e.g. awareness and empowerment of mass has become easy. Bank staff are getting pro to finance SHGs, which was not at initial years of the programme. He has explained to the researcher about the need to do more then what banks are presently doing as their role towards SHG's development in the district. He has discussed crucial issues and concern of banks, their role with SHGs and their microenterprises those are further discussed.

Banks district coordinators

The researcher could not be able to interview every bank manager during the study where the studied SHGs have opened their bank account, because bank managers get transferred and hardly the present managers would have been able to tell much about the SHGs studied even though branch is the same. So to know the particular experience of the banks in general all the district coordinators of various banks and the Lead District Manager of the district had been interviewed and discussed personally by the researcher. They had discussed their concerns regarding SHGs in length, their finance, microenterprises experiences and their own role performance in the district. The researcher had categorized the discussions and information shared by them further.

The issues and core concerns related with banks while performing their role against SHGs

1. The selection of the staffs at banks

Human aspect of organizations helps in realizations of the results, by implementing of policies and programmes through their institutions. So the quality and capacities of human resource of the institutions found to be an important aspect while looking at the performance and roles played by them.

The banks are hardly appointing staffs with training in rural development and related issues at their rural branches. When bank staff needs to work on SHGs' issues, they need to know the background of SHGs' members and their lives and rural environment around. The staffs that get rural posting and come to rural areas, see it as an obligation for their further promotions. And it is a mandatory posting, to spend certain years of service at rural branch. Most of the personnel are in hurry to complete their tenure as early as possible and want to go back to urban areas. The staff that works with SHGs in rural areas sincerely may get transfer altogether to different sections of bank, then his/ her experience with SHGs goes unused. This affects the motivation of staff at banks to come forward -to this new field of practice. Hence the LDM suggested that banks must have better transfer policies as well as selection of specific kind of staff, who has an interest for rural development, at the time of recruitment itself. This helps banks to have better personnel with self motivated interest, to work with rural poor and to contribute seriously to SHGs or other emerging issues of challenges in rural development.

At present the staff selection process of banks are of clerical in nature. SBI has recently started special recruitments and appointments, based on the interest and with specific professional degrees with rural development as well as degrees of agricultural development this has to be welcomed. This has been influenced by the potentials of work and pressure coming through SHGs in rural areas and as emerging new customers for banks. He further added that, the selected staff must be ready and able to go in the villages on motorbikes or on two wheelers but not with four-wheeler's, then only reach- ability, mobility to rural population for honest service delivery in the interior areas could be made possible by banks. This has to be made very clear while the selection of the staff itself. For sustainability and expansions of working areas of banks, it will be a mandatory for banks in coming years.

2. Training and capacity building of banking staff

The second aspect discussed by the LDM was the present capacities of the staff at banks. According to him, each bank must make a policy decision that the staff that are transferred to rural areas must be properly trained and educated about the rural realities as well as their specific roles in it. And SHGs work should be made compulsory in their job chart. At present it has only a bank mangers' responsibility. NABARD has a package for getting a training on the SHG's issue and banking business linkage. But hardly any of banks are sending their staffs regularly for training. Banks are paid by the NABARD for this. In most of the banks in the district, SHGs' concern has been seen as target but it is only concerned of the banks' manager and hardly to other staff. Bank managers alone are getting limitations to cater the needs of SHGs and constraints are like- time, language, work load etc. Banks' general staffs do lack the inputs, knowledge and information on SHGs' issue and concerns as well as on microenterprises development processes. Banking staff has hardly any past experience as well as training inputs on this subject- local economic development. So required capacities, skills are lacking with the staff at banks in general, when the customers of SHGs are getting increased by every year in banks.

3. Manpower planning of bank's staff and incentives for contributions

LDM suggested banks must do their manpower planning before sending their staff at rural postings. Staff should be compulsorily trained with required orientation inputs for the rural development and related projects must be introduced to them and their tenure in rural areas should be made in the phases e.g. like three years, five years, eight years and then their commitment and work in the rural areas must be rewarded by direct promotions, provisions of attractive monetary intensives etc. These kinds of mechanisms may not be leading to depressions to bank's staff who work in rural branches, when they compare with their counter parts in the urban areas, who get benefits of higher allowances due to their posting at cities. At present, rural staffs have hardly considered for their sacrifices of their life and of their families by living in rural areas with inconveniences. Otherwise without taking care of this human psychological aspect, the commitment and honest contribution by the bank staff may be difficult one.

4. Lack of uniformed approach by banks

Microfinance has been given mostly a last priority while practice comes at branches, even though it is a priority sector lending. Different banks are giving different weight age for the SHGs' component in their work. The state wise differences are also observed e.g. Syndicate Bank does well at Karnataka state which is the home state for bank, but in Maharashtra state SHGs work does lack. If Microfinance bill gets accepted, then it will be very easy to have more focused and unified approach towards the SHGs and microfinance activity by the banks. The government has to be serious in policy formation and its unified execution. Some time it happens that the policies and programmes are there but their execution, implementation, monitoring and serious review has not been given much importance by the authorities. This needs to change. At present various banks are charging various interest rates on credit provided to the SHGs. Some banks do ask mortgage from SHGs, while lending to them, which should not to be taken by banks while financing to SHGs as per the RBIs guidelines. Types of loans given to SHGs are not similar by the banks. Some banks provides Cash- Credit, some are giving Term- loans. Some banks give fixed installments for loan repayments and some do not specify. This brings confusions among the customers, SHGs and society at large. Hence the uniformed approach, and practice of banks may help better achievements and functioning for the SHGs related role performance.

5. SHGs members' motives do matters

Another worry expressed by the LDM is that about the SHGs itself. According to him SHGs in the district generally do lack long term vision and goals to achieve, rather than they are for petty benefits from the loan. This is one of the reasons some bankers get less involved with SHGs. The LDM had explained that banks are first to be a profit making organizations, if they get a possibility to earn profit, then only they will be taking more interest to get involved with SHGs. At present BPL-SHGs are more in numbers and APL-SHGs are less in numbers in the district. The present belief of banks about the BPL-SHGs i.e. after the loan sanction and after its repayment to bank and getting the subsidy amount, members may not be remained together. Because the BPL-SHGs in the district are informed about the subsidy component as benefit more than getting in to the sustainable practice of formal credit linkage access from bank. And hence the BPL-SHGs financing has not been considered of much important aspect of banking. To complete the government's target given to banks is an aim and not sustainable customers relations with the SHGs. But the researcher could see that, the BPL-SHGs are functioning even after the distribution of subsidy under the 'SGSY'. But hardly those are encouraged by the banks for further continuation of credit support for their economic activities. (SHGs - Dungeshwer and Ganesh are example in the study)

6. Profitability and commercial views over emphasized than social development

Another issue discussed is that, most of the banks at present those are asked to work on SHG and microfinance are the commercial banks and not the development banks in the country. And there the major difference comes in their working strategies. Profit earning is the motive in globalization era for banking institutions and one must understand they are not an exception for it. Profit has been considered the most important than the development of the poor or marginalized in the society by banks. And if this is so, then country need to develop another system of banking or new section in bank itself – where the development, poverty alleviation and microfinance etc. could be more focused attentions of bank's services and not the profit maximization. At present both aspect /aims are getting clashed with one another.

Due to the present strengths and opportunities in rural development it has to be looked differently, not just by adding to the present banking system which may hardly give justice to the cause. For SHGs and microfinance activity there is a special need for having of right personnel with certain qualities and knowledge, for delivery of the banking services for inclusion. Such personnel could be appointed for three to four branches of a bank and he/she can monitor, guide and direct SHGs for their business. At present, banks have technical staff, which provide such specialized services to branches for industries and agriculture sectors' financing and similar mechanisms can be developed or created for microfinance related work too. It is the government and RBI should be taking such initiatives. Banks are hardly having any independence for doing anything on these matters at present.

7. Infrastructural constraints

Next point shared by the LDM and some of the bank officers was an infrastructural shortage and inadequacy of infrastructural facilities with all the stakeholders including banks, while working with SHGs. This brings limitations for their performance. E.g. banks are not having any provisions for two wheelers for visiting the SHGs or rural village customers. The quality of trainings given to banks for SHGs is not adequate to respond to the challenges of microenterprises development. Lack of professional and technical support for microenterprises development is another constrain shared by the bank officers. From February 2010, the RBI has started a scheme Rural Self Employment Training Institution (*RSETI*) for skill building of SHGs in all districts of the country. The responsibility is with Lead District Bank of the districts, but for conducting these trainings, various inputs and resources are required like -class rooms, technology, machineries setups, vehicles, training programmes and material, business development service providers etc. But at present all the mentioned necessary requirements are lacking in the district. The lead district bank has to develop a training center for SHGs in the district with collaboration with the DRDA, where 70% BPL-SHGs and 30%APL-SHGs members can take trainings for their capacity building. Still the Lead bank has not got any clear understanding about the bank's role to be played for the SHGs in the district under the scheme.

The district coordinators of banks in the district had also shared their concerns like - staff shortage, most of the rural banks are having one or two officers and it is difficult to manage both indoor and outdoor banking works of branches. Staff of bank has hardly any experience of business development and management and so they find difficult to guide SHGs, as they ask for guidance.

Banks have much relation with NGOs in the district, but then those are not permanent but rather occasional. Banks do not have funds to provide to NGOs for taking their services regularly. The cost is involved for NGOs too for the charges and services they make avail to banks and hence long term relationship among the institutions/ organization hardly takes place, even though the need of intuitional cooperation and collaborations experienced beneficial for supporting SHGs. The DRDA staff lack the competencies to make viable project proposal for BPL-SHGs, which creates limitation to banks, to be very formal in their role and requirements while sanctioning loans to SHGs. Banks are lacking in, paying visits to SHGs', even once in a year, to the SHGs, to whom they have disbursed loans. Bankers' visit to SHGs makes positive influence to take up their activity with much seriousness and the recovery of a credit given to SHGs t ('Omkar' SHG shared with the researcher during the study). Banks as important and lasting support institutions for SHGs' financial support needs required to various adoptions at various levels for better performance, as the LDM and banks district coordinators discussed with the researcher.

According to the changing needs, institutions need to undergo a change which may be wanted or not wanted, liked or disliked by the functionaries or stakeholder institutions.

Conclusion

The study revealed to the researcher that the need to bring changes in the present banking institutions do exist and as banks are made as a responsible stakeholders by RBI in the process of micro-credit support to poor through SHGs must try to incorporate various changes seriously and indirectly to the task of development and promotion of microenterprises for creating self employment opportunities for the poor. Making of viable and vibrant institutions with qualitative human resource, supported with required necessary infrastructures, creating special sections and incentives/rewards for their work definitely would make a condition for positive sustainable contribution by them in their efforts towards providing positive output for SHGs' microenterprises task. If the SHGs could able to develop a sustainable microenterprises, those will be bringing employment and income to its members and so the development of poor and of marginalized who have organized in SHGs with hope and have become proactive for their self development. But responsible dynamic institutions and their good governance provide necessary investment climate.

References

1. Bagchi K.K (edited), Employment and Poverty Alleviation Programmes in India, Macro level studies with national perspectives, volume I & II, Abhijit Prakashan, Delhi,2007
2. Nabard- Andhra Pradesh Regional Office, Banking with Poor SHG-Bank Linkage Programme in Andhra Pradesh, 2007.
3. Ni-msme, Small Enterprises Development, Management, and Extension Journal,Vol-35,number 2, June 2008, Sendme, Yousufguda, Hyderabad.
4. P. Purushotham, Institutional Credit for Rural Livelihood, A study of SGSY in the Region of High Poverty, NIRD-Hyderabad, 2009.
5. North Douglass C., Institutions, Institutional Change and Economic Performance, Cambridge University press,28th edition, Cambridge, 2009.
6. Rhyne Elisabeth, Microfinance for Bankers and Investors understanding the opportunities and Challenges of the Market at the Bottom of The Pyramid, Tata McGraw Hill Education Private Limited, New Delhi, 2010.
7. Pleskovic Boris & Stern Nicholas (edited), Annual World Bank Conference on Development Economics 2001-2002, World Bank, Washington, Oxford University Press, NewYork,2002.

12

The Ethical Practices of small Enterprises in Twin Cities

Abstract

The growing importance of corporate governance is increasingly realized throughout the world, particularly in the rapidly changing international business scenario. The global ethical and governance scandals have placed corporations under intense scrutiny regarding their accountability. The ongoing trends ask for a system of checks and balances. Business ethics in this regard is an issue of great concern to businessmen and scholars. This paper attempts to examine the ethical practices and unethical practices in the small business organizations which they set In order to face the complexities encountered in turbulent waves of market. The study reveals the differential status of ethical practices varying by the form of ownership, type of industry and the business experience of the organizations.

The Ethical Practices of Small Enterprises In Twincities

Liberalization of the economy resulted in cut-throat competition in business. Globalization brought new opportunities and access to new and wider markets. The radical developments that have taken place in the fields of IT and transport have made the world shrunk to a village. In the present world of opportunities if the organizations fail to inculcate the values properly in their system, if they fail to provide good governance, their long term sustenance is questionable.

Satisfying the stakeholders, with the legal and regulatory requirements and also by meeting the environmental and social obligations is the main asking of the society from business today. In the era of many a scandal, there is a chorus of disapproval for nontransparent and hidden practices of the organization.

Wide range of discussions on corporate governance practices are increasingly becoming popular and considered as critical to stabilize and strengthen global markets to protect investors. Corporate governance is a term that refers broadly to the rules, processes or laws by which businesses are operated, regulated and controlled. Be trustful, keep an open mind, Meet obligations, Have clear documents, Become community involved, Maintain accounting control and be respectful are 7 principles of admirable business ethics proposed by Rober Moment. A harmonious line of balance between economic and social goals, between individual and communal goals must be drawn by the business entities.

Entrepreneurs were also significantly more permissive on the issues of padding expense accounts, Insider trading and copying computer software etc. Along with the efficient use of resources one must not overlook the accountability for the stewardship of those resources. Ethical consideration affect business organization of all sizes, indeed they affect all forms of human activity (Longenecker et.al, 1989).Trust makes the organization sustained through the turbulences over its life cycle. Uncomplicated way of seeding the trust is through transparency. Therefore, what is required today is contemplation towards the expansion and penetration of the practices of good governance which only can ensure a sustainable rate of development that can be absorbed by the society.

Ethics and Values in the Perspective of Small Businesses

While a great deal of discussion is going about the ethics and the corporate governance practices of business concerns around the world, the large part of it is limited in the domain of large industries. Small industrial sector contributes about for fifths of manufacturing employment in India. As per 2007-08 statistics the employment stood at 322 lakhs. The contribution of small scale sector in export earnings has been quite impressive and keeps on increasing by leaps and bounds. The share of small scale industries in the total export earnings stands at 31.1% in 2006-07. However, the studies pertain to small scale industries are scanty.

The small industries occupy a major place in the economy particularly in the globalised era the ethical dimension of those industries cannot be overlooked. Erika Wilson examined the perspectives of owner or managers of small business concerning social responsibilities. Irrespective of the size and structure every enterprise of today must give a serious glance to its ethical behaviors towards its internal and external stakeholders because responsibility lies with stakeholders rather than shareholders.

The management practices of small industries differ from those of large industries. Small industries typically employ fewer professional specialists, operate with less formality and reflect to a greater extent the personality and attitude of entrepreneur.

As the small and decentralized sector plays a very crucial for the economy, it is imperative to know the sense of responsibility towards the 'triple bottom line' consists of people, planet and profit (John Elkington, 1998). Sraboni dutta and Sharmishtha Banerjee made an attempt to study the relationship between ethical practices and ownership patterns. With the necessary changes the questionnaire was adopted for the present study.

In view of this general difference one might also expect to find difference in ethical environment, ethical percepts and ethical perceptions of small business. Alan.K.Simpson rightly said "If you have integrity nothing else matters, if you don't have integrity nothing else matters"

Objectives of the Study

The paper aims at studying the sense of ethical behavior in various managerial practices and day to day operations of small scale industries which may cause an impact on their internal and external stake holders. The interaction of the small enterprises with their stake holders varies remarkably from that of their counterparts. Their processes and practices are rather informal and 'easy go' kind.

'Employees' constitute a very important stakeholder of the small firm. Any discussion related to the employee is one of the crucial areas of ethical concern in these firms. It has to be scrutinized whether the firms follow ethical practices in selecting the employees, pay them proper periodical increments and abide by rules for the replacement of the employees.

Jenkins (1994) identifies that any issue regarding employees occupies very important position in the determination of their commitment towards ethics. Customer is the most important stakeholder to the organization. Irrespective of the size, structure or form of ownership every business organization is aware of how important customer satisfaction is for any organization. Compared to large industries, small industries have direct contact with the customers. They easily come to know the satisfaction levels of the customers. At the same time it is important to study whether the enterprises provide the right information to the customer about the product, whether standard weights and measures are used by the firm and about the quality consciousness of the firms. These three aspects are chosen to assess the ethical commitment of the firms towards their customers.

The business houses today are necessitated to have a strong committed approach toward the environment. It is widely accepted that environment is one of the most important internal stakeholder, since the irresponsible practices existing inside the firm may damage the environment. The firms need to admit the fact that only through their awareness and proactive steps towards the protection of environment their commitment is established. Therefore, the present study makes an attempt to assess the serious efforts put by the firms in this direction.

The ethical behavior of the firm is also reflected in its legal compliance towards Government. It covers several aspects such as reporting and payment of the taxes etc. Last but not the least they also have an ethical obligation towards community and the society. Taking all the above stakeholders in to consideration it is attempted to scan the ethical levels of the firms.

There are various issues that bring the ethical nature of the firm to the surface.

There are also various other aspects through which the ethical behavior of the entrepreneur gets revealed. As far as the issues of the employees are concerned the selection of the employee, the formal appraisal system exist in the organization, paying yearly increment to the staff and finally norms followed for replacing the employee are the key issues in reflecting the nature of the firm.

Out of all the above the present study is confined to only two issues. They are payment of yearly increments and the replacement mechanism. The reason is it is widely observed in the direct interviews that many of the firms under sole proprietorship recruit people from their own extended families or at least from native place. Many a time they may not follow a proper appraisal system as the appraisal is done rather in an informal way.

With respect to the ethics in marketing maintaining quality standards, using standard weights and measures and providing right information to the public are the chosen aspects of the study.

Similarly, as part of the macro environment every firm addresses certain responsibilities towards society, environment and also government. The firm with ethical norms maintains high legal compliance, develops awareness about environmental protection, takes proactive steps towards pollution control, and makes some charitable contribution for the welfare of the community.

Therefore the present study attempts to analyze the above aspects. Coming to certain unethical practices that are generally indulged by the firms, bribery or offering money to get the work done either in an easy manner or against the rules stands in the first place. Corrupt practices may be taken up to deal with government agencies in order to secure permits and clearances out of the way, or with financial institutions in order to get business loans. Other than corruption political or other kinds of influence can also be used for these purposes. Studying these issues is helpful in assessing the ethical behavior of the firms Small scale industries demonstrate variety of characteristic features. Their existence is the industry, the mode of ownership, the type of activities they deal with and the issues they come across in different business situations show a wide range of diversity. Above all the personal and moral bindings of the entrepreneur show more influence on these industries. Therefore, the ethical commitment towards the stakeholders as exhibited by the firm is to a great extent influenced by the nature of the entrepreneurs. Besides, it can also be hypothesized that the business experience gained throughout the period of operations also carves the ethical nature of the firms. As the learning through experience is the order of the day, due to the seniority gained in the field of its business a firm definitely forms certain rules and follows them.

The commitment towards ethics is also associated with the type of industry. Compared to manufacturing industries, the entrepreneurs of service industries are professionally qualified. Hence, the compliance with the law, awareness about environmental protection, transparency in HR practices is more seen in service industries compared to their counterparts.

Based on the three above propositions the present study aims at studying the association of ethical practices with respect to form of ownership, seniority of the business house and type of industry. The kind of behavior they show while encountering with various ethical and unethical issues is studied and attempt is made to understand the pattern it shows.

Data Collection

The data is taken from the District Industrial Centre Hyderabad. The study is confined to Secunderabad. The population for the study is small scale and micro enterprises having registration in the selected areas of Secunderabad. The list of industries who have filed Entrepreneurship Memorandum II was obtained. A sample of 50 industries was chosen from the population based on stratified random basis.

Data Collection Techniques

Data Is collected through primary survey. Entrepreneurs were selected and a structured questionnaire was given for them during the personal interview. The questionnaire developed for this was carefully designed covering many ethical issues come across in various business situations.

The first section of the questionnaire contains questions regarding the demographic and structural profiles of the business. The second section was about their attitudes towards ethical issues. Five point Liker scale was used to elicit the responses.

Results

Data regarding the profiles of the businesses included the form of ownership, qualification of the entrepreneur, annual turnover, nature of activity, number of employees and the years of experience. Based on the form of ownership the respondents were divided in sole proprietors, partnership, private limited company,

Based on the nature of the activity, the firms are divided into manufacturing and service industries. On the basis of business experience in the industry, once again the firms are classified into two. They are the firms with more than five years of establishment and firms with less than five years of establishment.

Out of the 50 firms surveyed 44% follow the ownership pattern of sole proprietorship, 28% are under partnership and the same percentage follow the ownership pattern of private limited company. Out of the firms from which data collected 52% are manufacturing industries and 48% are service industries.

Another aspect of the study is years of establishment. Under this category, 48% of sample units have less than 5 years of establishment, and 52% have more than 5 years of experience in the industry.

Association of ethical issues with reference to the form of ownership

Paying increments regularly and abiding by rules for replacing the employcc arc taken as two aspects of ethical HR practices. It is revealed from the study that 37.5% of proprietors only are paying yearly increments to their staff, without fail. Under partnership the percentage is 51%. The yearly increments are very well paid for the people working in private limited companies. The percentage is as high as 96.2 in this group. Nearly, 45% Of the firms under sole proprietorship abide to the rules for replacing the employee, which is lower than any of the two other forms.

According to the study 60.4% of partnership firms follow the rules, and 98% of the private limited companies fall in the same category.

In order to study the ethical practices in marketing measures taken for providing best quality product and providing sufficient information about the product to the customer are selected as the two aspects relevant for the study.

Approximately, 63.8% of sole proprietors accepted that they take all measures to provide the best quality product to the customer whereas the remaining people are not that quality conscious. The percentage is high both in partnership and in private limited companies at 94% and 97% respectively.

Coming to another aspect of marketing that is providing right and complete information to the customer the sole proprietors are still lagging behind. Only 35% of the people accept that they provide cent per cent right information to the customers, where as 60% of partnership firms and 83.3% of private limited companies follow this practice.

Environment is yet another important stakeholder for the business organizations. To assess the ethical commitment towards environment the proactive steps of the firm is taken as the aspect. It is evident from the study that 30.2% of the firms under sole proprietorship take proactive measures for the protection of environment whereas the percentages are 40% and 80% for partnership firms and private limited companics respectively.

Table 1

Form of Ownership - Ethical practices

	Proprietor	Partnership	Private Company
Paying yearly Increments	37.5	51	96.2
Replacing Employees as per rules	45	60.4	98
Measures taking Provide best quality products	63.8	94	97
Providing Information about the product	35	60	83
Proactive measures for environmental protection	30.2	40	80
Abiding by Legal formalities	35	30	45
Contribution to social welfare	31.6	49.1	98.3

Abiding to the legal formalities can be regarded as the manifestation of ethical practices of the organizations towards government. Payment of the taxes regularly, filing the tax particulars promptly etc. are various issues come under this category. Partnership firms and firms under sole proprietorship almost exhibit same tendency as 30% and 35% respectively of these firms satisfy fall under the category of high legal compliance. In the category of private limited companies the same is at 45.3%.

Organizations make certain contributions for community welfare as a demonstration of social responsibility. Undertaking such activities is also less prevalent among sole proprietary firms. It is as less as 31.6% in the case of sole proprietary firms. Partnership firms are slightly ahead of them and stood at 49.1%. In the case of private limited companies, the donations or contributions for charitable purposes are very high. Apparently 88.3% firms make such contributions.

A cross tabulation was also made for the unethical practices of the firms with reference to government, suppliers and financial institutions. Paying bribery in government offices, paying bribery for getting business loans sanctioned or any other kind of influence used for the same purpose, not paying the business loans promptly, not making payments to the suppliers in time and paying chandas to anti social elements are some of the general unethical practices followed by the firms.

From the table it is clearly evident that more than half of the partnership and small companies are involved in such practices. The percentages are

Table 2

Association of Unethical practices with reference to the form of ownership

	Proprietor	Partnership	Private Company
Pay bribery in Govt office	28.6	61.3	72.7
Bribery for business loans	37.3	30.6	73.2
Political Influence	44.5	71.6	71.8
Not Paying bank loans promptly	63.4	71.5	64.6
Not Paying to suppliers in time	35.7	1.8	14.9
Paying chandas	90.7	0	11.2

60.0 and 72.2 respectively. Somehow it is relatively less in the case of sole proprietorship at 27.8%. But coming to paying loans for securing business loans it is noteworthy that 73% of sole proprietors are involved some or other kind of corrupt practices. It is gradually less as the form of ownership evolves into a rather formal structure. While 50% of partnership firms involve in such practices only 37% of small companies take up such activities. If the usage of political or other kind of influence for securing either bank loans or any other grants or permits is taken into consideration, the above two are ahead of sole proprietary firms.

Among the sole proprietorship firms 43.3% firms involve in such practices, in the case of other two forms the it stands at 70.7% If the assessment is made for those entrepreneurs who do not take prompt payment of the bank loans seriously 63.4% of the sole proprietors fail in making prompt payments. Such practice is very high in the case of partnership firms at 71.5% and 64.6% for private limited companies.

Making payments to suppliers in time is also an important aspect in explaining the fair practices of the business organizations. Many small firms in the dearth of sufficient cash arrangement to meet working capital requirements may opt for a practice of not paying suppliers promptly. If the empirical evidence is seen with regard to the form of ownership, 35.7% Of sole proprietary firms are not paying their suppliers properly. This practice is very rare in the case of partnership companies and stands at 1.8% and 16.9% in the case of small companies.

Small businesses also come across certain incidental costs imposed by outlaws or anti social activists. The threat is very high in the case of sole proprietary firms, as it is revealed from the table that 9.6% of these entrepreneurs are compelled to pay any such amounts. Among the firms with partnership form of ownership 77.6% are paying such costs. However, it is very less for small companies. Only 11% companies are bound to pay such amounts.

Association of Ethical Issues with reference to type of Industry

The present research makes an attempt to examine the association of ethical practices with regard to the type of industry. The industries are broadly classified into manufacturing and service industries. In majority circumstances compared to manufacturing industries, the entrepreneurs of service industries are highly qualified. The activities encountered by manufacturing and service industries are to some extent different. The people working in service industries relatively are better qualified. Therefore it would definitely be interesting to look into the details of industry wise ethical practices.

The first two aspects of the study pertain to the ethical practices towards employees. There is clear evidence that compared to manufacturing industries service industries show more commitment towards ethics in a consistent manner. The policies that are followed with respect to employees are not an exception. Nearly 41.5% of manufacturing industries pay yearly increments whereas 80.4% of service industries pay increments regularly. Approximately, 53.8% of the goods producing industries follow strict rules to replace an employee. It is very high among service industries and as revealed it is 82.7%.

When ethical marketing practices are taken into consideration 87.3% of the manufacturing industries take measures to provide the best quality product. Cent per cent service industries make this kind of effort. Coming to providing information about the product, the cross tabulation reveals that 60.1% of the manufacturing and 98.6% of the service industries follow this. The table also depicts that 31.5% of the manufacturing industries and 83.6% of service industries take proactive steps towards pollution control.

Table 3

Ethical Pracices with reference to the Type of the firm

	Manufacturing	Service
Paying yearly Increments	41.5	80.4
Replacing Employees as per rules	53.8	82.7
Trying to provide best quality products	87.3	100
Providing Information to the customers	60.1	98.6
Proactive steps for environmental protection	31.5	83.6
Abiding by Legal formalities	57.4	49.3
Contribution to social welfare	41.1	53.7

However, with respect to the legal compliance manufacturing industries depict a slight edge over service industries. The percentages of the firms following legal formalities are 57.4% and 49.3% respectively. Another aspect of the study is making charitable contributions for the community. Approximately, 41.1% of goods producing industries make them. It is significantly higher in service industries and stand at 63.2%.

Table 4

	Manufacturing	Services
Pay bribery in Govt office	36.1	69.2
Bribery for business loans	43.3	67.4
Political Influence	57.3	60.1
Not Paying bank loans promptly	18.8	31.2
Not Paying to suppliers	23.3	11.4
Paying chandas	14.4	40.1

The study of various unethical practices brings out slightly different results. The bribery practices are high among service industries. Only 36.1% of manufacturing entrepreneurs are encouraging the practice of bribing the government officials to expedite their works whereas 69.2% of service industries are doing that. Paying bribe for securing business loans also demonstrate the same pattern. 43.3% of manufacturing industries and 67.4% of service industries have this unethical practice.

As far as using political or other influence for securing business loans is concerned the table does not show much variation between both the categories. The percentages are 57.3%, and 60.1% for manufacturing and service industries respectively. The manufacturing industries are paying the business loans promptly compared to service industries. Only 18.8% of them are not making timely payments while 31.2% of service industries come under default list.

Making delayed payments to suppliers is another aspect of unethical behavior. It is revealed that 23.3% of the owners of manufacturing industries agree that they follow this unethical practice and 11.4% of service industries exhibit this tendency. The payment of incidental amounts to outlaws is higher among service industries compared to manufacturing industries (40.1% and 14.4% respectively).

Association of ethical practices of the organizations with reference to the seniority of the firms

The entrepreneurs newly stepping into the business demonstrate dissimilarities with those who stayed in the business for longer time. The euphoric spirit, optimistic attitude and desire for success slowly and steadily get converted into practical approach towards life "Experience is the best teacher". The views about rules, regulations, society, social norms, community, environment and government mat subject lot of metamorphosis according to the rules of sustenance. Therefore it can be hypothesized that the ethical practices prevail in a better way among new firms compared to the firms which have been established long before. In the senior firms we may see certain practices which were set up out of experience.

In order to study how the ethical practices might vary between established and newly started business ventures the organizations were classified as firms established within 5 years and the firms having more than 5 years of age. The tabulated values reveal that 48.1% of young firms pay yearly increments whereas the percentage is 63% in case of senior firms. The higher percentage of senior firms strictly follows the rules for replacing the employee (74.3%) compared to their younger counterparts as only 55.2% of these firms give a serious thought for the formal replacement mechanism. Coming to the marketing aspects of the firms, the senior junior differentials are not muchnoteworthy. Apparently cent per cent of the newly entered firms take all measures to provide the best quality product while 91% of established firms have that practice. Another aspect considered for ethical commitment in marketing is providing the complete product information to the customer. As per the estimates 75.2% of young firms and 88.9% of senior firms provide right information to the customers.

Table 5

Association Between Ethical Practices and Experience of the Firms

	<=5	>5
Paying yearly Increments	48.1	63
Replacing Employees as per rules	55.2	74.3
Providing best quality products	100	91
Providing Information	75.2	88.9
Dispose waste in proper manner	23.3	66.2
Legal formalities	41.1	71
Contribution to social welfare	60.2	52.4

A very small segment of the young firms realizes its responsibility towards the environment. Only 23.3% of these firms take proactive measures toward protection of environment while 66.2% of senior firms take such measures. A significant percentage of established firms abide by the legal formalities while only 41.1% of new firms follow this practice. However, the charitable contributions are made almost equally by both the groups (60.2% and 52.4% for new firms and established firms respectively).

Newly established firms show higher tendency of corrupt practices. Approximately, 59.4% of them involve offer bribes for government officials at various levels to get the work done. The percentagc is 33.2% for their counterparts. The bribery of small young firms towards business loans go up to 64.3% and that of senior firms is 28.8%. Using political or other kind of influence in order to expedite the works or to secure business loans is equally practiced by both the categories as the percentages are 61.3 and 58.5 respectively.

Table 6

Association of Unethical practices with reference to the experience of the firms

	<=5	>5
Pay bribery in Govt. office	59.4	33.2
Bribery for business loans	64.3	28.8
Political Influence	61.3	58.5
Not Paying bank loans promptly	11.3	32.5
Not Paying to suppliers	61.9	10.7
Paying chandas	5.9	43.1

The newly established firms attach a great deal of importance for paying the bank installments promptly compared to the established firms. The percentage of default borrowers conspicuously stands at 11.3%, while that of its counterpart is 32.5%. Surprisingly, the established firms are ahead in making timely payments to the suppliers. A mere 10.7% of firms do not make the payments in time while in the case of new firms almost 61.9 are subject to this unhealthy practice.

Making payments for the outlaws is more prevalent in established firms as 43.1% of them have such practices. It is somehow less for new firms. It is praiseworthy to note that only 5.9% of new firms indulge in those activities.

Inferences of the study

The research reveals that the small industries maintain low levels of ethical standards. Generally threatened by the persisting problem of high mortality rate small industries find it unable to pay proper attention towards all the stakeholders. To fight out the incidental problems they resort to several compromises with the ethical principles and policies.

The study brings out the fact that the ethical practices do differ on the basis of form of ownership, the type of the activity taken up by the firm and the total business experiences of the firm.

In India the small scale industry is dominated by sole proprietorship firms. More than 85% of per cent of firms are run under sole proprietorship. These businesses do not have a separate legal identity. The owners are subject to unlimited liability. Their capacity to mobilize finances, to stay safe in the turbulent market conditions is very less. Their capacity to attract professionally qualified people is also questionable. All these issues drive the firms towards unethical practices. They dilute their commitment towards the stakeholder. On other hand limited companies have monitoring and control. They have to implement foolproof practices like maintaining records, make disclosure according to statutory needs.

The ethical practices of the firms reflect the difficulties they encounter in the present business scenario. The lack of fund mobilizing capacity pushes them towards default in repaying the loans, having connections with outlaws or not paying suppliers in time etc. But at the same time even limited companies are completely not away of such practices like corruption or using political influence etc.

These issues therefore have to be understood in the backdrop of the socio economic conditions, and the culture of our country. Business is just a subset of environment. It gets affected by the forces that condition the environment. The study also explores that compared to manufacturing industries service industries have more ethical practices. Many a time the entrepreneurs of these industries are highly qualified. In the absence of many professionals in the firm small businesses are like one man show. The business appears as a mirror image of the entrepreneur himself. In addition to that the existence of educated and qualified employees may compel the entrepreneur to abide by rules. It reveals the fact that ethical practices to certain extent vary by demographic profiles also.

However it is really shocking to note that the service industries are not showing any deep commitment of keeping away from unethical practices. The bribery practices, using influence for securing business loans is more common in these firms. Many times it is found that they are loan defaulters.

It may be an example of their dual value system. The study also proves that the seniority of the firm in the industry makes it to refine its practices, follow rules and feel the responsibility towards the stakeholders. It can be concluded that if the businesses are allowed to sustain for a longer period in the market by strengthening the incubators and the needed support system, if they are helped out properly in the times of difficulties definitely the ethical practices get enhanced.

Limitations

No research is an exception of limitations. The main limitation of the study is the sample number. The study is confined to a very small number of organizations. Majority of the industries were selected from a small part of the city which is an industrial area. It is expected that a more dispersed large sample is desirable for more reliable results. But due to resource and capacity constraints the researcher could not take it up. Researchers had a desire to extend the same analysis and see how the ethical practices differ by male female ratios, turnover of the firms and the educational qualification or professional qualifications of the entrepreneurs. But because of the constraint of length of the paper, the present study is confined to only few aspects of the entrepreneurs.

References

1. Elkington,J.(1997). Cannibals with Forks: The Triple Bottom Line of 21st Century Business. London: Capstone.
2. Hafrey,L.(2007). Small Business Ethics. IPA's Business Today, 2, 1.
3. Jamie D. Collins, Klans Uhlenbrut. "Why firms engage in corruption, A Top management perpective". Journal of Business ethics. Vol. 87, No.1 June 2009.
4. Jenkins,H.M. (2004). Corporate social responsibility- engaging SMEs in the debate. New Academy Review, 3, 3: 76 – 95.
5. Justin Longenecker, Joseph A. Mc Kinney Corlos W. Moore. Journal of small Business Management. Vol. 27, 1989.
6. Economic Environment of Business, Mishra & Puri ; Himalaya Publication, 2006.
7. Entrepreneurial Development, S.S.Khanka; S.Chand Publication, 1994.

13

Innovation, Entrepreneurship, Job Creation, Based on Incubators: International Experience

Abstract

The aim of this paper is to investigate, and to identify key critical factors that facilitate the outcomes of successful implementation of incubators such as innovation, entrepreneurship, and job creation. To achieve the aim, the research uses a mixed method approach consisting of survey questionnaire and multiple case studies. Specifically, eight case studies were conducted and data was mainly collected through electronic survey and organisational documents. The research findings suggest that there are four best practices for the implementation of incubators: 1) creating jobs and wealth, 2) fostering a community's entrepreneurial climate, 3) business creation and retention, and 4) financial module. The research adds value to current literature on incubator sustainability, benefits, and outcomes. It provides useful guidelines to both academicians and practitioners through experiences of worldwide incubator implementations.

Introduction

Countries and regions around the world are striving to be successful in today's dynamic global economy. Amid economic and political turbulence, each nation is looking for ways to improve and sustain its economy and to create more wealth for its citizens. With unemployment figures in many countries reaching all-time high, an urgent need is to create jobs. Creating a conducive environment for economic development, understandably, requires the presence of a supportive environment for start-up businesses. One of the most notable enterprises designed to support such initiative is "business incubators". EURP, 2010 define Business incubators as are programs designed to accelerate the successful development of entrepreneurial companies through an array of business support resources and services. These programs are developed and orchestrated by incubator management and offered both in the incubators and through their network of contacts.

According National Business Incubator Association (NBIA, 2010; Al-Mubaraki, 2008) the Incubators vary in the way they deliver their services, in their organizational structure, and in the types of clients they serve. Successful completion of a business incubation program increases the likelihood that a start-up company will stay in business for the long term. Historically, 87% of incubators that complete the program stay in business (Info DEV, 2009). (Monkman, 2010) Incubation originating in the United States over 50 years ago, worldwide incubation programs now include over 7,000 incubators worldwide.

The first business incubator, a privately owned for-profit centre, was started in Batavia, New York in 1959 (Brown, 2000). The concept of business incubators took off slowly with universities becoming the breeding ground for such development for the next twenty years (Smilor and Gill, 1986). In the beginning of 1973. The United States National Science Foundation supported a series of experiments with innovation centres through its Experimental Research and Development Program (Scheirer, 1985). By 1981, the program had expanded to include eleven centres which served as the basis for continuing university effort to turn research into innovative new businesses (Allen, & Weinberg, 1988).

The objective of this paper is to discuss and analyze the outcomes of successful implementation of incubator program. It will focus three specific outcomes namely, innovation, entrepreneurship, and job creation.

The paper is structured as follows: Section 2 provides a thorough review of the literature on incubator outcomes such as innovation, entrepreneurship, and job creation. In Section 4, we provide the survey results and eight successful case studies to illustrate different key performance such as value added incubators. In Section 5, we briefly discuss the guidelines drawn from quantitative and qualitative approaches of incubators. Section 6 concludes with implications of the innovation, entrepreneurship, job creation as incubators outcomes from successful countries.

Literature Review

Incubators: Overview

As stated in the introduction, the first incubator, a privately owned for-profit centre, was founded in 1959 in Batavia, New York (Brown, 2000). One of its tenants was a poultry producer and it is believed that this is where the name "incubator" was conceived (McKee, 1992). The incubator concept soon spread internationally. One of the first incubators in Europe was established at Cambridge Science Park and Sophia Antipolis in France in the late 1960s (Storey and Tether, 1998). The dispersion of incubators to the rest of Europe was relatively slow. The concept spread in United Kingdom (UK) more quickly with Business Innovation Centres (BIC) being developed more than 20 years ago (OECD, 1999). BICs and Science Parks are part of a continuum of such services offered in the UK. The only distinction between them is that Science Parks usually have formal and operational links to academic institutions while BICs being property-based initiatives, do not have these links (Storey and Tether, 1998).

In Europe, a uniformly accepted definition of business incubators does not exist (Monck, 1988) although they appear to apply the same model as seen in the United States (Colombo and Delmastro, 2002). A variety of names have been applied to these centres including Science Parks, Business Innovation Centres, Technology Centres, and Research Centres (Storey and Tether, 1998; Monck, 1988; Lindelof and Lofsten, 2002). The first incubator in Germany was built in Berlin (Berliner Innovation-und Grundersentrum-BIG) in 1983. It was set up jointly by the government and the Technical University to commercialise technology projects (OECD, 1999, p.49). The incubator concept was spread nation-wide, driven by city councils. German incubators are monitored by a special government program (Arbeitsgemeinschaft Deutscher Technologiezentren), which was established as part of the unification between East and West Germany and the economic restructuring of East Germany (OECD, 1999). As of 1999, there were 103 incubators in the east and 27 incubators in the west. Incubators are commonly linked with business support networks and technological innovation programs. Small business incubation is a dynamic process where young firms are nurtured to help them survive and grow during periods of uncertainty, particularly during the start-up phase. Incubator generally aids in the growth of new ventures (Campbell, 1989; Petree, 1997).

Incubators fosters technological innovation and industrial renewal (Allen and Rahman, 1985; Similor and Gill, 1986; Allen and McCluskey, 1990; Mian, 1996). In addition, it is supporting regional development through job creation (Allen and Levine, 1986; Mian, 1997; Thierstein and Wilhelm, 2001; Roper, 1999). National Business Incubation Association, 2010 (NBIA) estimates that there are now more than 7,000 business incubators worldwide. It is expected that the number will continue to grow as other nations also are looking in to business incubators as a way to stimulate economic growth (Monkman, 2010). There are more than 1000 incubators in Asia (European Commission Enterprise Directorate General, 2002; Lalkaka, 1996; Lalkaka, 2003).

Recently, in Europe alone, NBIA estimates there are more than 1,800 business incubation programs. The European Commission provides funding to nearly 160 business incubation programs, referred to as "Business Innovation Centres." In 2008, the EC invested just over $8,500 for each job created by a BIC. As referenced previously, the cost per job created by business incubators in the

United States tends to be much lower.

Today, in the United Kingdom, more than 300 business incubation programs are in operation. These programs directly support 12,000 companies while 40,000 additional firms experience indirect benefits from this support. Business incubators in the U.K. are credited with creating more than 50,000 jobs (NESTA 2010). Furthermore, the German Incubation Association of Technology (ADT, 2010) reveals that Germany currently has approximately 7,500 clients within its approximately 350 incubators. These firms have created about 56,000 jobs.

Germany's 9,000 graduate firms also employ 90,000 people – not including people hired after these firms have graduated from the incubator programs. Based on statistics from incubation associations in the United Kingdom and Germany, there are more incubation programs per capita in these nations than those in the United States (Monkman, 2010).

Innovation, Entrepreneurship, Job Creation based on Incubators

Innovation is the process of making change, difference and novelty in the products, services, add values and business manner to create economic and social benefit (EC, 2010). The OECD (2010) defines innovation as the implementation of a new or significantly improved product, service, process, a new marketing method, or a new organizational method in business practices, workplace organization or external relations the importance of innovation within the economic cycles, considered entrepreneurship with a specific emphasis on innovation. Innovation deals with: 1) new products, 2) new production methods, 3) new markets, and 4) new forms of organization.

Therefore, while the basic concepts of entrepreneurship, innovation and incubation and the associated terminology must be commonly accepted and shared, when putting into practice actions towards the creation of new IBIs (EC, 2010). EBN, 2010 was reported more than 25 years of practices and policies, lessons have been learned on the concept of innovation-based incubation and more specifically on the concept of innovation-based incubators (IBI). Today, it is possible to understand what are the key elements of their success, what to take into consideration as the tool to strengthen and carry out policies for innovation and SME support, and entrepreneurship (EC, 2010).

In 2010, the Strategy for American Innovation (White House, 2010) will shape the ideas and technologies suitable for building the 21st century. Innovation will create new jobs and catalyze broadly shared economic growth. The strategy consists of three parts: 1) to invest in the building blocks of American innovation and to ensure that the economic tools for successful innovation from research and development to transfer of those innovations, 2) to promote competitive markets that spur productive entrepreneurship to allow companies to be internationally competitive in innovation, and 3) to catalyze breakthroughs for national priorities. Innovation is the driver of our future growth (White House, 2010; EURP, 2010; EBN, 2010; EC, 2010 and Joseph and Eshun, 2009). This requires improving the quality of our education, strengthening our research performance, promoting innovation and knowledge transfer throughout the Union, making full use of information and communication technologies, and ensuring that innovative ideas can be turned into new products and services that create growth, quality jobs and help address European and global societal challenges. But, to succeed, this must be combined with entrepreneurship, finance, and a focus on user needs and market opportunities (EC, 2010).

Innovation-based incubators are local economic development tools (EURP, 2010; Al-Mubaraki and Busler, 2009; Joseph and Eshun, 2009;

Al-Mubaraki and Busler, 2010), which favoring the conditions for creation and growth of novel business activities, contribute actively to the development of the regions where they operate. In addition, innovation-based incubators support innovative business projects which could be either technologically-oriented or non-technologically oriented. Technology therefore is not the only unit on which to measure the degree of innovation of a business idea (EC, 2010).

NBIA, 2010 defines the incubation is a process which tends to be activated whenever there is a need to support entrepreneurs in developing their own business. The process, or parts of it, is to put in place whenever there is a need of nurturing would-be entrepreneurs to think over and further develop the business idea and transforming it into a viable and sustainable activity. There are three stages of incubation (NBIA, 2010; EURP, 2010; Al-Mubaraki, 2008):

1. Pre-incubation, relates to the overall activities needed to support the potential entrepreneur in developing his business idea, business model, and business plan, and to boost the chances to arrive to an effective start-up creation.

2. Incubation, concerns with the support given to the entrepreneur from the start-up to the expansion phase. Typically this is a mid-term process, lasting usually for the first three years of activity of the newly established company, which are the years in which it is safe to say whether the new venture is successful and has a good chance to develop into a fully mature company.

The actions activated generally are access to finance, direct coaching and mentoring services, as well as hosting services and specific training. Therefore, physical incubation, although a very important service, is a subset of the overall incubation process.

3. Post-incubation, relates to the activities to be carried out when the company has reached the maturity phase, and therefore is ready to walk on its own feet. The company will leave the incubator, if it has been physically incubated. Innovation-based incubators work in the intersection between the sets of innovation and entrepreneurship supporting entrepreneurs to profit from the added value of innovative ideas.

Incubators provide new high-tech venture creation, technological entrepreneurship, commercialization, and transfer of technology (Mian, 1994 and 1997; Phillips, 2002; McAdam and McAdam, 2008; Al-Mubaraki, 2008). According to (Monkman, 2010; NBIA, 2010) for 50 years, incubators have been helping entrepreneurs turning their ideas into viable businesses, promoting innovation, and creating jobs by providing emerging companies with business support services and resources tailored to young firms to increase their chances of success. Business incubators nurture the development of entrepreneurial companies, helping them survive and grow during the start-up period, when they are most vulnerable. These programs provide their client companies with business support services and resources tailored to young firms. The most common goals of incubation programs are creating jobs in a community, enhancing a community's entrepreneurial climate, retaining businesses in a community, building or accelerating growth in a local industry, and diversifying local economies.

European Business and Innovation Centre (BIC) observatory report (EBN, 2009) BIC are playing a leading role in Europe and supported more than 67,700 business plans. BICs have directly assisted the creation of more than 31,700 new jobs, and have identified more than 66,900 enterprises creation projects. More than 17,400 new innovative enterprises were created with the assistance of this centre. More than 15,300 tenants (enterprises) are located in the BICs incubators, supporting more than 92,200 jobs. The average survival rate of the enterprises supported by this centre is 89% (EBN, 2009).

Many reports by European demostrate (EBN, 2009; OCDE, 2010) that EBN network is instrumental in shaping the knowledge-based economy of the future, anchored in value-added jobs, robust economic models, technology and innovation-based enterprises, academic spin-off, dynamic clusters and efficient accelerators of the "Growth and Jobs" challenge. BICs are organisations which promote innovation and entrepreneurship. They help enterprises to innovate; they drive the creation of start-ups (support to innovation, incubation and internationalisation) and they promote economic development through job and enterprise creation and development.

Today, according to various reports from Europe (EBN, 2009; OCDE, 2010) the innovation R&D spending in Europe is below 2%, compared to 2.6% in the US and 3.4% in Japan, mainly as a result of lower levels of private investment. The aim of this is to re-focus R&D and innovation policy on the challenges facing our society. Every link needs to be strengthened in the innovation chain, from 'blue sky' research to commercialisation. The essential benefits of economic growth should reach the public because the direct relationship between the innovation, entrepreneurship and job creation is based on incubators (EBN, 2009; OCDE, 2010).

Research Methodologies

This study concentrates on a specific context, i.e. the innovation, entrepreneurial, job creation outcomes from incubators, making the case study method most appropriate. The investigation and analysis of literature is an accepted form of desk based research that compares the works of different authors (Hart, 1998). This type of approach is closely linked to mixed methods approach quantitative (survey questionnaire) and qualitative (multi-case studies, literature review) with qualitative research (Bryman and Bell, 2007).

This approach allows a broader assessment of a particular and real situation (Yin, 2004). Ronson (Saunders, 2003, p.93) defined case study as "a strategy for doing research which involves an empirical investigation of a particular contemporary phenomenon within its real life context". The case study allows researchers to gain an in-depth understanding of the phenomenon under investigation (Yin, 2009). Furthermore, it provides both an understanding of the research context and a rich insight into the issue being examined (Eisenhardt, 1989; Yin, 1994).

The objective of this research is to develop guidelines from best practices globally (Bryman and Bell, 2007) and identify the key critical factors that facilitate the successful implementation of incubators outcomes such as innovation, entrepreneurship and job creation. Moreover, the strategy in this research is linked to research based on a multi-case studies and survey questionnaire. It is important to identify key success conditions and factors that will develop better understanding of how innovation, entrepreneurial, job creation outcomes from incubators programs that are successfully managed, adopted, and implemented.

Survey Results

The survey questionnaire was intended to provide quantifiable information on the characteristics of business incubators around the world, including age of incubators, client catchment areas, location of incubators, primary functions and priority goals, sponsoring entities and stakeholders and client performance. The case studies were intended to collect more in-depth information about the operation and incubator outcomes such as innovation, entrepreneurship, job creation by drawing on the views and experiences of best practice. Of the 711 survey invitations that were emailed to NBIA members, 43 were returned as undeliverable, leaving a sample frame of 668. The total number of survey responses was 105, representing a response rate of about 16 percent. However, only 45 were completed in full, so data are available for less than 105 respondents on many of the variables.

Age of Incubators

A total of 79 respondents provided information on the time period when their incubator was founded. Nearly three-quarters (73 percent) had been founded in the period since 1996, with more than half (53 percent) founded between 2001 and 2006. Only about 14 percent of respondents (N = 11) said that their incubators had been founded before 1990. Overall, these results indicate that many business indicators are very well established, and it can be concluded that they are likely to be a contributing value to the economics and communities where they are based.

Type of Incubators

The 45 respondents who reported constituted the majority of their clients having the largest percentage (40 percent, N = 18) said that they were from urban areas, 31 percent (N = 14) from suburban areas, and 22 percent (N = 10) were from rural areas. Close to 16 percent (N = 7) said that they served a national catchment area, but very few (4.4 percent, N = 2) indicated they were multinational in scope.

Location of Incubators

A total of 78 respondents answered this question, of which 66 percent (N = 52) were from the United States and the rest were broadly distributed over the globe. Twelve (23 percent) incubators were located in developing countries.

Priority Goals of Incubators

Respondents were surveyed on the primary program function of their incubators. Less than half among them (N = 40, 43.96 percent) indicated that the primary purpose of their incubator was to foster the development of technology companies. This is followed by more than a third (N = 33, 36.26 percent) who indicated their program could best be described as supporting a mixture of businesses (i.e, mixed-use incubators). The rest described their programs as service-business oriented (N = 4, 4.4 percent), web-related (N = 3, 3.3 percent), manufacturing and community revitalization (N = 2, 2.2 percent), or others (N = 7, 7.69 percent).

Sponsoring Entities and Stakeholders

Seventy-five out of 79 respondents indicated they had a primary sponsoring entity, with academic institutions accounting for a third of all sponsors, followed by government agencies (N = 19, 25.33 percent). Economic development organizations also accounted for a significant number (N = 16, 21.33 percent) of sponsoring entities.

Client Performance

Respondents were asked the most likely reason that led to the graduation of clients from their incubator programs. A total of 45 respondents answered this question. The most common reasons given were outgrowing the space, spending the maximum time allowable, and having reached mutually agreed milestones (N = 30), followed by growth rate exceeding the limits of the program and achieving a liquidity event (N = 16). Acquiring an experienced management team (N = 9) and attracting another source of funding (N = 6) were the least common reasons for graduating.

Case Study Results

Usa Case Studies

Brief description

Technology continues to be the driving force for the new economy and is critical to Maryland's future. Maryland is richly endowed with technology assets – the largest concentration of federal laboratories of any State in the nation, nationally recognized research universities, a federal contractor base with a specialty in science, security and communications, and an emergent biotechnology cluster. The Maryland Technology Development Corporation (TEDCO) was created by the State Legislature in 1998. First, to assist in transferring to the private sector and commercializing the results and products of scientific research and development conducted by colleges and universities.

Second, to assist in the commercialization of technology developed in the private sector. Finally, to foster the commercialization of research and development and to create and sustain businesses throughout all regions of the State (TEDCO, 2010).

Key Performance Indicators: Entrepreneurs, Companies created, Jobs created, Incubator

RTI International (2007) conducted a comprehensive study of the

(TEDCO). Maryland currently has 19 Maryland technology incubators and seven proposed incubator projects. The key results and findings of RTI international are summarized below. All figures are related to TEDCO in 2006. 1) The gross increased in state of Maryland by $1.2 billion, 2) The total annual employment impact of technology incubators was 14,044 jobs, 3) New jobs contributed $845 million in annual salary, 4) The technology incubators in the state increased the state and local tax revenue by approximately $104 million per year, 5) Gross state product contributions totaled $1.2 billion to increase state output by $2.7 billion per year, 6) Contributed $104 million in state and local taxes, 7) For every $1 of incubator assistance funding provided by TEDCO tenant, companies contributed $1,800 dollars to Maryland's gross state product, and 8) TEDCO made an average investment of $120 per incubator company job.

UK Case Studies

Brief description

The North East Business and Innovation Centre (BIC) started in 1994, when the make-up of the North East region, and British industry itself, was undergoing a transformation. Traditional industries were being resigned to the history books, and with this followed a great deal of uncertainty. Eventually, however, their demise led to a new breed of businesses. Organisations like the BIC began to emerge, and helped to set the foundations for the development of an enterprising and innovative culture in the region. Designed to nurture new businesses by providing access to a network of experts, accommodation and business support, the BIC opened in June 1994, providing a home for 22 businesses and support for many more region-wide. In 2010, the BIC site can accommodate over 160 businesses from a range of sectors, and covers a 14-acre site. Their business support team assists over 300 businesses in the startup process each year. (EURP, 2010; EBN, 2010; EBN, 2008; 2009; Vanrie, 2009).

Key Performance Indicators: Entrepreneurs, Companies created, Jobs created, Incubator

Key Performance Indicators of 2009 indicated the number of tenants in incubators was 105 employing a total of 911. The number of tenants since the beginning of the incubator was 489; the number of start-ups created in 2009 was 111; the figure for jobs created are 4,502. The number of jobs created in SMEs (client companies of BICs) were 85 with enterprise survival rate of 75%. A total of 155 enterprise creation projects were developed and 167 existing SMEs were supported during 2009 (EURP 2010; EBN 2010; EBN, 2008; 2009; Vanrie, 2009).

France Case Studies

Brief description

During the last decades, institutions of higher education all over the world have experienced a transformation by broadening their traditional mission of teaching, research, and public service to include a more active participation in their region's economic development. This is the case of the University of Bourgogne which in 1999 decided to create with 7 other key regional stakeholders, PREMICE: "Pôle de Ressources et de Management de l'Innovation et de la Création d'Entreprises". PREMICE was founded in 2000 by French Research Ministry, Regional agencies and economic entities and the University of Bourgogne (EURP, 2010; EBN, 2010; Vanrie, 2009).

PREMICE mission is to promote, encourage and develop high innovative and technology firms companies based on university or R&D centres discoveries. For that reason, the centre works intensively with universities and research centres in the region, in order to identify new ideas that have commercial potential and help to bring them to the market. Moreover, PREMICE have extended its services to SMEs in the region which are involved in innovative activities. (EURP 2010; EBN 2010; Vanrie 2009).

Key Performance Indicators: Entrepreneurs, Companies created, Jobs created, Incubator

Results confirmed that incubator programs in France in 2007 assisted 15 entrepreneurs and since the start of BIC, 25. In 2007, 17 companies were formed creating 112 jobs; cumulatively 44 companies were created with BIC support generating 155 jobs. The number of companies in the incubator in 2007 was 11 which created 44 jobs and graduated 75 companies (EBN, 2008; 2009; Vanrie 2009).

Germany Case Studies

Brief description

Anwendungszentrum GmbH Oberpfaffenhofen (AZO) incubation centre is located in Bavaria in Oberpfaffenhofen, near Munich. The region has a population of 12,520,000 and approximately 560,000 companies. Anwendungszentrum GmbH Oberpfaffenhofen –AZO has helped to found

38 companies and create 650 new jobs since 2002. Phase I ran as a German Aerospace Center (DLR) project between 2002 and 2005 and was one of the most successful business incubators in the European aviation industry. The AZO Incubation Centre accepts ten incuabtees per year for duration of four years until 2013. Their 2005-2009 funding was •1,842,000 (EURP, 2010; EBN, 2008; 2009; 2010).

Key Performance Indicators: Entrepreneurs, Companies created, Jobs created, Incubator

Key Performance Indicators of 2009 indicated that the number of tenants in incubators were 3 out of a total of 16 employed. The number of start-ups created in 2009 were 6; however, figures for jobs created are not available. The number of jobs created in SMEs (client companies of BICs) were 16 with Enterprise Survival Rate of 100%. Six enterprise creation projects were developed and 10 existing SMEs were supported during 2009 (EBN, 2008; 2009).

Spain Case Studies

Brief description

BIC Berrilan is a non-profit-making Public Limited Company, founded in 1993 by a group of public and private bodies in accordance with the 'Business and Innovation Centre (BIC)' model of the European Commission. BIC Berrilan aim is to promote the self-generation of wealth and employment in Gipuzkoa through the creation of innovative businesses with capacity for growth and long-term stability and the incorporation of innovation in existing SMEs. The centre does this by means of active industrial promotion, the mobilisation of resources and the competitive added value contribution and the incorporation of innovation in existing SME (EURP, 2010; EBN, 2010, Vanrie, 2009).

Within the creation of the Basque Network of Science, Technology and Innovation, BIC Berrilan is an intermediate agent which facilitates and enables the Technology and Knowledge transfer processes to the market through the creation of innovative and technology based start-ups and the incorporation of innovation in SME's. BIC Gipuzkoa Berrilan's main objectives are to be the preferred instrument for qualified entrepreneurs as a support for the creation and development of innovative, technology-based businesses and to be recognised for guaranteeing the satisfaction of customers, partners and collaborators, as well as its own workforce. (EURP, 2010; EBN, 2010; Vanrie, 2009).

Key Performance Indicators: Entrepreneurs, Companies created, Jobs created, Incubator

Results confirmed that since the start of BIC, 163 incubator programs in Spain during 2007 assisted 33 entrepreneurs. In 2007, 23 companies were formed creating 99 jobs; cumulatively 83 companies were created with BIC support generating 640 jobs. The number of companies in the incubator in 2007 was 23 and graduated 60 companies (EURP, 2010; EBN 2008; 2009; 2010; Vanrie, 2009).

Sweden Case Studies

Brief description

Innovatum Technology Park is a development centre packed with research projects and inspirational activities. It consists of a science centre, a project arena and an incubator. The incubator is an environment conducive for innovative ideas within three focus areas: production technology, clean tech and creative industry. Innovatum offers entrepreneurs a network of professional advisors, access to external financing and guidance through the complexity of managing a business. Since 2003 it is founded in Trollhättan, Sweden by Governmental funding, more than 40 companies have developed and several of them are now working with international brands in a global market (EURP, 2010; EBN, 2010, Vanrie, 2009).

Key Performance Indicators: Entrepreneurs, Companies created, Jobs created, Incubator

Key Performance Indicators of 2009 indicated the number of tenants in incubators was 13 employing a total of 35. The number of start-ups created in 2009 was 6; however, figures for jobs created are not available. The number of jobs created in SMEs (client companies of BICs) was 20 with Enterprise Survival Rate of 85%. Twenty enterprise creation projects were supported during 2009 (EBN, 2008; 2009; Vanrie, 2009).

Portugal Case Study

Brief description

BIC Madeira was found in 1997 by Madeira Regional Government which main goal was to contribute to the diversification and growth of the economy in Madeira Autonomous Region, focusing specifically on innovative business activity and entrepreneurship promotion. Furthermore, The Madeira´s mission is to give a full range of support to promoters of innovative projects and ideas, for the creation and modernization of enterprises in all economic sectors. In addition, the main objective is the creation and promotion in Madeira Region of a new entrepreneurial culture of innovation and competitiveness. Finally, the Madeira main activity are 1) the promotion of entrepreneurship and business innovation, 2) is an instrument of regional development and optimizes public and private resources to support through their innovative nature, 3) economic relevance to wealth 4) job creation 5) economic diversification, and 6) on technology transfer as the innovation results and connections between research and development entities and the entrepreneurial activity. (EURP 2010; EBN 2010; Vanrie, 2009).

Key Performance Indicators: Entrepreneurs, Companies created, Jobs created, Incubator

Results confirmed that incubator programs in Portugal in 2007 assisted 11 entrepreneurs and since the start of BIC, 100. In 2007, 3 companies were formed creating 4 jobs; cumulatively 200 companies were created with BIC support generating 267 jobs. The number of companies in the incubator in 2007 was 11 generating 35 jobs and graduated 54 companies generating 172 jobs. (EURP, 2010; EBN, 2008; 2009; 2010; Vanrie, 2009).

Belgium Case Study

Brief description

Since 2005 the Wallonia government has been putting in place a new revival plan aimed at regenerating Wallonia's economy. This plan tries to 1) promote the setting up and development of new companies, 2) to stimulate economic activity through among other initiatives,3) a straightforward and attractive system of business incentives 4) promoting the entrepreneurship spirit. La Maison de l'Entreprise, a LTD founded in 1996 by two Economic Development Agencies with main activity is working with the companies for the revitalizing of the area. There are four different sites in Wallonia: Mons, Binche, Tournai and Enghien, and funded by the EU and the Ministry of Economic Affairs. (EURP, 2010; EBN, 2010, Vanrie, 2009).

Key Performance Indicators: Entrepreneurs, Companies created, Jobs created, Incubator

Results confirmed that incubator programs in Belgium in 2007 assisted

138 entrepreneurs and since the start of BIC, it has helped 1302 entrepreneurs. In 2007, 11 companies were formed creating 34 jobs; cumulatively 174 companies were created with BIC support generating 582 jobs. The number of companies in the incubator in 2007 was 46 generating 158 jobs and graduated 174 companies generating 582 jobs. (EURP, 2010; EBN, 2008; 2009; 2010; Vanrie, 2009).

Guidelines From International Countries Best Practice

An incubator is a place where the incubation activities are carried out, and where the would-be entrepreneurs and the existing SMEs find a suitable place, in terms of facilities and expertise, to address their needs and develop their business ideas, and transforms them into sustainable realities. Business incubation outcomes have been identified as a means of meeting a variety of benefits which may include:

1- Creating jobs and wealth: incubators are seen as effective tools for creating self-employment opportunities, conventional product or service companies, and high-growth companies. Incubators also are used to develop innovation, transfer technology, and impart an entrepreneurial spirit.

2- Fostering a community's entrepreneurial climate: flexibility and adaptability in a wide range of contexts and they are increasingly becoming centers for international interaction that help entrepreneurs get in contact with difficult to access overseas networks. However, it is symbolic places, bearers of the entrepreneurial climate. Finally, Incubators are places of communication to making them effective in numerous.

3- Business creation and retention Incubators also can be used to develop international networks of small- and medium-sized companies. Also incubator is a tool to gather and orchestrate existing forces to facilitate company creation.

4- Financial modle incubators is a financial module used for economic development this measured by the number of job created per year and the number of companies in the market. In addition, the total number of incubation is increasing gradually to reach 7000 programs around the world.

1. Conclusions and Reflection

It has been widely acknowledged that innovation, entrepreneurship, job creation are based on the incubators. Understanding the significance of successfully implementing of incubators in many countries. Incubator is a place where the incubation activities are carried out, and entrepreneurs find a suitable place, in terms of facilities and expertise, to address their needs and develop their business ideas, and transform them into sustainable realities.

Business incubation outcomes has been identified from international countries best practice which may include: 1) creating jobs and wealth, 2) fostering a community's entrepreneurial climate, 3) business creation and retention, and 4) financial modle. The authors in this paper have highlighted the importance of incubators as the innovation, entrepreneurship, job creation are based on the incubators and success tool of the of economic development as indicated specifically in sections 1, 2, 3,4 and 5 of this paper. Also, the authors have identified the guidelines from best practice of differences countries, as mentioned in section 6. Therefore, this paper attempts to provide a new line of thinking and further scope for researchers in areas of business incubation. The research findings suggest that there are four set of guidelines from international counties best practice. A full understanding of these incubators outcomes such as innovation, entrepreneurship and job creation, and the best practice guidelines to lead countries implementation successfully that are vital keys to reducing the risk of failure and increase of survival rate around 90%.

This paper is based on a mixed-method approach using both qualitative and quantitative methods, would provide a deeper insight and understanding into the phenomenon under investigation. Each case study has investigated, addressed and explained the Key Performance Indicators such as Entrepreneurs, Companies created, Jobs created, and Incubator companies graduated. For future research and from the findings that highlighted in this paper, the authors aim to conduct more case studies and survey on implementation of business incubation in different Middle Eastern and Gulf states. Hence the authors are planning to develop a model applicable to the GCC countries.

References

1. Allen, D.N. and Rahman, S. (1985). 'Small Business Incubators: A Positive Environment for Entrepreneurship'. Journal of Small Business Management, 23 (July): 12–22.
2. Allen, D. and Levine, V. (1986). Nurturing Advanced Technology Enterprises: Emerging Issues in State and Local Economic Development Policy. New York: Prager.

3. Allen, D.N., and Weinberg, M.L. (1988). 'State investment in business incubators'. Public Administration Quarterly, 12(2), 196–215.
4. Allen D.N. and McCluskey (1990). Structure, Policy, Services, and Performance in the Incubator Industry, Entrepreneurship, Theory and Practice, Winter 1990: 61-77.
5. Al-Mubaraki, H. (2008). "Procurement of International Business Incubation– Quantitative and Qualitative approaches". Melrose Books, United Kingdome. www.melrosebooks.com
6. Al-Mubaraki, H. and Busler, M. (2009). Business incubators: findings from worldwide survey and guidance for the G.C.C states. World Sustainable Development Outlook, 83- 91.
7. Al-Mubaraki, H. and Busler, M. (2010). "Business incubators: Findings from worldwide survey, and guidance for the G.C.C states". Global Business Review, Vol.11(1), January-April, 2010.
8. Al-Mubaraki, H., Al-Karaghouli, W. and Busler, M. (2010). "The Creation of Business Incubators in Supporting Economic Developments". European, Mediterranean & Middle Eastern Conference on Information Systems 2010 (EMCIS2010), April 12-13, 2010, Abu Dhabi.
9. Al-Mubaraki, H. and Busler, M. (2010). "Sustainable development through the inclusion of incubator: A SWOT analysis. World Sustainable Development Outlook; pp 51-63.
10. Brown, M., Harrell, M.P. and Regner, W. (2000). Internet Incubators: How to invest in the new economy without becoming as investment company, Business Lawyer, 56(1): 273- 284.
11. Bryman, A. and Bell, E. (2007). 'Business Research Methods'. 3rd ed. Oxford University Press.
12. Campbell, C. (1989). Change Agents in the New Economy, Business Incubators and Economic Development, Economic development Review, 7(2): 56-59
13. Colombo, M.G. and Delmastro, M. (2002). How effective are technology incubators? Evidence from Italy. Research Policy, 31: 1103-1122.
14. Eisenhardt, K. (1989). "Building theories from case study research". Academy of Management Review, Vol. 14 No. 4, pp. 532-50.
15. Europe business & innovation centre network EBN. (2009). Innovation with Vision Incubation in Action Networking by Passion. Access date August 1, 2010. Available online.http://www.ebn.eu/assets/assets/pdf/brochure%20corporate%20- %20version%2008.pdf.

16. Europe business & innovation centre network (EBN). (2010) the Smart Guide to Innovation-Based Incubators (IBI) Available online. http://ec.europa.eu/regional_policy/sources/docoffic/2007/working/innova tion_incubator.pdf.
17. European Business and Innovation Centre Network (EBN). (2008). BIC Observatory Facts and Figures.
18. European Business and Innovation Centre Network (EBN). (2009). BIC Observatory Facts and Figures.
19. European Commission (EC). (2010). "EUROPE 2020: A strategy for smart, sustainable and inclusive growth". Available online. http://ec.europa.eu/eu2020/pdf/COMPLET% 20EN% 20BARROSO% 20%20%20007%20%20Europe%202020%20-% 20EN % 20version. pdf. Access date August 1, 2010.
20. European Commission Enterprise Directorate-General (2002), Final Report Benchmarking of Business Incubators, Centre for Strategy & Evaluation Services.
21. European Union Regional Policy (EURP). (2010). The smart guide to innovation based incubators. Retrieved on August 5, 2010 from:
22. Http://www.ebn.eu/assets/assets/pdf/news/final_case-studies-nma- 07042010.pdf.
23. German Association of Technology Center (ADT), 2010. "Technology Incubation" Available on line: http://www.adt-online. ge. home-page.html.
24. Hart, C. (1998). Doing a literature Review: Releasing the Social Science Research Imagination. SAGE publications Ltd, London.
25. Info DEV. (2009). Mixed-use Incubator Handbook: A Start-up Guide for Incubator Developers. Retrieved on July 5, 2010, from http://www.infodev.org/en/Publication.733.html.
26. Joseph, P. and Eshun, Jr. (2009). Business Incubation as strategy, Business Strategy Series, 10(3), 156-166. Retrieved August 2, 2010, from ABI/INFORM Global. (Document ID: 1882777971). (2009).
27. Lalkaka, R. and Bishop, J. (1996). Business Incubators in Economic Development: an initial assessment in industrialising countries, United Nations Development Programme, New York, Organisation of American States, Washington DC, United Nations Industrial Development Organisation, Vienna.
28. Lalkaka, D. (2003). Best Practices in Asian Business Incubation. NBIA 17th International Conference on Business Incubation, Richmond, Virginia, May 20, 2003.
29. Lindelof, P. and Lofsten, H. (2002). Growth, management and financing of new technology –based firms-assessing value added

contributions of firms located on and off Science Parks, The International Journal of Management Science, 30: 143-154.

30. Maryland Technology Development Corporation (TEDCO), (May 20, 2010). Annual Report, fiscal year 2008, Development. Retrieved from ABI/INFORM Global. (Document ID: 1105634131),13(3), 454-468.
31. McAdam, M. and McAdam, R. (2008). 'High Tech Start-ups in University Science Park Incubators: The Relationship Between The Start-Up's Lifecycle Progression and Use of The Incubator's Resources'. Technovation, 28 (5): 277–90.
32. McKee, B. (1992). A boost for start-ups, Nations Business, August: 40-42.
33. Mian, S.A. (1994). 'Are University Technology Incubators Providing a Milieu For Technology- Based Entrepreneurship?' Technology Management, 1: 86–93.
34. Mian, S. (1996). Assessing the value-added contributions of university technology business incubators to tenant firms, Research Policy, 25: 325-335.
35. Mian, S. (1997). Assessing and managing the university technology Incubator: An Integrative Framework, Journal of Business Venturing, 12: 251-285.
36. Monck, C.S.P., Porter, R.B., Quintas, P., Storey, D.J. and Wynarezyk, P. (1988). Science Parks and the Growth of High Technology Firms, Croom Helm, London.
37. Monkman, D. (2010). Business Incubators and Their Role in Job Creation. President & CEO National Business Incubation Association (NBIA), Athens, Ohio. Retrieved on June 30, 2010 from www.n bia.org.
38. NBIA (National Business Incubator Association). (2010). Retrieved on May 26, 2010, from http://www.nbia.org/resource_library/faq/ #13.
39. NESTA. (2010). Business Incubation in Challenging Times. NESTA Policy Briefing, BI/29 (2008). Retrieved on May 7, 2010 from:
40. http://www.nesta.org.uk/library/documents/Business-incubators.pdf.
41. OECD (1999). Business Incubation- International Case Studies, Organisation for Economic Cooperation and Development Publications, Paris, accessed on August 2, 2010 from http://www.oecd.org.
42. OECD (2003). Organization for Economic Cooperation and Development 'OECD government studies: The government imperative', OECD Publishing.

43. OECD (2010). Ministerial report on the OECD Innovation Strategy. Innovation to strengthen growth and address global and social challenges Key Findings.
44. Petree, R., Petkov, R. and Spiro, E. (1997). Technology Parks-Concept and Organisation, Summary Report prepared for Center for Economic Development, Sofia, accessed 24/8/2002 at http://www.ced.bg.
45. Phillips, R.G. (2002). 'Technology Business Incubators: How Effective as Technology Transfer Mechanism?' Technology in Society, 24: 299–316.
46. Roper, S. (1999). 'Israel's Technology Incubators: Repeatable Success or Costly Failures'. Regional Studies, 33 (2): 175–80.
47. Saunders, M. Lewis, P. and Thornhill, A. (2003). 'Research Methods for Business Students'. 3rd ed. Financial Times/Prentice Hall, New Jersey.
48. Scheirer, M.A, Nieva V.F, Gaertner G.H, Newman P.D, and Ramsey, V. (1985). Innovation and Enterprise: A Study of NSF's Innovation Centres Program, Report prepared for the National Science Foundation, December.
49. Smilor, R.W. and Gill, M.D. (1986). The New Business Incubator: Linking Talent, Technology, Capital, and Know-How, Massachusetts: Lexington Books.
50. Storey, D.J. and Tether, B.S. (1998). Public Policy measures to support new technology based firms in the European Union Research Policy.
51. Thierstein, A. and Wilhelm, B. (2001). 'Incubator, Technology and Innovation Centres in Switzerland: Features and Policy Implications'. Entrepreneurship and Regional Development, 13 (4): 315–31.
52. Vanrie, P. (2009). "Case Studies A Survey of 14 BICs in Action" Europe business & innovation centre network (EBN).
53. White House. 2010. "A Strategy For American Innovation: Driving Towards Sustainable Growth and Quality Jobs". Available online. Access June 20.
54. http://www.whitehouse.gov/assets/documents/SEPT20 Innovation Whitepaper FINAL. pdf.
55. Yin, R. (1994). 'Case Study Research: Design and Methods'. 2nd ed. Sage publications. Newbury, CA.
56. Yin, R. (2004). 'The case study anthology'. 1st ed. Sage publications, Inc.
57. Yin, R. (2009). 'Case study research: Design and methods'. 4th ed. Sage publications, US.

14

Innovation Reconsidered: Industry Meeting Global Challenges

Abstract

Covering any aspect, India is developing dynamically. It's accompanying economic re-invention assigns comprehensive tasks to innovation. Adaptation is replaced by genuinely India-specific innovations – see e.g. Tatra. The entire performance cycle demands innovative changes: applying to the producing industry, to services, but also to public economy-related institutions. Innovations need be pro-active to enter worldwide markets. Innovative competition e.g. from China, the US and Europe is to be met. Innovation has to secure its base e.g. in material and human resources, namely education. In close co-operation with business and economy the innovation carrying infrastructure has to be built up by innovative measures, e.g. the use of mobile phones, or securing energy, transport and water supply. Entrepreneurial management of innovation includes the innovation of management itself. Preconditions of the innovative enterprise need be specified and developed: as well in the outer natural/ societal as in the inner organizational 'environments'. It is the 'environment' which shapes successful innovation. Innovative operation – structure follows process - will be supplemented by investment strategy as to ensure tomorrows innovativeness to open and develop markets. Innovation on sight acts as an investment into the future. Future challenges tie innovation likewise to technology and the product/ service/ market sector. A process of continuous constructive learning, it demands the 'Learning enterprise` as part of the learning Information Society. New forms of business conduct will emerge. Examples from business practice will be demonstrated.

Innovation is the pivot and the heart of enterprise. Entrepreneurial management of innovation includes the innovation of management itself. Preconditions of the innovative enterprise need be specified and developed: as well in the outer natural/societal as in the inner organizational 'environments'. It is the 'environment' which shapes successful innovation. Innovative operation – structure follows process - will be supplemented by investment strategy as to ensure tomorrows innovativeness to open and develop markets. Innovation on sight acts as an investment into the future. Future challenges tie innovation likewise to technology and the product/ service/ market sector. A process of continuous constructive learning, it demands the 'Learning Enterprise` as part of the Learning Information Society. New forms of business conduct will emerge.

Prologue: Function and Faces of Innovation

Innovation is essential to all life systems, so to the enterprise. Life and economic life are signified by change and *evolvement*; innovation embodies passive as well as pro-active adaptation. Innovate, or decline and perish. In ontogenesis as well as in phylogenies innovation represents directed growth and rejuvenation. The dictum applies to the individual as well as to society and societal institutions. It is therefore that the phenomenon entrepreneurial innovation must not be conceived as separate. Entrepreneurial innovation is closely networked with *social and societal innovation.*

What does *innovation* comprehend? It contains the answer to simple questions as: which performance on the market will earn which returns on investment within the next three, five, fifteen years? What products do you want to sell to whom? Where is your base in the general economy/ company set up? Or turning to the market: emerging markets provide new challenges, new chances. Will you invest more in expensive luxury goods or into cheap, durable and easy to serve mass products? Frames to decide from will be given by the phase of societal and economic development, the competition existing inside and outside India. Which challenges, which chances can be distinguished? Where is need, where are niches to fill profitably for both enterprise and the customers? In the next decades India will re-invent base societal and economic structures. Crisis's will occur, enterprises from other countries and continents will compete. How to stay operational and thriving, if not by steady innovation?

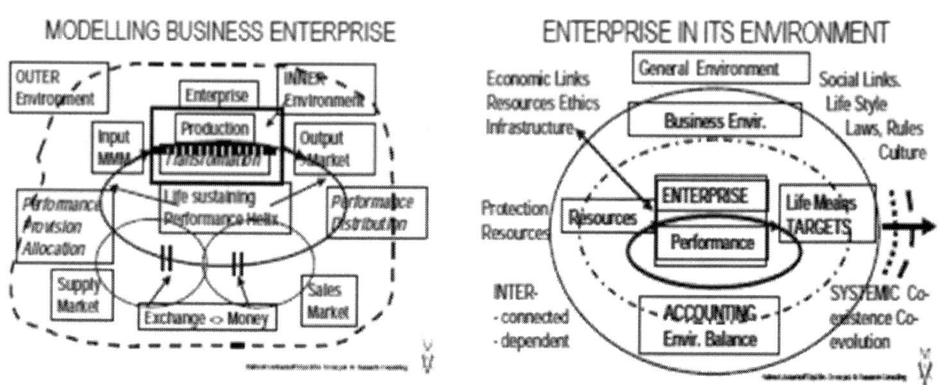

An entrepreneurial *concept of innovation* reflects and complements these aspects. Innovation begins with an idea, an idea might lead into an invention, which in turn is transferred into a product, a service. Such a potential 'product for market' is designed for customer preferences as it is constructed for economic production and for effective sales activity. It usually proves a long and troublesome, a costly way to the innovation ready for market entrance. If, and only if, the invention is sustainably accepted by the market it is truly rendered an 'innovation'. More than an established product, an innovative one needs be: – producible ; - useful for the customer – economic: cost and benefit in balance; and – affordable by the target market. It needs by a accepted solution for a problem to be solved or a desire of the customer to be fulfilled.

The *character of an innovative product* and the markets for its useful application is diverse and may be located in any sector of societal performance. For example a new ICT technique may affect machine control, the taxation systems or entertainment gadgets as well. How far the influence carries depends among others whether a limited *application product* or a general *methods and procedures innovation* is at stake. E.g. the battle between the big ICT companies rages mostly about procedure patents. Also the particular new performance aspect comes in a multitude of forms and applications. It may consist in cutting down waste or energy consumption, convert nuclear waste, facilitate handicraft work or simplify complex operation procedures. It may improve safety (in medicine technology) or reduce material input and weight in the construction of bridges (using textile instead of steel reinforcement). New sophisticated materials as different as smart fiber or nano-tubes carry the potential for vast changes in chip clothing respectively in chip production. The vastly differing examples show that innovation can – and by that *needs* - happen in any phase, concerning any aspect of any performance or activity cycle in economical and societal fields. Vice versa it endorses that any part of the societal systems needs innovation to cope with change and to meet challenges. Not only the merging countries need re-invent themselves economically as well as socially/societal. The old industrialized areas are forced to do so as well. The necessities in the background are the same: shortage of resources, of raw materials, of energy, of natural resources in particular as water and clean air. In the course of a rapidly technological civilization a fast growing *complexity*, differing rates of change and growth produce imbalances and tensions. The latter is often overlooked or underestimated (see Nano). In consequence, around a nucleus of performance, also the enterprise, has constantly to re-invent itself and in particular its (necessarily innovation focused) management. The paper will spotlight on the entrepreneurial side and the impacts of such a general environment e.g. on the entrepreneurial inner and outer environments.

Now from the technical/procedural aspect: *which elements do constitute an innovation?* Research into creativity has corroborated that novelties arise more often than not from *re-thinking basic assumptions* taken for granted so far. Innovation includes questioning the well established solutions as it does request to combine existing ones with new potentials. Innovation is seldom simple nor rooting in only one new technological or marketing feature. Normally a novel mode to devise a technical function will exploit the novel qualities of new materials *combining* them with new procedures and new techniques now possible to realize. They will fit into and eventually change an existing system, improving it to new improved qualities. Examples are provided by the ongoing development of the combustion engine, but also relating to the strategy not to pivot on the single automobile and its qualities but on the *entire system of mobility* instead. Another exemplification is given by systems in Middle and North European climates for house heating in wintertime. Novelties are transferred into useful application by the persistent innovative exploitation of given preconditions. The same applies to the *market attractiveness* – as e.g. the Apple I-Pod displays. Concerning markets the cost side must be taken into account, and what may be called the commodity or the value of emotional and show consumption.

For emerging countries in particular *high-tech* and *low-tech* may form a fruitful alliance. Cheap solar technology will help to local sources of electric energy, simple cooking devices use solar energy instead of scarce organic matter. *Cheap and foolproof* computers in various forms may upgrade the infrastructure, as the famous cheap mobile phones accomplished. The innovation, the construction and re-constriction of the *infrastructure* comes a very complex, intrinsically networked task implying virtually any kind of the social/societal system. In particular novel everyday commodity items need improve *locally (!) and countrywide* the base communication system. Water and energy provision as food production will be crucial points of departure for the development of the infrastructure.

The Enterprise: A Co-Learning, Innovating System

The base of creativity, of thinking in novel modes, of conceptualizing innovative products, is constituted by *learning*. Innovation in particular is the result of open, constructive learning (as contrasted to mere mimetic and repetitive learning). Degree, quality and consistency of learning determine failure and success of the enterprise, in particular in the medium and the long run. *Life systems, as the enterprise*, are equipped with a *memory holding a model of the past and the future of the system*. In case of the *company planning and control*, institutionalized memories as accounting store and learn from the *past performance and anticipate the future* open to business and to be realized by management. Accordingly, the concept of controlling assesses the results of past operation under the auspices of *potentials* open for the corporation policy in the future.

Simplified, *controlling* provides the base information on which fields of business operations need innovation as to meet challenges and chances in the future. These *incremental* innovation process is prompted by policies as *continuous improvement*, quality circles, logistics development and similar organizationally 'diagonal' team activities. It constitutes the fundament whereupon *basic innovations* changing the business will grow. Necessarily innovation qualifies a *continuous, ubiquitous, comprehensive, networked effort* pointing into the future. It does not suffice to be competitive today. The challenge is to secure to be *competitive tomorrow;* granted that competing companies will act the same way. To fail in the *competitive innovation race* e.g. by a gap in innovation may prove deadly. (Therefore informal monopolies and oligopolies conveniently 'smooth' the innovation path). The need for innovation pertains to the *entire performance cycle* of the enterprise and its long term foundations. In practice it is a closely *networked and balanced system of innovations* which drives the enterprise. The first innovation normally proves the driver for other complementing innovations. But consequentially any single or any succession of innovative changes will be linked by the power of factual networking to all other sectors. In particular the markets are involved: the *actual customer* as well as the *potential markets,* as the *demand* to be expected in the future. Today's innovation is the first step of a *strategic innovative path* to be commenced by *investments on sight* and to be finances (ideally) by the *operation profit.*

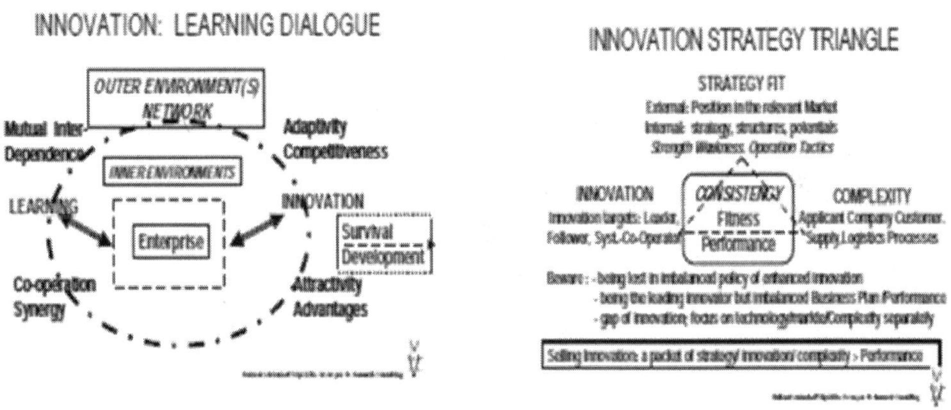

It must not be forgotten that innovations use *scarce resources* and bear a *risks.* Any innovative projects needs carefully be weighted. The key indicator to assess innovation is on the marketing side represented by *'value added' for the customer.* Fast, flexible and punctual delivery and service are an integral part.

On the operation side any phase of the productive cycle must contribute. But in consequence the innovation process increasingly includes customers and suppliers as immediate 'environments'. In some cases knowledge sharing leads to a close *co-operation* involving *joint ventures* in innovation. Another salient factor is the right point of time: if possible ahead of the competition and when the market changes. As aforementioned the actual innovation represents in but few cases *base innovations,* e.g. changing a technology. More frequent are *intelligent combinations,* complements, alterations of existing items brought into a *new performance context.* Knowledge organisation and *knowledge exchange* constitute a vital condition sine qua non for innovativeness. Within the enterprise the *'tacit knowledge'* needs be vitalized. To keep the capacity of the individual as well as of the institutions, stored knowledge ought be updated actually and regularly. Entrepreneurship on any level roots in *information exchange.*

In particular in the technology sector joint ventures between *universities, research institutes* (as Fraunhofer or Max Planck in Germany) acts as a mutually advantageous *transmission belts.* They connect demands from practice to research; and in reverse transfers research results into practice. Increasingly joint venture ripe innovative solutions taking advantage from a direct theory-practice dialogue.

The need to co-operate on a broad level gaining knowledge instantly fostered various concepts of *'open innovation'.* Namely small and middle sized enterprises (SME) co-operate in well defined areas, thus bundling scare resources for research and development. Joint ventures *sharing r&d capacities*, focussing on complementing performance segments, need a well balanced policy and mutual trust behind. The general idea throughout relies on avoiding double investments on the same field and profiting from different approaches to the same issue. In spectacular cases (Gold mining company, Proctor & Gamble) even the help of the general public has been included.

Inner and Outer Environments of the Innovative Enterprise

Research into creativity revealed environments as the decisive factor for creative innovation. Looking at the enterprise as a life system, an *inner* and an *outer* environment can be distinguished. The *inner environment* harbours the *performance metabolism*; the *outer environment* the preconditions offered by the 'world around' to exchange with information and energy that is resources. Both are closely connected by the *process of exchange*; the outcome of the performance gaining new resources to survive and hopefully strive and develop.

Innovation is requested, stimulated and driven by mutual networking. The *inner environment* roughly coincides with the performance cycle and the institutions/organization around. As indicated above, on the floor level *continuous improvement, quality control and other 'diagonal' services* provide an experience and data base for innovations in particular concerning the performance cycle. Vital comes the data flow along the *operation* processes. Report from *sales* will supply insight into customer satisfaction and market trends. Such institutional preconditions on the control facet furnish not merely the organizational frame and scaffold. They become vital and effective only when augmented by an *atmosphere encouraging* novel approaches, innovative ideas, even *unconventional musings.* 'Needs this be necessarily so? Or shouldn't it be done else wise?' It is this spirit, penetrating the enterprise from the CEO to the blue collar worker and the sale representative, to look openly and actively for new opportunities. It is *motivation* inherently mobilizing into novel considerations and proposals, transferred into innovative action.

Such an successfully creative atmosphere rests on a deliberate *policy* and on an appropriate *organisation.* Appraising in-company solutions as well as models offered by outside consulting firms some treats can be singled out. First, they involve every employee, *fostering self-responsibility,* individual learning, and what could be called an attitude of *conscious awareness* of the own person and of its professional duties. Second, management, namely personnel management, *appraisal and reward* systems are installed. A VP for Innovation and a specific training of middle management respectively the stewards on the floor will fill them with life. Third, the *culture arising* needs allow to make mistakes as not to curb motivation and mobilisation of tacit creativity. Controversial to hard reality as it may sound, even *creative isles of leisure* (!) are recommended. To *focus* faculties and capacities *innovation stages are carefully designed* from idea generation over testing and appraisals to inventions ready to be tested for market acceptance. Procedural designs range from models near to production *(design factory*) to establishing, on a philosophical and psychological behavioural grounding, a *creative atmosphere* (ex. IBM) prompting astonishing success stories. Hierarchy tends to erect barriers for creativity – as seems too, by the way, *forced* team working. It must be stressed, however, that to institute a sustainable, prolific state of the enterprise is precondition to integrate the creative innovation process.

It has also to be acknowledged that *innovation as a normal part of the business cycle* will take much efforts in *investment* and in time. *Relearning to learn continuously* can turn out a troublesome process, which needs be carefully und patiently be *guided and controlled.* Not least a turn to the consciously and focused innovative enterprise implies *'change management'* in the double sense: management centred on change; and changing the management itself to meet the demands of an innovative guidance and control. Such a change may include targeted *divestment* towards to shift capacities to future potentials.

Apart from 'virtual institutes' of shared co-operation as discussed above, the *outer environment* counts, concerning the preconditions of economic as well as social/societal exchange.

The general *atmospheric/mental state of the country,* well known to politicians, influences strongly the attitudes and the behaviour down to the production floor. Emerging countries furnish surprising positive examples, as do in reverse negative ones areas where *private initiative* is stifled. In European countries several *government and semi-government institutions support developmental projects* (as the electric car, battery or solar) to contribute initial investment to product fields not likely to be financed sufficiently by the private industry. The provision with adequate *venture capital* still is and will probably remain a problem. It is not the place here to discuss in detail the impact of *economic cycles and crisises* as the last and enduring one. They prove often deadly for however innovative start-ups without sound financial backing.

Crucial proves the *openness of the market.* In spite of anti cartel legislation markets are often by tacit understanding *closed to innovation from outside.* Innovations are turned down if not within a course of innovation scheduled by the company and affiliated oligopolies themselves. Restraining policies are to prevent that the power balance between competitors is disturbed. *Vested interests* and capital must not be endangered. To repeat: In open markets the right time of market approach and *market entrance* needs be carefully chosen. To succeed, an innovation must fit into the *entire network of relevant systems. Infrastructure* will be decisive not only for supply and sales markets, but e.g. for the cost, quality, logistics. It begins at the local market and the immediate product field. It may end at the international division of labour and the international technology race. Both are heavily influenced by *political intervention* and only partly if at all predictable. Cost per unit, the labour intensity of a product, trade rules, taxation and power targets will exert impacts. An increasingly difficult problem proves the *legal system(s);* the protection of patents, of *property rights.* To defend legal rights encounters high costs of access and the widespread (mis-)use of law and courts for policy.

Re-Inventing the Business: Innovating the Performance Cycle

Again, innovation affects necessarily the *entire value adding performance cycle.* Innovations of differing depth and at different phases of the process will change its innovative character, if not abruptly, then incrementally. Imbalances will occur. To eliminate them an in tendency complete *re-consideration of the business model* will be necessary. Or arguing from the business concept: it needs be continually tested concerning its constancy and aptness for the future.

The testing will retake into awareness the chances and risks the state of the inner and outer *potentials of the enterprise* and its business offer. Which performance capacities could be better employed, extended or adapted to market conditions? Which opportunities does the emerging – or changing or shrinking – market suggest? A most dangerous challenge appears a turnover driven too fast, neglecting traps not provided for e.g. in financing and organisation of business processes. In particular start ups need keep a keen eye on *core qualities* and competences, on *competitive advantages*, on the *appropriate management* and organisation. With the crises and the following recovery the well known priority choice became actual between *cost reduction* and *innovation.* A simple rule states that in saturated *market cost reduction* is presupposed, but gains can be won only by *innovative products.* Another often overlooked – and eventually tricky – choice can be to exploit the *scaling* effect before innovating. The decision depends on the developmental position of the product: on the short, the middle and the long term developmental curve. For mobile phones e.g. with little space for innovation left, scaling has become a complementing competition policy. The decisive question arising also here concerns whether the innovation should focus on *technology* or on the *price and performance/ service* market - or on both successively. The market for mobile phones (Blackberry) and I-pods holds striking lessons. The general lecture to be derived teaches, that innovations like any other business activity needs be *planned and controlled* (see below 4. Of this paper).

Precondition to *planned innovation* is a clear concept of the business and the enterprise carrying it. The *properties of markets* have to be defined, in particular as to their volatility in the middle and long range. They have to be scrutinized to their potentials for change in quality and quantity, for expansion or shrinking. *Business processes* are to be analysed and stream-lined. For innovative projects a specific *project management* is introduced. Ideally it covers, divided into *mile stones*, the stage-gate progress from the classical aspects: time, cost, results achieved, and project specific other aspects. A triviality should be reminded: *Any innovation is a special case to be treated as such.* An analysis will appropriately follow the performance process and its parameters as extensively investigated from market, production and technology aspects. In addition *inventions with innovation potential* need be assessed to their position in a scale.

Innovations begin with mere *adaptations* as the usual upgrading of products and end by *novelties*, displaying new technologies and/or opening new markets. A *product innovation* confined to one or more applications is to value differently from a *method and procedure* patent with a wide range of possible applications. Innovations but supporting or extending running concerns are to treat otherwise than those opening new potentials into the future. Quite another kind of innovations relate to what can be called *the sales and service periphery* of the product sold as immediate delivery, extended guarantee and the like. They belong to the complementary fields of marketing.

With economic change and innovation in the long run, or in some cases even at short notice, the *entire business model* may be at stake; a new business model is to be invented. Examples are provided e.g. in local marketing by local farmers. A company roasting coffee e.g. expanded to coffee and general food trade. Or re-thinking the business model of automotive industry from selling cars to providing mobility. Or the expanding and changing the business model by Amazon. Or the turn-around by IBM from production to services.–Outsourcing of essential parts of the performance process pose together with advantages eventually serious disadvantages. Foxconn for example actually produces the bulk of hardware for Apple and e.g. most of the mobile phone and entertainment electronics business. In the long run the supplier relation will foster a dependency on the cost and price frontier as well. It will, that is even more dangerous, transfer research and development and technological competence to the hardware supplier. Foreshortened: the *innovation authority* will be diminished if not lost.

Guiding/Controlling Innovation and Innovation Potential

Deliberately the *concept of innovation* has been depicted in a rather general and broad mode. In ubiquitous and fast change, all sectors of entrepreneurial activity need be adapted if not re-invented. Innovation is to be perceived as an essential developmental activity central to the overall business strategy and to the actual policy. In consequence innovation becomes the *task and the responsibility of management throughout* from top management to the blue collar level. Innovation does rarely emerge by itself; it has to be stimulated and fostered. Likewise, the process from idea to production to market success to business model has deliberately to be guided, managed and controlled. Preconditions of the innovative enterprise are to be carefully designed and updated.

The *innovation helix* represents the core of entrepreneurial survival and development. Innovative ideas do not arise as a coincidence but as the result of a long term policy. Innovative leadership emerges from strategy and control. As indicated above, the policy involves all aspects and time spans. It has to think in entire systems, in closed loops as well as in helices. Preferably is has to begin with the achievements desired, from the target end. *'Designing' innovation* comprehensively models the enterprise in its markets.

Innovation controlling commences with a thorough *orientation. Mega-Trends* delineate worldwide fundamental changes in the long run. Well known is the energy and resources shortage, the rise of the emerging countries (in particular Asia) and the resulting shift of economic and political power; but also technology advances as continuing in ICT or nanotechnology. New markets are emerging in e.g. personal security (privacy lost already), or in the growing role of public and para-fiscal, quasi-entrepreneurial public activities. Responding, the enterprise strategy will define its *actual position* in the short, middle and long term developmental curves. It will examine the potentials of its inner environments, the chances offered by the external environments. Upon the result it will decide on a feasible policy. *Targeting* will search for and fix a balance between *potentials open, risks to be acceptable, and optional politics.*

A first step defines the *strategy fields*, followed by estimating the middle term *investments* necessary and the actual operational profits supporting them. The next phase *Planning* transfers *targets into measure* and activity programs, in detail for the first three years; where only the first year is the base for point for point control. Actual *Controlling*, normally spanning two years in an overlapping 1-2 years 'rolling' plan, controls the results. It states and comments differences plan-actual outcome as to its causes and prompts *corrective action.*

Apart from individual project management the general controlling cycle provides separate assessments of the actual innovative results and the development of the *innovative potentials*. An important part is to detect *gaps* in a ideally continuous unbroken *innovation chain*.

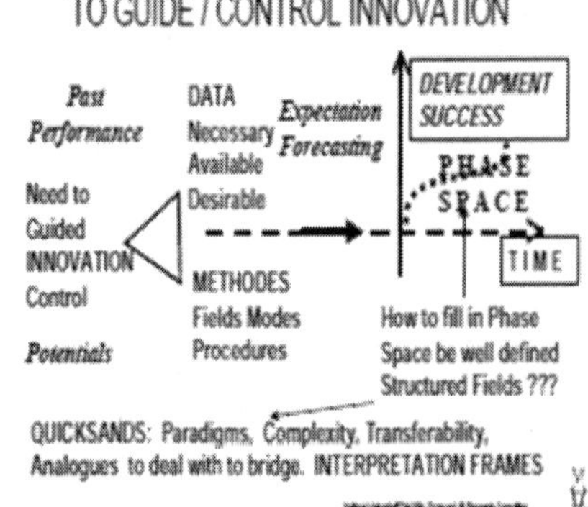

Reports –regular or specific from projects – pertain to the entire performance cycle. They scrutinize the necessity of improvement, the innovative measures in sight and investments necessary. Maintenance and upgrading of the performance capacities prove a valuable source to identify activities, and those of *replacement/extension innovations* due. A *scrolling planning and reporting* system has proved feasible. It must be noted here, that such running innovation planning on the company level presupposes the involvement of virtually any employee in an innovative 'environment' as described above. – *Risk management* is a vital part to detect failures at an early stage and to limit losses.

Innovation Controlling is known as an intriguing task. Innovation demands scarce resources competing with other targets. Depending from the measure, only 20- 30 % of innovations are reasonably successful; the quota can be doubled by sensible project control. The benefit lies not least in learning form mistakes – and, as a side effect, improving insight into relevant business processes and knowledge management. It helps to see innovations in an innovative network, as parts of an *innovation strategy* related to the enterprise strategy as in *portfolio* and *scenario* frames. Innovations should be *bundled* into a *systems innovation frame. Life Cycle Management* provides a vertical example for products or product groups.

A very sensible management is requested in *open innovation*, ripening the advantages of co-operation without losing competitiveness. In Germany open *inter-company platforms*, supported by government or chambers of commerce, develop successful namely in the SMU environment. But also trusts like Swarovsky, GoldCorp Mining, and Bombardier launched if differing but successful projects.

Depending from its quality, any innovation triggers changes often *less desired* and in scarcely expected areas. In sum they often enhance *complexity,* concerning technology, production, maintenance, even marketing and sales. Again the entire performance cycle is prone to rising complexity as well as *complicatedness.* Cars for example become more and more complex (see e.g. a caterpillar), so does aircraft (see e.g. EADS). Among other disadvantages, complexity means higher costs to maintain *quality and reliability.* That may well happen also on the scale of a small company; it is endemic with fast growing star-ups. ICT alone will in most cases but superficially help; it may even trigger *additional complexity.* Keeping complexity of business processes as well as e.g. the use of products by the customer (remind user's manuals) often will be a follow-up of innovative changes.

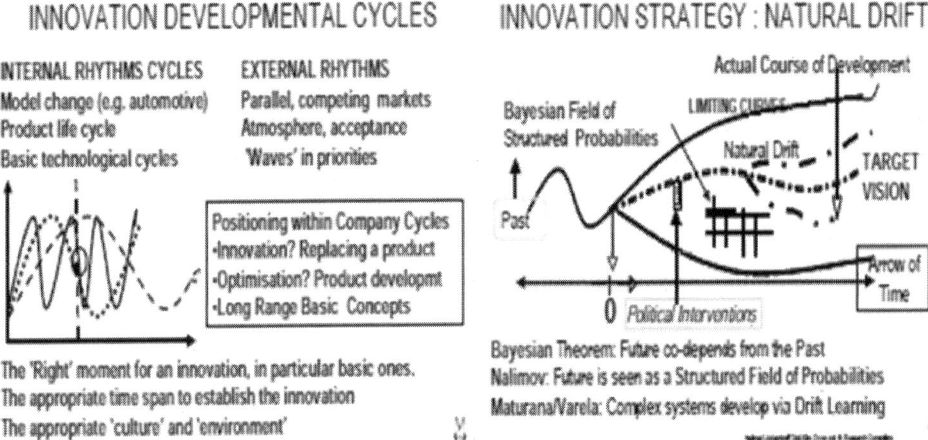

As experience from practice tells, a solution has to be attempted re-designing the entire *value-adding and logistic chain.* A regular analysis where innovative changes are called for, for long has become part of Controlling. Particular attention should be given to preventing respectively reducing the relevant degrees of complexity - see above. Managing innovation has to face a host of *impediments and obstacles* connected with the institutional environment of the societal and economical *constitution* – the written constitution less than factual. The topic is to be touched here only. *Bureaucracy,* open or hidden *corruption, lobbies, corporatism, ideological narrowness,* insufficient infrastructure, difficulties in patenting, high and sometimes insurmountable costs to fight for ones legal rights, are everyday reality. They and other constitutional lags point out but some of the more obvious hurdles for any innovative society on a broad base. As mentioned, tacit de- facto monopolies and oligopolies have effective ways to prevent innovations which might disturb the running business or endanger vested interests. It seems that innovation has to find a way to live with it.

Epilogue: Innovation: a Continuous, Comprehensive Learning Effort

From any point of entrepreneurial view, successful innovation resembles an act of *creative learning.* Such learning must be open, constructive, comprehensive and not least guided and controlled. Change and innovation proceed in waves and tides. Learning needs be an never ceasing continuous effort not only of r&d, but involving the entire company and any employee. It needs a continuous *culture* of innovation.

Management, Planning and Controlling are institutionalized instruments of *companywide learning*. Innovation is an essential feature of such future oriented controlling. Supporting the work force of the enterprise to learn as to innovate is perceived as a central function of management. *Human Resources* as the backbone of an innovating enterprise must be maintained and developed. 'Change Management' managing change and changing, that is innovating management itself, arises the consequential necessity.

The present change is part of an epochal conversion of *cultures*, of worldview, the reconciliation of values and thus of self-understanding, of *identity*. It is accompanied by a *power shift*, economically, politically, culturally. Continents and their cultures are competing for priority. An encompassing restructuring of our life world is under way and incrementally reaching a critical stage. It coincides with awareness of the limits of the 'space ship earth' or of 'Gaya', the conceptualization of the earth's life body. It is understood, that even the view on science and the ensuing technology is tainted by culture. To be aware of the influence, to respond to, to employ and transfer it sensibly will be paramount.

Following these and similar trends, the handling of innovation experiences a necessary turn to *life systems*. It focuses on concepts observable in *nature*, on principles of *bio-physics*, of *bio-chemistry*. Technology has began to think not only in high pressure, high temperatures and short spans of time. It does so now in low pressure, low temperatures and long process time. *Recycling* simulates natural *metabolisms*, a so called *green technology* sets on to develop techniques with minimum exploitation and distributions of natural (and social) environments. For two decennia *bionics* undertakes to understand the 'secret techniques of nature' and to transfer them into physical-chemical technologies for industrial production. It is for example the function of the insect facets eye, the chemistry of the spider net, or the glue of the mussel shell that opens new modes to achieve mechanical or chemical effects in an often revolutionizing way. *Biotechnology* is experimenting with 'white technology; using algae for production processes. Systems sciences and ICT research explore e.g. the 'minibrains` of insects or molluscs for control hard-and software surprisingly simple and efficient. Recently in pharmacy 'biosimilars' simulate natural procedures to produce medicines. Of course similars are not the original and can display missing of not-wanted qualities.

The above development stays but in its very beginning. It is paralleled by an altering *awareness*, which also pertains to what is understood as *'design' in the comprehensive sense.* It is emerging from a changing awareness of, to use the philosophical term, of 'man in his world'. Still opaque, it seems to combine a holistic comprehension with responsibility for natural and social environments expressed in a attempted concord (?) of the product with its environment where it is employed. For example Puma will encase shoes no longer in boxes, but in brightly coloured bags to be used afterwards for shopping.

The movements sketched above can be summarized in their essence as efforts to learn in a new way. It implies a heightened sensitivity for the *'soft' factors* of a technology based civilisation and for the consequences concerning the natural, social and cultural sequels. The observation applies to societies, groups, to institutes and individuals as well. *Aestetics* are re-discovered in a wider meaning extending over and above the feeling of beauty and fitting-in, appropriateness to the technical employ. Business administration and business management models begin to reflect *business ethics.*

Not yet fully explored is the *learning connection via internet.* It thrives between customers themselves, customers and seller and via the seller to the producer. Experience indicates that the new learning will affect innovative product design as described above. As an additional trend it can be identified, that the customer expects not single products, but combined service, newness, fitting in, aesthetic pleasantness, and gain for personal well feeling and self-estimation. All this is well known, but gaining via internet a new intenseness and quality.

Acknowledgement and Reference

The paper rests on lifelong industrial practice, teaching and consulting. Freelance research added systemic insights. It appears futile to select references from the abundance of literature and personal contacts, other than mentioned within the text. I summarily acknowledge indebtness and gratefulness to contributing sources. The vital structures of the paper are, of course, my own responsibility. In case I overlooked a debt I shall be glad to be informed and to comply accordingly. C.J. Touhill G.J Touhill; Th.A. O'Riordan: Commercialisation of Innovative Technologies. Bringing good ideas to the market place. Wiley-VCS 2008 (Note of the author: Actual text and slides have been extracted and adapted from a general text to be published elsewhere; the copyright fully remaining with the author).

15

Product and Service Innovations in Rural Markets of India: Market Penetration through Development of Local Entrepreneurship

Abstract

Rural markets provide numerous advantages to the marketers. They are characterized by a vast consumer base and have an enormous potential. These are the markets of the future as they provide numerous opportunities for the marketers. These markets will provide larger in dimension compared to the urban markets in the near future.

The growth of rural markets is attributed to the saturation in the urban markets. There are various products and services that have become obsolete in urban markets due to technological developments and product innovations, these products have a ready market in rural markets, as these are new for the rural customers. The marketers can extend the life of their products and brands by exploring rural markets. Today, rural markets provide new marketing opportunities. Infrastructural development and development in information and communication technology are other reasons contributing to the growth of the rural markets. The growth of rural markets has also seen opportunities for the development of local level entrepreneurs.

Rural Marketing

Rural markets provide numerous advantages to the marketers. They are characterized by a vast consumer base and have an enormous potential. These are the markets of the future as they provide numerous opportunities for the marketers. These markets will provide larger in dimension compared to the urban markets in the near future. Another feature of rural markets is that they are heterogeneous in the nature. There are variations in the needs and requirements of the customers in the different rural markets. There are many small sub-segments of the customers within one segment, which makes these markets heterogeneous. Another feature which differentiates the rural markets from the urban markets is the dependency of the purchasing power of rural consumers on agricultural output, which ultimately again depends on the monsoon. If the monsoon is good, the purchasing power of the rural consumers is proportionately increased.

The growth of rural markets is attributed to the saturation in the urban markets. There are various products and services that have become obsolete in urban markets due to technological developments and product innovations, these products have a ready market in rural markets, as these are new for the rural customers. The marketers can extend the life of their products and brands by exploring rural markets. Today, rural markets provide new marketing opportunities. Infrastructural development and development in information and communication technology are other reasons contributing to the growth of the rural markets.

Challenges and problems

In the recent years, Indian rural market has been receiving ever greater attention of the marketers, policymakers, consultants, multilateral agencies and academicians as well as researchers. The saturation and relative growth slowdown in the urban markets heightened competition.

The realization of rural markets being underserved, increasing focus of the policymakers on injecting money to pump the rural economy have all contributed towards an increased interest of businesses towards rural India. The numbers associated with rural India and the rural markets are truly mind boggling. The annual rural market potential of India is in excess of Rs. 1230 billion. There are over 627,000 villages in which 70% of India's population resides. There are many product categories, where the rural buyers' share in the demand pie is over 60 percent. The reach of television has doubled from 13% in 1993 to 26% in 2002 in rural India. There are 25,000 *melas* which are held annually, 47,000 *haats* are held across 18 states, 7,000 pure grain *mandis* and 450 regulated Sugar mills. Each one of these is a handy marketing window for the rural marketing initiative. The developments in agriculture and other village based occupations in the last decade have led to affluent villagers closing in on to their urban counterparts in terms of income gaps.

Notwithstanding these attractive metrics, the rural market comes with its own challenges; it is not homogeneous. The individual sections of this market are small, although the aggregate size is large. There are geographical, demographic, statistical and logistical differences. Positioning and realities regarding the potential of each of these market segments differ and lie at the very core of forming the strategy for the rural markets.

The first and foremost problem of rural markets is their heterogeneity. These are immensely diversified markets in terms of consumer taste and preferences. A product satisfying one rural market may not find favour in another market, probably due to the geographical conditions. Rural markets are still in the process of development unlike many urban markets which are developed. The rural markets are underdeveloped in terms of channels of distribution, communication and other strategic focus. These markets are highly unorganized and unstructured. Another challenge for rural marketers relates to communicating with the rural consumers. The standardized methods of advertising and sales promotion cannot be carried out in the rural markets due to low literacy levels of the rural consumers and less technological development in these areas.

Other problems include smaller shops, less penetration of internet, poor purchasing power, heterogeneous language and dialects and the vastness of the rural markets.

The Emergence of Rural Markets

The Indian rural market with its vast size and demand base offers great opportunities to marketers. Two-thirds of country's consumers live in rural areas and almost half of the national income is generated here. It is only natural that rural markets form an important part of the total market of India. Our nation is classified into 450 districts and 638,365 villages, which can be sorted in different parameters such as literacy levels, accessibility, income levels, penetration, distances from nearest towns etc.

The rural India offers a tremendous market potential. A mere one percent increase in India's rural income translates to a mind boggling Rs. 100,000 crore of buying power. Nearly two-thirds of all middle-income households in the country are in the rural India and close to half of India's buying potential lies in its villages. Thus, for the country's marketers, small and big, rural reach is on the rise. Realizing this, corporate India is now investing in a sizeable chunk of its marketing budget to target the rural consumers.

Changing Face of Rural Markets

Increased focus of the market on rural markets

Today rural markets are proving to be vital for the growth of many marketers. With the urban markets saturating fast the present day urban marketers have been forced to find newer markets with high volumes and penetration possibilities. Obviously they have turned towards the rural markets of India. These markets not only offer great penetration possibilities but also are source of high profits because of their Herculean volume markets.

Increased Education

With the increase in education facilities at primary and higher education level the new generation is increasingly becoming more educated. The number of youth taking college education has also increased manifold in recent years. This has made the newer rural consumers more aware about their needs and the various products, services and practices that are available in the urban markets. They also aspire to use

Increased awareness due to spread of TV

Rural India is also increasingly recognized for Rising Awareness Levels and its Consequent Influence on Lifestyle, this is primarily being led by development of telecommunications, exposure to televisions & media and rise in literacy levels that are dramatically affecting rural perceptions. As a result, rural India is registering Changing Consumption Patterns; which is again being catalyzed by the transition towards varied economic activities like manufacturing, fisheries and services. With this changing economic scenario, rural consumers are not only becoming more aware about the availability of a large number of products but are also willing to try out brands.

Need to emulate urban life style

With the increasing awareness about different products and services the new age rural consumer also wants to emulate the life style of his/her urban counterpart. They want to buy the latest gadgets, wear pretty clothes, drive bikes, use mobile phones, eat urban food, try out new FMCG products etc.

Exposure to mall culture

With better road and other connectivity the rural customer on one hand and the penetration of various retail formats in small towns, the rural customers have now tasted and seen the glamorous world of shopping malls and supermarkets. This exposure to the mall culture has also increased the need of rural consumers to try out new products, brands and services.

New sources of income

Non-farm activities in rural areas are witnessing a rise in entrepreneurship and employment, which are growing at a faster rate than urban areas. These trends can be seen in the findings of the Fifth Economic Census 2005, excluding crop production and plantation, which puts about 25.81 million enterprises (61.3 per cent of total enterprises) operating out of rural areas. These rural enterprises are clocking an average annual growth of about 5.53 per cent and employ more than 50 million people (51 per cent of the total). Further, rural enterprises are recording an average annual growth of 3.33 per cent in total employment, which is higher than that of urban enterprises. What is striking about rural enterprise is the rising level of entrepreneurship, which is indicated through low number of hired workers (presently standing at about 2/5 of total persons employed).

Major Variables present in the Rural Markets

As one moves from the urban to the rural markets the following variables become very vital :

1. Heterogeneity and size of markets
2. Market Constraints: Purchasing Power, Buyer Awareness, Logistics
3. Product and Service Innovations
4. Rural Marketing Mix
5. Social Influence on buying behavior
6. Availability of Local Brands

Product, Service and Practice Innovations in Rural Markets

The increasing stature and importance of rural markets have forced most of the modern day businesses to look for ways and means to crack the rural market code. 'Go Rural' is the new mantra for many players in the markets; especially in the FMCG, Insurance, Banks and other areas.

Today we are witnessing many product, service and practice innovations offered by many players across product categories to reach out to the rural customers.

What are the existing models?

Project Shakti by Hul

To expand its markets, the challenge for Hindustan Lever (Unilever's business in India) was how to reach millions of potential consumers in small remote villages where there is no retail distribution network, no advertising coverage, and poor roads and transport.

The solution was Project Shakti, launched in 2000 in partnership with nongovernmental organizations, banks and government. Women in self-help groups across India are invited to become direct-to-consumer sales distributors for Hindustan Lever's soaps and shampoos. The company provides training in selling, commercial knowledge and bookkeeping to help them become micro entrepreneurs. By the end of 2009 there were more than 45 000 Shakti entrepreneurs covering 3 million homes in 100 000 villages in 15 states in India. HUL has plans to roll out similar initiatives in Sri Lanka and Bangladesh. *(www.unilever.com)*

Itc E-Chaupal

E-Chaupal is an initiative by ITC to serve two purposes: First it gives direct access to the farm produces from across India and secondly it has enabled the local farmers to sell directly to the manufacturer which has helped them to get a fair price of their produce. So in a way E-Chaupal is a win-win solution created by ITC.

A powerful illustration of corporate strategy linking business purpose to larger societal purpose, e-Choupal leverages the Internet to empower small and marginal farmers – who constitute a majority of the 75% of the population below the poverty line. By providing them with farming know-how and services, timely and relevant weather information, transparent price discovery and access to wider markets, e-Choupal enabled economic capacity to proliferate at the base of the rural economy. Today 4 million farmers use e-Choupal to advantage – bargaining as virtual buyers' co-operatives, adopting best practices, matching up to food safety norms. Being linked to futures markets is helping small farmers to better manage risk. e-Choupal has been specially cited in the Government of India's Economic Survey of 2006-07, for its transformational impact on rural lives.

ITC's strategic intent is to develop e-Choupal as a significant two-way multidimensional delivery channel, efficiently carrying goods and services out of and into rural India. By progressively linking the digital infrastructure to a physical network of rural business hubs and agro-extension services, ITC is transforming the way farmers do business, and the way rural markets work. The network of 6,500 e-Choupal centres spread across 40,000 villages has emerged as the gateway of an expanding spectrum of commodities leaving farms – wheat, rice, pulses, soya, maize, spices, coffee, and aqua-products. The reverse flow carries FMCG, durables, automotives and banking services back to villages. (www.itcportal.com)

Kisan Sewa Pumps by IOC

Kisan Seva Kendra (KSK) is an award-winning retail outlet model pioneered by IndianOil to cater to the needs of customers in the rural segment. Today, KSK outlets have emerged as dominant players in the rural markets, riding on the rapid growth of upcoming second and third tier roads in the rural areas. The KSK come with a fresh perspective enabling dealers to tap the huge demand driven in by consumers there. In addition, non-fuel retail facilities like convenience stores have been added to the KSK to sell pesticides, vegetables, banking products and stationery items. IndianOil has tied up with Indo-Gulf for fertilizers, National Seeds Corporation for marketing seeds and agricultural inputs as well as alliances with Nabard, Oriental Bank of Commerce and Bank of Baroda for banking products. Some KSK have installed internet kiosks, communication facilities, etc. Business alliances have been signed to market products from Dabur, Airtel, Tata Chemicals, Godavari Fertilisers, Gokulam Fertilisers, Hindustan Unilever and Godrej Agrovet. Other alliance partners are Emami for personal care products, Money Gram for money transfer, MILMA and OMFED for milk products, and Supplyco for convenience stores. *(www.iocl.com)*

Product and Service Innovations found in the rural markets:

Sachets of small sizes at very affordable prices:

One very common approach adopted by FMCG companies in the rural markets is launching their products in affordable price brackets in smaller sachet packs. Today you get hair oil, shampoo, biscuits, ketchup, soft drink concentrate, cheese, butter etc. in sachet pouches in the price of Rs.1 to Rs. 5.

Customized marketing campaigns

One other common approach is to customize the marketing communication mix to specially cater to the needs of the rural markets. With given limited technology and rampant illiteracy of the target audience in rural markets, the marketers are using customized campaigns to reach the rural consumers. They use of public health centres, melas, Haats, local festivals to reach out their customers. Audio and visual mediums are extensively used keeping in mind the illiteracy rate among the target audience.

Financial Products : Biometric cards by ICICI , SBI

ICICI Prudential Life Insurance, one of India's leading life insurance companies, launched the biometric smart cards for their rural policyholders, making it the first life insurance company in India to provide this service to its rural customers. The cards will enable policyholders carry all their policy details without the hassle of carrying policy documents for any policy related activity. The unique biometric smart card will enable ICICI Prudential Life's rural policyholders to:

1. Carry all policy details without any papers
2. Store transaction details
3. Pay renewal premiums and service transactions (service to be launched)
4. Help customers during the time of claim

In a similar model, four villages in Mizoram boast of being at the helm of a rural banking initiative, which uses the mobile phone instead of the ATM to connect banks to their rural customer base.

In a pilot project initiated by the State Bank of India in November 2007, in three states, Mizoram, Uttarakhand and Andhra Pradesh, over 5,000 people are using biometric smart cards. These store the user's thumbprint information.

Vardaan TV by Philips

Shailesh Prabhu who is currently a senior manager for Philips CTV in Mumbai has completed five years in Philips in appliances sales, and, then in CTV marketing. Since past one year, Prabhu has been involved in marketing Vardaan CTV series in rural markets and the challenges faced were on the availability, affordability, awareness, and, providing after-sales service.

As a first step, Prabhu took the initiative of launching Vardaan range of CTV and understanding the villagers concerns made the Philips CTV more affordable without compromising on the quality of the product.

For the purpose, he implemented rural promotion programmes in Tamil Nadu and Karnataka, among other states. In terms of availability, the biggest bottleneck was making it cost-effective to the distributors. Prabhu says the total CTV market size is around 8 million in units of which 40% of the market is in the less than one lakh population.

The all India market is growing at about 9%, whereas, in rural India, the market is growing at the pace of 20%. Now, the penetration of CTV in rural India is only 7% compared to all India penetration of 24%.

He says the factors of growth in rural India are the electrification drive by the government, the direct-to-home facility which is available now in the rural India, upgradation from black and white television to colour television, and, finally, good monsoon is expected even this year which will result in more disposable income in rural India.

In order to meet the evolving needs of villagers, Prabhu took the right step in promoting and establishing the Vardaan brand in the rural India. "What I observed was Philips had a very good equity in rural India due to its radio penetration in these markets, and, the consumers saw Philips as a reliable, trustworthy and good value-for-money brand," he says.

The biggest challenge which Philips has faced in the rural markets is to have a service set-up in the rural market, cost-effective distribution model, making hire purchase options available for rural consumers, and, finally, to promote the Philips brand in these markets.

Philips is planning to appoint new distributors exclusive for Vardaan range to improve its coverage of rural India from about 100 to 150 distributors. As for after-sales-service, Philips plans to expand the service network by appointing franchise service centres in smaller towns as authorised service dealers. This programme started in the second quarter of 2005. Philips has gone rural... (http://www.financialexpress.com/news/the-four-as-of-ruralmarketing/ 136842/)

Rugged phones by NOKIA and Samsung

The phone makers like NOKIA and Samsung have also customized their products by launching rugged phone with long battery life. These phones are specially designed keeping in mind the tough conditions of rural markets and also the difficulties the rural consumers have face in charging phones.

Insurance Products

Many customized insurance products both in life and non-life segments are available especially for the rural markets. Recently announcing its foray into rural and micro-finance segment, Reliance Life Insurance Company Limited has announced the launch of two new insurance products, Reliance Jan Samridhi Plan and Reliance Traditional Super Invest Assure Plan (RTSIP).

The company is targeting Rs 100 crore from micro insurance segment this year. The Jan Samridhi Plan is rural-centric product that lowered the entry level for providing life cover and savings opportunities with premium as low as Rs 50 a month and the Reliance Traditional Super Invest Plan is a regular premium scheme designed to meet the regular savings, protection and income needs of customers having a risk-averse profile. At present 95 per cent of the insurance products sold by company are Unit Linked Insurance Policies while only 5 per cent non linked policies. (www. businessstandard.com)

HDFC Standard Life Insurance, a joint venture between HDFC and Standard Life

Assurance Company has identified the rural market as an important thrust area for its future growth.

The company, ranked number 4 among the private players in the insurance sector thus far in terms of number of policies sold, presently has 100 rural consultants already in four rural belts namely Amravati in Maharashtra, Nelikuppam in Tamil Nadu, Panipat in Haryana and areas near Pune and Nagpur.

The company has pegged business from rural markets to increase from 4.5 per cent of the total business turnover last fiscal to around 7 to 7.5 per cent this fiscal. Also on the anvil are plans to expand the country-wide retail network base of the company, from the existing 32 centres to around 50 by the end of the current financial year.

The company has aimed to build up infrastructure, which would have the right kind of people selling the right kind of products to ensure that the customers get a good deal and good returns in the long run. (www. financial express.com)

Banking in Rural Markets

Getting the poor to bank and bank profitably is the new motto! India's largest bank, State Bank of India (SBI), has a breathtaking rural branch network of 6,600 with 972 specialized branches. These branches have been set up in different parts of the country with the sole purpose of developing agriculture through credit deployment. In addition, SBI has also developed rural agricultural business units, education programmes for local farmers and "kisan" cards. State Bank of India has gradually evolved to become the leader in agricultural finance with a portfolio of Rs. 18,000 crore in loans to around 50 lakh farmers. One of their recent endeavors is the tie-up with National Agricultural Cooperative Marketing Federation (NAFED) to finance farmers for cultivation of various crops like soyabean, paddy, jute and potato. Private sector banks too, have geared up for a piece of the cake. ICICI Bank, the country's second largest bank, has adopted the franchise model of operation in rural markets. Unconventional indeed! A one man office (known as "kendra") in the village forms an interface between the villager and the Bank's products and facilities. Crop loans, housing loans, automobile loans, farm equipment, seed financing and insurance policies are all on offer. The number of borrowers has risen from 130 in 2000 to over 42,000 today, and the rural loan book has crossed Rs. 16,000 crore. What's more, the bank's default rate in the rural retail sector is 1 – 2 % as compared to 2 – 3% in the rural wholesale sector and 5% for the banking sector as a whole.

Canara bank has launched aggressive grass-root level plans, in a bid to achieve 100% financial inclusion in 1,400 villages all over India, which could bring 7 lakh families into their net. Under this programme, every adult member of a rural household in the selected villages would be encouraged to open a 'No Frills' account with minimum entry-level formalities.

The FMCG Juggernaut

With rural consumers warming up to branded products, the urban rural divide is fading away faster than one can imagine. There is now very little difference between the aspirations of rural consumers and their urban counterparts. Certain growth statistics have shattered the myth that the rural consumer is content with unbranded or mass end products alone and gives a strong indication that rural market consumptions has picked up and is accelerating faster than urban markets . This has led to their changing consumption pattern.

Demand for top of the drawer FMCG products is no longer restricted to urban India. The rural consumer has emerged as an important cog in the sales growth of premium offerings Clever pricing rising aspirations and new marketing mantras are driving this trend. Dove shampoo a premium end product reported a growth of over 100% in rural market during January - October 2010 over the same period last year. In fact, Dove grew faster than its lower priced cousin, Sunsilk shampoo which reported a growth of around 14% in rural India during the period.

So it is not just mass brands like lifebuoy, Nirma or Wheel which have for decades met the need of rural India. Take a look at the growth numbers of a beauty care products like Pond's white Beauty and the figures are mind boggling. The brand grew 4,200% in January October 2010 in rural markets over the same period last year.

Although analysts explain that the high growth is due to a lower base and that actual sales number would be smaller given the recent introduction of the brand, one cannot overlook the fact that there is a demand for such products and marketers can no longer underestimate the aspirations of the rural consumers.

Gone are the days when the rural consumer was content with using mustard oil and plain soap. Today, he/she is seeking special branded products daily skin and healthcare needs. Rural consumers across income segments are showing a marked propensity towards spending on premium high quality products which are backed by strong brand values.

For instance take food products. Not only has the demand for cream biscuits gone up in rural markets the sale of instant noodles, too is growing nearly twice as fast in the rural market compared to the urban on What's more one in every six rural buyer hair dye now uses colors other than black – something which would have been dubbed. Indulgence a decade ago. Even seemingly urbane brands in categories like deodorants and fabric softeners are said to be growing much faster in rural Indian than urban.

Variety biscuits (creams, cookies) are growing significantly faster that glucose. Even in rural market, they are taking away significant consumption from glucose biscuits.

According to a retail audit, the share of glucose biscuits in overall market has changed from 30% to 26% in the last 18 months. Clearly consumers are valuing superior quality and better delivery in product experience and are willing to pay a higher price for it. The trend particularly serves as a wakeup call for those marketers, who still do not have a deep rural reach. It is also broad based cutting across categories The year on year rural growth of premium soap brand Cinthol original during April September was higher this year at around 28% as compared to 12.5% in the corresponding period last year. Similarly the rural growth of mosquito repellent brand double that it's urban market growth this year.

Summing Up

Looking at the pace with which the rural consumers are embracing conventional and innovative products, it seems very clear that the next decade is going to see an exponential growth in strategies and practices to penetrate deeper in the rural markets. More and more product, service and practice innovations would be seen to capture this voluptuous and humungous market. There are several roads ahead. One of them would of course take care of what kind of products and services to offer in these markets. The second would be create models of distribution and penetration in this very difficult market to enter. And, finally the third important road would be to create media strategies to reach out and create awareness among this special set of customers.

Bibliography

1. Raj, S John Mano and P Selvaraj, "Social Changes and the Growth of Indian Rural Market : An Invitation to FMCG"; 2007
2. Chandramouli S, "Innovations as Cutting Edge Solutions in Rural Marketing" at Rural Marketing Summit; FICCI- 2007
3. Sanyal Kumar Velayudhan and Guda Sridhar, Marketing To Rural Consumers, excel books, New Delhi, 2009

16

Categorizing & Chustering of Innovators: New Dimension in Grassroots invention

Abstract

Curiosity and Necessity are the parents of invention. Creativity has a central role to play in the development of the country. Creativity kick starts the virtuous cycle of enterprise creation and employment generation. Inventions are not only done in the laboratories of bricks and cement, but are also explored in the laboratories of life. Indians per se are very creative as they are educated in the schools of hardships and deficiency of resources. The highest level of creativity is depicted among the rural poor who struggle to survive as they are associated with constraints of either resources, or income, or at times become victim of different unfavourable environmental conditions. Necessity also strengthens such people to become inventors. Such creative or ignited minds are not given a formal designation of scientist nationally or internationally, but are recognized as "odd balls" in their limited periphery of village.

Introduction

Indian villages are think tanks resources bubbling with practical and creative ideas. Villagers are creative scientist who does not hold a formal degree but they do possess a master's degree while graduating the lessons in the laboratories of life. Villagers should be credited for such intuition and god gifted creativity to think out of the box. Every inventor has a distinctive personality and his invention is the sum total of his first hand experiences and problems faced by him. Inventors are basically resourceful, ingenious and imaginative people. Some inventors invent things to satisfy their curiosity and thereafter cease to take audacious steps of starting an enterprise. Only idiosyncratic inventors come up with an initiative to start an enterprise. Prof. Anil Gupta of IIM(A) is honored for scouting such "odd balls" by pioneering the idea of mining the goldmine of rural India for marketable innovations. He strongly points out in his various literary works that there is a large reservoir of knowledge and skills with India's economic poor which is untapped to the surprise of others. He plays a fatherly role for barefoot inventors. Such creative inventors or innovators are aloof from organized business world and are simultaneously unaware of their own worth, rights and opportunities. According to him a grassroots innovator is a person who is unaided (not helped by anyone), unqualified (does not have formal education) and he or she is an individual from informal sector with no work experience. Such grassroots innovator must be recognized, respected, rewarded and reciprocated for their innovative ideas. Dr. Abdul Kalam also believes that such ignited minds must be honored by our government. Recently in the Convocation ceremony of Ahmedabad University Dr. Kalam rightly pointed out that 21st century is the Knowledge century. When we talk about knowledge it is not only the formal degree holders but also traditional, community and individual intuition knowledge holders who are unqualified as per education system but well qualified with respect to the application of the knowledge they hold. Time has come to learn from well qualified application oriented knowledge holders.

Objective and research methodology of the study

The basic objective of this descriptive study was to collect information from grassroots innovators about their invention. Effort was made to know the present status of their invention. An attempt was also made to explore the problems faced by grassroots inventors and the measures taken to overcome the problems. A detailed questionnaire consisting of eleven pages and fifty six questions was framed to collect the primary data. Questionnaire contained open ended as well as close ended questions. Database of innovators was taken from GIAN (Grassroots Innovation Augmentation Network) Ahmedabad. The sampling frame revealed the total number of 43 innovators, out of which a sample size of 30 innovators (sampling element) who are exclusively based at Gujarat are taken for the study.

The sampling area was across remote villages of Gujarat namely Kalol, Mansa, Ahmedabad, Gandhinagar, Vaktapur, Rajkot, Atkot, Vankaner, Movaiya, Upleta, Pikhor, Kalavad, Galvav, Vavdi, Sitala, Sankheda, Talav, Kursad, Surat, Vijalpur, Mota Devaliya, Chittal, Ghogha Samadi, Hansalpur and Kamalpur. The respondents of the research were men describing a single cross sectional research. To explore the literary work done and to gauge the knowledge of various types of innovators various websites were surfed.

In the data collection phase during the research it was found that every innovator had a different dimension to look at his invention. Certain things were found to very common across all the innovators who were surveyed. Couple of uncommon things was found to be rare in some innovators. Qualitative data extracted from innovators had lot of insights and it also keeps one thinking of the basic qualities of innovator. Some innovators simply invented things to satisfy their curiosity and give shape to their creativity. Other invented to make either their work easy or other's work easy. Some inventors started their own enterprise on tiny scale or they transferred the rights to prospective entrepreneur and made good out of his invention.

In order to group and identify the various categories of innovators to form a cluster which exhibited typical characteristics initially a thorough analysis was made of the available information. Appropriate statistical technique of cluster analysis was not applied as the sample size is too small to administer such test and which may be insignificant to furnish transparent result for analysis. Therefore, to overcome this statistical error a model was proposed by using the answers of qualitative questions and simultaneously analyzing it with quantitative data to reach to logical conclusion. Three broad clusters are suggested based on number of inventions, enterprise and technology transfer and no enterprise start up. The first cluster was based on number of invention, which was categorized as singular invention and multiple inventions. Second cluster was based on enterprise and technology which included one part on the basis of commencement of enterprise and non transfer of technology i.e. it was referred as exclusive entrepreneurs, which were then categorized as contributors and qualifiers. The second part consisted of commencing enterprise and technology transfer and was referred as Optimizers.

The last cluster was done on the basis of no enterprise start up which were further categorized as strugglers and thrivers. The detailed discussion of the same is done further in the paper. Diagrammatically it is shown in the Annexure-I (Figure.5) attached to this paper.

Findings of Major Demographic Details

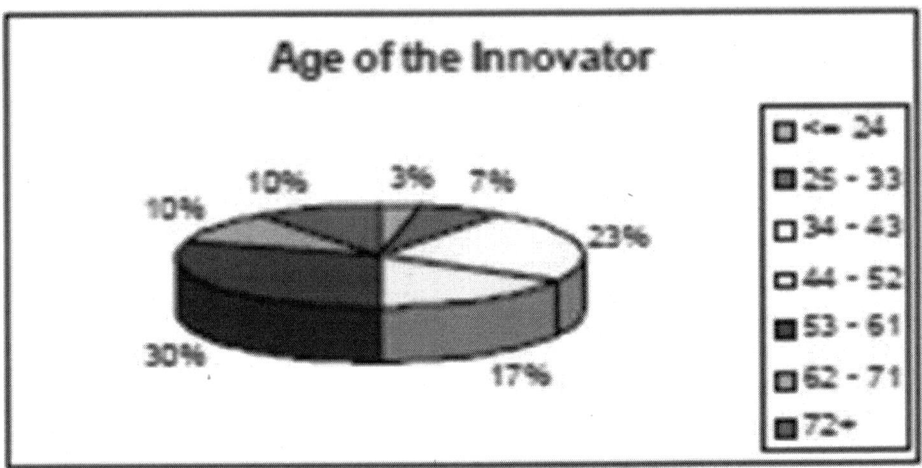

Figure.1 Age of the Innovator

Interpretation: Majority of the innovators were in the age group of 53-61 years (30%) which were followed by the age group between 34-43 years (23%) and still further 44-52 years (17%). The youngest innovator in the survey was of age equal to 24 years (3%). 7% respondents were falling in the age group of 25-33 years. 10% each respondents belonged to the age category of 62-71 years and 72 years and above. The respondents who are below 50 years are experimental and above 50 years are experienced and experimental.

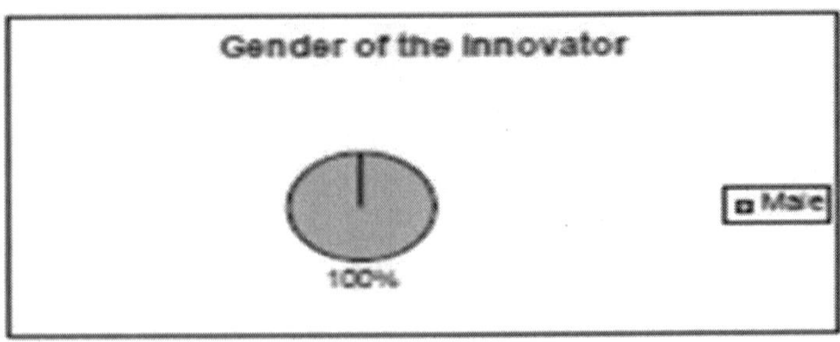

Figure.2 Gender of the Innovator

Interpretation: Out of 30 respondents it was found that all the respondents (100%) in the survey are males. Thus survey is thus single cross sectional research. It can be concluded that till date no female innovator has been scouted by GIAN. It can also be presumed that as females are pre-occupied with their routine chores they hardly find time to think and invent technological invention. Generally men have high level of technical curiosity which motivates them to experiment technical things and in the process of exploration and adoption of trial and error they succeed to a new discovery or invention.

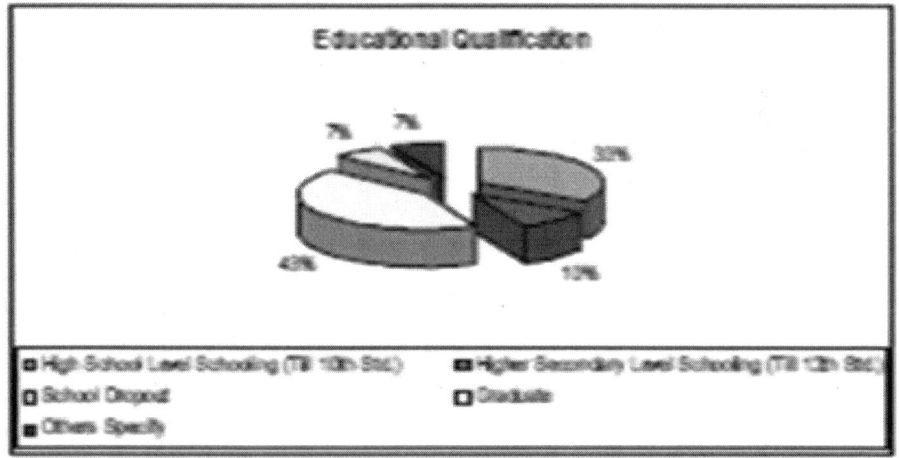

Figure.3 Educational Qualification

Interpretation: The profiling of the innovator suggests that highest 43% of the innovators are school dropouts who have not even completed their schooling up to primary level. 33% respondents have managed to complete their studies up to class 10th. 10% respondents appear to be bit inclined to studies who hold a higher secondary certificate. Graduation degree holders in the survey are found to be just 7%. 7% of the respondents have never been to school at all. The survey clearly points out the universal fact that formal degrees do not play a major role in invention it is the inquisitiveness, creativity and zeal which leads to discovery of new inventions. A recognized educational degree is not a yardstick to measure intelligent quotient (IQ) of the innovator but is the creativity quotient (CQ) which leads to invention.

Interpretation: Out of 30 respondents it was found that all the

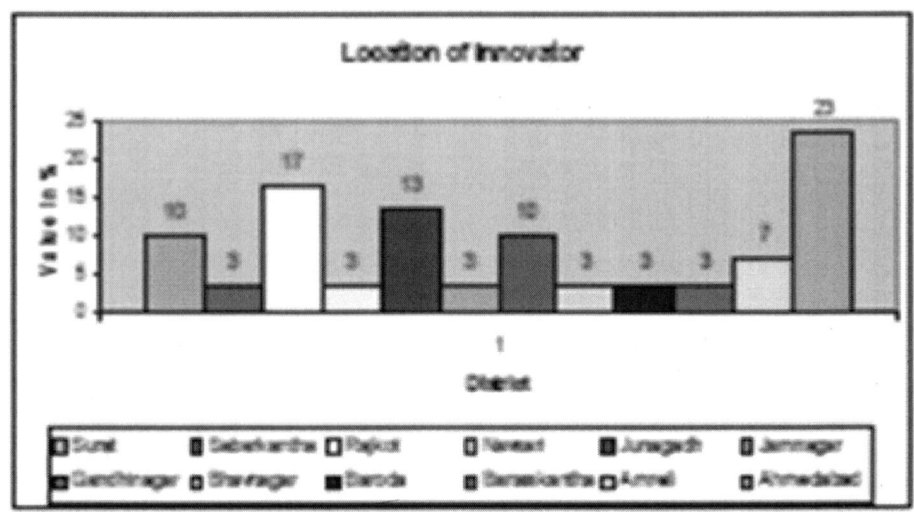

Figure.4 Location of Innovator

respondents (100%) in the survey are males. Thus survey is thus single cross sectional research. It can be concluded that till date no female innovator has been scouted by GIAN. It can also be presumed that as females are pre-occupied with their routine chores they hardly find time to think and invent technological invention. Generally men have high level of technical curiosity which motivates them to experiment technical things and in the process of exploration and adoption of trial and error they succeed to a new discovery or invention.

Discussion of Various Proposed Cluster Model

Cluster. 1: Proposition of Cluster based on Number of Invention: It can be segregated in two parts viz. Singular Invention and Multiple Inventions

Cluster.1.1: Cluster Based on Singular Invention

Contribution made by such inventors is unitary. Inventors who have one invention to their credit can be stated as *'Problem Solver'*. They try to solve a problem by finding a solution, which till date nobody has struck open. Such inventors either try to overcome their personal difficulty or problems encountered in their routine work. Such inventors are *perfectionist* by nature. They always strive to make their invention perfect. These inventors do not surrender to constraints. They can also be called as

'Domain Innovator' who have deep domain knowledge and are aware of the *'devilish details'* (See Julian Keith Loren). The outcome of a domain innovator is in terms of product, service and technology invention.

In our research the outcome of product inventions are Maruti Jhula, Innovative Sickle, Energy Saving Stove, Washing brush, Tongs, Motorcycle mounted sprayer. The examples of technology invention comprises of Mini Tractor, Cotton Stripper Machine, Rotovator, Small Diesel Engine and Paddy Thresher. The inventors carry out constant research to upgrade and make their invention from better to best. In this race of improvement they are also called as *'Improvers'* who have an unwavering ability to run their business with high level of integrity and ethics (See Sbininformation). They can also be named as *'Builders or Creators'* as they are driven to create something tangible where it did not exist before (See Business Opportunities).They exhibit trait of an *'Idealist Entrepreneur'* where he likes invention, enjoys working on something new or creative or something personally meaningful (See Developing Eyes). 40% inventors have been identified in this category.

Cluster.1.2: Cluster Based on Multiple Inventions

The inventors who have more than one invention to their credit are called as 'Multiple Designer Inventor'. Such inventor can also be called as *'Serial Inventor'* as they keep on inventing new things. Such inventor always experiments new things. They are forever determined to try out new things. They not only have inherent quality of *'Problem Solver'* type of innovator, but they are also blessed with a curious nature of exploring new surroundings, new materials, new ideas and new methods etc. Such innovators are sharp observer. They not only try to shoot up the problems they face but also solve the problems faced by others in their work. Such innovators always try to find a new option of doing things in different way, which can reduce the work fatigue and drudgery. Serial innovators can also be labeled as *'Creative Innovators'*. They often employ trial and error method of experimentation to explore an invention. Creative innovators may not be a *'Perfectionist'* in his invention as his urge to satisfy creative need is so strong that he quickly switches to instigate for multiple invention. Once the level of curiosity is satisfied in one invention he immediately takes up other invention. The curiosity level is very high and so such innovators are often called as *'mad'* by their neighbours, fellow villagers and friends. Such innovators are crazy behind the number of invention to have in their innovation portfolio. They are restless in nature. They meticulously and regularly devote time for carrying out experiments. They are described as

'Artist' whose personality is reserved but highly creative type. (See Sbininformation). 60% inventors have been identified in this category.

Cluster. 2: Proposition of Cluster based on Based on Enterprise & Technology: It can be separated in two broad parts viz cluster based on commencing enterprise and technology transfer and cluster based on exclusive commencement of enterprise and non transfer of technology. Exclusive entrepreneurs are further divided into two parts as contributors and qualifiers.

Cluster. 2.1: Proposition of Cluster based on Exclusive Commencement of Enterprise and Non Transfer of Technology

Cluster.2.1.1: Cluster Based on Contributor Entrepreneurs

Contributor entrepreneurs are like *'Social Entrepreneurs'*. Their primary goal is not profit. Such entrepreneurs run the enterprise for self-sufficiency. Their aim is not to mint money, so they cannot be referred as money chaser. An irony is seen in this set of self sufficient entrepreneur, who have high level of self actualization need. Such set of entrepreneurs can be referred as 'Society developers' as they disseminate their invention to the society without charging any technology transfer fee. Such entrepreneurs believe in the principle of brotherhood. They are like *'Saint Preachers'*, who believe in spreading knowledge not only by sharing but also by teaching the invention to the person who is in dire need and for the benefit of their community domain. These entrepreneurs believe that if invention is shared to the counterparty then they may also commercialize the invention and earn their livelihood. Such entrepreneurs do not believe in cut throat competition, but believes in the principle of collaborative growth. 20% inventors have been identified in this category.

Cluster.2.1.2: Cluster Based on Qualifier Entrepreneurs

Qualified Entrepreneurs are the people who are developing and promising high growth. These set of people carry an innate quality of becoming an entrepreneur. They are therefore referred as *'born entrepreneur'*. They are often referred as 'hard worker entrepreneurs' who enjoy putting long hours to build a larger more profitable business. They like to accept challenge and reap the rewards if the business turns out to be successful (See Developing Eyes). Qualified entrepreneurs are synonymously called as *'Commercial Entrepreneur'* who also cares to disseminate the invention to society for its benefit at large, by venturing into own enterprise. In fact such entrepreneurs start the enterprise as the activity pertains to their hobby of discovery. Qualified entrepreneurs exhibit high degree of self confidence, managerial ability and have good knowledge pertaining to their field. A serial innovator who is also a qualified entrepreneur often carries out horizontal invention.

At times if the creative idea pursued is strong he may also go for diversified invention, unrelated to his core business. Such entrepreneurs are called *'Visionary Entrepreneurs'.* They can foresee the demand of such new products and therefore with their existing financial backup of ongoing business they deploy funds for experimentation of new ideas and if found successful may establish a new Strategic Business Unit (SBU). 23% inventors have been identified in this category.

Cluster. 2.2: Proposition of Cluster based on Commencing Enterprise and Technology Transfer

In this cluster we include both the type of innovator viz singular invention and multiple inventions. Such innovators can be called as 'Optimizers' as they are content with the personal satisfaction of simply being a business owner (See Developing Eyes). The set of innovators who start their own enterprise have a great zeal to work and are mainly self motivated and self starters. They start the business because they are ready to take up new challenges and it closely pertains to their interest areas or hobby. Drive for money and supporting the family also plays a vital role to commence the venture. As observed a 'problem solver' or 'domain innovator' is perfectionist by nature so they enjoy doing the business in their unitary invention. They try to modify and carry out research to make their product best. Such innovators use business concepts partially to sell their product.

They often brand their product before selling it example: a swing cum chair is sold in the brand name of "Maruti Jhula" by the innovator. A domain innovator transfers his technology on non-exclusive basis to third party so that the reach of invention becomes wider and society can benefit from the invention. Problem solvers unitary invention becomes bread and butter for him when he becomes an entrepreneur.

Therefore, he remains committed to his business by improving on turnover on consistent basis. A serial innovator has multiple inventions to his credit. His entrepreneurial venture is usually based on number of orders. He is not engaged in full-fledged business activity. A serial innovator transfers his technology on nonexclusive basis to third party for socictal benefits. At times the reason for transfer could be associated to concentrate on other experimentation of invention thereby satisfying the quest for curiosity. Such serial innovator has other sources of income so they are not worried about earning income to sustain their family, therefore they do not ply into full fledge enterprise. A serial innovator transfers technology of the multiple products and earns a considerable amount of technology transfer fees and royalty which helps him to deploy funds for other invention. Serial innovator prepares the product as per customer's requirement. He is more into customized product. 13% inventors have been identified in this category.

Cluster. 3: Proposition of Cluster based on No Enterprise Start up: It can be alienated in two parts viz Strugglers and Thrivers

Cluster.3.1: Cluster Based on Strugglers

'Strugglers' are the set of people who have good ideas, but they are deficient in basic entrepreneurial traits. At times their invention is in nascent stage of either working model or prototype so they are not confident in starting the enterprise. If the invention pertains to high technology then even funds are a constraint for such set of people to move ahead for making of more number of prototypes for the purpose of test marketing. Such people are in search of 'Hand holders' or 'Venture Capitalist' or 'Angle Investor' who can come forward and invest in their raw and nascent ideas. Strugglers by default are very creative and have high desire for invention but they rank low on entrepreneurial and risk taking aspect23% inventors have been identified in this category.

Cluster.3.2: Cluster Based on Thrivers

'Thrivers' can be referred to the set of people who are already occupied in their business. Thrivers existing business is well established and is satisfied with their economic condition. They are more focused with their core activity. They are reluctant to shift their attention from core business and diversify in to unrelated areas. Their invention may at times not be perfect, as they do not devotee full time behind discrete invention. They have carried out invention to satisfy their creative urge or their *'observant'* personality has lead to the discovery of new a thing. Such existing entrepreneur behaves like a commercial entrepreneur. He would not like to share his invention in the form of gratitude to the society but would either like to transfer it by accepting technology transfer fees or by starting a joint venture with other entrepreneur. They are *'opportunist'* and are aware how to make money from their invention. 20% inventors have been identified in this category.

Conclusion

Various Categorizations & Clustering of Innovators reveals the true personality of the inventor. The experimenting nature of people does not require any concrete platform of cement, mortar and bricks i.e. laboratories. Grassroots innovators experiment and invent new things in the laboratories of life. The inventions brought out by the grassroots innovators are quite different and distant from conventional inventions. These inventions have the capability to solve the societal problem in major way. The brought out inventions are not only cost reducing apparatus but it is cost effective at the same time. An inventor who has solved the problem faced in work is credited with a singular invention. Such innovators are highly satisfied with their invention, they constantly think of improving existing invention rather than experimenting new things. The constant urge to invent new things puts the innovator in the category of discovering multiple inventions. Those Grassroots innovators whose motto is not mint money teach their invention to fellow occupant without charging any technology transfer fees. A qualified innovator who has high degree of enthusiasm to start his own enterprise does not part with his inventions. A genius set of innovators not only start their own enterprise but they also sell their invention to other budding or established enterprises for handsome one time amount of consideration for a pre defined and identified territory. Such innovators sell their rights on non-exclusive basis with respect to either marketing or manufacturing the products with a condition of receipt of revenue payment in the form of royalty. That innovator whose existing business is well established does not think of devoting time for his new inventions, as he is highly occupied in his existing set up. Dearth of finance and infrastructure hinders other set of highly ambitious innovators to keep away from establishing own enterprise.

To take our country from transformational phase to development phase we need to appreciate the knowledge of such creative minds. A quick clearance system should be established by setting up a Grassroots Invention Upliftment and Entrepreneurship Promotion Cell (GIUEPC) in various States for encouraging grassroots innovators to start the enterprise. Struggler innovators should be put in contact with enthusiastic entrepreneur or angle investor who can genuinely start the business by proper reciprocity to the inventor for his ideas. The database of such inventions can readily be accessed from the websites of www.gian.org, www.nifindia.org and www.sristi.org. Here we need to link a golden triangle of investment, idea and enterprise. Thrivers can be linked to budding first generation entrepreneurs of various engineering or management schools who are eager to start their venture under the mentorship of thrivers by providing necessary share or technology transfer fees to them. Our countries burning problem of unemployment and poverty can be removed if we accept the concept of inverted pyramid, i.e start acknowledging the knowledge rich poor people. We should start tiny or micro enterprises with the ideas of grassroots innovators. We should give them a fair chance to show their latent talents. An incremental step towards the same is done by Gujarat government by establishing (GIAN) for providing micro venture innovation finance to grassroots level innovators. A major recommendation in the survey was that government should provide infrastructural facility to establish a workshop with adequate different types of tools, machines and modern technology, so that the experimental spirit of the grassroots innovator is not marred due to constraints of money and distance from apparatus of experiments in villages. It is just the beginning and much more needs to be done to either invert the pyramid in true sense or reshape the pyramid into diamond.

Reference

1. See Julian Keith Loren: http://www.slideshare.net/jkloren/innovationteam- topic01-3-innovator-types

Annexure. I

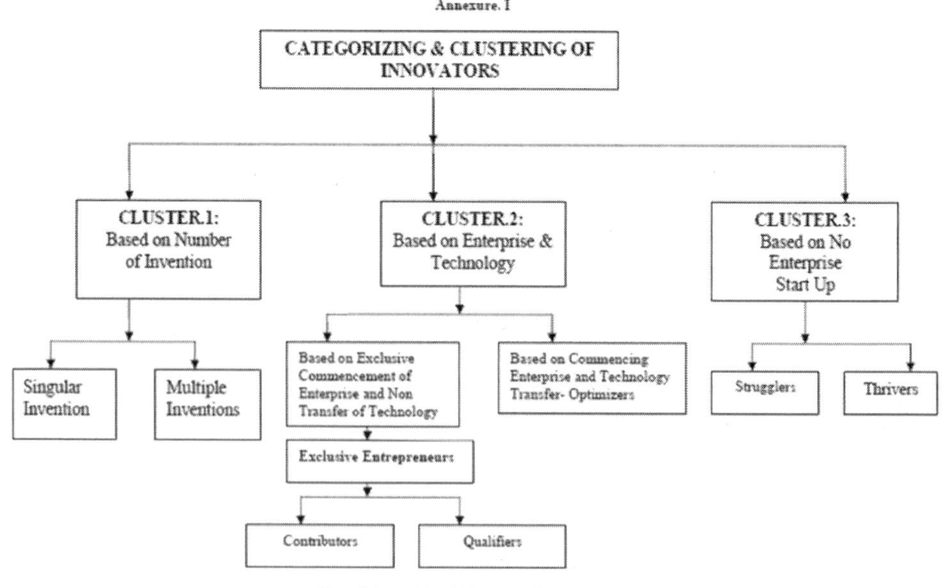

Figure.5 Categorizing & Clustering of Innovators
(Source: Own Creation)

2. See Business Opportunities:http://www.businessopportunities.biz/2006/08/22/nine-types-of-entrepreneurs/
3. See Developing Eyes: http://www.developingeyes.com/five-types-ofentrepreneurs/
4. See Sbininformation: http://sbinformation.about.com/cs/development/a/personality.htm

17

A Comparative Study of Entrepreneurial Innovations in Formal and Informal Sectors

Abstract

The paper focuses on three issues- a) innovations are knowledge based resulting from the synthesis and application of the tacit and the coded knowledge; b) the role of entrepreneur (as knowledge manager) is important for exploiting the tacit knowledge and making use of the coded knowledge; and c) for the diffusion of innovations, variety of actors (as individuals or institutions) participate which leads to the formation of innovation networks. An attempt has been made to elaborate upon the above issues through two case studies from diverse sectors – formal and informal. One case study is related to the diffusion of new technology (plant biotechnology) at the field level. The process from technological innovation to diffusion level involved interaction amongst public and private institutions. The change was mainly based on the coded knowledge (the adoption of new technology) and in the process of change, the tacit knowledge played substantial role (in how to make use of the new technology) in accomplishing the technical change. In the second case of informal sector (the adoption of floriculture by traditional crop growing farmers), entrepreneurs' tacit knowledge initiated the change process. Tacit knowledge was used to fulfill customers needs and thus was used to capture the market. The new knowledge was created by combining the tacit one with the explicit and then applied meaningfully by the entrepreneurs so as to reap the economic benefits. The participation of different institutions in the later case was not so much differentiated and direct as it was in the first case. The role of the government, influenced by the circumstances, for the sustenance of the technical change was apparent.

Introduction

The economic condition of any nation or a region depends on natural and the created resources and then organizing activities around them. For its sustenance or growth, the production systems need to be dynamic so that they can accommodate the changes from time to time. The changes are nothing but are the outcome of innovations. The process of innovation is the creative use of various forms of knowledge to respond to market articulated demands and other social needs. Innovation is the key process that characterizes a knowledge economy understood from a dynamic perspective (Archibugi and Lundvall, 2000). Lundvall and Johnson (1986) suggested 'learning economy' according to which knowledge contributes to development and promoting innovation. It emphasizes the dynamic perspective of knowledge. The learning economy is about new knowledge replacing new knowledge and is very close to Schumpeter's concept of 'creative destruction' (Conceicao and Heitor, 2003).

Innovation is associated with creativity, with generation of new ideas but also with initiative and risk taking ((Conceicao and Heitor, 2003). Innovation entails bringing new ideas to fruition in the market place, satisfying demands or creating new needs, in a process that overall improves overall welfare. Further to creation of knowledge, its articulation to the production system and its diffusion in the society necessitates the participation of variety of actors (as individuals or as institutions). Depending on the type of knowledge used and the way the various types of actors participate in providing the infrastructure and environment for the change to take place, different kinds of innovation networks are formed. The present paper deals with dynamic perspective of the knowledge economy through two case studies. An attempt has been made to reflect the role of the tacit and the explicit knowledge in the field level technical change. It highlights the role of entrepreneurs in ' to create new knowledge' by synthesizing the two types of knowledge and apply it for their own economic gain and bringing a technical change in the society. The two diverse cases-from formal and informal sector compare the nature and process of innovation networks formed in bringing about the technical changes.

Background

The diffusion of innovation at the societal level leads to technical change. The term 'Innovation' has been defined in various ways in the literature and broadly, it amounts to 'doing something new' for the benefit of the enterprise/society. Innovations are the new things applied in producing, distributing, and consuming products or services (Beije, 1998). Schumpeter (1968) made a practical classification of innovation consisting of – a) new products and processes, b) new distribution methods, c) ways to penetrate new markets and d) the use of new management practices and organizational structures. All these categories bring in the role of entrepreneur for opting any of these new activities to earn more money. Thus one can derive that a firm is said to be innovative if it produces a new good or service or applies a new method or material and thus brings about some technical change. The knowledge is the critical requirement for any kind of innovation to take place.

The process could be based on tacit (or embedded) and/ or coded (explicit) types of knowledge having scientific, technical, production engineering, managerial or any other kind of knowledge dimensions. Tacit knowledge was described by Polanyi (1966) as the knowledge we possess but 'cannot tell' and it is more or less intuition, the knowledge we have without 'access-rules' to our memory. Nonaka and Takeuchi (1995) mean the tacit knowledge is personal, context specific and therefore hard to formalise and communicate. According to them, explicit knowledge, in contrast, can be articulated in formal language and transmitted across individuals formally and easily. In case of 'explicit knowledge', we know the 'access-rules' to our personal memory and to its written or electronic storage. It can be routinized, codified and formalized (Boekama et. al, 2000).

Tacit knowledge is argued to be the most important kind of knowledge and through knowledge creation model, explained the transfer of tacit to explicit knowledge through externalisation process (Nonaka and Teakeuchi, 1995). Nonaka et. al (2003) have emphasized that more than managing the explicit knowledge, it is important to create the new knowledge by synthesizing the tacit and explicit knowledge and to incorporate that synthesized knowledge into organisational activities.

An innovative firm may not be deriving all the technological knowledge from within the firm but from external sources as well (Beije, 1998). The innovative firm thus interacts with several kind of external partners and is involved in one or many innovation networks. Such innovation networks may cover private and public organizations and they are the facilitators of technological innovations. Based on the concept of networking, National System of Innovation (NSI) has become very popular (Orsenigo, 1989; Fransman, 1991 and Fransman and Tanaka, 1995). NSI is defined as the "Set of distinct institutions which jointly and individually contribute to the development and diffusion of new technologies and which provides a framework within which governments form and implement policies to influence the innovation process. As such it is a system of interconnected institutions to create, store and transfer the knowledge, skills and artifacts which define new technologies" (Metcafe, 1995) .

NSI encompasses the innovation as well as its diffusion by the participation of public and private institutions (Beije, 1998 and Mehra, 2001). Porter (1990) discussed the issue of national boundaries in the concept of NSI by considering it as the relationships between innovators and their customers and suppliers. Beije (1998) describes NSI by involving more organizations and institutions along with the role of government in promoting technological co-operations and knowledge transfers and the focus of interactions within the national territory.

After considering innovation as the basis for the growth of an economy, and the role of institutions in the technical change, some attention needs to be given to the role of entrepreneurs in the process discussed. Freeman (1982) emphasized the role of entrepreneur to be crucial in the linking of novel ideas and the market together. Schumpeter (1934) put the human agent at the center of the process of economic development. Drucker (1985) considered innovation and entrepreneurship as an integral component for sustaining of life in any organization, economy and society. In the present paper, role of entrepreneurs in managing the knowledge has been elaborated. Through two different case studies, in different settings, the role of two types of knowledge (tacit and explicit) and the participation of different actors/institution for the technical change have been analysed.

Case Studies from India: Knowledge management and Entrepreneurial Innovations

Formal Sector - A Case of application of Plant Biotechnology in Cardamom crop:

This is the case of adoption of a process developed through plant tissue culture technology for the rapid large scale multiplication of elite cardamom planting materials. It describes the need for the new knowledge (explicit knowledge), its generation and utilization 9by synthesizing with tacit knowledge) at commercial scale by the entrepreneur. The involvement and interaction of various institutions and especially the role of government found to be evident have accomplished the diffusion of technology.

Knowledge inflow: There had been a steep fall in the export of cardamom (Elettaria cardamom Maton) from the country since 1980s. India's share in the world export of cardamom declined from 56 per cent in 1970-71 to just 4 per cent in 1994-95. Since mid 1980s, Guatemala had been bringing its produce into the international market and threatening the Indian dominance.

Why had been the fall in the export of cardamom from India? It was due to higher costs of production that in turn was due to low productivity of plantations. Crops had been infested with number of diseases and the most common of them was the 'katte' disease. For maintaining yields, growers had to replant their areas prematurely and to do so; there have been insufficient supply of high yielding disease-free planting material to the cardamom growers.

When such a situation was prevailing in the country, many research laboratories in India became interested in developing a protocol through plant tissue culture for the rapid multiplication of disease free planting material of cardamom which was highly desired to replant the cardamom farms. A national laboratory of Council of Scientific and Industrial Research succeeded in the endeavor and published its finding as a research paper in one of the popular science journal (Nadgauda et. al, 1983). An entrepreneur owning a big cardamom exporting firm came across the article about tissue culture technology and explored the possibility of employing it for his fields so as to overcome the problem of low yields of plantations.

The entrepreneur, without losing any time, managed to acquire the tissue culture technology for multiplication of desired cardamom plant material maintained as stock by the firm. The technology was further upgraded with the help of a foreign company, which was already in the business of commercial multiplication of horticultural plants. The firm set up a tissue culture laboratory with the help of an experienced scientist who had worked abroad in a commercial tissue culture plant production unit in U.K. All these steps show the inflow of knowledge into the firm through various channels. Apart from this, the firm was already having a skilled and unskilled workforce for maintaining a genetic garden with hundreds of clones of healthy cardamom varieties. This was a part of firm's activities and on the basis of experience, the firm was maintaining such a vast collection of superior planting material. Thus, the firm employed the technique of micropropagation (multiplication of elite plant material in huge numbers and in short time through plant tissue culture technology) and replaced the diseased plantations with the healthy plantlets. It resulted in higher productivity, better capsule size and color and in early maturation of crop.

Entrepreneur innovativeness: The entrepreneur was–

1. Aware of the reasons of low productivity of the plantations (tacit knowledge)
2. Targeting to achieve his goals of export
3. Maintaining a genetic garden of healthy, superior high yielding genetic lines. It was due to farming experience (tacit knowledge) and the scientific approach by which healthy plant materials was isolated from the infected ones. He was aiming to multiply the healthy material but conventional method was too slow to multiply the limited plant material for commercial requirements.
4. Having the vision, enterprising and very quick in decision making. With this background and making use of his earlier experience (tacit knowledge), acquired the technology (explicit/ coded knowledge) and employed it for commercial production.

Innovation Network: The entrepreneur succeeded in achieving his targets by making use of the R&D efforts of National research laboratory, by having inputs from abroad, hiring a well trained staff and also utilizing his own experience in cultivation of cardamom and maintaining a stock of superior genetic material. Apart from the manpower and knowledge, he must have interacted with many ancillary (secondary) actors, supplying lots of material inputs but those are not under consideration in the present discussion. The next step was the diffusion of innovation in the society by participation of variety of private and public institutions. The entrepreneur of the firm under discussion, was linked to Spices Board (Ministry of Commerce) and Indian Cardamom Research Institute (public research institution) through various committees. Through these channel he was able to convey the use of plants tissue culture technology to combat the menace of 'katte' and other diseases in cardamom fields, and this was the great concern of various government departments too. The Spices Board linked to Department of Biotechnology (DBT- Ministry of Science and Technology) through various projects also came to know the potential of technology experienced by the firm in the multiplication of high fielding healthy varieties of cardamom.

DBT in the late 1980s was formulating many policies to make use of the new biotechnology and at this juncture when cardamom export was under threat and some developments were taking place, Plant Tissue Culture technology was declared as an industrial activity by DBT. Another government intervention came by launching a multi-institutional project in cardamom for the multiplication of high yielding varieties of cardamom to attend to the problem of diseases in cardamom fields. The project involved number of institutions like private firm, the public research laboratory, Ministry of commerce and Ministry of Science and Technology and the participation of the farmers. The firm was to multiply the elite plant material supplied by the public institution so as to meet the demand of cardamom planting material. The two ministries were involved to finance the project and monitor the adoption of technology by the farmers (diffusion of technology). During this project, healthy plants produced through tissue culture were offered to the farmers at subsidized rates. Government made use of audio/visual media for the popularisation of technology amongst farmers. Farmers developed the faith in technology after comparing the yields of tissue culture raised plants with the control plants on their own fields (Department of Biotechnology, 1989-90) .

In the above case the generation of know-how was the outcome of R&D by a National Research Laboratory and diffusion of the new technology at field level was due to the interaction amongst well differentiated institutions. In this process, the government interventions played an important role in completing the innovation chain.

Informal sector – A Case of Floriculture Sector

It describes the innovativeness of farmers in bringing about the farm level technical change by exploiting their tacit knowledge in farming to capture the market demand. It has been examined for Delhi area and the region around it. The growth in floriculture sector under open field conditions took place due to replacement of traditional crops such as wheat and sugarcane by flower crops marketed as cut flowers. The adoption of crop substitution and thereafter the changes brought in the practices by the farmers for better yields has been accepted as the entrepreneurs innovativeness. The farm level technical change is accomplished when the government is induced to take part. So, contrary to the last case study, the innovations at the field demanded government interventions (induced institutional change) to accommodate the change so that it can survive for the benefit of economy.

***Sources of Innovation*:** India has a long tradition of floriculture but in the last 15-20 years, it has assumed a commercial status. Flower production can be put under two categories- traditional flowers (loose flowers) and cut flowers (with stems). More than one third of total area at the national level is devoted to cut flowers cultivation. The area under cut flowers is gradually expanding and it has increased from 30,000 hectares to 36,000 hectares (Export-Import Bank paper, 1996) has been reported. The area should have expanded further by this time. The promotion in the activity has been due to the replacement of other crops (e.g. sugarcane and wheat) by the farmers who were untrained for the floriculture activity. The sector grew several times to the size of early 1990s. The significant contribution came through open field cultivation of gladiolus, tuberose, rose, carnation, and some other seasonal flowers. The growing affluence, people's interest in using flowers and the favourable policies of the government towards floriculture has made the floriculture as a lucrative business and has created demand for cut flowers. Production of cut flowers for exports is also a thrust area for export. The Agricultural and Processed Food Products Export Development Authority (APEDA), the nodal organisation for promotion of Agri-exports including flowers has introduced several schemes for the promotion of floriculture exports from the country. These relate to development of infrastructure, market development, freight subsidy etc. The 100% Export Oriented Units have several benefits like duty free imports of capital goods, etc. It led to large investments in this area and as a result, 186 projects with a production capacity of 1833 million stems per annum were approved by Indian Government till 1998. Nearly 70 units have already commenced production (APEDA report, 1999).

All these efforts indicate the government's commitment for improving the sector and create a positive climate for entrepreneurship development in the field. Though these products are mainly exported, domestic market also receives a good amount and in spite of higher costs, gets very speedily consumed in the market.

***Entrepreneur innovativeness*:** The farmers who were growing traditional varieties of rose, gladiolus and other flowers could notice the sharp increase in the sale of high quality cut flowers produced under green house conditions. In addition to high market demand, the government policies announced to promote the cultivation of flowers in green house conditions for the export purpose, created an environment to educate the scientifically informed farmers (even those growing traditional crops like wheat and sugarcane) about the cultivation of superior quality cut flowers. The regular Kisan Melas (Farmer fairs) to display the new technologies and products also brought awareness amongst the traditional small and medium farmers. Many of them got inspired by the successful attempts made by their neighbours/relatives/friends in the field of floriculture. It was a case of 'seing is believing' It helped the farmers to think and go for crop substitution may be on experimental basis. Thus, the capturing of the market demand and utilisation of the tacit knowledge of farming, without any kind of formal, outside supply of scientific and technical knowledge remains the basis of innovativeness of the farmers (Mehra, 2002).

They used high quality planting material being used by green houses for their open field conditions. They brought about number of changes by themselves on the basis of 'learning by doing':

1. The quality of product has been improved by manipulating the input supply e.g. supply of potash etc made the flowers look bright. They also incorporated gypsum which otherwise is not used in other crops.
2. The preservation of the planting material (bulbs) has been standarised. Bulbs of flowers are commonly kept in cold storage. Some farmers have developed alternative method of preserving bulbs by burying them in sand and controlling the room temperature through ventilation etc.
3. The flowering time has been manipulated by them to get the maximum flowering on the peak demand days as the is very well irrigated, 3-4 days prior to specific demand day.
4. Manipulation of the sowing times has increased the number of harvests during the year.
5. Standardisation has been achieved for the depth of the pit for sowing the bulb, inter bulb distance.
6. Methods of harvesting and packaging been standardized to maintain moisture and quality of cut flower intact.

Networking of institutions- induced institutional innovation: By mid 1990's, adoption of floriculture by more and more farmers under open field conditions by the use of superior planting material led to the production of better quality cut flowers in large volumes. All the produce of the fields started flowing into Delhi market for sale. With the increase in volumes, there was an increase in the number of wholesalers whereas in the early 1990s, hardly one could find any wholesaler (Mehra et. al,1996).

Since it was the beginning infrastructure for the sale of flowers was lacking. Initially, small volumes of flowers brought by individual grower from near or far off Delhi were being sold at Cannaught Place outside Hanuman Temple in an informal way. Some amount was also being sold at Chattarpur, which was the produce of local farmhouses. By mid 1990s larger volumes of produce started coming from hundreds of kilometers away to Cannaught Place market on regular basis. There was remarkable difference in the quantum and variety of products. The market became unmanageable without any infrastructure and permission of authorities, sellers started facing problems. Municipal Corporation of Delhi started harassing sellers. Sellers having no option but continue to sell with a great risk. Under these circumstances, need for the togetherness arose and it resulted in the formation of societies or associations. Within a period of one year, three societies were registered and managed to get permission from the government to continue to sell the produce at the existing places, till alternative permanent market place is arranged for them. The kind of network formed during this period was very important. No initiative from government to promote the business rather it was the demand from the growers and sellers for the support from government. These developments indicating a step towards formalization of the informal field level innovation. There was an induced institutional by the setting up of a "Pushp Samiti" to look after the welfare of the business of cut flowers in the Delhi region. The government has announced for the setting up a big whole sale flower market with appropriate infrastructure (Das, 1999). In this case, no well defined 'innovation network' was formed. The policies of the government, role of private firms for the sale of planting materials, financial institutions etc. were not meant for promotion of open field cultivation.

Conclusion

'Knowledge management describes all methods, instruments and tools that in a holistic approach contribute to promotion of the core knowledge processes –to generate knowledge, to store knowledge, to distribute knowledge and to apply knowledge - in all areas and levels of organizations' (Mertins et. al, 2001). The paper also discussed the process of promotion of core knowledge and its application at the production level in two diverse conditions of economic activity. During the course, role of entrepreneurs and the interplay of tacit and explicit knowledge and the participation of various actors/institutions have been compared.

The process of innovation in case of cardamom was a planned activity. The entrepreneur had the skill of growing cardamom and exporting it. He could make out the reasons of low productivity of his fields. He used his tacit knowledge in maintaining a genetic stock of superior planting material in a scientific way. However, limitation was there, as it was not possible to multiply the maintained stock to meet the commercial requirements in a short time. The entrepreneur thus utilized R&D based protocol of micropropagation (coded knowledge) of cardamom developed in a laboratory. It was a case of the utilization of tacit and coded knowledge by the entrepreneur. However the process was dominated by the plant biotechnology based knowledge (coded form). The innovation chain had participation from variety of actors and institutions describing an national system of innovation in plant biotechnology in India.

Case study in floriculture, a case of informal sector, describes the innovativeness of the farmers in bringing about farm level technical change. The change occurred gradually without any kind of planning. The farmer could notice the sudden growth of cut flower market and employed the tacit knowledge and skills for capturing the market. The source for such knowledge had been the market surroundings. There was no direct involvement of the government. In fact the policies and the infrastructure created for the promotion of production of green house technology based production and export of superior quality cut flowers, served the purpose of informing the 'scientifically' informed farmers who were growing traditional crops. Foreign companies were selling superior quality planting material (bulbs) in India and it was a product of innovation of foreign companies. The farmers made use of that easily available coded knowledge and exploiting their tacit knowledge. Thus, the process in informal sector (floriculture) was dominated by the tacit knowledge.

In the latter case of innovations, not many institutions directly played any part. The innovation discussed was a byproduct of the efforts of public institutions for export promotion of green house technology based production. The market circumstances forced individuals to form association and societies force the government to participate in the making of organized flower market and it resulted in the creation of infrastructure. 'Innovation network' formed in the informal sector is thus different from the network formed in case of formal sector. A comparison of the innovation network formation in two sectors discussed above has been summarized in Table1.

Both the case studies have one thing in common- the role of tacit knowledge in the farm level technical change. This part of knowledge got transformed as new knowledge by getting synthesized with the explicit knowledge.

Table 1: Formation of Innovation Networks : Formal and Informal Sectors

Innovation Network/ issues	Formal Sector	Informal Sector
Activity	Planned	Non planned
Type of knowledge used	Primarily new knowledge Mainly the use of coded knowledge	Knowledge through experience base Mainly the use of tacit knowledge and skills
Sources of knowledge	R&D	Learning through experience, knowledge spill over through interaction with the environment
Investments on the knowledge generation	Yes	No
Role of Government	In creating the infrastructure	Not directly, but in informing the society, scientifically informed entrepreneurs get the signals
Participation of actors and institutions	Variety of actors/ institutions	Individuals mainly, no defined organisation or institutions directly participate
Sustenance of change	On completion of innovation chain	For the institutionalization of change, participation of the government is desirable

References

1. Annual Reports, (Department of Biotechnology, Ministry of Science and Technology, 1989-90 to 95-96).
2. Archibugi,D. and Lundvall,B. *The Globalizing learning economy,* (Oxford University press , 2000).
3. Beije, P. (1998). Technological Change in the Modern Economy. Edward Elgar, U.K.
4. Boekema, F., Morgan, K., Bakkers, S. & Rutten,R. (2000). Knowledge, Innovation and Economic Growth. Edward Elgar, U.K.
5. Conceicao, P. and Heitor, M.V. 'Systems of innovation and competence building across diversity: learning from the portuguese path in the European context.in : L.V.Shavinina (ed.), *The Internation Handbook on Innovation,(* Elsevier Science ,2003).
6. Das, A.K., 'AC flower market for Delhi soon' in *Hindustan Times*, a daily newspaper, Delhi,India (1999).

7. Drucker, P.F. *Innovation and Entrepreneurship-Practice and Principles.* (Heinmann, London, 1985).
8. Freeman, C. *The Economics of Industrial Innovation,*(Francis Pinter, London, 1982).
9. Fransman, M. *Biotechnology: Generation, Diffusion and Policy-An Imperative Survey* (UNU/INTEC Working Paper No. 1, 1991).
10. M. Fransman, M. and Tanaka , S. 'The strengths and weaknesses of the Japanese innovation system in biotechnology' in: M. Fransman, G.Junne and A.Roobeek (eds.), *The Biotechnology Revolution?* (Blackwell Publishers, UK,1995).
11. *'Floriculture: a sector study'* (Occasional paper no.50, Export-Import Bank of India 1996).
12. Lundvall, B.A. and .Johnson, B. 'The learning economy', *Journal of Industry studies,* 1/2, 1994, p.23-42.
13. Mehra, K., Entrepreneurial spirit of the Indian farmers, *AI&Society,* 16, 2002, p. 112-118.
14. Mehra, K., Kapoor, R. and Nabi, S. *'Floriculture Market Study – A case of wholesale market in Delhi '* (Agricultural and Processed Food Development Authority, Ministry of Commerce, Government of India , 1996).
15. Mehra, K. 'Indian System of Innovation in Biotechnology-A case study of Cardamom.' *Technovation , 2*, 2001, p.15-23.
16. Mertins, I.K. Heisig, P. and Vorbeck, J. 'Introduction' in: Mertins, K., Heisig, P. and Vorbeck, J.(eds.), *Knowledge management -Best Practices in Europe,* (Springer, 2001).
17. Metcalfe, S. 'The economic foundation of technology policy: Equilibrium and evolutionary perspective' in: Stoneman, P. (ed.), *Handbook of the Economics of Innovation and Technical Change,* (Blackwell, London, 1995).
18. Nadgauda, R.S., Mascarenhas, A.F. and Madhsudan, K.K. 'Clonal multiplication of cardamom (Elettaria cardamom) Mat. by tissue culture' *Journal of Plantation Crops, 11*, 1983, p. 60 .
19. Nonaka, I. and Takeuchi, H. *The knowledge- creating company,* (Oxford University press, 1995).
20. Nonaka, I, Sasaki, K. and Ahmed, M.. 'Continuos Innovation: The power of tacit knowledge' in : Shavinina, L.V. (ed.), *The Internation Handbook on Innovation,(* Elsevier Science ,2003).
21. Orsenigo, L. *The Emergence of Biotechnology* (Pinters Publishers , London, 1989).
22. Porter, M. *The Competitive Advantage of Nations*, (Macmillan Press, London,1990).

23. Polanyi, K. (1966). The Tacit Dimensions. Bantam Doubleday Dell Publishing Group, USA
24. Schumpeter, J.A. (1968). The Theory of Economic Development, Harvard University Press, Cambridge (MA).
25. Schumpeter, J.A. *The Theory of Economic Development* (Harvard University Press, Cambridge, Mass, 1934).

18

Public–Private Technology Transfer Stimulates Innovation and Propel Entrepreneurship

Abstract

India has a large number of public sector undertakings. Research & Development is an integral part of many of these undertakings, the R& D centres of these public sector establishments have contributed to research in India in a big way, whether it is product innovation, process innovation and in general technology development. Many of the Public undertakings are entering into public-private partnership for promotion of technology transfer. This joint effort can stimulate further innovation in technologies and result in growth of entrepreneurship. There are several examples of such transfer leading to entrepreneurship. The present paper is to study the issues, challenges and analyze the factors that can contribute to the growth of public-private participation in technology transfer resulting in entrepreneurship.

Introduction

In 1990's the economic environment in India had undergone a drastic change the economy was guided by three buzzwords liberalization, privatization and c globalization. The de licensing of many industries encouraged growth of private enterprises. The private sector today is playing a significant role in contributing to the revenue of the country. The private sector is partnering public sector in improving the basic infrastructure, delivery systems and also in bringing new technologies into the country. Public-Private partnerships are increasing in many sectors to day especially in technology transfers and in boosting entrepreneurial growth. India has a large number of government controlled research institutions and premier institutes established after the country's independence. These institutions today are known for their quality and research. These institutes have made valuable contribution in the field of scientific and technological research. The organizations like ICMR, ICAR, CSIR, DRDO, ISRO, DBT, CFTRI are in the forefront in technology transfer. The indigenous technology transfer from these companies to private individuals or to organizations can stimulate innovation and propel entrepreneurial growth. As the number of educated people increase the government faces the challenges of providing suitable employment to these people. The technology transfer between public-private enterprises can increase the growth of private sector and provide a large section of people employment as well as entrepreneurial opportunities. The Technology transfer from the government-owned research organizations is proving to be catalyst in propelling and stimulating entrepreneurship and innovation. The commercialization of technology by the institutes helped in improvisation and adaptability to their environment and the entrepreneurial spirit that was gaining prominence during this period was becoming even more important. The present study is undertaken to analyze the opportunities the technology transfer between public and private enterprises offers for innovation and for entrepreneurship in the country.

Objectives of the study are to:

1. Study the Technology Transfers by various government controlled institutions
2. Study the opportunities for innovation and entrepreneurship.
3. Conclusions to be drawn based on the above analysis.

Methodology for the study

The study is undertaken using the data available on the Internet and other secondary sources. The study is descriptive in nature.

Limitation of the study

Limitation of the study is, the study is undertaken using the data available from secondary sources like Internet.

2. Technology Transfer – Stimulants of Growth And Innovation

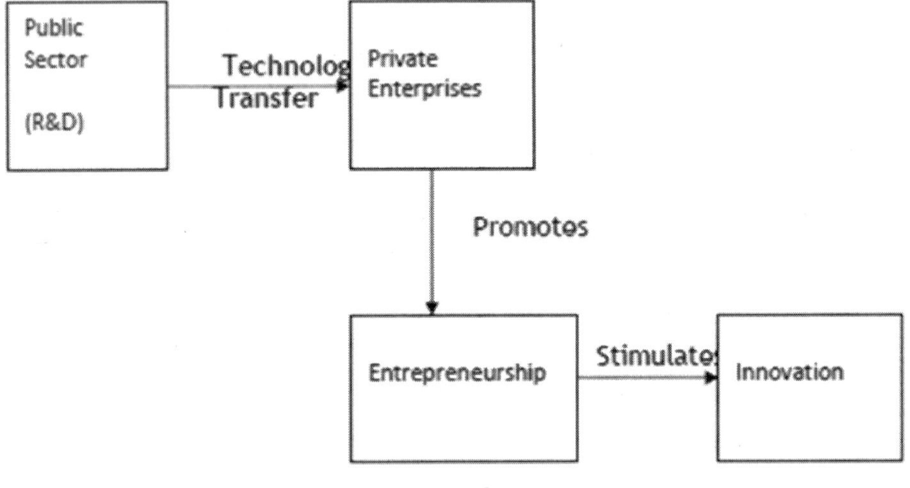

Figure 1

The above diagrammatic representation shows the relationship between Technology Transfer, Entrepreneurship and Innovation. The Process can be initiated, funded or made to succeed through intermediaries called coordinators, cells or agency which can guide the different parties involved. These intermediaries can accelerate technology transfer to foster entrepreneurship environment in the country.

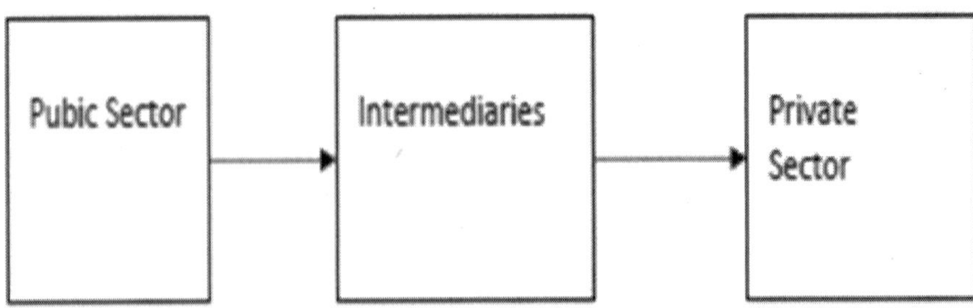

Figure 2

The Intermediary or the Agency can play a proactive role for the all parties concerned For Public Sector: The agency or the cell (like Financial Institution or voluntary organizations) can identify the right set of private enterprises who have genuine interest in acquiring and innovating it through their private venture can transfer the benefits of the same to people at large.

For Private sector: The agency or cell can play the role of a guardian in helping the individual or group to identify the appropriate technology based on individual skills and expertise by interacting with the participating public sectors

For Agency itself: In case the agency or cell is a financial institution this is not only an opportunity to provide the prospective private party money but also help the agency in monitoring them easily.

In case the agency or cell is a voluntary agency interested in transfer of important technologies for public for good it can play the role of monitor in seeing the appropriate technologies reaches the targeted people and in a cost effective way through public-private partnership.

The ultimate beneficiaries of the technology transfer are the people because they are able to get goods or services at cheaper cost, there increased scope for employment generation and new technologies are available to them.

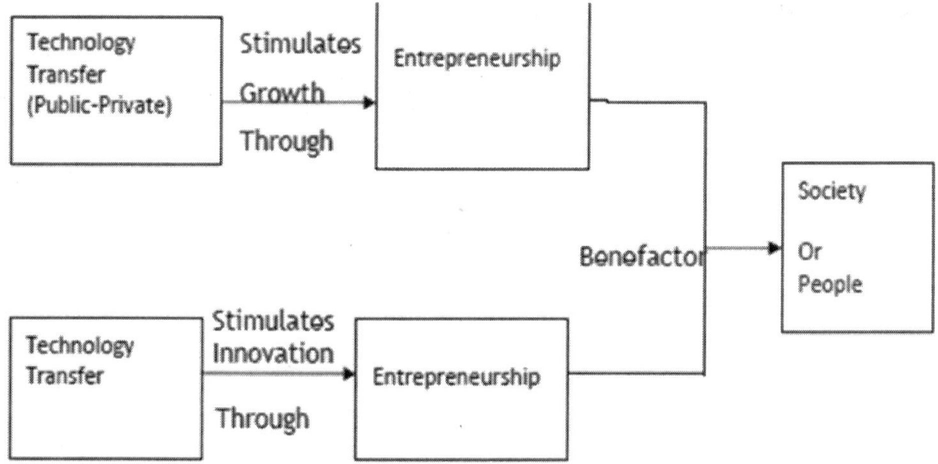

The examples given below explain the advantage of public- private technology to general public:

I. Jaipur Foot was improvised by the technology provided by the DRDO. Jaipur foot is boon for many accident victims who lost their legs for any reason.
II. Ready-To-Make and Ready-To-Eat food items, available in the market are because of technology developed by CFTRI, Mysore.
III. Kalam-Care Heart Stunt used in heart related a problem is a collaborative effort of DRDO and Care Hospitals, Hyderabad.

Technology Transfer–Indian Scenario

Technology Transfer in India by Government owned research and development organizations is gaining importance. The coming in of patenting regime in the country has created a sense of responsibility and a challenge for many scientific and technology research institutes to make their research available to public. The R& D organizations have realized the importance of publishing their new findings and filing patents for their discoveries, their organizations have created infrastructure for patenting by individuals and organizations and commercializing their discoveries. This has created a new scientific temper and also boosting the entrepreneurship among the youth of country. The indigenous technologies are affordable for aspiring techno entrepreneurs. A brief look into the technology transfer and their commercialization in India provides analyst optimism for growth.

National Research and Development Agency (NRDC) established in 1953 under the Ministry of Science and Technology, Government of India is a nodal agency in transfer of technology for commercial purposes. It has been acting as a bridging agent between scientific establishments and industry. NRDC has provided valuable assistance to budding entrepreneurs. NRDC has conducted special programs on entrepreneurship amongst youth in North East states and also conducted programs with special emphasis on women entrepreneurship.

According NRDC's annual report 2008-09

Details regarding processes assigned and agreements concluded with entrepreneurs during 2008-09:

	2007-08	2008-09
A. Processes Assigned	58	55
B. New License Agreements Concluded	41	36

These programs are carried out to promote entrepreneurship among women and during the programs the corporation provides information on appropriate technologies. The corporation has conducted in all 14 such programs in southern states at various universities.

In India, technology transfer from public funded research institutions to industry happens in various ways, either the research organizations have a special cell or department for a liaison between the research organization and industry e.g.

1. Antrix — Indian Space Research Organisation (ISRO)
2. C-Tech — Defence Research and Development Organisation (DRDO)
3. Centre for Scientific and Industrial Consultancy (CSIC) — Indian Institute of Science
4. Industrial Research & Consultancy Centre (IRCC) — Indian Institute of technology, Bombay
5. Foundation for Innovation and Technology Transfer (FITT) - Indian Institute of Technology, Delhi
6. Sponsored Research and Industrial Consultancy (SRIC) — Indian Institute Technology, Kharagpur
7. Technology Licensing Cell (TLC) of Research Institutes like TLC - Bhabha Atomic Research Centre
8. Or there is an organization as interface between research organizations and Industry e.g. National Research Development Corporation (NRDC) and Biotech Consortium India Limited (BCIL). [Ref 1]

No. of technologies received (without technology duplication over the years) from various sources during 2003-04 to 2007-08 (Based on information received from NRDC)

Source: Technology Transfer by Kavita Mehra cited at ref 1

CSIR on the recommendations of Abid Hussain committee CSIR laboratories was given freedom to commercialize their technologies on their own without the assistance of NRDC.

Government Research Institutes like Central Food Technology Research Institute (CFTRI), Mysore set up in 1950s has made significant contributions to technology creation and technology transfer in the area food processing and other related areas According Dr. P. K. Gupta, Scientist, CFTRI writes- In order to ensure that fruits of its wide ranging endeavors in technology reach the right user at the right time and in the right way, CFTRI transfers classified technologies against prescribed fee for each process. [Ref 1]

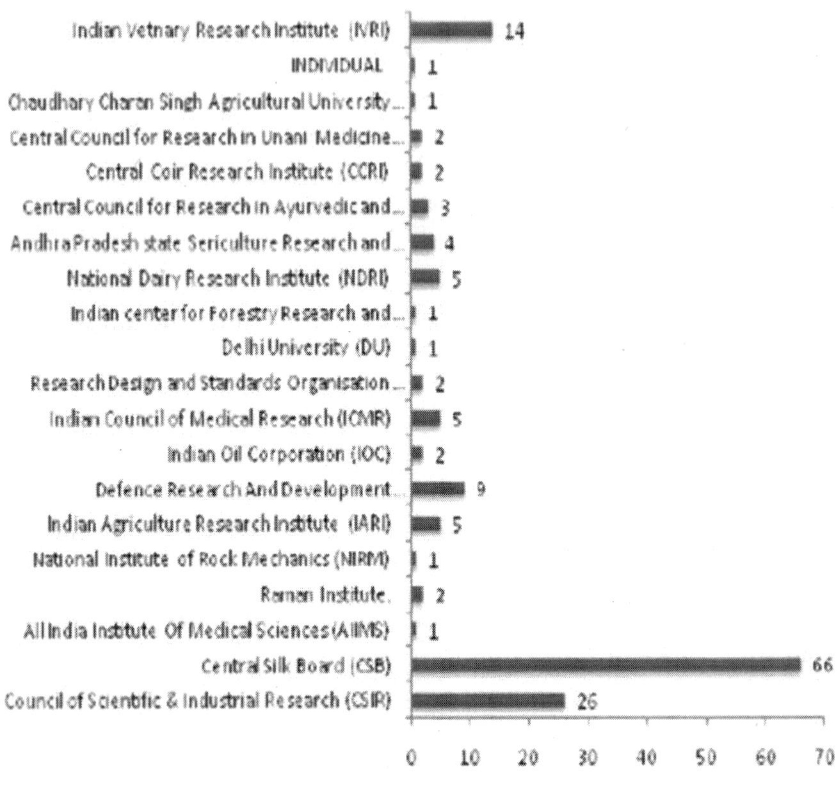

According to CFTRI it has created a major social impact in India with its role in developing technologies for low-cost nutritious food supplements and specialty foods for several vulnerable sections of the society. During the last 5 years CFTRI has played an important role transferring these technologies to socially conscious entrepreneurs. It has run 500 programs of technology awareness, entrepreneurship development, Demonstration and Training across the country, particularly in rural and tribal areas and for women entrepreneurs.

Indian Space Research Organization (ISRO), The organization under department of Space has transferred a number of technologies to industry. Technology Transfer Group of ISRO initiates and guides all technology transfer of ISRO. According to ISRO - The technology transfer mechanism established during early eighties enables licensing of know-how from various centres for commercial exploitation. Over 290 technologies have successfully transferred and productionised in industries in the field of electronic and computer-based systems, specialty polymer chemicals and materials, electro-optical instruments, mechanical equipments and ground systems related to satellite communications, broadcasting and meteorology. Industries in the large, medium and small-scale sectors have largely been beneficiaries of the technology transfer scheme. ISRO have executed over 270 consultancy projects in high technology areas to provide support to various industries [ref 2].

Defense Research And Development Organization under Ministry of Defense is commercializing its research and new technologies developed in their laboratories. DRDO Labs have been undertaking a large number of projects in wide ranging areas of science and technology related to Indian Armed forces.

Though the end products are for military use, many of the technologies that are developed to realize these systems can have civilian applications. These applications and products may have large commercial potential and wide application in India and abroad. DRDO in January 2010 signed six MOU with Industry for Technology Transfer through FICCI. To unearth the hidden potential in the commercial market, DRDO through launched the ATAC program. This Commercialization process is aimed at filling the technology gap in Indian Industries. [Ref 4].

BHEL, another navratna public sector has an R&D centre that plays an active in acquiring for their own requirement from outside the country and improvising them and transferring them for peoples good. Indian Council for Medical Research (ICMR) also has a number of technologies, which developed indigenously. ICMR established in 1911 is one of the oldest medical research organizations in the world. The Council has 27 permanent institutes/centres actively pursuing in need based research. ICMR has identified the importance of public-private partnership ad means of achieving its goal of providing affordable health care to the needy and also realization that such joint ventures could help health care products reach needy public more efficiently and quickly. So it has given a lot of impetus to IPR and Technology Transfer.

ICAR or Indian Council for Agricultural Research is also an old organization established in 1929 as an autonomous organization under the department of agricultural research and education in the Ministry of Agriculture and is actively involved in carrying out research in agriculture and related areas. The Organization has realized the importance of technology transfer and the need for private partnership in transferring the technologies to the large sections of small and medium farmers. ICMR has endeavored to contribute towards technology-led growth of Indian agriculture through grater partnership with different stakeholders.

The Organizations like Accelerator India through their ACTIV (Accelerated Commercialization of Technology and Innovation) workshops. The Organization is playing a proactive role in creating an entrepreneurial environment through scientific research and technology transfer. Through their works the hope to achieve their outlined objectives such as

- o Strengthen competencies in public research institutions and technology transfer and commercialization organizations in India in the area of Technology based entrepreneurship, i.e. taking an idea from the lab to the market in the form of new products and services.
- o Build new capabilities for commercialization through a variety of business models such as licensing, technology transfer and new venture creation.
- o Transform a small but significant section of India's science and technology manpower and technology transfer and commercialization manpower from job seekers to job-generators, by promoting new knowledge driven enterprises. [Ref 9].

Federation Indian Chamber of Commerce and Industry or FICCI has established a centre for Technology Commercialization to provide an organized structure to link the mind to market. According to Dr. Amit Mitra, Secretary General, FICCIwe would be supporting all Public and Private funded research organizations under this centre. We will continue to provide commercialization support to DRDO, DST and look forward to supporting organizations like CSIR as well. [Ref 4].

Technology Transfer and Entrepreneurship Development –Role Of Academic Institutes

In India Government controlled R&D organization have set up cells or centres to transfer or commercialize their scientific research and technologies developed indigenously. These centres are responsible for identifying the right private persons for technology transfer and promote socio-economic growth. The Institutes of excellence such as IITs, IIMs, Universities have centres for technology creation, transfer. These Institutes and Universities also have Entrepreneurship Development Cells or some IIMs have Business Incubation Centres as well to promote entrepreneurship through indigenous technologies.

IITs like Chennai, Bombay, Kanpur and Kharagpur have centres for developing promoting indigenously developed technologies and inculcating the spirit of entrepreneurship among the youth.

In IIT Chennai there is centre for industrial consultancy and sponsored research, this centre is responsible for co-ordinating the sponsored research and industrial consultancy projects. It identifies and protects IP rights and manages transfer of technology and commercialization.

In IIT, Bombay – Society for innovation and entrepreneurship or SINE administers a business incubator that provides technology-based entrepreneurship. IIT Bombay also has an entrepreneurship cell that not only motivates the youth to startup their own enterprises but also makes efforts to provide them with necessary resources. IIT, Kanpur has set up a centre in collaboration with Small IndustriesDevelopment Board of India (SIBDI) called SIBDI Innovation and Incubator Centre to promote and foster innovation, research and entrepreneurial activities in technology based areas.

IIT Kharagpur has set up Rajendra Mishra School of Engineering Entrepreneurship and student Entrepreneurship cell. The aim of this school is to provide the opportunities for undergraduate engineering students to design a product or a service during their period of study.

IIT Delhi has Industrial R& D set up to provide specialized administrative and managerial support for the operation of sponsored research, consultancy and other related R&D activities of the institute. The Institute also has Entrepreneurship Development Cell to promote entrepreneurship among students of IIT Delhi. The Premier Science and technology institute the IISc Bangalore also has a number of centres to study and conduct research in frontier and need based technologies. The Centre for scientific and industrial consultancy is set up to promote sponsored and industrial research and interaction for the industry.

The well known Management institutes in India like IIMs are playing an active role in promoting entrepreneurial environment amongst youth of India. IIM Ahmedabad has centre for Innovation, Incubation and Entrepreneurship set up with the support from Gujarat Government and Department of Science and Technology, Government of India to promote innovation and entrepreneurship.

Similarly IIM Bangalore set up NS Raghavan Centre for entrepreneurial learning (NSRCEL) for seeding, nurturing and promoting entrepreneurship. This centre not trains and promotes entrepreneurship cell but also acts as an incubator cell for startup companies. IIM Kolkata 's centre for entrepreneurship and innovation is an initiative to achieve greater understanding of the process as well as stimulate its development for social benefit. Centre for Entrepreneurial Ventures and Innovation & Incubation Centre of IIM Lucknow are playing an important role in providing linkages with industry, support and required facilities for students to take up entrepreneurial ideas into workable business ideas. Wadhwani Centre for Entrepreneurship Development of Indian School of Business empowers and encourages entrepreneurship by incubating business ideas.

In addition to all the above formal academic institutes, Government set up institutes for promotion and development of entrepreneurship. Institutes like EDI, Ahmedabad, IIE Guwahati, MSME, Hyderabad are playing an important role in helping the prospective entrepreneur not only in identifying the right technology but also providing the necessary training to run an enterprise.

Future Prospects

a. India with vast pool of Government Controlled R&D Laboratories that doing a lot of valuable research can contribute a lot to development and commercialization of technologies. However these laboratories must concentrate on identifying right technologies for research and creation technologies for societal benefit.
b. The Public sector companies which like BHEL, ISRO, DRDO, DAE etc can play a more active in identifying right technology for transfer and also tie up with entrepreneurship development institutes for commercializing their technologies and promotion of private entrepreneurship.
c. The Academic Institutes and Specialized institutes for entrepreneurship promotion must co-ordinate with R&D institutes in identifying need based technologies and their transfer for promoting entrepreneurship among technical and management students and others interested in taking up entrepreneurship.
d. The Growing public interest especially among educated middle class towards entrepreneurship can hasten the technology development and transfer and foster entrepreneurial environment in the country.

Conclusions

The above study outlines the scope for greater participation of both public and private sectors for promotion of indigenous technology transfer for prospective entrepreneurs. The Government Owned R&D institutions are contributing immensely for technology transfer that can stimulate innovation to make the product, process or service suitable for the local environment and this will propel entrepreneurship amongst the students and youth of the country. The premier institutes of Technology and Management in India are contributing in their own way to promote the spirit of creativity, innovation and entrepreneurial culture among students studying in their institutes.

References

1. Kavita Mehra, India, Science and Technology; 2008, S&T Structure, Infrastructure and Public Space-Technology Transfer, NISTADS/ CSIR
2. P.K.Gupta, Technology for Commercialization: CFTRI, www.cftri.com
3. Prabhu Ram, Technology Transfer in the Public Research System, www.sathguru.com
4. Technology Transfer and Business Development, CFTRI
5. DRDO signs six MoUs with industry for technology transfer, Inside Kerala,
6. http://www.isro.gov.in/ttg
7. www.icmr.nic.in/ipr
8. www.icar.org.in
9. www.nrdc.com
10. http://www.venturecenter.co.in/activ/
11. www.iitm.ac.in
12. www.iitb.ac.in
13. www.iitd.ac.in

19

Entrepreneurial Leadership and New Venture Innovations: The two faces of R&D

Abstract

This study aims to contribute to the knowledge of leadership styles and entrepreneurial orientation at small and medium enterprises (SMEs) as well as their effects on business performance. Entrepreneurial leadership and continuous innovation are vital components of twenty-first-century communities and organizations. The concept of 'visionary leadership' has been changed to 'entrepreneurial leadership' in 21st century. Leadership is one of the most essential ingredients for entrepreneurial success yet it is conceptually elusive. Most business leaders would agree that innovation is vital for delivering business results and maintaining competitive advantages. The climate demands that organizations must adopt a new model for improving profitability, increasing competitiveness, allowing for globalization and providing superior customer care. Entrepreneurial leaders must realize the importance of environmental, social, and global issues while creating an atmosphere of innovation designed to help followers become more entrepreneurial themselves. Research and Development (R&D) culture is the engine for sustained product innovations and key driver of continual growth. R&D fuels sustainable economic expansion by creating high-wage jobs, world class exports and the growth of productivity. A model has also been developed to test the effectiveness of the leadership and innovations in Indian SMEs.

Introduction

"Courage-not complacency-is our need today. Leadership not salesmanship. And the only valid test of leadership is the ability to lead. Our ends will not be won by rhetoric. We can have faith in the future only if we have faith in ourselves."

John F Kennedy

Entrepreneur basically means 'Capitalist' and 'Industrialist' i.e., 'Producer', 'Maker', 'Manufacturer'. Here in the broader sense, the macro vision, entrepreneur does mean the producer of new things, new ideas, languages and all those innovations in the world. Thus an entrepreneur is the crown of all the present day academic, spiritual, cultural, scientific and technological innovations and developments in the world. Had not there been an entrepreneur we all would have been still in the primitive age moving in the jungles without proper food, clothing and shelter. It is by the zeal and perseverance of the entrepreneurs of the past that it has become possible for us to live in this modern age quite cozily with all the comforts in life. Unless one makes efforts and becomes a successful entrepreneur he will have to lead a stagnant and mundane life.

The entrepreneur must be able to recognize and seize external opportunities that relate to innovation in a specific industry. Specifically, it is important to apply innovation when sources of opportunity are presented through the entrepreneurial environment. There are three sources of innovative opportunities which are very much essential for smooth functioning of the business. They are incongruities, demographics, and perception change. An important aspect of these motivational models is the role of entrepreneurial goals in motivating business founders to sustain their pursuit of entrepreneurial activity.

What makes a good entrepreneur? What attributes do successful entrepreneurs possess? What are the qualities that make an entrepreneur effective? The answer to these questions must arise from an understanding of either what entrepreneurs actually do or what they are expected to do; it would require, in other words, an analysis of the entrepreneurial skills. Essential qualities of an entrepreneur are as follows:

Entrepreneurship is essential for international, social and economic well-being, as new ventures are the dominant source of job creation, market innovation, and economic growth in many societies. Entrepreneurship is a major contributing factor to the economic well-being of a country, both in terms of economic growth and job creation. Traditionally, entrepreneurial ability tended to be defined by the following four attributes:

1. Initiative – the entrepreneur takes the initiative to bring together the economic resources of land, labour and capital to produce a commodity (whether a good or a service), with the hope that such production will create a profitable business venture.
2. Decision-making - the entrepreneur makes the basic business policy decisions for the business, thereby setting the course of the enterprise.
3. Innovation – the entrepreneur is an innovator who attempts to introduce new products and new ways of doing things.
4. Risk-taker – the entrepreneur risks his or her time, effort, business reputation and invested funds in the entrepreneurial venture.

Literature Review

"Entrepreneurship, in its narrowest sense, involves capturing ideas, converting them into products and/or services and then building a venture to take the product to market" (Johnson, 2001, p. 138). Drucker (1994) made an important contribution to the theoretical construct of entrepreneurship in large organisations when he referred to "corporate entrepreneurship" or "intrapreneurship." Antoncic and Hisrich (2003) argued that intrapreneurship goes on within organisations, regardless of their size. Intrapreneurship research has studied the individual intrapreneur, the formation of new corporate ventures, and the characteristics of entrepreneurial organization (Antoncic & Hisrich, 2003). Innovation can be radical *and* incremental. Radical innovations refer to pathbreaking, discontinuous, revolutionary, original, pioneering, basic, or major innovations (Green, Gavin, & Aiman-Smith, 1995). Incremental innovations are small improvements made to enhance and extend the established processes, products, and services. However, this contradiction does not "necessarily correspond to the more fine-tuned reality" because "radicality is a continuum" (Katila, 2002 p. 307). The spirit of entrepreneurship includes imagination, inventiveness and openness to the *new*. This spirit of creative response aligns with the capacity to exercise moral imagination and to see ethical problems in a new light. To be sure, our most fundamental ethical values — values such as honesty, avoiding doing harm, keeping commitments – are grounded in timeless traditions and are not likely to be soon abandoned. But it is in the application of these ethical values to emerging, unique situations, where moral imagination and the entrepreneurial spirit can make a decisive difference.

Entrepreneurial Leadership: A New Paradigm

Leadership is one of the essential ingredients for entrepreneurial success yet it is conceptually clusive. We recognize leadership when we see it but it is very hard to say what we are recognizing. The challenge is not just to understand leadership but also to provide recommendations on how leadership skills can be developed and used to enhance organizational performance. Entrepreneurial leadership can be classified into following eight categories. Thinking about leadership is developing rapidly. In some ways a new post-transformational integration which draws from the whole tradition on leadership thinking is emerging. By distilling this integration, entrepreneurial leadership can be thought of as having eight key elements.

1. Personal Vision: The entrepreneur's vision is the driving force behind leadership. It is the vision which transforms a disparate group of stakeholders into the people who will act to move the venture forward.
2. Communication with stakeholders: An entrepreneur must relate their vision to stakeholders through a variety of communication channels and forums. Such communications is not simply a passion of information; it is a call to action.
3. Organisational culture: It is the web of rules which define how it goes about its tasks. The relationship between leadership and culture is reciprocal. Leadership creates the organization's culture and in return, the organization's culture creates a space to be filled by a leader.
4. Knowledge and expertise: Entrepreneurs develops expertise in some specialist technology. For example, Bill Gate's knowledge of computing is an example of the above.
5. Desire to lead: The thing which ultimately underpins leadership is the desire to lead. No-one can be an effective leader unless he really wants to take on the role of leader.
6. Credibility: It is critical for leadership. If credibility can be built-up, then leadership becomes easier. If an entrepreneur loses credibility, then leadership is likely to be made more problematic if not lost altogether.

7. Performance of the venture: Credibility comes from the decisions which lead to successful outcomes. If credibility comes from being associated with success, it is not necessarily true that credibility is automatically lost as a result of the occasional failure.
8. Leadership role: The entrepreneur will usually be the most senior manager in the venture. They will be expected to take on a leadership role merely by virtue of being an entrepreneur.

Research Design: Innovation and Entrepreneurship Equation

According to Frederic Sautet, *"Entrepreneurship in Everything: Management Is Doing Things Right; Leadership is doing the Right Thing."* Innovation is a continual process of creative destruction where unproductive and irrelevant ideas, systems and mechanisms are replaced by new and more productive ones.

Innovation is generally a response to a change in the environment. However, innovations in financial products also have given rise to some new challenges for market participants and their supervisors in the areas of corporate governance and compliance. The process of innovation is not always painless as individually all innovations are not necessarily successful but collectively it is the process of innovations that leads us ahead in the path of progress. Recently we have seen this process of creative destruction at work more closely in the financial sector. The business environment across the globe has been witnessing an unprecedented turmoil over the last couple of years. Financial innovations have become a conventional and popular phenomenon for the contemporary world of finance. These innovations have enabled them to win new customers by increasing demand for their products and have also increased their importance in the eyes of other businesses. The customers of today have become smarter and more knowledgeable. As a result, their demands and standards have also risen. In order to meet those demands, financial institutions have come up with their own set of innovations that they employ to achieve a high degree of customer satisfaction.

Leading innovation is a delicate and challenging process. You need to encourage expansive out-of-the-box thinking to generate new ideas, but also filter through these ideas to decide which to commercialize. Use a balanced "loose-tight" style of leadership for this purpose. "Loose-tight leadership alternates the creation of space for idea generation and free exploration with a deliberate tightening that selects and tests specific ideas for further investment and development2".

Looseness usually dominates the early stages of the innovation process; in the later stages, tightening becomes more important to scrutinize the concepts and bring the selected ones to the market. A balanced approach is essential to loose-tight leadership. Those who remain loose too long generate plenty of ideas but have difficulty commercializing them. Those who lock into the tight mode choke off all but most obvious ideas, thus confining innovation to incremental line extensions of existing products that add little value.

The fast growth and business successes of eBay, Amazon.com, travel.com, priceline.com, and so forth, and the bankruptcy of numerous dot-com firms worldwide in 2000 have held potent management implications for IT innovation and entrepreneurial organizations worldwide. E-entrepreneurship and einnovation are emerging disciplines for proactively responding to changes in the e-business world. The dot-com crash presented new challenges as well as new opportunities to e-business entrepreneurs and managers to rethink and reshape their business strategy. This author argues that a combination of entrepreneurship and innovation is a crucial factor to the long-term sustainability of ecommerce and e-businesses. In this frenetically changing competitive landscape, an integrative approach to e-entrepreneurship and einnovation will enable organizations to gain competitive advantage and hold the key to e-business success.

Innovation=Idea + Leader + Team + Plan

Innovation= Invention X Entrepreneurship

Customer Value

Source: Adapted from Govindarajan & Trimble (2010, L 439), Kim & Mauborgne (2005) and Pinchot & Pellman (1999)

Entrepreneurial Learning: the Battle of the Decade

In order to compete in the environment, the right mix of innovation and entrepreneurship is essential. To encourage each kind of innovation, entrepreneurial process needs to vet ideas effectively and move them forward systematically. With the recent focus on innovation, it can be easy for any organization to become wrapped around building a better axle. However, innovation alone does not breed success. There is a battle brewing between the time tested practice of entrepreneurship and the requirements of the emerging innovation economy. The question is whether innovation or entrepreneurship can exist in this new environment without the other, finding the right mix, and understanding the difference. In this article, we explore the critical differences between and the many types of innovation and entrepreneurship, as well as how to find the balance between the two and your optimal mix for competitive advantage.

Innovation is about new ideas. It may be new products, processes, services, business models and more. Entrepreneurship, however, is about realizing profit. The difference between innovation and entrepreneurship is key. You can build it, but they may not come. Delia Smith of Green Field Ventures gives a concise view of the difference when she notes that, “If innovation is the creation of new capacities for wealth creation, entrepreneurship is the exploitation of these capacities.”

In the accelerating business environment and evolving innovation economy, differentiators are key. Your business has to be unique in some advantageous way that draws your customers. The right mix of innovation and entrepreneurship is at the heart of creating advantage in this evolving economy.

Steve Epner suggests, “an entrepreneur with an innovative idea is a rare and valuable find...everyone is capable of coming up with the idea. Put that together with someone who can execute a plan—and watch out.”

Differences In Leadership Types

Particulars	Transactional	Transformational	Entrepreneurial
Communications	As conditions demand	Symbolic	Intimate and personal
Investment	Immediate payback	Committed investment	Staged investment
Strategy	Situational analysis	Long term	Medium term
Focus	Day-to-day activities	Organization Change	Opportunity Building
Approach	Development of tasks	Creative rearrangement	Creative destruction then rearrangement

LEADERSHIP AND INNOVATIONS: THE TWO FACES OF R & D

According to Jeff Timmons, "*Entrepreneurship is the transformation of an idea into an opportunity.*" Entrepreneur provides a bridge between the small business manager and the chief executive of large firms. In growing the venture, the entrepreneur transforms the role of acquiring resources into that of creating an intaining structures to management. Growth is a critical to entrepreneurial success. Organisational growth, however, means more than just an increase in size. It involves development and change within the organisation and changes in the way in which the organisation grows as coherent whole, organizational growth itself is best understood in a multi-faceted way. We have to steer it in the right direction with the abilities of a good entrepreneur.

According to Peter F. Drucker, The Father of Modern Management, "*Innovation is the specific tool of entrepreneurs, the means by which they exploit change as an opportunity for a different business or a different service. It is capable of being presented as a discipline, capable of being learned, capable of being practiced. Entrepreneurs need to search purposefully for the sources of innovation, the changes and their symptoms that indicate opportunities for successful innovation. And they need to know and to apply the principles of successful innovation.*" Investing in new and better products or services requires innovation "*the successful exploitation of new ideas*". No idea or innovation is successful, until its commercial manifestation is purchased in significant amounts. The evidence shows that innovative businesses deliver above average sales growth and profitability. New and better products or services may be created from new technology, a new application of old technology, by new design, through a new delivery model or just by better business processes. The stimulus for innovation can arise from either *"technology push"* or "*market pull*" or sometimes a conjunction of the two. Often, novelty is created by the fusion of different technologies to meet a technical need in the market place. Involvement in R&D can provide technology, knowledge and expertise, but this can also be obtained from elsewhere. An important pre requisite, however, is to have the necessary skill to recognise, translate and apply the technology, wherever it comes from.

Findings

Leadership is crucial for enhancing innovation practices and achieving strategic competitiveness in organizations. To sum up, the present research investigated the relationship of transformational leadership with technological innovation and the moderating effects of organizational culture and incentive compensation on these relationships. There are three levels of innovative practices i.e., Statesmanship, Entrepreneurship and Innovation. Statesmanship is the ability to work with and through other people, where as entrepreneurship is the ability to achieve results, regardless of obstacles. Innovation is the ability to generate new and usable ideas. Below mentioned a model which developed relationship among these three.

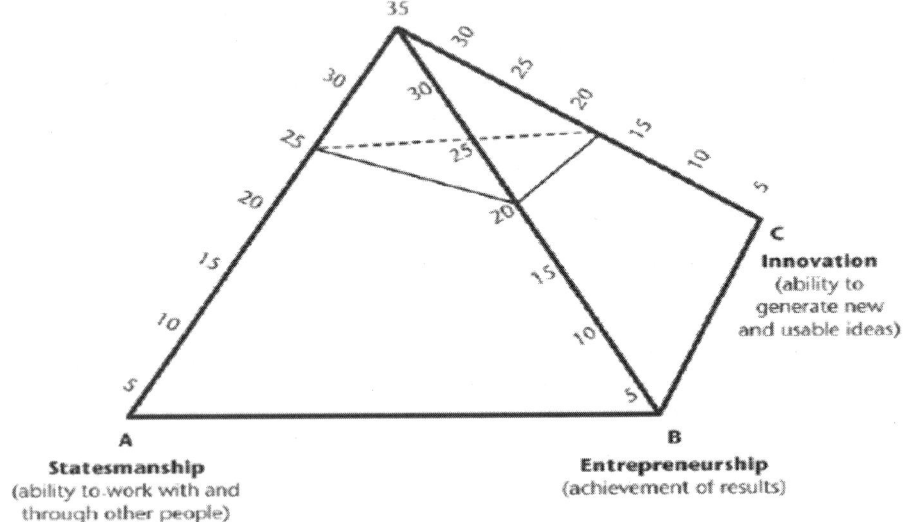

Conclusions

Entrepreneurs have an important effect on world economies and playing an important role in maintaining and developing to create new values. Organisational growth, however, means more than just an increase in size. It involves development and change within the organisation and changes in the way in which the organisation grows as coherent whole. Entrepreneurship education is a common course of study in educational settings. A question, which is always raised whether entrepreneurs born or are they taught?

Educational institutions seem to have an answer to this old question i.e., entrepreneurs can be taught. Universities, technical institutes, colleges, high schools, elementary schools, and out-of-school programs are teaching entrepreneurship. It involves development and change within the organization and changes in the way in which the organisation grows as coherent and sets out a rationale for entrepreneurship in higher education. To be successful, an entrepreneur must not only identify an opportunity but also understand it in great depth through the acquiring of various skills.

References

1. Johnson, D. (2001). What is innovation and entrepreneurship? Lessons for large organizations. *Industrial and Commercial Training, 33*(4), 135-140.
2. Antoncic, B., & Hisrich, R.D. (2003). Clarifying the intrapreneurship concept. *Journal of Small Business and Enterprise Development, 10*(1), 7-24.
3. Drucker, P.F. (1994). *Innovation and entrepreneurship: Practice and principles.* London: Heinemann.
4. Katila, R. (2002). Measuring innovation performance. In A. Neely (Ed.), *Business performance measurement: Theory and practice* (pp. 304-318). Cambridge: Cambridge University Press.
5. Green, S., Gavin, M., & Aiman-Smith, L. (1995). Assessing a multidimensional measure of radical technological innovation, *IEEE Transactions on Engineering Management, 42*(3), 203-214.

20

Innovation and Entrepreneurship in India: Some Concerns, Some Directions

Abstract

The paper makes a serious attempt to find and analyze the present scenario of innovation based entrepreneurship in India. The policy rationales and foundations of innovation and entrepreneurship are well discussed and debated. Various problems of innovation as well as entrepreneurship are delved into, to search for reforms required in India. It also mentions how the shift from government controlled environment to market-based environment, in postreform era, has generated additional economic growth by fostering entrepreneurial activity within its border. The problem with tax system, bureaucracy and land/real estate laws are dealt with, to augment the culture of innovation based entrepreneurship in our country. Priority areas like financing hi-tech startups, education and training in entrepreneurship, networking of entrepreneurs, boosting R & D spending and fostering more inclusive innovation were identified and discussed. A work jointly conducted by Columbia University and Indian Institute of Management, Bangalore is incorporated in this paper. The work defines the optimal role for individual entrepreneurs, whether Indian entrepreneurs playing their optimal roles, if not, what are the obstacles stands in their way.

One of the unique features of this paper is to highlight the problem of startup fund required by brilliant, young, middle and lower middle-class entrepreneurs from I.I.T, I.I.M, N.I.T and other reputed institutes. The problem is they do not have money, land or any security required for mortgaging a commercial loan. Many experts proposes venture capital, but this has it's demerits like equity ownership and interference in management of the hi-tech startups. The solution provided is high value 100% hypothecation route of financing the hi-tech startups, with minor reforms in hypothecation loan laws and policies.

Introduction

The paper makes a genuine attempt to highlight the status of the innovation and entrepreneurship scenario in India from the point of view of policy makers, innovators and entrepreneurs.

India is increasingly becoming a top global innovator for hi-tech products and services. Still the country is underperforming relative to its innovation potential-with direct implications for long-term industrial competitiveness and economic growth.

Although India is plagued with under employment, as well as, low productivity and low skill activities, but still India has stepped up the gas for rapid growth and alleviate poverty through entrepreneurship development.

We all know more than half the population of India is under 25 years. In the present context providing them with a living is an enormous burden for the government as well as private sector industries. Entrepreneurship is the way out. People trained to become entrepreneur not only boosts the national income but also acts as an agent for growth in employment.

The body of the paper has four parts. The first part deals with the policy implications regarding innovation and entrepreneurship in India. In the second part the role of individual enterprise is discussed from an economic angle. Third part of findings elucidates the findings of the researchers from Columbia University an Indian Institute of Management, Bangalore. The fourth part provides a roadmap and subsequent reforms required to boost innovation led entrepreneurship in India. One of the unique feature of this paper is to highlight the problem of startup funds required by middle and lower middle-class entrepreneurs form I.I.T, I.I.M, N.I.T hand other reputed institutes. The solution provided is the hypothecation route of financing the hi-tech startups.

The paper also delves into inclusive innovation-by promoting formal R & D efforts for poor people and more creative grassroots efforts by them to exploit existing knowledge.

2.0 Characteristics of Innovation-Policy Implications.

2.1 The National Innovation System as a Policy Concept: In a time of globalization, it may appear strange to argue that any kind of national approach to innovation or any other domain of policy is relevant. It is sometimes argued that globalization is rendering the state obsolete, and that integration of product and capital markets removes the possibility of effective policy intervention by government. However it is important to know that structural elements of the system are either predominantly or wholly national in character: they are built up largely by use of national resources in national contexts. They are subject to national decision making, even where there may be increasing transnational elements. For example how much country spends on R & D, what kind of education system it constructs and operates, how much it spends on education, how it builds and finances its knowledge infrastructures, how it's areas of specialization are managed, are matters for that country alone. Certainly financing such assets faces budget constraints and in the area of institutions there is an increasing zone of transnational bargaining and regulation (for e.g. agreements like TRIPS, TRIMS or GATS). These considerations suggest that, at least with respect to the core elements of the innovation system there is no reason to believe that government is any less important in setting the context and framework for economic behavior than it ever was. The real problem is how to think about what desirable performance of the system looks like and why and how government should act towards it.

2.2 Policy Rationales and Foundations: Innovation and entrepreneurship rests on structures of institution and organization and that performance depends on how the structures functions operationally. This suggests an approach to policy that rests on assessments of evaluations how specific organization or structures contribute to system functionality.

System approaches, at whatever level, tend to see innovation performance as a result of how sets of institutions and organizations work. Both analytical and policy issues then turn on the nature of the components of the system, the nature of links between them and how well those linkages work. The link may take various forms. They may be economic or they may involve the transmission of knowledge, or they may involve the joint use of infrastructures, and so on: the precise connections cannot be specified in advance, and often need detailed empirical investigations to uncover. But the point is that innovation performance can be seen in large part as a forum of coordination problem— components of the system must work in a coherent way (that is, all moving in more or less the same direction, with more or less compatible objectives) towards the development and use of the new technology which is the object of the innovation process.

Where institutions, infrastructures or inter-firm connections are well established within a particular technological frame work, the coordination needed for innovation may be unproblematic (although even stable technologies and business can run into novel problem). But where a new technology involves major disruption, co-ordination can be very difficult. Some innovations are radical with respect to existing procedures, engineering capabilities or technical knowledge bases- they involve major discontinuities, and shocks to the existing technological system. The co-ordination problems that arise are relevant at all levels of innovations. Even if innovation is seen in terms of incremental improvements to existing technology then current organizations and regulations systems can readily run into technological or economic problem that requires new forms of co-ordination to solve. But if you see task of innovation in a more radical way, as shifting the fundamental technological systems on which the current industrial economy is based, then co-ordination problems become really critical. A systems approach would suggest that the identification of coordination failures, the design of policy instruments to overcome them and development of relevant actors are likely to be an important rational for public policy intervention and important also in deciding its scope and objectives. The argument here is that co-ordination problems with respect to innovation system relate primarily to institutional action that precedes the operation of markets, or organizational action that creates a new arena for economic behavior. There seem to be two types of problem. One is that we might be able to conceptualize a market for some benign outcome, but the real issue is to see how the market could be institutionalized. So issues related to corporate governance, accounting procedures or risk management devices and so on, are issues to do with the shaping of markets or substitution for them, rather than interventions in market operation. A second problem is that it may not be possible to create a market at all. That is, the relevant problems are simply not amenable to a market solution, and could only be resolved by some other coordination mechanism. The main alternative is some form of administrative coordination that may be more or less democratic, or more or less hierarchical. Overcoming problems related to knowledge creation, education and training or lock-in and specialization, require institution building and not market rectification.

Economic Development in India: The role of individual Enterprise (and entrepreneurial spirit)

The Indian economy provides a revealing contrast between how individuals react under a government-controlled environment and how they respond to a marketbased environment. Evidence suggests that recent market reforms that encourage individual enterprise, have led to higher economic growth in India. India can generate additional economic growth by fostering entrepreneurial activity within its border. To pursue further the entrepreneurial approach to economic growth, India must now provide opportunities for (1) education directed specifically at entrepreneurial skills (2) financing of entrepreneurial efforts and (3) networking among potential entrepreneurs and their experienced counter parts. Further, although the government of India should establish policies supportive of entrepreneurial efforts, its role overall should be minimized, so that the influence of the free market in individual self-interest can be fully realized.

Given recent economic reforms, the Indian government should devise policies that rely more on individual enterprise with its emphasis upon individual initiative and self-interest, to spur economic development of India by a greater emphasis on entrepreneurship.

Post Reform situation

Due to government intervention, particularly the high levels of government subsidies, it was clear by 1990 that India was living beyond its means. The result was severe payment crisis in which, for the first time, the government of India physically transferred gold overseas to prevent defaulting on foreign commitments. To meet its immediate balance of payment crisis, India also entered into a structural loan adjustment agreement with I.M.F. However one condition of this loan required India to undertake economic reforms, to move from a centrally-planned development strategy to one based on market-based resource allocation. As a result, government of India undertook a package of economic reforms between1991-93, with the intent of placing the market in place of government controls as the prime mover in the economic development process. Today there is no doubt the economic reforms of 1991 have led to considerable economic progress in India.

However, even though India has made substantial economic progress in recent years, it still has several areas in need of major market-based reform. Below we identify three examples from India's economy that reveal a restriction of the pursuit of individual self-interest and diversion of resources away from their most efficient use. The first example concern the obstacle still presented by the Indian tax system, the second highlight the inefficiencies of the Indian civil services and the third describes the need for land reform in India.

1. In spite of recent tax reform in India, the present tax system still work against the individual self-interest to survive and accumulate wealth and as a result, still leads to the hiding of income, wealth and expenditures. Indeed whereas in the U.S and South Korea, the highest tax rate applies to an income level of \$250,000 and \$60,000 respectively. In India the same tax rate applies to an income of only \$3400.
2. We believe that the policies, underlying compensation to government employees should be reformed such that they are based primarily on market principals. The advantage of doing so include eliminating departments known for corrupt practices, making explicit the true cost of a government employee's performance and giving government employee's good sense of their market worth.
3. Finally considerable reform is needed in the Indian real estate sector. A large proportion of land is owned by the government and any land made available for private use is governed by archaic ownership, zoning, and tenancy and rent laws. Further this government controlled land has reduced the amount of land available for trading purposes. The result is that Indian land prices are the highest among all Asian nations relative to average incomes. Further the officially assessed values of real estate are low, while the true market price is high. The situation leads, among other things, to higher levels of corruption as individuals use real estate as a major hiding place for investments of illegally acquired income.

Examples such as these indicate that there are still large numbers of areas where the individual self-interest of survival and wealth accumulation are not respected.

In the next section, we examine how one fairly new approach to microeconomic policy- the encouragement of entrepreneurship- can help India to continue its recent economic growth.

3.2 The role of Entrepreneurship in India's Future Economic Development

India can do more, however to, further advance its economic development. Indeed, one of the more recent micro-economic approaches to economic growth is the promotion of entrepreneurial activities. Entrepreneurial efforts have been found to generate a wide range of economic benefits, including new businesses, new jobs, innovative products and services, and increased wealth for future community investment.

In Indian context three priority areas are: (1) availability of financing of new entrepreneurs, (2) the need for government policies which are supportive of entrepreneurial efforts, (3) the opportunities for education and training in entrepreneurship.

Recent research on entrepreneurship around the world indicates that the cultural characteristics that can foster successful entrepreneurial activities and its related economic benefits are a strong education base: financial support, opportunities of networking among entrepreneurs and a well defined minimal role for the government.

Opportunities should lead to consider entrepreneurial activities as a way to economic growth. At least one major threat is growth of population of 80-100 million people seeking jobs which is not there. Entrepreneurial efforts can help to provide those jobs.

India now has an extraordinary talent pool suited for entrepreneurs. However, the government must ensure that new entrepreneurs have access to both functional (such as areas in marketing, finance, and product development only) and entrepreneurial (such as managing risk, building an effective team and raising funds) skills. It is observed that both sets of skills somewhat lacking in India. Indian educational institutes can play a major role in the development of these skills. Given India's extra-ordinary talent pool, it is possible to shift—by entrepreneurs- from low technology product export to high technology oriented product export, because this will yield the competitive advantage necessary for broader economic growth.

Consider next the financial support required to produce successful entrepreneurial efforts. Among other things, India must ensure that its new entrepreneurs will have access to venture capital. An establishment of a global support network of venture capitalists and other funding sources like angels, hypothecation etc. should be provided to the new entrepreneurs.

Providing opportunities for networking among entrepreneurs themselves also can help new business get started on the right foot. It is suggested that India needs to foster networking and exchange, among both new and established entrepreneurs. The obvious reason is that entrepreneurs can learn not only through their own experiences but also through that of others. Conferences and seminars must be held by government of India and educational institutes where the entrepreneurs can share their views and discuss their problem. Another additional thrust area is the voters and tax payers should be made aware with reasons why Indian government is investing in anything as new as entrepreneurship.

Some Concerns

According to a survey conducted by a team from I.I.M. Bangalore headed by Prof. Amar Bhide from Columbia University, who all tried to answer three questions. First, how and why optimal role for individual entrepreneurs is likely to be different in India than in advanced economy? Second, are Indian entrepreneurs playing the optimal role? Third, if they are not, what obstacles stand in their way?

In order to answer the above questions the team collected data on five percent of all registered shop, commercial establishment and factories and on more than 90% on the software and software related companies located in Bangalore.

Optimal Role

A system of entrepreneurship has evolved in U.S that has been very successful and possesses economic dynamism. However the system needs modification when applied to India. The optimal role for Indian entrepreneurs is somewhat different than in an advanced economy.

In a developing economy like India, however, do not require U.S style technological innovation to increase living standard. Rapid growth can be achieved merely by the introduction and diffusion of superior technology from advanced economy with indigenization required for local use. However the returns from investing in new technologies are generally lower than the returns from acquiring and implementing existing technologies from the developed nations. Since these technologies are proven and ready to use, the basic technical and market- risks are long gone. Therefore one of the important roles that entrepreneurs play in advanced nations, their role in early- stage innovation, has relatively little value in India. Moreover in India individual entrepreneurs do not have capital and personal required to acquire technologies from abroad. A proven technology usually requires large scale operation and because of this, the technology lies outside the reach of wealth constrained individual entrepreneurs.

This does not mean, individual entrepreneurs in India cannot try out novel ideas which have value not just in the very early stages of a new technology. Successful implementation of technologies that are proven in advanced nations and are new to India will certainly require a host of complimentary goods and services to make them suitable for local use. Individual entrepreneurs can play a critical role in developing such low budget small-scale complements; many of them unique to India or less developed nations. For instance, large companies may have an advantage in acquiring and implementing modern, proven technology to build automobiles; however widespread diffusion of new automobiles requires a host of new distribution, servicing outlets as well as low cost component manufacturing. Individual entrepreneurs may enjoy advantages in starting these outlets.

Failures to Play Optimal Roles

In the developed nation, the individual entrepreneurs never competed with large companies. They concentrated on niche market and may be competed with smaller startups firms, where as in Bangalore great many startup companies competed head on with larger businesses. The Bangalore entrepreneurs preferred to diversify into new businesses rather than expand, where as in U.S there are serial entrepreneurs but they sale their prior business, often to parties who believe they can realize greater economies of scale.

By competing with, instead of complimenting the activities of large organization, Indian entrepreneurs are likely to hinder economic development; not only of the nation but also their own startups.

It has also been recorded that startup median capitals of U.S entrepreneurs and Bangalore entrepreneurs are same i.e. $20,000. But this is 10 times the local per capita income in Bangalore where as it is one-half or one-third of U.S per capita incomes. This is a matter of concern. More over the differences in revenues are even starker: the median Bangalore Company booked under $6, 66,000 in revenues, where as U.S entrepreneurs with the same level of investment earned $5.5 million in revenues, or more than 8 times the Bangalore Company. The limited- and possibly negative- contribution of Bangalore entrepreneur is reflected in their low contribution to job creation compared to startup companies in U.S.

Possible Explanations for the Failures

Why do Bangalore entrepreneurs operate small units in domains that in the developed world would be dominated by large companies? Historically, the government reserved certain sectors for small units. Today however, many of these reservations have been removed. But, several other factors continue to encourage entrepreneurs to start sub-scale units and to avoid growth. The tax system appears to play a major role. From colonial times, indirect taxes (such as excise duties and sales taxes) have been a major source of government's revenues. Today such indirect taxes account from about 20 to 40 percent of final prices. The tax regime exempts small businesses from paying some of these taxes; small units apparently can also evade indirect taxes more easily than large businesses through off the books transactions. These tax effects can more than offset the disadvantages of operating below technologically efficient scale.

The tax system encourages the formation of sub-scale businesses in other ways as well. The black money that it engenders can be more easily recycled into the assets of many small units rather than one small unit. The government also periodically grants indirect tax exemptions and holidays to promote causes it deems to be worthy or in response to lobbying. But tax benefits for particular businesses can make competing businesses unviable. And the unpredictable grant of benefits increases the risks of making large scale investments. Rules intended to protect workers also contribute to the reluctance to operate on a large scale. In particular, the respondents expressed concerns that employing more than 20 workers makes them liable for inspections under the Factories Act and requires them to contribute to health insurance and retirement plans that increase their labor costs.

Restrictions on layoffs and terminations however, did not seem to concern any of the entrepreneurs interviewed. One entrepreneur said that as workers see signs of business failure they leave for greener pastures of their own accord: this explanation would be consistent with the widespread unwillingness of employers to pay efficiency wages. Another entrepreneur claimed that when employers run short of funds, they often stop contributing to their employees' insurance schemes and retirement plans and may even stop paying salaries. The employers' subsequent inability to clear these unpaid dues (which can lead to criminal prosecutions) then makes it impossible to terminate unwanted employees.

Survey findings suggested reasons for relatively low efficiency in the use of capital by Bangalore entrepreneurs- why they require more funds (compared to local incomes) to start their businesses and why the revenues and number of employees is smaller. In Bangalore, entrepreneurs usually:

1. Pay a deposit equal to 11 months of rent to lease space (instead of one month in the U.S).

2. Extend credit for 90 days or longer, (instead of 30 days).
3. Acquire their own premises as soon as they can, instead of renting them. The acquisition of real estate obviously ties up capital. More subtly, it can also limit the entrepreneur's ability to grow (if that requires more space) and thus limits the revenues the business can achieve.
4. Purchase equipment like copiers that U.S entrepreneurs lease, because the leasing market is thin or non-existent.
5. 'Make' goods and services that the U.S entrepreneurs routinely 'buy'. For instance, more than half of the entrepreneurs that were interviewed have their own electrical generators- something not observed in the U.S. The propensity to make rather than buy increases absolute capital requirements.

And because entrepreneurs typically forgo economies of scale when they 'make' in – house, their output (and revenue) to capital ratios are also reduced. Some of the factors that impair the relatively inefficient use of capital can be traced to defects in the regulatory and legal system. The market for copier leases collapsed because the legal system could not limit the disappearance of leased copiers to levels that would allow the market to function. The erratic supply of electricity boards by poorly regulated and misgoverned utilities encourages businesses to install their own generators. Poorly maintained land records, the shortages of plots with access to basic municipal services (i.e. roads, water and electricity) and the sale of plots at below market prices to favored individuals and organizations create incentives for businesses to buy instead of renting their premises.

Innovation & Entrepreneurship In India-the Road Ahead

To unleash India's innovation and entrepreneurship potential, India needs to develop a three-pronged strategy.

1. India would benefit from increasing competition as part of efforts to improve the investment climate, supported by stronger skills, better information infrastructure, and more finance-public and private.
2. Competition is vital to unleash innovation. India must encourage stronger competition among enterprises. Since the Indian economy was opened up in 1991, the private sector has invested the most in research and development (R&D) in the sectors most open to competition. In 2004, enterprise R&D was more than seven times higher than in 1991. Recommended actions to spur competition

include removing nonessential regulations and applying essential ones more transparently in product, land, labor, capital, and infrastructure services markets – for example, easing limits on small industries, restrictions on foreign direct investment (FDI), and barriers to import competition, as well as introducing bankruptcy reforms and modernizing the Industrial Disputes Act.

3. Limited skills and training are a major bottleneck. Only 16 percent of Indian manufacturing firms offer in-service training compared with 92 percent in China and 42 percent in the Republic of Korea. The Indian firms that provide in-service training are 23-28 percent more productive than those that do not. Moreover, gross enrollment in higher education is only 12 percent in India, compared with 90 percent in Korea and 68 percent in the Russian Federation. The skills bottleneck could be unblocked by providing public matching funds for firms to invest in training, increasing the fiscal and managerial autonomy of universities and colleges, and increasing private participation in higher education.
4. Better information flows are needed. India is already the world's fastestgrowing market for mobile phones. However, disparity persists between rural and urban areas. And while high-speed national research and education networks accelerate the pace of new discoveries and the expansion of knowledge, India's connectivity is lower than China, Korea, the United States, and European Union countries. Information-related actions could include expediting the allocation of radio and wireless broadband spectrums, increasing targeted subsidies for rolling out rural mobile and broadband, and agreeing on an organizational structure to deploy and manage a national research and education network.
5. More early-stage funding is needed. In 2005, just 13 percent of deals by venture capital and private equity providers were for early-stage funding. In dollar terms, early-stage deals accounted for even less of such investments: 4-6 percent. Cumulative start-up capital provided for seed financing in India is estimated to be $25 million-$35 million – enough for 75-100 start-ups, many fewer than the 450-600 start-ups needed. Financerelated actions could include facilitating regulations for early-stage venture capital investments, and government provision of leveraged returns for private investments in innovation areas overlooked by the market (such as rural industry and pro-poor, grassroots innovations) by creating a fund of funds – with distinct windows for pro-growth innovations and inclusive innovation – with venture capital funds managed by the private sector.

6. Funding with hypothecation loan: The main problem for the brilliant innovators of India (people from I.I.T., I.I.M., N.I.T and others) generally come from lower or middle class environment. They possess good ideas & innovations, and have excellent drive to become an innovator cum entrepreneur. But the security money or mortgage assets is what most of them do not have. This is required for any commercial loan. Institutional investors or venture capitalists provide seed capital and commercial loans for startups. But these loans are not 100 percent of the project cost and require security or mortgaging of assets or ownership in the form of equity. One solution that can be proposed is to reform the "Hypothecation" loan.

Today in India hypothecation loans are provided for agri-equipments, crops, vehicles, other factory equipments, and to some extent to real estate developers (against notes from time sharing customers).

Hypothecation loans are cheaper than commercial loans. Moreover, the lender possesses lesser risk, because the lender hold, the ownership of the assets created by the borrower till the loan is paid back.

Hypothecation loans may be 100% loan given against the total cost of the project. Moreover the lender does not claim any equity ownership unlike venture capitalists.

It is suggested that high value hypothecation loan, covering the total project cost, must be introduced for hi-tech startups. This will attract the Indian talent pool to become an entrepreneur with their ideas and innovations.

As mentioned earlier venture capital way of funding is another option. But the problems with venture capital are as follows:

1. Venture capital is appropriate for high growth companies that are capable of reaching at least $ 25 million in sales in five years.
2. Cost of fund is expensive. Institutional venture capitalists demand significant equity ownership in a business. The earlier the investment stage, the more equity is required to convince an institutional venture capitalist & to invest. The range of fund typically available is $ 5, 00,000 to $ 10 million.
3. Ease of acquisition is difficult; venture capitalists are choosy.
4. The better solution, in the Indian context, is to provide 100% high value hypothecation loans with some minor reforms in policies & laws; if required. Covering the entire project cost is what is desired via hypothecation loan.

India would benefit from strengthening efforts to create and commercialize knowledge, as well as better diffuse existing global and local knowledge and increase the capacity of smaller enterprises to absorb it. If all enterprises could costlessly achieve national best practices based on knowledge already in use in India, economic output could more than quintuple.

Variations in productivity highlight the need for better knowledge diffusion. Average enterprise productivity in finance, insurance, and real estate companies is nearly 23 times that in agriculture. But these industries account for only 1.3 percent of employment, while agriculture accounts for 60 percent. Actions to better diffuse existing knowledge could include increasing openness to trade and FDI, coupled with strengthening and expanding public support for technology at the cluster level and modernizing infrastructure for metrology, standards, testing, and quality (especially metrology). India could also consider strengthening its support infrastructure for technology licensing by creating a public private technology acquisition fund, building on intellectual property that is already locally available.

Private enterprises need to increase R&D spending. Aggregate domestic R&D spending has never exceeded 1 percent of GDP. And 75-80 percent comes from the public sector. However, between 1998 and 2003, multinational corporations spent $1.3 billion on R&D in India – showing that its valuable assets could be exploited more effectively. Actions to spur private R&D could include consolidating and expanding public early stage technology development programs, as well as developing a policy and action plan to use public procurement to promote innovation.

Reforms to existing early-stage technology development programs could include establishing a streamlined matching grant program building on India's Sponsored Research and Development program and Small Business Innovation Research Initiative – targeted mainly at smaller enterprises and promoting more collaboration.

New domestic knowledge needs to be converted to commercial use. Of the top 50 applicants for patents in India between 1995 and 2005, 44 were foreign firms. Only six were Indian; three of these were public institutions and one, a public corporation, just two were private Indian firms, both in the pharmaceutical industry. Actions to promote commercia-lization and strengthen links among industry, universities and public laboratories could include providing support to technology transfer offices, creating a patent management corporation, developing technology parks and incubators, and improving India's regime for intellectual property rights, India should also consider enhancing support for higher-risk technology parks and incubators, and improving India's regime for intellectual property rights.

India should also consider enhancing support for higher-risk technology R&D and commercialization by strengthening its New Millennium India Technology Leadership Initiative including by opening the program to international collaboration and giving grants to both research institutions and private enterprises, with sharing of any resulting royalties. To further spur international collaboration, India could create a Global Research and Industrial Partnership program to promote advanced R&D and commercialization efforts conducted jointly by domestic and foreign enterprises.

The Diaspora needs to be tapped more effectively. About 2 percent of India's population -20 million people – live abroad, where they earn the equivalent of two-thirds of India's GDP. Actions to effectively tap India's overseas talent could include supporting a larger Diaspora network, building on existing groups that aggregate this population's talent and capital for use in India.

India would benefit from fostering more inclusive innovation – by promoting more formal R&D efforts for poor people and more creative grassroots efforts by them, and by improving the ability of informal enterprises to exploit existing knowledge. Existing pro-poor initiatives need to be scaled up. Inclusive innovation can play a critical role in lowering the costs of goods and services and in creating income-earning opportunities for poor people. The Council of Scientific and Industrial Research have developed technology applications for rural India, and university and formal private initiatives (such as e-Chou pal and Amida's Simputer) have delivered benefits. The National Innovation Foundation has a repository of more than 50,000 grassroots innovations and traditional knowledge practices. And a number of initiatives exist to help the informal sector better absorb knowledge. More favorable matching grant support for pro-poor early-stage technology development could significantly increase collaboration among public R&D entities, universities, nongovernmental organizations, national industries, and global networks. Increased support for grassroots innovators could be provided to the Innovation Foundation to scale up impact. To leverage traditional knowledge into revenue, a policy-oriented intellectual property rights think tank could propose how to implement a cheaper intellectual property regime. Finally, successful technology upgrading programs could be extended to help informal and rural enterprises make better use of existing knowledge.

The action-oriented recommendations that form part of this volume's three-pronged innovation strategy require a realistic, time-bound implementation plan. This may best be accomplished through a consensusbuilding process that includes a task force of Indian policy makers working with business and social leaders – who would be in the best position to set priorities among the recommendations and develop and appropriate sequencing of activities. To help capture the nation's imagination, it may be desirable to focus on "grand challenges" such as access to clean water throughout the country or mitigating road congestion in cities. A light Paper touch public-private oversight mechanism may be required to evaluate and address the fragmentation of India's current innovation a entrepreneurship system; encourage collaboration and facilitate streamlining of the system's constituent programs, using public-private partnerships wherever appropriate; and monitor the achievement of realistic targets, with periodic international benchmarking as India's innovation potential is unleashed. India's successes with inclusive innovation will be of particular interest to other developing and emerging market economies also seeking to harness innovation for poverty reduction and economic development.

Conclusion

In order to conclude, what is emphasized is Indian's need a great awakening to innovate and commercialize it. The mass should be awakened and motivated to create a culture, a determination, to grow and prosper with the innovation and entrepreneurship route. Otherwise all the policies, plans, rationales and foundations, discussed become a day dream. Not only culture to innovate and commercialize,- though most important- but also what is required in India is vibrant institutions and organizations along with availability of funds to support the Government of India's genuine effort in this direction.

21

Progressive Metamorphosis of Workforce: Leader creating Leaders

Abstract

In the light of volatile and dynamic work scenarios where things are changing in the spur of the moment, as there is more of instability and less of monotony; it is well said that the only change is constant. Technology, product, services etc no more form the competitive advantage for the firm, the customer is becoming more demanding and all these aforesaid things are masked by the fear of obsolescence. Under such vagueness, the true competitive advantage upon which any company can find anchorage is the quality Human Resource. But with the changing times as the required skill set is changing and the dearth of quality people is there, work force has assumed more power and assertion. To cater to such work scenario, we need more flexible and dynamical leaders who are ready to shun their egos so as to respect individual creativity and thus set arena for giving out a vent to innovation. Today concept of leadership is experiencing overhauling as leadership not only demands accomplishment of organizational goals but also demands that the leader should be a liaison, an interface that recognizes the worth of each employee and thus aligning individual aspirations to organizational goals so as to pacify an individual's thirst to exceed and develop. An individual always chalks out a career plan for him, the effectiveness of leadership lies in not being myopic but being proactive enough to develop the career graph for each employee according to individual worth and try to bring about a tradeoff between the two career plans keeping the organizational and individual welfare in mind. This is what one can expect only under the mentor ship of transformational leaders. This paper makes a humble attempt to draw out positive relationship between transformational leaders and intrapreneurs by the retrospection of the cases of historical leaders and eventually extrapolating the drawn out implications and inferences in the modern corporate culture.

Introduction

"He that will not apply new remedies must expect new evils: For time is the greatest innovator" Francis Bacon (1561 - 1626)

Intrapreneuring is suddenly becoming more important because bureaucracy can't respond rapidly enough to respond to challenges like climate change and cultural turbulence. Gifford Pinchot coined the term *"intrapreneur"*. Intrapreneur is a person who focuses on innovation and creativity and who transforms a dream or an idea into a profitable venture, by operating within the organizational environment. The Civilization is at a turning point. We are becoming aware that our economies and lifestyles need massive amounts of innovation to remain viable. Only those institutions that can reinvent themselves will survive. In order to maintain full employment in the face of low cost global competitors, nations, must innovate far faster and more cost effectively than they do today. Corporate bureaucracy is often depicted as the direct opposite of the entrepreneurial spirit, innovation and does not allow for adjustment or change in response to opportunities in the environment. Creating the climate for intrapreneuring is an effective way increasing innovation and sustainable innovation manifold. Fortunately, this attitude is changing meaning that the terms 'corporation' and 'entrepreneur' are not necessarily as contradictory as one might think. According to Ross (1987), the corporate entrepreneur who operates within the complexities of a large organisation, but who manages to find a way to encourage the entrepreneurial spirit and release the innovative potential of the workforce, has the best of both worlds.

In studying hundreds of innovations inside larger organizations, it is found that in every case a passionate and persistent intrapreneur drove the project towards success. This does not mean Intrapreneuring was company policy, in most cases it happened despite the rules. Intrapreneurs are essential to drive innovation in large organizations. For this reason it pays to create a culture that encourages Intrapreneurial activity. Not doing so in today's innovation hungry world will lead to an organization's extinction. Our current trend towards innovation and creativity effects the process of leadership by speeding up the inputs, requiring faster and more personal transformation of the product and people, all in a business climate that builds competition through "response time" to customer demands. The function of leadership in the future will see a sea change where the leaders will be entrusted with the more demanding job of not just coaching their followers but of mentoring them. They are responsible not just for the growth of their followers but also are accountable for their development.

Statement of the Problem: Transition From Knowledge Based Economy To Knowledge Economy

Today the expanse of human resource management is not limited only to the functions like hiring and firing, pay, benefits, training, and administration. The knowledge today is not the means or a tool to attain competitive edge rather knowledge has become a product or a competitive advantage in itself. As, the global economy is in the transition phase towards a "knowledge economy" where knowledge and education (often referred to as "human capital") can be treated as one of the following two:

- A business product, as educational and innovative intellectual products and services can be exported for a high value return.
- A productive asset

This concept thus supports creation of knowledge by organizational employees, which in turn helps and encourages them to transfer and better utilize their knowledge in line with company/organization goals. The concept of manual worker is being replaced by the concept of knowledge worker; the manual worker works with his hands and produces goods or services. In contrast, a knowledge worker works with his or her head not hands, and produces ideas, knowledge, and information. This gives altogether a new perspective to the economy; the economics are not of scarcity, but rather of abundance. Unlike most resources that become depleted when used, information, knowledge and skills can be shared, and actually grow through application. This new economy is extending radically, creating a pattern in which even ideas are being recognized and identified as a commodity.

Few companies have started reporting the competency levels of their human capital in annual reports. These developments compel the researchers to go for deep insight into the things as to what possible changes these would bring into the human relations at work place. In the light of these dynamics, the present paper makes an attempt to study the importance of intrapreneurship in the present scenario and also to conceptualize the role of the transformational leader to elevate his follower from the level of the worker to an intrapreneur.

Literature Review

Knowledge Economy Defined

In coining the phrase "knowledge society" Peter Drucker convincingly argued that land, labor, and capital – the classical factors of production – had been largely replaced by knowledge (Drucker, 1993), "that knowledge has become *the* resource, rather than *a* resource, is what makes our society 'postcapitalist'"(p. 45). Rowley (1999) suggested that "the knowledge based society has arrived, and those organizations that can succeed in the global information society are those that can identify, value, create, and evolve their knowledge assets" (p. 416). For the last two hundred years, neo-classical economics has recognised only two factors of production: labour and capital. Knowledge, productivity, education, and intellectual capital were all regarded as exogenous factors – that is, falling outside the system. New Growth Theory is based on work by Stanford economist Paul Romer and others who have attempted to deal with the causes of long-term growth, something that traditional economic models have had difficulty with. Following from the work of economists such as Joseph Schumpeter, Robert Solow and others, Romer has proposed a change to the neoclassical model by seeing technology (and the knowledge on which it is based) as an intrinsic part of the economic system. Knowledge has become the third factor of production in leading economies. (Romer,1986; 1990).

Transformational Leadership Defined

Burns (1978) held that leadership could be broadly classified into two forms, *transactional* and *transformational leadership*. *Transactional leadership* occurs when one person takes the initiative in making contact with others for the exchange of valued things. The relationship does not go beyond this exchange of expected goods. Most of the earlier theories of leadership fall under transactional leadership because "they seem too narrow and simplistic to explain leaders in change agent roles" (Conger, 1999: 147). Transformational leadership, on the other hand, focuses only on leading change. A transformational leader focuses on "transforming" others to help each other, to look out for each other, be encouraging, harmonious, and look out for the organization as a whole. The transformational leader enhances the motivation, moral and performance of the followers. Meta-analyses have shown that it is significantly related to important effectiveness dimensions, e.g., higher performance ratings, enhanced innovativeness, etc. (DeGroot, Kiker, & Cross, 2000; Dumdum, Lowe, & Avolio, 2002). Studies have also shown that transformational leaders significantly energized followers and enhanced their motivation, morality, and empowerment (Dvir, Eden, Avolio, & Shamir, 2002).

According to Oden (1997), leaders in intrapreneurial companies take the longrange view, looking down the road and striving to anticipate every contingency. The greatest challenge for the leader is not shifting from an entrepreneurial to a more managerial style as a company grows, but rather maintaining the intrapreneurial spirit and style while leading a growing and increasingly complex organisation (Smilor & Sexton, 1996).

Intrapreneurship Defined

It is seen as an imperative for the organizations to survive and prosper amidst increasing global competition, rapid technological progress and major structural changes in the organizations (Dess, Lumpkin and Mc Ghee, 1999). An analogy for the intrapreneur would be the chess player, who may make a bold move yet understands the parameters of the game and anticipates the possible countermoves (Smilor & Sexton, 1996). According to Fry (1993), intrapreneurship exists in different forms, and the form that is appropriate in one organisation may not work for another. These forms vary in terms of management's commitment and can thus be placed on a continuum from high to low managerial commitment.

The different forms of intrapreneurship include the *organic organisation*, the *new products group*, the *new products subsidiary*, the *venture capital company* and the *training section*. Each of these forms of intrapreneurship varies in terms of the extent of the organisation's managerial commitment.

Cases From the Corporate

Company: 3M

Intrapreneurs: Spencer Silver and Art Fry

Year Launched: 1980

The Post-it, now as indispensable to the typical office worker as a chair and desk, might never have made it to market without 3M's longstanding "bootlegging" policy. The company's program allows employees to spend up to 15 percent of their time at work developing their ideas. That's how 3M scientist Spencer Silver invented a light, repositionable adhesive in 1968, although he was unsure how best to use it. He gave seminar after seminar, explaining the advantages of his adhesive to co-workers, but he was unable to drum up much enthusiasm for his not-so-sticky stickum. Five years later, Art Frey, one of Silver's colleagues, noticed his bookmarks were constantly falling out of his hymnals during choir practice. He remembered Silver's seminars, and in that "Eureka" moment, the Post-it was born. The product languished until a marketing manager, Bill Shoonenberg, designed a campaign called the "Boise

Blitz" to drive sales and blanketed the state of Idaho in Post-its. The sticky notes went national in 1980 and quickly became an office-supply and household standard.

Company: Sony Computer Entertainment Inc.

Intrapreneur: Ken Kutaragi

Year Launched: 1994

Ken Kutaragi was working in Sony's sound labs when he bought his daughter a Nintendo game console. Watching her play, he was dismayed by the system's primitive sound effects. He realized that a digital chip dedicated solely to sound would improve the quality of the games — and the product itself. Keeping his job at Sony, Kutaragi developed the SPC7000 for the next generation of Nintendo machines. Sony execs nearly fired him after discovering his sideline project, but then-CEO Norio Ohga realized the value of his innovation and encouraged Kutaragi's efforts. With Sony's blessing, Kutaragi worked with Nintendo to develop a CD-ROM-based Nintendo. But Nintendo decided not to go forward with it, so Kutaragi helped Sony develop its own gaming system, which became the PlayStation. The first PlayStation made Sony a major player in the games market, but the PlayStation 2 did even better, becoming the best-selling game console of all time. Kutaragi founded Sony Computer Entertainment, one of the Sony's most profitable divisions.

Company:Sun Microsystems Intrapreneurs:Patrick Naughton, James Gosling, Bill Joy Year Launched:1995

The circuitous route Java took to market began when Patrick Naughton, a 25- year-old, up-and-coming programmer, told Sun CEO Scott McNealy he was leaving the company. McNealy asked Naughton to give him an assessment of what Sun was doing wrong, and the programmer responded that Sun, then known for its business workstations, was missing out on the fast-growing PC consumer market. His 12-page e-mail quickly became a rallying cry to change Sun's direction. Naughton stayed, and Sun set up a group dedicated to breaking into the consumer market. Group member James Gosling created an elegant object-oriented programming language called Oak (renamed Java), which Sun initially hoped would be used by Time Warner in its cable set-top boxes. When that deal fell through, it looked like the language would be abandoned. It took Bill Joy, a Sun co-founder, to champion the project. Joy realized that with the explosion of the Web, a programming language like Oak could be used across different platforms — computers, cell phones, PDAs, and more. Joy also understood that the key to making Java a cross-platform linchpin was to give the language and development kit away. By the end of 1996, Java had nearly 100 licensees and had attracted 6,000 developers.

Company: W.L. Gore

Intrapreneurs: Dave Myers and John Spencer

Year Launched: 1997

W.L. Gore, known primarily as the maker of Gore-Tex rain gear, encourages employees to develop new ideas through its "dabble time" policy: Ten percent of a work day can be devoted to personal projects. In 1995, the company was experimenting with ePTFE, a chemical cousin to Teflon, to coat push-pull cables for use in animatronics. Dave Myers, an associate in the company's medical unit, thought the coating might be good for guitar strings and recruited both marketing and manufacturing personnel to work on the project. Myers' team originally believed that the coating's appeal would be in making strings more comfortable to use. But extensive market research, piloted by John Spencer, and more than 15,000 guitar-player field tests led the team to realize their real selling point: better sound. The coated strings were only nominally more comfortable than non-coated strings, but they kept their tone longer than conventional guitar strings. W.L. Gore launched them under the brand name ELIXIR Strings, now the No. 1 seller of acoustic guitar strings and the overall No. 2 seller in the guitar string market.

Findings and Recommendations

In the modern form of the bourgeois society, when multinational corporations are displacing the family owned businesses, and are having the stakeholders spread across the globe, the entrepreneurship is gaining popularity in all new face of intrapreneurship where employees under the mentorship of their leaders can possibly work as entrepreneurs within the domain of their organization thus benefiting the organization with their talent, spontaneity and creativity. Following changes in the business dynamics further suggest the incorporation of the trait of intrapreneurhip amongst the employees:

- **Intrapreneurs can pave way for Creative destruction:** From the 1950s onwards, the term "creative destruction" has become more readily identified with the Austrian-American economist Joseph Schumpeter who adapted and popularized it as a theory of economic innovation and progress. Since, it refers to the incessant product and process innovation mechanism by which new production units replace outdated ones, innovative entry by entrepreneurs was the force that sustained long-term economic growth as they guaranteed innovation. But as the trend of large organizations is gaining ground intrapreneurs are asserting more importance and voice as they alone have the power to change the rules of the game and help the firm to attain competitive advantage derived from challenging the previous technological, organizational, regulatory, and economic paradigms.
- **Intrapreneurship can be a precursor to creative problem- solving within an organization:** Creative problem solving is the mental process of creating a solution to a problem. It is a special form of problem solving in which the solution is independently created rather than learned with assistance. To qualify as creative problem solving the solution must either have value or be appreciated by organisation for which the situation improves, if this creative solution becomes widely used it becomes an innovation and in modern organizations intrapreneurs beyond all doubts are the drivers of the innovation.
- **Transformational leadership for the intrapreneurship:** According to the latest Global Innovation Index published in March 2009, the study that measured both innovation inputs and outputs. Innovation inputs included government and fiscal policy, education policy and the innovation environment. Outputs included patents, technology transfer, and other R&D results; business performance, such as labor productivity and total shareholder returns; and the impact of innovation on business migration and economic growth, India takes the 12th slot behind the developed giants like U.S.A, France, Germany and developing nations like China and South Africa. To elevate India on this index, one of the ways could be encourage

innovation within an organization facilitated by intrapreneurship. Since to ease the functioning and make the system ordered most of the organizations opt for the traditional bureaucratic structure for that reason leaders or the supervisors with their charismatic personas and transformational leadership style can pave the way for the innovation an novelty amongst their followers and subordinates.

Prospects For Future Research and Conclusion

This paper can act as a prelude to empirically test the relationship between transformational leadership and intrapreneurship thus the outcomes can be extrapolated to revise and redefine HR policies of the company so as to incorporate intrapreneurial behavior in performance and potential appraisals. In nutshell, this paper brings to the light, the importance and indispensability of the intrapreneurial activities for the modern enterprise under the mentorship and encouragement of the transformational leader who by all chance happens to be the real force behind the long-term sustainability and viability of the organization. No organization can deny the importance of Innovating with the times as *Innovation Saturation* applies to every product, every corporation, every industry, every sector, and every factor of production and labour being one of them, so to reinvent the labour factor of production, encouragement of intrapreneurship by the superior can be the effective means.

References

1. Burns, J. M. (1978). Leadership. New York: Harper & Row.
2. Dess, G., Lumpkin, G. and McGee, J., 1999. Linking Corporate Entrepreneurship to Strategy, Structure, and Process: Suggested Research Directions. Entrepreneurship: Theory & Practice 23 (3), 85-102.
3. Drucker, P. (1969). The Age of Discontinuity; Guidelines to Our changing Society. New York: Harper and Row.
4. Dumdum, U. R., Lowe, K. B., & Avolio, B. J. (2002). A meta-analysis of transformational and transactional leadership correlates of effectiveness and satisfaction: An update and extension. In B. J. Avolio, & F. J. Yammarino (Eds.), Transformational and charismatic leadership: The road ahead (pp. 35-66). Oxford: Elsevier Science.
5. Dvir, T., Eden, D., Avolio, B.J., & Shamir, B. (2002). Impact of transformational leadership on follower development and performance: A field experiment. The Academy of Management Journal, 45: 735-744.

6. Hunt, J.G. & Conger, J.A. (1999) "Charismatic and Transformational Leadership: Taking Stock of the Present and Future (Part II)", Leadership Quarterly, vol. 10, no. 3.
7. Romer, Paul (1995) Beyond the Knowledge Worker, Worldlink, January/February 1995.
8. Schumpeter, J. (1942). Capitalism, Socialism, and Democracy. New York: Harper & Bros.
9. Smilor, R.W. and Sexton, D.L. (1996). Leadership and Entrepreneurship: Personal and Organizational Development in Entrepreneurial Ventures, Quorum, Westport, Connecticut.

22

Role of Women in Family Managed Businesses: A Study in Andhra Pradesh

Abstract

Family businesses constitute most businesses in India, as anywhere else. Economic liberalization and rapid expansion in the industrial base in recent years have not only created growth opportunities for many but also have tested their resource capabilities to respond to them- some have chosen to follow the role of a custodian of their existing wealth and followed the preservation route, while some others have followed more of an entrepreneurial route of exploiting opportunities with or without relevant resources, with mixed results. One of the key resources for all of them is their family, and their prime concern is wealth and welfare of their family. A major dilemma many of them have faced particularly in the last decade since economic liberalization began, is to choose between combination of risks and returns of business growth and conservation of wealth of the family. This, of course, is intertwined with the missions of their businesses and families (Ramachandra, 2003). Research conducted over the past 15 years has increased our knowledge of family-owned firms. Unfortunately relatively little empirical research has been conducted on women and their participation in family owned businesses (Dumas, 1998). In collaboration with the above, Lyman, Salganicoff and Hollander, (1985), cited in (Rowe and Hong, 2000), state that the strength of traditional family roles, both within society and within individual families, kept women's business contributions from being acknowledged. An attempt is made in this paper to empirically examine the role of women and highlight the issues/ challenges women face in family managed businesses in Andhra Pradesh. The results of the study along with the implications for further research and practice are discussed in the paper.

The Context

The contemporary era forces every country to stay competitive in the globalize world. It is possible not only through economic growth, but sustained economic growth. This presupposes all round growth which includes social, political, cultural and other dimensions of development. A major task therefore, is to stimulate the people to undertake productive economic activity. Today, this has been the only strategy to bring many into the main stream of development, as the old model of employment generation in the economy by expanding government and public sector could not pay off the expected results. Thus, the concepts of *self employment* and *entrepreneurship* have been thought of as viable alternatives to tackle the problem of unemployment in many countries.

Alongside, evidence also suggests that businesses existed and were carried on by the families all over the world. India is no exception to this and there are several business houses in the family business mode.

Entrepreneurship and Family Business- According to Lavoisier, (2009) for millennia, scientists believed that the entire world was composed of only four substances: earth, water, air, and fire. Fire was by far the most elusive. It was dramatic, and powerful, but no one knew what actually caused fire to burn.

Entrepreneurship is like fire- rapid, dramatic, and powerful. Sometimes its destructive side decimates standing forests, sometimes its power carries innovation throughout the world like a firestorm. From a contextual stand point, these decades of investigation have, however, taught us the same lesson that Lavoisier proved with regards to fire – entrepreneurship is fed by the oxygen of family, financial resources, human resources, education, economic conditions etc. although family permeates most business ventures, surrounding virtually every entrepreneur, contributing financial and human resources for most ventures, and providing a major source and origin of education and values that are critical to entrepreneurs. Yet the components that constitute or promote success or effectiveness in a family firm remain elusive, as does the interrelated nature of family and business activities within family firms of utmost importance is, understanding the impact of the family on the business and vice-versa. It also will open many opportunities to the economic development like providing job opportunities to the society; increasing government's tax revenue and multiple effects to the country's economy as a whole (Reishana Hoosen,2007). Research into entrepreneurship had generally side – stepped investigating family as a source of oxygen for the entrepreneurial fire, seeking instead to identify a magic, unique substance to explain entrepreneurship.

The Concept of Family Business - What is a "*family business*"? Not unlike a related concept, "*entrepreneurship*", there appears to be no stand and definition of family business. It has even been suggested that the definition of family business varies with culture. Even the term "*family*" lacks a common meaning in all societies (Basu, 2008). William Dennis, writing on behalf of the US – based National Federation of Independent Businesses, states that the term "*Family Business*" generally lacks meaning from wither a practical or conceptual standpoint (Dennis,2002). His survey yielded 5 definitions, which he felt were equally good, because each of the definitions offers a different perspective and each is intuitively appealing.

Probably the most comprehensive exploration of family business concepts was provided by Chua, Chrisman and Sharma (1999). They identified a total of 21 definitions. They felt that a definition of family business "should distinguish one entity from another based on a conceptual foundation of how the entity is different and why the difference matter. Such a definition is preferable to an operational definition that merely identifies observable characteristics that differentiate one entity from another" Family ownership and family control merely observes characteristics about certain aspects of the businesses. They will render a business truly a family business only if characteristics will facilitate the perpetuation of the business across generations. So, according to these three authors" a family business is one where there is a dominant family, which owns and controls the business and where there is also a clearly established vision to keep the business in the family across generations. In other words, it is not a truly family business its owners and managers do not have any plans to keep the business in the family beyond their retirement or death.

Shanker and Astrachan (1996) noted that the criteria used to define a family business can include: Percentage of ownership, Voting control; Power over strategic decisions; Involvement of multiple generations and active management of family members. Whatever may be the definition and thinking on family business, family businesses have been considered instrumental in initiating and sustaining social economic development. Evidence suggests that countries with more number of family businesses have developed faster as compared to countries with fewer entrepreneurs in society (ILO, 2002).

Family Business: The Indian Scenario - India, too, is dominated by small, family-owned and family-managed businesses. With few exceptions, there appears to be a cultural resistance among Indian firms to institutionalize themselves. As a result, there are relatively few large, hierarchical, professionally managed corporations of the kind that exist in Japan and the United States. Inspite of this limitation, family businesses constitute most businesses in India, as anywhere else. Economic liberalization and rapid expansion in the industrial base in recent years have not only created growth opportunities for many but also have tested their resource capabilities to respond to them, - some have chosen to follow the role of a custodian of their existing wealth and followed the preservation route, while some others have followed more of an entrepreneurial route of exploiting opportunities with or without relevant resources, with mixed results. One of the key resources for all of them is their family, and their prime concern is wealth and welfare of their family. A major dilemma many of them have faced particularly in the last decade since economic liberalization began is to choose between combination of risks and returns of business growth and conservation of wealth of the family. This, of course, is intertwined with the missions of their businesses and families (Ramachandra, 2003).

The Indian economy, currently in a state of rapid development, is burgeoning with innumerable small and medium-sized family-run enterprises. Family businesses in India initially started in the 1890s as a means to promote import substitution and attain economic freedom from the British. These enterprises were an integral part of India's freedom struggle, and as part of the Swadeshi movement, got special treatment and subsidies from the government. The businesses consolidated their positions as near monopolies under the protective environment of the licence raj and their inefficiencies did not get exposed to the indefatigable market realities. Some of the prominent business families during the 1960s were the Modis, Thapars, Shrirams, Singhanias, Birlas, Wadias and Godrej.

Women in Business- The Global Scenario - Since, the early times women have been uniquely viewed as a creative source of human life. Women just like men have been involved in economic activities since early years. Their involvement has been in addition to their participation in the domestic sector. However, their economic activities have focused primarily on meeting basic needs, yet lack of resources and control of resources has been common. Their contribution in micro- entrepreneurship has been equally unpaid, unrecognized and undervalued. It is only of late such discrepancies are being looked into and being corrected all over the world.

Women in Indian Family Business - Across centuries and across time, the role of women remains rooted into eternity. It forever remains the same and at the same time goes through many transitions. It took centuries for women's role to unfold in different forms, shapes and sizes and move in new directions. Once upon a time the large part of the world was designed such that men could only set up enterprises, and then there were women who by compulsion of circumstances took up income generating activities to sustain themselves and their family. The men of these women were either not there or if they were there would not or could not take the responsibilities of sustaining the family (Indira Parikh and Bharthi Kollan, 2005). The role of women in the Indian society has important implications for women in businesses and in turn is shaped by the institutional environment which included various historical, political, economic and cultural factors.

The recent shifts in policy evidence a trend towards encouraging women to explore their hidden entrepreneurial potential. Education, rising awareness levels are not only making a women increasing conscious of their existence, rights and work situation but also some of them are exploring newer avenues of economic participation and development. Among the reasons - betterment, their skills and knowledge, talents and abilities and more importantly a compelling desire and urge to excel are cited from women taking to entrepreneurship/ or taking part in family business management. (Sita, 2007).

As a part of this economic and social development it is clear that the role of women entrepreneurs is important. But there is dearth of research on women in family business to gain clearer insight about them. Holmquist (1997) points out that empirical studies of women entrepreneurs and the development of theories is a neglected subject in descriptive and prescriptive research work. This set the scene for developing country like India to fully grasp the opportunities as part of their drive towards economic growth and prosperity well into this millennium. Inadequate literature and dearth of documentation on the role of women in business is one possible reason for such apprehensions on the role of women in family business management.

Research conducted over the past decade has increased our knowledge of family-owned firms. Unfortunately relatively little empirical research has been conducted on women and their participation in family owned businesses (Dumas, 1998). In collaboration with the above, Lyman, Salganicoff and Hollander, (1985), cited in (Rowe and Hong, 2000), state that the strength of traditional family roles, both within society and within individual families, kept women's business contributions from being acknowledged.

There are many reasons for women eventually joining family businesses. An interesting study by Hollander and Burkowiitz (1990), reveal the following reasons: wanting to help the family, filling a position that no other family member wanted, and being dissatisfied with another job. Dumas (1989) similarly concluded that, in general, women do not plan a career in their family business, do not aspire to ownership, and see their work as a job rather than a career. In addition, some became interested because they saw the potential when the business began to grow, in the same study; it was found that some of the women came into the business to help the family in a time of crisis.

Contrary to these limitations, it is cited in Cole (1997), that some women perceive their family business as a reservoir of great careers. When they work outside the family domain, they may face the "glass ceiling" no matter how talented they are. In concurrence with this, it has also been reported that better positions, higher incomes and more flexibility in work schedules are available for females who work with family, as well as more latitude for personal concerns, which is particularly important for woman who must juggle home and work (Rome and Hong, 2000).

From the 1990s onwards-new research has considered the way the family business has contributed to general economic development in a positive light. On the micro side, the main themes have been the relationship between strategies and structures of family owned firms and family ownership, the introduction of professional managers, and the succession process. In a macro perspective, the research has examined the contribution of family firms to the wealth of the nation and the relationship between the diffusion of family firms, their persistence and the cultural and institutional environment.

Despite all the research that has already been done in the field of family businesses, thus far few researchers have investigated the link between family business and women in family business. One can thus say the information available on women in family businesses is rather limited. Given the current knowledge-based society and its emphasis on business, combined with the economic importance of both family firms and women entrepreneurs, it is surprising that there has not yet been more research done to find out more about women in family businesses. The family business and the steady growth of women in family business implies wide use and relevance to today's managerial practice. A large and still growing number of family business and practitioners needs to deal with issues involved in the formation and management of women in family business in its many forms.

Although managing family business is critical for women, this area has been virtually unexplored in academic work. In the context of women in family businesses, there appear to be specific aspects associated to the characteristics of family businesses, which might set family businesses apart. These specific characteristics of family businesses can have a significant impact and, therefore, must not be neglected in studying women in family businesses.

Along with the importance, family business research over the past decade has also changed significantly. Today, family business and its impact on society is a subject of a growing body of research in various disciplines- Economic, Geography, Psychology, Sociology, Management etc. It is a sub field in most of the disciples. The professionals have organized themselves into several family business- related professional organizations. These include the family Firm Institute (FFI), Family Owned Business Educators (FOBE), and the International Family Business Program Association (IFERA). The newly formed IFBPA is the premier organization for academicians and directors involved with centers and programs of entrepreneurship and family businesses and serves across the United States and Internationally. The literature in the past decades was fragmented, but the last few years saw the emergence of journals specific to family business and the literature expanded since then. The result of family business became an existing field for all those who had passion for research in the field. Though the broad range of subject is strength for any field, lack of focus might lead to lack of rigor as a field of research. The dividing line was clear in so far as two schools of thought emerged where some argued that it should developed as a distinctive domain, while others wanted to see family business having a wide range. This throws up the question of distinctive domain of family business.

Over 60 universities now have family business programs (Vinturellas, Elstrott and Galiano, 1993) and a small group of programs exist as private non- university entities. Many of these university programs are associated with Centers for Entrepreneurship. Schools such as Harvard University, Cornell University, Baylor University, University of Southern California, University of St. Louis, and the University of St. Thomas have held family business conferences, developed cases and state of the art curriculum, and participated in family business research consortiums. The interest in the family business area is increasing over time. The field of family business has caught the attention of major financial institutions and corporation and many sponsored university programs. These sponsors include Ernst and Young, Mass Mutual, Arthur Anderson, U.S. Trust, Banker Trust, Coopers and Lybrand, Boston Company and the Melton Group. There is a dearth of research on family businesses and many aspects of such firms merit attention from both the business side and the family side. Although the importance of entrepreneurship and family businesses can be documented, the study of entrepreneurship as it matures into a family business and changes over time has only recently emerged. Such study is critically tied to the study of both the business and the family business can reveal new knowledge about business formation, growth and expansion, professionalizing, strategic management, and succession. From the business side for example, we know very little about the family firms within minority sub populations, the differences of family firms between the large scale versus micro enterprises, and the dynamic of change over the life course of the family firm, the problems of strategic regeneration in the family firm, and the nature of the strategies used to grow have not been addressed. Study of the family behind the business is essential in understanding not only the business activities but learning more about the environments within which entrepreneurs live and flourish (IFPA, et al.)

On the whole, it can be concluded that the family has a significant impact on the upper echelons of the family business and can, thereby, influence the business significantly. Family business as an academic field of study is of recent origin, although the Indian business scenario reflects businesses only in the nature of *family business*. The result is discussions in seminars / conferences the subject has been dealt with only in the past decade or so and scholarly journals as well. Very few courses are offered in the area in the Indian context and hence the conceptual development took several turns often disjointed to each other.

Research Gap and the Need for the Study - The focus of research studies on women in family business in the Indian context not only reflects the smaller number of studies but also evidence studies in different contexts. There are many issues in the family business which has to be studied and very little work has been done on it. Despite the impressive contribution, women owned businesses is comparatively understudied in the entrepreneurial domain (Brush and Hisrich, 1998). As against this background, Baker (1997) in a comprehensive review of both practitioners and scholarly journals found that the number of articles about women in business declined from 44% in 1980 to 14% in 1995. Furthermore, the bulk of these studies only included women in their research samples. In particular, studies that systematically analyzed the business age, size, strategy, policy, managerial capabilities, and business opportunities and analyze their perceptions and opinions on business are nearly absent from the existing literature. This also has an impact on the role of women in family business management. Though women in India were large entrants into business, it is all the more saddening to find that this area was not found worth exploring by scholars other than a few and that too women wither in academics or practitioners, leaves the field limited in documentation. The knowledge about the characteristics of women business owners and the existence of women in family business in other countries due to political, economic, cultural, and institutional difference. Thus, the investigation of women in family businesses in self-employment in other countries is seen as a promising direction for new research (McManus, 2001). The available literature on women in family business in the countries from centrally planned to market economy apart from being scare suffers from some important limitations, mainly lack of methodological rigor and lack of contingent and explanatory investigations in the issues of women in family business which contributes to the development in family business. This provides for a considerable research gap and need for studies in this direction. Most of questions relating to the profiles, motivation, enterprises data along with the opinions and perceptions of women in family business management are left unanswered. Thus, the concepts of *self employment* and *entrepreneurship* have been thought of as viable alternatives to tackle the problem of unemployment in many countries. More particularly the following issues can be figured out. They are-

1. The demographic and psychographic profile of women in family business age, education, work experience, career goal, income, family background etc.

2. The enterprise data in family business terms of year of establishment, location, nature of unit, nature of product, employees, values and decision making in business.
3. The problems faced by the women in family business.
4. The factors which influence the women the most in managing the family businesses.

Thus, the above issues evidence significant research gaps which need to be addressed to generate data and literature in the area and also to further research. Moreover, India as the geographical area, in terms of business climate and the promising role and interest being showed by women makes the study worth exploring. Family businesses have existed in India for quite long but very few women participated professionally in managing the businesses which makes both the research and the literature scanty, thus needing studies in the direction. The available literature though does not throw light on the issues that women face in family businesses, they however, help in arriving at a *conceptual framework* to guide the empirical investigation.

Methodology of the Study– The Concept - The literature has a number of definitions of the term 'family business". Vera and Dean (2005), proposes that a family business is any business where the majority ownership is controlled by the family, decisions about management are influenced by the family and two or more family members are employed and actively participate in management of the firm. From this definition it is clear that family members must be involved in the business. This formed the concept for the study.

The Framework – The conceptual framework for the study was arrived at after incorporating the major constructs previously identified in the family. Literature in terms of the family which is an important responsibility of a woman in the Indian context (Poza and Messer (2001) and business concerns for those with an entrepreneurial spirit are significant in family business management. (Danes, Haberman and McTavish 2005; Curimbaba , Rowe and Hong 2000; Danes and Olson 2003; Foley and Powell 1997; Cosier and Harvey 1998), Family issues like motivation (Singh, 1993; Sharma, 2004), Kahn and Henderson (1992) the impact of family criteria on business decisions, boards of family businesses (Barach, 1984) (Ward, 1988; Harris, Martinez & Ward, 1994), family communication in planning (Ward, 1988), stakeholders: founders, next generation members, women and non-family members (Sharma, 2004) , family business culture (Hollander and Burkowitz, 1996) assume significance in the context.

Objectives- The Study empirically examines the role of women in family managed businesses in Andhra Pradesh. More specifically, it aims at the following objectives :

1. To examine the position of women in family managed businesses
2. To examine the family, business and individual factors that influence Indian women in the family managed business
3. Profiling the women in family managed business
4. To analyze the enterprise growth in family managed businesses
5. To analyze the issues which women face in family managed business
6. To highlight the challenges which women face in family managed business

Scope of the Study - The scope of the study was determined based on the geographical area to be covered (Andhra Pradesh) managed by women along with other members of the family in terms of decision making. Though, no sector specific limits have been identified, all those industries which are family owned and managed businesses, have been considered for the study. In a way, while there was no upper limit for the number of years, the minimum enterprise age was determined with the cut off year of establishment as 2007. All women spending time on the activities of business and continuously invested in the growth of the firm were other criteria followed in deciding the scope for the study.

Research Area - Andhra Pradesh, an upcoming state in Southern India, in terms of the business climate is the research area for the study. Based on the criteria identified , it was decided to select at least one city/town representing each of the three regions of Andhra Pradesh, but criteria adopted for the study limited the research area to the business environs of Hyderabad, Vijayawada and Bhongir areas of Andhra Pradesh.

Research Design-The study is exploratory in nature. Literature evidences very little information on the problems and issues concerning the family managed businesses. This entailed the construction of the conceptual framework based on isolated studies conducted in different contexts. Documentation in the Indian context is much more limited due to the relatively new phenomena of women managing professionally in business families. A lot of qualitative data had to be collected to comprehend the problem and understand the phenomena in the absence of a validated framework. Since the study is aimed at finding out the profile of women in family business in respect of their traits/characteristics, the enterprise performance in terms of nature of product, level of employees, business related information and their assertive opinions on the reasons for strengthening women in business, business opportunities, and issues related to family, a descriptive research design was used to capture the relevant information which included both qualitative and quantitative data.

Assumptions of the Study - The findings of the research studies were inconclusive on certain dimensions of the women in family business. Eisenhardt (1989) states that theory building research should begin as closely as possible to the idea of no theory under consideration and no hypothesis to test. However, some assumptions could form a starting point for the study to prevent *data dredging*. Studies on women in family business - starting, managing a business was inconclusive and hence, the study starts with some assumptions. They are:

(a) The socio-economic profile of women in family business is different from those women who own and operate managed business unlike the other enterprises.
(b) Women in family business face challenges of a different order.
(c) The family, business, and individual factors influence the role of women in family
(d) The role of women in family business is different from the roles – played and they negotiate these roles between the family and business.

Data Collection - Data in the nature of both primary and secondary was collected from the respondents. The secondary data related to the information containing the literature review in journals, books and the information/manuals/websites of the respective enterprises. The primary data was collected from a specifically designed schedule, which was standardized after pre testing on a limited number of sampled respondents. The schedule was designed to elicit the socio-economic profile of the entrepreneur, profile of the enterprise, business related information, problems in family business and their reaction on certain issues relating to women in family business – family issues, dealing with issues , decision making, succession, business values vs. family values etc.

Visit to their enterprises, collecting relevant information through an agenda for discussion on how they identified the opportunity, evaluated the business idea, the process of entrepreneurship and their future agenda in family business was also collected. Thus, data collection including the documentation started in June 2009 and ended in February, 2010.

Tools and Techniques - A specifically designed questionnaire which captured the factual information about the entrepreneurs and the enterprise along with their opinions and perceptions was specifically administered to each of the respondents after taking time from them. Some of the women entrepreneurs were also contacted telephonically to fill certain gaps and ascertain information from them.

Sample - Women in family business were identified based on a set criteria. It was originally decided to select all the three regions in Andhra Pradesh but the sample was drawn based on the set criteria and was limited to Hyderabad, Bhongir, Vijayawada. The help and assistance of the Association of Lady Entrepreneurs in Andhra Pradesh (ALEAP), Confederation of Women Entrepreneurs (COWE), Confederation of Indian Industry (A.P Region) and the Association of Indian Manufacturers Organization (AIMO) was taken to identify the sampling frame. After taking the list of registered entrepreneurs from these organizations, it was found that all of them were either affiliated to ALEAP or COWE. The details of each enterprise along with the entrepreneur, location, address of the enterprise and residence along with the telephone number/mobile number was provided to select the sample. Based on the criteria, 80 women were selected as sample for the study. About 52 responded for the study with a response rate of 63%. The rest of them were either busy or were not willing to participate in the study.

Data Analysis - Data was analyzed using descriptive statistics such as frequencies and percentages for analyzing the factual information regarding the entrepreneur and the enterprise and presented using graphs wherever found necessary. To understand the opinion of women on *issues* in family business a 4 point scale was used. The mean and standard deviation was calculated to check consistency in their perception. In addition, a factor analysis was done to resolve a large set of variables into factors. The data collected from the respondents was subjected to principal component, factor analysis by Varimax Rotation with Kaizer Normalization method by using the criterion that factors with Eigen value > 1.00 were retained. Loadings exceeding 0.5 were considered for determining factors. To avoid the crowding of factors, this measure was taken although the literature allows a loading of 0.33 to be the absolute minimum value to be interpreted. This criterion is being used more or less by way of convention (Vasanthi and Rayappan, 2006). Thus, content analysis, interpretation of the various statistical tests is done to arrive at inferences and satisfy the objectives of the study.

The field of family business has invited interesting questions and these have been explored with increasing sophistication as times changed.

However, the critics of scholarships in the field point out to a lack of central research paradigm thus forcing the scholars to devote inadequate attention to the issues of validity and reliability resulting in analytical methods used by other researchers. When there is no agreement on such issues it is difficult to bring in the rigor called for in the investigations in entrepreneurship (Cooper, 2005)

Conclusion and Recommendations - The broad conclusions are–

1. In terms of the profile, women were in the thirty five plus age group, educated and had previous work experience before entering the family business. As in the other contexts, urban women showed inclination to manage the family business. Culturally, they were married and belonged to the Hindu Undivided Family to participate in the business. This trend appears to match with the women entrepreneurs who are on their own managing enterprises – big and small. Since the education levels of women are on the rise, women should be inducted into business at an early age. They also feel exposure to the work place and their experience helps them in taking the plunge into the family business smooth. Experience does help them in networking and getting the necessary contacts. Probably exposing them to the family business instead of the other work contexts may allow more insights into their own business and help the business flourish with their fresh ideas at a relatively young age. The urban women by virtue of their education and exposure are able to involve themselves well with business but this should be encouraged from the rural women too.
2. In terms of the profile of the enterprise, it could be said that a majority of the enterprises were started around the economic reform process in India in the 1990s, which showed that family businesses nurtured their enterprises and sustained in the dynamic and volatile business environment for quite long. Majority of enterprises were inherited and the size and scale of the operation was limited. Manufacturing appears to be the activity of the enterprises. Women should take the opportunities available from the service economy and diversify into areas both related and unrelated to take the best out of the given situation.
3. The opinions and perceptions of women in family business revealed that work life balance, transparency, disagreement on family issues as the major family issues embedded in family business management. The family spending a lot of time away from business though is a healthy trend and speaks of the close knit family, appears

to be an issue of concern from the business point of view and the business success. Work-life balance always has been a deterrent for women to take up any productive activity. Taking the available services to take care of children and being more organized is of course the best option but women should try and bring in a change the cultural moors of family life and make their partners feel the responsibility of familial life will go a long way in solving the issue. With the changes happening in every aspect, it should not be a long time to overcome this problem. The time being spent outside with the family should be utilized to take care of such issues.

4. Planning and organizing seem to be the strategies for dealing with family issues. However, the family interest in their over anxiety relating to family business should not end up in muddling with business. The need for planning in business in general and family business in particular is essential and understood. Thus efforts towards plan and organize accordingly assumes significance in this context.
5. The process of decision making in family matters, their performance individually and with partners/family appears to be the significant factors in family managed businesses. The same trend continued over decision on business matters. However, non-employed owners involved in business decision making appeared to be the area of concern in the decision making matters. Decision making is central to family business management. Decisions are taken after all family members agree on issues connected with business. Consensus however, emerges only if the issues are dealt with in a professional manner. Thus decisions even in family business management needs to be taken with at most professionalism even with the non employed stakeholders in the processes. Professional management should precede personal dreams and fancies.
6. Balancing work and family was found to be the challenge for women in family business like any other business women managing enterprises. The overlap between the business and family fears leading to potential conflicts was an area of concern for women. Better time management, better planning, getting more organized and try to bring a change in the familial life are some of the areas which could be explored for a better work and family life.
7. Governance issues like the role of independent directors and family members along with the conflicts in ownership are the significant issues. Issues like not trusting the board of directors appear to be the area of concern in governance. Professionalism in governance

on the part of the family members and imposing trust on the role of independent directors would take care of the governance issues in the family business matters.

8. Business relationships, family events , family values , entrepreneurial climate, process of business values, family traditions and business results in that order were the factors included in business values and family values. This was stressed as the most important influencers for both the family and business and society at large. Values – both business and family values – are important for family business management. Women are known to carry the house hold traditions, values, customs generation after generation and keep the spirit of the family intact. The same spirit could also be extended to an integration of family and business values which will go a long way in sustaining the business.
9. Leadership, control, future plans of succession and list of family successors in that order are issues in succession planning. Appropriately identifying the future business leader was a challenge women thought in family managed business. Culturally and socially Indian women are not encouraged to takeover and have control over businesses when there are sons in the family. This is true even in the current context with education, experience and exposure of Indian women to the work place, which hampers the succession issues for women in family managed businesses and inhibits the leadership capabilities of women. Practices do evidence a small beginning on leadership and succession issues which needs to be stepped up for grater roles of women in family managed businesses.
10. The family image along with business image was the two factors considered important in image issues. Like the issue of leadership, in the name of family and business image women are again not preferred, which needs to be corrected in the contemporary globalized era.
11. Organizational design, business strategy, business skills, family communication and management of the company in that order were the factors which contributed to the professional management of family managed businesses. Equal focus on strategic orientation and the operational aspects of business were areas of concerns for women in family managed business. Business strategy and the day to day operational aspects of business are taken to be business concerns and hence are managed by the seasoned business men in the family. Evidence suggests that a women's role is at the best is a sleeping partner or a member of the business with not much of a

management control , even if the women poses business acumen and skills.

12. Two way communication between family and others was a significant factor in running the family managed business. Irrespective of levels/ positions/role lending one voice to the managers in running the business was the significant factor which had to be dealt with caution. Communication is an important factor in business success. Miscommunication and too many orders/direction in managing the business will affect the business.
13. Family support, business success, family prestige and long term interest of the family in business were the others issues in family managed business. The future of business and its fate was an area on concern in family managed business. The contemporary organizational context is categorized by competition. The family managed businesses are no exception to this fact. They have to be managed and manage successfully with full family support and long term business concerns in view. Women with their education, exposure and experience can play an important role in taking care of the business in future and business success in particular.

References

1. Alcorn, P. B. 1982. Success and survival in the family-owned business. New York, NY: McGraw-Hill.
2. Business Gyan (2007), "50 Years of Indian Entrepreneurship", The Author, Bangalore, pp. 69 – 71.
3. Business World (2007) "Lessons from the Banyan Tree Beyond the Family Fued", The Author, Mumbai, 17
4. Barach, J. A. 1984. Is there a cure for the paralyzed family board. Sloan Management Review, 25 (1): 3–12.
5. Barach, J. A., & Gratinsky, J. 1995. Successful succession in family business. Family Business Review, 8 (2): 131–155.
6. Barkema, H. G., Shenkar, O., Vermeulen, F., & Bell, J. H. J. 1997. Working abroad, working with others: How firms learn to operate international joint ventures. Academy of Management Journal, 40 (2): 426–442.
7. Barnes, L. B., & Hershon, S. A. 1976. Transferring power in the family business. Harvard Business Review, 54 (4): 105–114. - 173 –
8. Beamish, P. W. 1999. The role of alliances in international entrepreneurship. In Wright, R. (Ed.), Research in global strategic management - Vol. 7 International Entrepreneurship: Globalization and Emerging Businesses: 43–61 Greenwich, CT: JAI Press.

9. Beckhard, R., & Dyer, W. G., Jr. 1983a. Managing change in the family firm - issues and strategies. Sloan Management Review, 24 (1): 59–66.
10. Beckhard, R., & Dyer, W. G., Jr. 1983b. Managing continuity in the familyowned business, Organizational Dynamics, 5 (1): 5–12.
11. Christman, J. J., Chua, J. H., & Sharma, P. 1988. Important attributes of successors in family businesses: An exploratory study. Family Business Review, 11 (1): 19–34.
12. Churchill, N. C., & Hatten, K. J. 1987. Non-market-based transfer of wealth and power: A research framework for small businesses. American Journal for Small Businesses, 11 (3): 51–64.
13. Daily, R. C., & Dollinger, M. J. 1993. Ownership structure, strategic posture, and firm growth: An empirical examination. Journal of Small Business Management, 31 (2): 25–34.
14. Daily, R. C., & Dollinger, M. J. 1994. An empirical examination of ownership structure in family and professionally managed firms. Family Business Review, 5 (2): 117–136.
15. Daily, R. C., & Thompson S. S. 1994. Ownership structure, strategic posture, and firm growth: An empirical examination. Family Business Review, 7 (3): 237–250.
16. Davis, P. 1983. Realizing the potential of the family business. Organizational Dynamics, 5 (1): 47–56.
17. Davis, P. S., & Harveston, P. D. 1999. In the founder's shadow: Conflict in the family firm, Family Business Review, 12 (4): 311–323.
18. Davis, P., & Tagiuri, R. 1982. The influence of life-stages on father-son work relationships in family companies. Family Business Review, 2 (1): 47–74.
19. Doz, Y. L., & Hamel, G. 1998. Alliance advantage: The art of creating value through partnering. Boston, MA: Harvard Business School Press.
20. Dunn, B. 1995. The challenges facing Scotland's family enterprises. Glasgow, UK: Centre For Family Enterprise.
21. Dyer, W. G., Jr. 1986. Cultural change in family firms: Anticipating and managing business and family transition. San Francisco, CA: Jossey-Bass.
22. Dyer, W. G., Jr., & Sánchez, M. 1998. Current state of family business theory and practice as reflected in Family Business Review 1988 - 1997. Family Business Review, 11 (4): 287–295.
23. Dyer, W. G., Jr., & Wilkins, A. L. 1991. Better stories, not better constructs, to generate better theory: A rejoinder to Eisenhardt. Academy of Management Review, 16 (3): 613–619.

24. Fletcher, D. E. ed (2002) Understanding the Small Family Businesses, London and New York: Routledge.
25. Franko, L. G. 1971. Joint venture survival in multinational corporations. New York, NY: Praeger Publishers.
26. Friedman, M. & Friedman, S. 1994. How to run a family business. Cincinnati, OH: Betterway Books.
27. Gallo, M.A. 1995. The role of family business and its distinctive characteristic behavior in industrial activity. Family Business Review, 8 (2): 83–98.
28. Gallo, M. A., & Garcia-Pont, C. 1994. Internationalizing family firms. Family Business Advisor, 3 (4): 1.
29. Gallo, M. A., & Garcia-Pont, C. 1996. Important factors in family business internationalization, Family Business Review, 9 (1): 45–59.
30. Gallo, M. A., & Sveen J. 1991. Internationalizing the family business: Facilitating and restraining factors. Family Business Review, 4 (2): 181–190.
31. Geeraerts, G. 1984. The effect of ownership on the organization structure in small firms, Administrative Science Quarterly, 29: 232–237.
32. Gersick, K. E., Lansberg, I., Desjardins, M., & Dunn, B. 1999. Stages and transitions: Managing change in the family businesses. Family Business Review, 12 (4): 287–297.
33. Gomes-Casseres, B. 1987. Joint venture instability: Is it a problem? Columbia Journal of World Business, 22 (2): 97–102.
34. Gomes-Casseres, B. 1989. Joint ventures in the face of global competition. Sloan Management Review, 30 (3): 17–25.
35. Gomes-Casseres, B. 1994. Group versus group. How alliance networks compete. Harvard Business Review, 72 (4): 62–74. Gomes-Casseres, B. 1996. The alliance revolution: The new shape of business rivalry. Cambridge, MA: Harvard Business Press.
36. Gudmundson, D., Hartman, E. A., & Tower, C. B. 1999. Stratcgic orientation:
37. Differences between family and non-family firms. Family Business Review, 12 (1): 27–39.
38. Gulati, R. 1995. Does familiarity breed trust? The implications of repeated ties for contractual choice in alliances. Academy of Management Journal, 38 (1): 85– 112.
39. Gummesson, E. 1991. Qualitative methods in management research. Newbury Park, CA: Sage

40. Handler, W. C. 1989. Methodological issues and considerations in studying family business. Family Business Review, 2 (3): 257–276.
41. Handler, W. C. 1992. The succession experience of the next generation. Family Business Review, 5 (3): 283–307.
42. Handler, W. C. 1994. Succession in family business: A review of the research. Family Business Review, 7 (2): 133–157.
43. Handler, W. C., & Elman, N. S. 1988. Family owned business: An emerging field of inquiry. Family Business Review, 1 (2): 145–164.
44. Handler, W. C., & Kram, K. E. 1988. Succession in family firms: The problem of resistance. Family Business Review, 1 (4): 361–381.
45. Harris, R., Martinez, J. I., & Ward, J. L. 1994. Is strategy different for the family-owned business? Family Business Review, 7 (2): 159–174.
46. Harvey, M., & Evans, R. 1994. Family business and multiple levels of conflict. Family Business Review, 7 (4): 331–348.
47. Hayes, G. W., Walker, R., Rowe, B. R., & Hong, G.-S. 1999. The intermingling of business and family finances in family owned businesses. Family Business Review, 12 (3): 225–239
48. Hisrich Robert and Brush, C. G. (1985) Women and minority entrepreneurs: A comparative analysis, Frontiers of Entrepreneurship Research, Wellsley, MA: Babson College.
49. Hisrich Robert and Brush, C. G. (1987) Women entrepreneurs: A longitudinal study. Frontiers of Entrepreneurship Research, 1987.
50. Hisrich, R. D. And Brush, C.G. (1983), The Women entrepreneurs: Implications of family, educational and occupational experience, Frontiers of Entrepreneurship Research, 1983
51. Hisrich, R. D. And Brush, C.G. (1986). The woman entrepreneur: A comparative analysis. Leadership and Organization Development Journal, 1986,
52. Holland, P. G., & Boulton, W. R. 1984. Balancing the family and the business in a family business. Business Horizons, 27 (2): 16–21.
53. Holland, P. G., & Oliver, J. E. 1992. An empirical examination of the stages of development of family business. Journal of Business and Entrepreneurship, 4 (3): 27–38.
54. Hollander, B. S., & Bukowitz, W. R. 1990. Women, family culture, and family business. Family Business Review, 3 (2): 139–151.
55. Hollander, B. S., & Elman, N. S. 1988. Family-owned businesses: An emerging field of inquiry. Family Business Review, 1 (2): 145–164.

56. Indira Parikh J and Bharthi (2005) A reflection of Indian women in entrepreneurial world , IIM, Ahmedabad
57. Kanter, R. M. 1983. The change masters: Innovation and entrepreneurship in the American corporation. New York, NY: Simon & Schuster,
58. Kaye, K. 1992. Penetrating the cycle of sustained conflict. Family Business Review, 4 (1): 21–44.
59. Kepner, E. 1983. The family and the firm: A coevolutionary perspective. Organizational Dynamics, 12 (1): 57–70.
60. Kepner E. 1991. The family and the firm: A coevolutionary perspective . Family Business Review, 4 (4): 445-461.
61. Kets de Vries, M. F. R. 1993. Leaders, fools and imposters. San Francisco, CA: Jossey-Bass.
62. Kleinsorge, I. K. 1994. Financial and efficiency differences in family-owned nursing homes: An Oregon study. Family Business Review, 7 (1): 73–86.
63. Landsberg, I. S. 1983. Managing human resources in the family business: The problem of institutional overlap. Organizational Dynamics, 12 (1): 39–46.
64. Landsberg, I. S. 1988. The succession conspiracy. Family Business Review, 1 (2): 119–143.
65. Landsberg, I. S., & Astrachan, J. H. 1994. Influence of family relationships on succession planning and training: The importance of mediating factors. Family Business Review, 7 (1): 39–59.
66. Landsberg, I. S., Perrow, E. L. & Rogolsky, S. 1988. Family business as an emerging field. Family Business Review, 1 (1): 1–8.
67. Levinson, H. 1971. Conflicts that plague family businesses. Harvard Business Review, 52 (6): 53–62.
68. Levinson, H. 1983. Consulting with family businesses: What to look for, what to look out for. Organizational Dynamics, 12 (1): 71–80.
69. Levinson, R. E. 1987. Problems in managing a family-owned business. U.S. Small Business Administration Management, No. 2.004.
70. Litz, R. A. 1995. The family business: Toward definitional clarity. Family Business Review, 8 (2): 71–81.
71. Longenecker, J. G., & Schoen, J. E. 1978. Management succession in the family business. Journal of Small Business Management, 16 (3): 1–6.
72. Malone, S. C. 1989. Selected correlates of business continuity planning in the family business. Family Business Review, 2 (4): 341–353.

73. Mathews, G. H. 1984. Run your own business or build an organization? Harvard Business Review, 62 (2): 34–44.
74. Miller, Danny and Lebreton Miller, Isabel (2005), "Managing for the Long Run: Lesson in Competitive Advantage from Great Family Businesses", Harvard Business School Press, Boston.
75. Moores, K. & Mula, J. 2000. The Salience of Market, Bureaucratic, and Clan Controls in the Management of Family Firm Transitions "Some Tentative Australian Evidence". Family Business Review, 13 (2).
76. Okoroafo, S. C. 1999. Internationalization of family businesses: Evidence from Northwest Ohio, U.S.A. Family Business Review, 12 (2): 147–152.
77. P. L. Rika Fatimah Æ J. Abdul Aziz Æ K. Ibrahim, 2007) Women–Family in Quality Perspective Accepted: 8 October 2007 / Published online: 24 October 2007, Springer Science Business Media B.V. 2007
78. Ramachandran K (2006 & 2007), "Case Studies on Family Business", Indian School of Business (Mimeo). Retailer – 2007, Vol. 2, No. 7, December, pp. 36
79. Rogoff, E. G. and Heck, R. K. Z. (2003) 'Evolving Research in Entrepreneurship and Family Business: Recognizing Family as the Oxygen that Feeds the Fire of Entrepreneurship', Journal of Business Venturing, 18, 5, 559-566.
80. Rumelt, R. P. 1987. Theory, strategy, and entrepreneurship. In Teece, D. (Ed.), The competitive challenge: Strategies for industrial innovation and renewal: 137–158. New York, NY: Harper & Row.
81. Schwarz, M. A., & Barnes, L. B. 1991. Outside boards and family: Another look. Family Business Review, 4 (3): 268–285.
82. Shanthi Nachiappan, Ms.Devi and Ms.Kiran (2006) "Family Business Management - Small and Medium Enterprises in Tamil Nadu"
83. Sharma, P., Christman, J. J., & Chua, J. H. 1997. Strategic management of the family business: Past research and future challenges. Family Business Review, 10 (1): 1–35.
84. Sonnenfeld, J. A., & Spence, P. L. 1989. The parting patriarch of a family firm. Family Business Review, 2 (3): 355–375. Sorensen, R. L. 1999. Conflict management strategies used in successful family businesses. Family Business Review, 12 (2): 133–146.
85. Stern, M. H. 1986. Inside the family held business. New York, NY: Harcourt Brace Jovanovich.
86. Swogger, G., Jr. 1993. Assessing the successor generation in family businesses. Family Business Review, 4 (4): 397–411.

87. Ward, J. L. 1987. Keeping the family business healthy: How to plan for continued growth, profitability, and family leadership. San Francisco, CA: Jossey-Bass.
88. Ward, J. L., & Handy, J. L. 1988. A study of board practices. Family Business Review, 1 (3): 289–308.
89. Wilkie, R., & Young, J. N. 1971. The owner-managers and managers of small firms: A study in depth. Strathclyde, Scotland: University of Strathclyde.
90. Wilcosin family forum, (2003),"Women in Family Business: Challenges and Opportunities", Buttedes Morts Country Club, Appleton
91. Wortman, M. S. 1994. Theoretical foundations for family-owned business: A conceptual and research-based paradigm. Family Business Review, 7 (1): 3–27.

23

An Analytical Study of the Impact of Women Entrepreneurship Development Measures Promoted By The Government and Financial Institutions in Kerala

Abstract

PURPOSE - This paper is based on a probe carried out to critically analyze the pros and cons of various measures initiated by the state, central governments and financial institutions for the promotion of women entrepreneurship in Kerala. Even though a large number of measures have been carried out women entrepreneurship development is still in a dormant state in Kerala.

METHODOLOGY- The study is a field level investigation done among the women entrepreneurs and the officials of the various institutions rendering support to women entrepreneurs. The method is broadly descriptive and evaluator. Intensive interviews were carried out personally by the researcher over a period of seven months on the basis of a comprehensive schedule. The study is confined to women entrepreneurship ventures in six districts of the state. Multistage random sampling and Probability sampling were used. Trend analysis, Regression analysis and

Anova were the important statistical tools used to substantiate the major findings of the study.

FINDINGS- The study revealed that the reality on ground regarding the development measures for promoting women entrepreneurship does not match the blueprint of the programme in official writing .This implies that women entrepreneurship development in the state is still in a rudimentary state and adequate measures are to be initiated to promote women entrepreneurship which is an imperative necessity for mitigating the mounting unemployment problem. There is presently enormous entrepreneurial qualities and intense desire in our women it merely remains dormant and needs to be nurtured and developed.

CONCLUSION- The study gives a number of constructive suggestions for making changes in the existing schemes of assistance, launching new schemes and making cordial relations between officials of the agencies and women entrepreneurs.

Introduction

Entrepreneurship is a purposeful activity indulged in initiating, promoting and maintaining economic activities for the production and distribution of wealth. The individual as an entrepreneur is a critical factor in economic development and an integral part of socio-economic transformation. Therefore, the basic concept of entrepreneurship connotes effectiveness, an urge to take risk in the face of uncertainties and intuition. Entrepreneurs are the real heroes of economic life. They are the ones who have shown that genus is sweat and toil and sacrifice and that natural resources gain value only by the ingenuity and labour of man1. From their knowledge and failure, they forge success. In accepting risk they achieve security for all. The importance of entrepreneurs to progress cannot be more succinctly expressed than zinkins statement, “no entrepreneur, no development”2.

No nation can transform into a developed nation without making optimum use of all its resources including its human resource. It is imperative that women constituting half of the population must be given their due share in the development process at all the three stages. Viz. formation, utilization and remuneration of resources. Women entrepreneurship has great importance for future economic prosperity and empowerment of Indian women. Specific policies and strategies must be adopted to remove the hurdles of women entrepreneurs and to develop the entrepreneurship among them. Actually, the potentials of women are largely unrealized.

Our society is always doubtful regarding the ability and success of women in the entrepreneurial world. In India, a huge potential of women is left unutilized and untapped. It should be tapped towards entrepreneurial pursuits and a concerted effort would change the socio-economic scene of our country3. Schumpeter, the first major writer to highlight the human agent in the process of economic development, believed that the economy was propelled by the activities of persons" who wanted to promote new goods and new methods of production, or to exploit new sources of materials or new market', not merely for profit but also for the purpose of creating. The Government of India has defined women entrepreneur as 'an enterprise owned and controlled by a women having a minimum financial interest of 51% as capital and giving at least 50% employment to women.

Whatever is the definition, across the world entrepreneurs have been considered instrumental in initiating and sustaining socio-economic development. There are evidences to believe that countries which have proportionately higher percentage of entrepreneurs in their population have developed much faster as compared to countries which have lesser percentage of them in the society. Various definitions of entrepreneurship exist, but researcher likes to adopt a simple one, "the creation of new businesses that prosper and create jobs".

Kerala is one of the states located at the southwestern tip of the country, According to 2001 census of India, the total population of the state is 3, 18,38,619 of which the women population accounts for 1,63,69,955 i.e. 51% and, therefore, empowerment of women assumes greater significance for the industrial development of the state for a socio-economic transformation. Of the state's total literacy rate of 90.92 % women accounts for 86%. The female sex ratio of the state depicts a unique feature of 1058 females per 1000 males against 933 females per 1000 males at All India level. Despite these advantages, role of women in the economic activity is at low ebb and their contribution towards industrial development is meager. One reason that could be attributed for the slow pace of progress of women with particular reference to the industrial sector is the lack of 'entrepreneurship' warranting qualities like determination, desire and courage. Women of Kerala lag behind these areas resulting in little contribution to the industrial economy of the state when compared to other states in the country. Although the indicators of social development of women are remarkable, the same degree of achievement is not recorded in the economic front as employees and entrepreneurs4. Women are employed in the low earning sectors of the economy. The Kerala model /

experiences of development have been much discussed in national and international forums. Kerala ranked first among the Indian states in terms of performance on the Human Development Index (HDI), Gender Equality Index (GEI) and Gender Empowerment Measure (GEM). Work participation among women in Kerala is 22.9 percent (NSS 1999-2000), which is one of the lowest in India. This low labor force is accompanied by high rates of unemployment. Kerala has the highest incidence of unemployment both for males and females and in rural areas as well as urban areas. The overall unemployment rate in Kerala is 12 percent showing a wide gender gap with 24.3 percent for women and 6.5 percent for men.

However the role of Kerala women in the small enterprises sector remains unenviable. According to the third all India census of SSI-2004, in Kerala 22.44 %of the women enterprises and 19.70 % of women managed units were in the registered sector and the corresponding percentage in unregistered sector was 34.74 and 35.51 respectively. A comparison with the percentage of women SSI units in Kerala (in the total SSI sector) with that of the all India level shows that the percentage of women enterprises and women managed units in Kerala was three times that of the national average. Before 1978 there were only 73 SSI units registered in the name of women in Kerala. In Kerala about 80 percent of the women enterprises were promoted during the period 1991-2000.The total number of women enterprises in the state increased from 6967 in 1989-1990 to 38364 in 1999-2000 and to 44,116 in 2009. However, the fact is that most of them are not sustainable. Main reasons often are placed on the lack of enabling and sustaining facilities of entrepreneurial environment in general. Even, then there are success cases of women- run business units, details of which can motivate the women entrepreneurs in the scene.

Various institutions at the state and national levels, apart from financial institutions, and research and development organizations have been making special provisions to assist women entering small enterprises. The focus is on providing counseling and escort services, organizing training on entrepreneurial and managerial aspects exclusively for women entrepreneurs, apart from general programmes where women can participate, and encouraging women entrepreneurs association to play a greater proactive role in guiding , and molding prospective and existing women entrepreneurs to benefit from the conducive environment to give them a helping hand in shaping their dream of becoming successful entrepreneurs a reality5. The following are the major institutions rendering support to women entrepreneurs.

1. National Level Standing Committee On Women Entrepreneurs
2. Small Industries Development Organization (SIDO)
3. National Institute For Entrepreneurship and Small Business Development (NIESBUD)
4. Entrepreneurship Development Institute (EDI)
5. National Institute of Small Industries Extension Training, Hyderabad (NIESIET)
6. National Research Development Corporation of India
7. National Commission on the Self Employed Women in the Informal Sector
8. National Association of Women Entrepreneurs and Executives (NAWEE)
9. Small Industries Development Bank of India (SIDBI)
10. National Small Industries Corporation Ltd (NSIC)
11. IFCI Scheme of Interest Subsidy For Women Entrepreneurs
12. National Bank For Agriculture And Rural Development
13. Bank Of India-Priyadarshini Yojana
14. State Bank of India Schemes
15. Industrial Development Bank Of India
16. Prime Ministers Employment Generation Programme (PMEGP)
17. Tread Related Entrepreneurship Assistance And Development Scheme For Women (TREAD)
18. Micro and Small Enterprises Cluster Development Programme (MSE-CDP)
19. Credit Guarantee Fund Scheme

State Level Institutions

1. Kerala Financial Corporation
2. Kerala Small Industries Development Corporation Ltd. (Kerala SIDCO)
3. District Industries Centre
4. Kerala State Women's Development Corporation
5. Khadi and Village Industries Commission
6. Kerala State Electronics Development Corporation Kerala Industrial Infrastructural Corporation (KINFRA)
7. Khadi and Village Industries Board
8. Kerala Bureau of Industrial Promotion (K-bip)
9. Kerala Industrial and Technical Consultancy Organization (KITCO)
10. Kerala Institute of Entrepreneurship Development (KIED)
11. Centre for Management Development (CMD)

But, in spite of the efforts the participation of women in the wealth creation process is far from satisfactory. By and large , the pronouncements in this regard have turned out to be mere political rhetoric. Much needs to be done. The SSI have not been able to play their role to full extent as envisaged in our plans. This has been ascribed as mainly due to financial and marketing difficulties. Many units get sick during the first two or three years of their inception itself., without making any inroad into developing a market for their products. The rate of growth in the number of sick units is much higher in Kerala than the rest of the country. In the light of institutional and financial support to the women entrepreneurs from different sources in the present years an assessment of women enterprises and women entrepreneurship promotional programmes in the state of Kerala is of utmost importance. All these important reasons embolden the researcher to choose a probe in this direction

Objectives

1. To find out the efficacy of the various women entrepreneurship promotional measures being promoted by the government and financial institutions in the state and to identify gaps if any.
2. To find out the motivational factors behind women entrepreneurship and also to know the type of supports received by the entrepreneurs from the government, financial institutions, family members, community etc.

Data

The study is a field level investigation done among 300 respondents. The method is broadly descriptive and analytical. Six districts of Kerala state constitute the universe for the study The list of the names and addresses of registered unit was collected from the District Industries Centers (DIC). The women entrepreneurs who registered their units on or before 31st march 2006 were selected . According to the Data of the industrial records, there were 53204 units registered in the name of women as on 31st March, 2006. And the total numbers in the selected six districts are 29,969 numbers of units. One percentage was taken from these and so the units for the study constitute 300 units. Intensive interviews were carried out personally by the researcher over a period of five months on the basis of a comprehensive schedule. But during the collection of data it was found that only half of this number is actually functioning. Others were closed down or could not be traced either because the firms had gone out of existence /changed name , ownership , location or were only paper organization and had never been in the field. More over half of the functioning units were found to be managed by men in the family. The proportion of jointly managed units was equally high. Very few units were run entirely by women. There were many units which were registered as garment manufacturing units but when the researcher visited the units it was founded they were only service units with only one or two sewing machine in the house of the entrepreneur. As there is no follow up from the industrial department it was easy for the entrepreneur to arrange the required infrastructure at the time of inspection by the officials.

Findings and Discussion

One important feature of the study was the information relating to the entrepreneur, age, qualification and family background. Majority of the sample respondents started their entrepreneurial career while they were in the age group of 30 to 40 years (46.67%). This means that maximum number of the women entrepreneurs started their units at a comparatively young age after completing their educational qualifications, discharging their matrimonial engagements.

Even though Kerala women possess high levels of education which is a favorable condition for the development of entrepreneurship, only a few women with technical and professional qualification are entering the entrepreneurial field. This leads to the conclusion that formal education is not enough to attract women to the entrepreneurial sector.

Majority of the women entrepreneurs were married (85.67%) when they started their entrepreneurial careers. This proves that women have a tendency to start their enterprises only after marriage. This may be because of a profound deeply seated in their own competence which begins in early childhood to have a protection if they want to survive. This belief is instilled into women by misguided social expectations and by fear of parents. 5.33% were divorced and 2.33 % were widow. During the course of field visit some of the women respondents opined to the researcher that an unmarried women entrepreneur faces a lot of difficulty in finding a prospective groom for marriage. As a result getting the daughter married first becomes priority for parents. More over the parents prefer spending money on the marriage of their daughter instead of investing on establishment of her enterprise.

Analysis of family background reveals that the emergence of first generation 'small scale entrepreneurs was evident. Majority of the women entrepreneurs had nuclear families (76.67%). These women started their enterprises and became successful after fighting heavy odds. Stacked against them because they have to look after the family and simultaneously face the rig ours of an entrepreneurial career especially the initial hiccups. Majority (52.66%) belonged to Hindu community, 37.33 Christian and 10% Muslim community. Majority of the respondents (53.72 %) were found to be presently operating Manufacturing, Manufacturing cum trading , Manufacturing cum servicing businesses .This was followed by 39.81 % who were in service sector. And 6.47 were engaged in trading.

Motivating Factor

'Out of compulsion 'was the most dominant motive for 35.66 % of the respondents. The compulsions cited were; unemployment, to supplement meager income at home and adopt better lifestyle, death of husband who was in business, dissatisfaction with the job held. This was followed by 25% of respondents said that because of encouragement by Husband, Parents, friends they took up the entrepreneurial path .Unemployment was the reason for 20.67% of respondents. 12% of the respondents were motivated by the interest /inclination to do business.(Table 1.1)

Awareness of the schemes of assistance

The respondents were asked to whether they were aware of the various schemes of assistance which the government has launched for entrepreneurs in general and for women entrepreneurs in particular. A total of 53.33% of the respondents were aware of the schemes.(Table 1.2) . It is pertinent here to mention that even amongst those who were aware of the existence of such schemes, only 20% were fully aware of the schemes. The remaining 46.67% said that they are oblivious of the availability of such schemes. Lack of adequate promotional efforts on the part of support agencies could be the main reason behind ignorance of a big chunk of the respondent regarding the various schemes of assistance.

Agencies Approached

As the list of the women entrepreneurs were taken from the DIC, 300 of them had approached DIC for registration purposes, so DIC ranks first among the agencies approached. Also they had utilized subsidy schemes, training and benefits of PMRY. 26.33% of the respondents were financed by various commercial banks in terms of obtaining financial assistance for their projects under different schemes. The second rank goes to various commercial banks for assisting the respondents financially. 64 respondents have approached Kerala State Women's Development Corporation . The third rank is to KSWDC. Under the self employment loan scheme of the Corporation, credit facility is extended to women belonging to families below the poverty line to take up any income generating and self-sustaining activity. Loans are presently extended to women belonging to backward classes, minority communities, scheduled castes, handicapped women and economically marginalized women of forward communities. The prime motto of MSMED Institute is to provide timely and adequate techno-economic and managerial assistance to prospective and existing entrepreneurs. It acts as a technology resource centre, training centre, service provider of industry, implementing agency of MSME schemes and assistance of Government of India. The Kerala Small Industries Development Corporation provides infrastructure facilities such as land, work shed, water supply arrangements, power connections, distribution of raw Material assistance, etc for strengthening the SSI sector in the State by setting up of industrial estates, mini industrial estates and industrial parks. Execution of construction works for Industries department and public sector undertakings are the other activities of SIDCO.

K-BIP Kerala Bureau of Industrial Promotion is envisaged for promoting the potential business opportunities of the state to the foresighted entrepreneurs and to highlight the ideal business climate prevailing in Kerala. KINFRA is developing the sector specific industrial parks based on the availability of raw materials and natural resources in the region. It places emphasis on small and tiny industries as a priority sector. It is involved in providing Industrial infrastructure in Kerala and is not directly involved in providing any financial assistance or industrial units coming up in KINFRA. Industrial Parks can avail the financial incentives and benefits announced by the state Government and other organizations. It may be noted that some of the beneficiary respondents availed of more than one scheme of assistance from different entrepreneurial support organizations.

Development /Support services utilized

The support agencies are organizing a host of training programmes for women entrepreneurs to acquire knowledge about their proposed business, develop personality traits, business skills and also for future expansion of business. Among the support services utilized, training programme ranks the first. The type of training utilized are PMRY training, skill up gradation, EDP training, Management development training. The major skills developed through training are communication, leadership quality, management, self confidence, technical skill.(Table 1.4). The major service utilized was training because the certificate issued by the training agencies helped them to avail themselves of loan easily from banks and also to get other concessions. The subsidy and incentive by the government agencies was utilized by 47.37 %. 45.71% respondents got benefit from various commercial banks in terms of obtaining financial assistance for their projects under different schemes. Only 5.26% have utilized the industrial estate / shed facilities.

It was found that the assistances provided by the government are mainly financial assistance aimed to attract women to start new units. Though a number of institutions are functioning in the state, only a few women entrepreneurs could avail the services rendered by them. Lack of information and procedural complications are the main causes. The study shows that the present institutional support system is not sufficient to support the sustainable development of women entrepreneurship in the state.

Perception of Women Entrepreneurs about Support Agencies

Assistance to be provided by the support agencies is largely on papers". Majority of the respondents were of the view that officials of these agencies pay lip services rather do the actual work. The paper work is tremendous and the entrepreneurs have to comply with too many formalities. Compliance with lengthy and outdated rules and regulations frustrate the entrepreneur to such an extent that she starts thinking as to whether the assistance she may be going to ultimately get worth the crucial time and energy wasted in procuring the same.

Unending procedural delays and a plethora of formalities have made the task of getting assistance too cumbersome resulting in wastage of time and resultantly cost overruns. There is no co- ordination between the various agencies engaged in the support of women entrepreneurs. Some times their cases gets through in one agency but gets delayed in another agency Majority of the respondents were also critical of the role played by support agencies in not expanding the pool of women entrepreneurs. They were of the opinion that support agencies are not properly discharging their role of motivating the budding entrepreneurs to opt for self employment as a career option. Some of the respondents opined that the officials of the support agencies doubt the intentions of the women entrepreneurs. Majority of them were critical of the role popularizing their schemes of assistance. This also gets validated by the low level of awareness amongst majority of the sample respondents.

The respondents said that nothing special is being done to attract the potential women entrepreneurs into starting of their own ventures. Women entrepreneurs face difficulties in getting finance which is a critical resource for venture creation. Women believe that lending practices of banks and Government funding agencies were too restrictive for them.

They said that although the facilities and incentives being provided by the support agencies act as a catalyst in establishment of an enterprise, yet the determined entrepreneurs can also do without it and it is basically the zeal or the lack of it which decides the success or failure of an enterprise.(Table 1.5) The researcher for the purpose of the study had visited for more than 35 institutions supporting women entrepreneurs in one way or the other. The agencies can play a more effective role. The numbers of educated women seeking employment have aggravated the unemployment problem in the state and have created so many economic as well as sociological problems. It is clear that no governmental machinery can provide employment to all these women. Hence, it is absolutely necessary that many of them will have to find out employment for themselves.

Suggestions

1. Entrepreneurial support organizations need to make intensive promotional efforts to popularize their schemes of assistance for entrepreneurs in general and for women entrepreneurs in particular.
2. Entrepreneurial support organizations need to tap the huge reservoir of technically / professionally qualified women by offering them better schemes of assistance and ensuring their proper implementation. Comprehensive entrepreneurship development programmes for desirous women intending to pursue entrepreneurial careers.
3. The problems of women entrepreneur are multi dimensional. These can be solved by the co-ordinated efforts of entrepreneurs, coordinated functioning of promotional agencies, and governmental assistance without red tape or bureaucratic delays. The entrepreneur has to be educated ; and she should have a proper training in acquiring the necessary skill in running an enterprise. In fact, the entrepreneur is the kingpin of the industrial spectrum.
4. No collateral security should be insisted upon from the women entrepreneurs. In addition, women –owned enterprises should get

at least 90-95 % funding as women have barely any money or property or other assets in their name. With a view to further attract more number of women into entrepreneurial careers, a tax holiday for five years should be given to the enterprises promoted by women.

5. Separate cells could be created in support agencies exclusively for women entrepreneurs. These cells should be managed by women officials.
6. There is a need to make concerted efforts to popularize the various associations meant for women entrepreneurs. Strengthening of these associations by having young and enthusiastic office bearers in them is also required.
7. Institutions imparting training in entrepreneurship development should cater to the needs of rural women also. These institutions should play a more proactive role and should fan out in rural areas also with a view to tap those rural women who possess the potential to become successful entrepreneurs. This hither to relatively untapped segment needs to be tapped in the right earnest.
8. The entry of proxy/ dummy women entrepreneurs needs to be checked so that the benefits trickle down only to genuine women entrepreneurs.
9. Good policy provisions for development of women entrepreneurship followed by their effective implementation and some sort of business incubators so that a women entrepreneur can withstand the initial hiccups of one or two years in business will go a long way in creating a right type environment for women to join entrepreneurial bandwagon.
10. To make women entrepreneurship movement a success, cohesive efforts of all the concerned institutions viz. training, financial and marketing are greatly required. They are needed to work in collaboration with each other. A single coordinating agency , which facilitates the flow of adequate working capital , technology power, and marketing of finished products is desirable.
11. Information centers should be set up at appropriate places, in both rural and urban areas so that the information related to entrepreneurship (whether it is regarding training, finance, marketing or any other) is easily accessible to aspiring women entrepreneurs, and to those who are already in the field. Information should also be disseminated using other media of communication.
12. More finance should be given for small units started by women at lower interest rate without stress on collateral security. There should be improvement in the method of accessing credit. There should

not be any delay in sanctioning and receiving of funds. It is also very necessary to identify the poorest women in rural and urban areas to provide financial assistance by banks.

13. Training component should include skill formation knowledge on different technologies, handling of better equipments, legal aspects of running a business, preparation of feasibility reports, better marketing and communications. The content of the training programme should be planned keeping in mind the intelligence level and interest of the target group. The venue of the programme should be such that more and more women come to participate in it.
14. Depending upon the resources available, entrepreneurial activity should be decided upon. The type of enterprise feasible at one place might prove out to be completely unsuccessful at another. The easy availability of the raw materials should be considered.
15. If the individual lacks enough motivation and confidence, the efforts made by the concerned organizations are of no significance. Counseling centre must be established where women can be helped to overcome their weaknesses and encouraged to take up entrepreneurial programme.

Conclusion

There is an increasing realization in the recent years that the industrialization process should be stimulated in the state to solve the problems of slow growth and worsening unemployment. Very high literacy rate and lack of employment opportunities paved way for many unemployed youth including women to take up small scale business units in Kerala. In order to utilize this potential and to keep their growth continuum, it is necessary to formulate strategies suitable for stimulating, supporting and sustaining the development of women entrepreneurship. Such a strategy needs to be in congruence with realities, and especially take cognizance of the problems those women entrepreneurs face within the current economic system of liberalization and globalization. The need of the hour is to provide an opportunity in a conducive atmosphere free from gender differences to promote women entrepreneurship.

References

1. Guilder George,' The spirit of enterprise-Penguin Books, England
2. Zinkin,Maurice,'Entrepreneurs;Keyto Growth,"Stanford Research Institute Journal, Second Quarter,1961

3. Rajashree Saxena, Prof. R.K Tripathi, Rashmi Saxena, 'Women Entrepreneurship, A Source of Empowerment, Radha Publications, New Delhi, 2004.
4. Koshy, N.P and Joseph,M.T, 2000 , women entrepreneurship in small scale industrial units; A study of Kerala, southern economist, 41(7), 19-21.